Planning Law

Planning Law

by

MICHAEL O'DONNELL

B.A., M.R.U.P, LL.B.
Barrister-at-Law

Consultant Editor
The Hon. Mr. Justice Philip O'Sullivan

Butterworths

Ireland	Butterworth (Ireland) Ltd, 26 Upper Ormond Quay, DUBLIN 7
United Kingdom	Butterworths a Division of Reed Elsevier (UK) Ltd, Halsbury House, 35 Chancery Lane, LONDON WC2A 1EL and 4 Hill Street, EDINBURGH EH2 3JZ
Australia	Butterworths, a Division of Reed International Books Australia Pty Ltd, Chatswood, NEW SOUTH WALES
Canada	Butterworths Canada Ltd, Markham, ONTARIO
Hong Kong	Butterworths Asia (Hong Kong), HONG KONG
India	Butterworths India, NEW DELHI
Malaysia	Malayan Law Journal Sdn Bhd, KUALA LUMPUR
New Zealand	Butterworths of New Zealand Ltd, WELLINGTON
Singapore	Butterworths Asia, SINGAPORE
South Africa	Butterworths Legal Publishers (Pty) Ltd, DURBAN
USA	Lexis Law Publishing, Charlottesville, VIRGINIA

© Butterworths Ireland Ltd 1999

A CIP Catalogue record for this book is available from the British Library.

ISBN 1 85475 8616

ISBN 1-85475-861-6

9 781854 758613

Printed and bound by Bookcraft (Bath) Ltd, Midsomer Norton, Avon

Visit us at our website: http//www.butterworthsireland.com

Contents

Acronyms

Statutes

BCA 1990	Building Control Act 1990
EPAA 1992	Environmental Protection Agency Act 1992
LGA 1991	Local Government Act 1991
LGA 1994	Local Government Act 1994
LG(PD)A 1963	Local Government (Planning and Development) Act 1963
LG(PD)A 1976	Local Government (Planning and Development) Act 1976
LG(PD)A 1982	Local Government (Planning and Development) Act 1982
LG(PD)A 1983	Local Government (Planning and Development) Act 1983
LG(PD)A 1990	Local Government (Planning and Development) Act 1990
LG(PD)A 1992	Local Government (Planning and Development) Act 1992
LG(PD)A 1993	Local Government (Planning and Development) Act 1993
LG(PD)A 1998	Local Government (Planning and Development) Act 1998
LG(PD)A 1999	Local Government (Planning and Development) Act 1999

Regulations

EC(EIA)R 1989	European Communities (Environmental Impact Assessment) Regulations 1989 (SI 349/1989)
EC(EIA)(A)R 1994	European Communities (Environmental Impact Assessment) (Amendment) Regulations 1994 (SI 84/1994)
EC(EIA)(A)R 1998	European Communities (Environmental Impact Assessment) (Amendment) Regulations 1998 (SI 351/ 1998)
EC(EIA)(A)R 1999	European Communities (Environmental Impact Assessment) (Amendment) Regulations 1999 (SI 93/1999)
EC(NH)R 1997	European Communities (Natural Habitats) Regulations 1997 (SI 94/1997)
LG(PD)R 1994	Local Government (Planning and Development) Regulations 1994 (SI 86/1994)
LG(PD)R 1995	Local Government (Planning and Development) Regulations 1995 (SI 69/1995)
LG(PD)(No 2)R 1995	Local Government (Planning and Development) (No 2) Regulations 1995 (SI 75/1995)
LG(PD)R 1996	Local Government (Planning and Development) Regulations 1996 (SI 100/1996)
LG(PD)R 1997	Local Government (Planning and Development) Regulations 1997 (SI 78/1997)
LG(PD)(No 2)R 1997	Local Government (Planning and Development) (No 2) Regulations 1997 (SI 121/1997)

LG(PD)(No 3)R 1997   Local Government (Planning and Development) (No 3) Regulations 1997 (SI 261/1997)

LG(PD)(F)(A)R 1998   Local Government (Planning and Development) (Fees) (Amendment) Regulations 1998 (SI 119/1998)

LG(PD)(F)(A)(No 2)R 1998   Local Government (Planning and Development) (Fees) (Amendment) (No 2) Regulations 1998 (SI 128/1998)

LG(PD)(No 2)R 1998   Local Government (Planning and Development) (No 2) Regulations 1998 (SI 194/1998)

LG(PD)R 1999   Local Government (Planning and Development) Regulations 1999 (SI 92/1999)

Table of Cases

Note: References are to paragraph numbers

D

E

F

G

H

R

S

Part I
The Statutes

LOCAL GOVERNMENT (PLANNING AND DEVELOPMENT) ACT, 1963

(No 28 of 1963)

Part I

PRELIMINARY AND GENERAL

Part II

FINANCIAL PROVISIONS

Part III

DEVELOPMENT PLANS

Part IV

CONTROL OF DEVELOPMENT AND OF RETENTION OF CERTAIN STRUCTURES, ETC.

Part V

AMENITIES

Part VI

COMPENSATION

Part VII

ACQUISITION OF LAND, ETC.

Part VIII

MISCELLANEOUS

An Act to make provision, in the interests of the common good, for the proper planning and development of cities, towns and other areas, whether urban or rural (including the preservation and improvement of the amenities thereof), to make certain provisions with respect to acquisition of land, to repeal the Town and Regional Planning Acts, 1934 and 1939, and certain other enactments and to make provisions for other matters connected with the matters aforesaid. [7th August, 1963]

Be it enacted by the Oireachtas as follows:

Part I

PRELIMINARY AND GENERAL

1. Short title and commencement

(1) This Act may be cited as the Local Government (Planning and Development) Act, 1963.

(2) This Act shall come into operation as follows:

   (a) this section shall come into operation on the passing of this Act,

   (b) ...[1a]

   (c) if an order is made under paragraph (a) of subsection (3) of this section, the rest of this Act shall come into operation on the day appointed by that order,[3a]

   (d) if an order is not made under paragraph (a) of subsection (3) of this section, the rest of this Act shall come into operation in an area on the day appointed with respect to that area by order made under paragraph (b) of that subsection.

(3) The Minister for Local Government[3b] –

   (a) may by order appoint a day[3a] to be the day appointed under this Act, or

   (b) may by orders appoint two or more different days to be, with respect to different areas respectively, the days appointed under this Act.   **[1]**

---

1 Amendments

a   Section 1(2)(b) was repealed by the BCA 1990, s 24.

3 Notes

a   The "appointed day" was 1 October 1964 for the whole country.

b   Now the Minister for the Environment.

4 Commentary

The Planning Acts became operative on 1 October 1964. Before that date a degree of planning control had existed under the Town and Regional Planning Act 1934 and the Town and Regional Planning (Amendment) Act 1939. A planning permission granted under these latter Acts may still have some application: see s 92(2) of the LG(PD)A 1963 and *Molumby v Kearns,* High Court, unrep 19 January 1999, O'Sullivan J.

---

2. Interpretation

(1) In this Act, save where the context otherwise requires –

"the Act of 1919" means the Acquisition of Land (Assessment of Compensation) Act, 1919;

"the Act of 1934" means the Town and Regional Planning Act, 1934 (repealed by this Act);

"advertisement" means any word, letter, model, balloon, kite, poster, notice, device or representation employed for the purpose of advertisement, announcement or direction;[3a]

"advertisement structure" means any structure which is a hoarding, scaffold, framework, pole, standard, device or sign (whether illuminated or not) and which is used or intended for use for exhibiting advertisements;

"**agriculture**" includes horticulture, fruit growing, seed growing, dairy farming, the breeding and keeping of livestock (including any creature[3b] kept for the production of food, wool, skins or fur, or for the purpose of its use in the farming of land), the use of land as grazing land, meadow land, osier land, market gardens and nursery grounds, the use of land for turbary, and the use of land for woodlands where that use is ancillary to the farming of land for other agricultural purposes, and "**agricultural**" shall be construed accordingly;

"**alteration**"[2a] includes any plastering or painting which materially alters the external appearance of a structure so as to render such appearance inconsistent with the character of the structure or of neighbouring structures;

"**appointed day**"[3c] means –

    (a) if a day is appointed under paragraph (a) of subsection (3) of section 1 of this Act, that day, and

    (b) if a day is not appointed under that paragraph, the day appointed under paragraph (b) of that subsection with respect to the relevant area;

["**the Birds Directive**" means Council Directive No. 79/409/EEC of 2 April 1979 on the conservation of wild birds;][1a]

"**car park**" has the same meaning as in section 101 of the Road Traffic Act, 1961;

["**Council Directive**" means the Council Directive of 27 June 1985 (No 85/337/ EEC, OJ No 175/40 5 July 1985) on the assessment of the effects of certain public and private projects on the environment, and any Directive amending or replacing that Directive;][1b]

"**development**" has the meaning assigned to it by section 3, and "**develop**" shall be construed accordingly;

"**development plan**" has the meaning appropriate in accordance with subsection (9) of section 19;

["**environmental impact statement**" means a statement of the effects, if any, which proposed development, if carried out, would have on the environment;][1b]

["**European site**" means –

    (a) a special area of conservation;

    (b) a site of Community importance which has been placed on the list referred to in the third sub-paragraph of Article 4(2) of the Habitats Directive;

    (c) an area classified pursuant to paragraph (1) or (2) of Article 4 of the Birds Directive;][1a]

"**exempted development**" has the meaning specified in section 4;

"**exhibit**", in relation to an advertisement, includes affix, inscribe, print, paint and otherwise delineate;

"**fence**" includes a hoarding or similar structure;

"**functions**" includes powers and duties;

["**the Habitats Directive**" means Council Directive No. 92/43/EEC of 21 May, 1992, on the conservation of natural habitats and of wild fauna and flora;][1a]

"**land**" includes any structure and any land covered with water (whether inland or coastal) and, in relation to the acquisition of land, includes any interest or right in or over land (including an interest or right granted by or held from the authority acquiring the land);

"**local authority**" means a local authority for the purposes of the Local Government Act, 1941;

"**the Minister**" means the Minister for Local Government;[3d]

"**non-municipal town**" means a place (not being a county borough, borough, urban district or town in which the Towns Improvement (Ireland) Act, 1854, is in operation) which is designated a town in the report of the census of population taken in the year 1956;[2b]

"**obsolete area**" means an area consisting of land (in this definition referred to as the principal land) which, in the opinion of the planning authority, is badly laid out or the development of which has, in their opinion, become obsolete, together with such land contiguous or adjacent to the principal land as, in the opinion of the planning authority, is necessary for the satisfactory development or user of the principal land;

"**owner**" in relation to land, means, a person, other than a mortgagee not in possession, who, whether in his own right or as trustee or agent for any other person, is entitled to receive the rack rent of the land or, where the land is not let at a rack rent, would be so entitled if it were so let;

"**prescribed**" means prescribed by regulations made by the Minister;

"**public place**" means any street, road, seashore or other place to which the public have access whether as of right or by permission and whether subject to or free of charge;

"**public road**" has the same meaning as in the Road Traffic Act, 1961;

"**the register**"[3e] means the register kept under section 8;

"**reserved function**"[3f] means –

(a) with respect to the council of a county or an elective body for the purposes of the County Management Acts, 1940 to 1955, a reserved function for the purposes of the County Management Acts, 1940 to 1955,

(b) with respect to the corporation of a county borough, a reserved function for the purposes of the Acts relating to the management of the county borough;

"**road**" has the same meaning as in the Road Traffic Act, 1961;

"**scheduled town**" means –

(a) any town specified in Part I of the First Schedule to this Act, or

(b) any non-municipal town specified in Part II of that Schedule;

"**seashore**" has the same meaning as in the Foreshore Act, 1933;

"**special amenity area order**"[3g] means an order confirmed under section 43;

"**statutory undertaker**" means a person authorised by a British or Saorstát Éireann statute or an Act of the Oireachtas or an order having statutory force to construct, work, or carry on a railway, canal, inland navigation, dock, harbour, gas, electricity, or other public undertaking;

"**structure**" means any building, erection, structure, excavation, or other thing constructed, erected, or made on, in, or under any land, or any part of a structure so defined, and, where the context so admits, includes the land on, in, or under which the structure is situate:

"unauthorised structure" means –

(a) in relation to a structure in an area in relation to which a resolution under section 26 of the Act of 1934 was passed, a structure other than –

    (i) a structure in existence when that resolution was passed,

    (ii) a structure for which there was a general or special permission under that Act, being a permission which has not been revoked,

    (iii) a structure the construction, erection or making of which was the subject of a permission for development granted under section 26 of this Act, being a permission which has not been revoked, or which exists as a result of the carrying out on or after the appointed day of exempted development,

    (iv) a structure for the retention of which a permission was granted under section 27 of this Act, being a permission which has not been revoked,

    (v) a structure which, immediately before the appointed day, had the protection afforded by section 15 of the Act of 1934, or –

(b) in relation to a structure in any other area, a structure other than –

    (i) a structure in existence on the commencement of the appointed day, or

    (ii) a structure the construction, erection or making of which was the subject of a permission for development granted under section 26 of this Act, being a permission which has not been revoked, or which exists as a result of the carrying out on or after the appointed day of exempted development;

"unauthorised use" means, in relation to land, use commenced on or after the appointed day, the change in use being a material change and being development other than development the subject of a permission granted under section 26 of this Act or exempted development;

"use" in relation to land, does not include the use of the land by the carrying out of any works thereon;[3h]

"works" includes any act or operation of construction, excavation, demolition, extension, alteration, repair or renewal.[3i]

(2) In this Act **"planning authority"** means –

(a) in the case of a county exclusive of any borough or urban district therein, the council of the county,

(b) in the case of a county or other borough, the corporation of the borough, and

(c) in the case of an urban district, the council of the district,

and references to the area of the planning authority shall be construed accordingly.

(3) A reference in this Act to contravention of a provision includes, where appropriate, a reference to refusal or failure to comply with that provision.

(4) Any reference in this Act to performance of functions includes, with respect to powers, a reference to exercise of powers.

(5) Any reference in this Act to any other enactment shall, except so far as the context otherwise requires, be construed as a reference to that enactment as amended by or under any other enactment, including this Act.

(6) (a) A town specified in Part II of the First Schedule to this Act shall be taken for the purposes of this Act as comprising the area declared by the council of the county in which the town is situate to be comprised therein for those purposes.

(b) Declaration of any such area shall be a reserved function.

[(c) A declaration made under this subsection may be amended by the council of a county by whom it was made and the making of any such amendment shall be a reserved function.][1c]

(7) In subsection (1) of section 22, subsection (1) of section 26, subsection (1) of section 27, subsection (2) of section 30, subsection (2) of section 31, subsection (2) of section 32, subsection (2) of section 33, subsection (2) of section 35, subsection (3) of section 36 and subsection (3) of section 37 of this Act –

(a) the references to the provisions of the development plan shall, until that plan is made, be construed as references to the provisions which the planning authority consider will be included in that plan;[3j]

(b) the references to the provisions of any special amenity area order relating to the area of the planning authority shall be construed as including references to any provisions which the planning authority consider will be included in a special amenity order relating to their area.

(8) The Minister may by order vary the First Schedule to this Act by addition or deletion, but, where any such order is proposed to be made, a draft thereof shall be laid before each House of the Oireachtas and the order shall not be made until a resolution approving of the draft has been passed by each such House.   [2]

---

1 Amendments

a   Inserted by EC(NH)R 1997 (SI 94/1997).

b   Inserted by EC(EIA)R 1989, art 5 (SI 349/1989).

c   Subsection (6)(c) was inserted by LG(PD)A 1976, s 43(1)(a).

2 Cross References

a   See s 4(1)(g) of this Act and *Cairnduff v O'Connell* [1986] IR 73 for a discussion of the precise meaning of these words.

b   See now s 62 of the LGA 1994 which modifies the application of the Town Improvements (Ireland) Act 1854 to certain areas.

3 Notes

a   See *Dublin Corporation v Regan Advertising* [1989] IR 61 which dealt with a change of use from one kind of advertisement to another. In that case, the court held that this change was a material change of use.

b   Does this cover farming of salmon parr, eg, in an inland lake?

c   The "appointed day" was 1 October 1964 for the whole country.

d   Now the Minister for the Environment.

e   The important role of the register in court proceedings, eg, was stressed by Henchy J in *Readymix (Eire) Ltd v Dublin County Council* Supreme Court, unrep, 30 July 1974.

f   In *P & F Sharpe Ltd v Dublin City & County Manager* [1989] IR 701, the Supreme Court held that in the case of a "section 4" direction, the decision-making function (normally carried out by a manager) is carried out by the councillors. They are bound to act judicially, in accordance with LG(PD)A 1963, s 26, but once they have done this, the manager must give effect to their direction.

g   The three Dublin planning authorities have made such orders. Only two, the Liffey Valley and North Bull Island special amenity area orders have been confirmed.

h   *Re Viscount Securities; Viscount Securities Ltd v Dublin County Council* 112 ILTR 17. See also *Kildare County Council v Goode* High Court, unrep 13 June 1997 where the distinction between "use" and "works" was considered in the context of an application under s 27 of LG(PD)A 1976. See also *Irish Wild Bird Conservancy v Clonakilty Golf & Country Club* High Court, unrep, 23 July 1993 for similar dicta re s 4(1) of LG(PD)A 1963.

i   See *Lennon v Kingdom Plant Hire* High Court, unrep, 13 December 1991.

j   A planning authority is accordingly authorised to have regard to the draft development plan. But see now *Chawke v Limerick County Council* High Court, unrep, February 1991.

4 Commentary

Section 2(2) specifies the geographical areas within which the Planning Acts operate, that is within County Council areas, County Boroughs, Corporations, and Urban District Councils. There may therefore be a number of separate planning authorities operating within a County. Powers under the Planning Acts are divided between the elected members, known as reserved powers, and the powers given to the County Manager, known as executive powers. The making of development plans and special amenity area orders is a matter reserved to the elected members, whereas the making of decisions on planning applications is an executive function.

---

3.   Development[3a]

(1) **"Development"** in this Act means, save where the context otherwise requires, the carrying out of any works on, in, or under land[3b] or the making of any material change[3c] in the use of any structures or other land.[3d]

(2) For the purposes of subsection (1) of this section and without prejudice to the generality thereof –

   (a)   where any structure or other land or any tree or other object on land becomes used for the exhibition of advertisements, or

   (b)   where land becomes used for any of the following purposes:

      (i)   the placing or keeping of any vans, tents or other objects, whether or not moveable and whether or not collapsible, for the purpose of caravanning or camping or the sale of goods,

      (ii)   the storage of caravans or tents,

      (iii)   the deposit of bodies or other parts of vehicles, old metal, mining or industrial waste, builders' waste, rubble or debris,

the use of the land shall be taken as having materially changed.

(3) For the avoidance of doubt it is hereby declared that for the purposes of this section the use as two or more dwellings of any structure previously used as a single dwelling involves a material change in the use of the structure and of each part thereof which is so used.[3e]   **[3]**

3 Notes

a   See the definition of "development" in the Dun Laoghaire Harbour (Amendment) Act 1994 which broadens the definition of "land" to include foreshore. See s (1)(1).

b   See *Lennon v Kingdom Plant Hire* High Court, unrep, 13 December 1991; *Tralee UDC v Stack* High Court, unrep, 13 January 1984; *Patterson v Murphy Trading Services Ltd* [1978] ILRM 85. *Westmeath County Council v Quirke* High Court, unrep, 28 May 1996, in particular, contains an excellent summary of the law.

c   Trivial changes or very brief changes of use may be ignored for planning purposes, see *McGrath Limestone Works Ltd v Galway County Council* [1989] ILRM 602, and it is the act of development itself and not the use which constitutes the change of use, see *Dublin Corporation v Moore* [1984] ILRM 339; see also *Dublin County Council v Carty Builders* [1987] IR 355 and *McGrath Limestone Works Ltd v Galway County Council* [1989] ILRM 602 where it was held that a change of use had not occurred. See also *Meath County Council v Daly* [1987] IR 391 on successive changes of use. See also the definition of "use" in s 2. See also *Kildare County Council v Goode* High Court, unrep 13 June 1997; *Mountcharles (Earl of) v Meath County Council* [1997] ILRM 446 which considers temporary intermittent uses, and *McMahon v Dublin Corporation* [1997] 1 ILRM 227. See also *South Dublin County Council v Balfe* High Court, unrep 3 November 1995.

d   See *Patterson v Murphy Trading Services Ltd* [1978] ILRM 85; *Cork Corporation v O'Connell* [1982] ILRM 505; *Dublin County Council v Tallaght Block Ltd* [1982] ILRM 534; Supreme Court, unrep, 17 May 1983; *Carrickhall Holdings v Dublin Corporation* [1983] ILRM 268; *Cusack and McKenna v Minister for Local Government and Dublin Corporation* High Court, unrep, 4 November 1980; *Dublin County Council v Sellwood Quarries* [1981] ILRM 23; *Monaghan County Council v Brogam* [1987] IR 333; [1987] ILRM 564; *Galway County Council v Lackagh Rock Ltd* [1985] IR 120 and *Dublin County Council v Macken* High Court, unrep, 13 May 1994. See also *Westmeath County Council v Quirke* High Court, unrep, 23 May 1996 where the law in this regard is extensively set out. See also *Kildare County Council v Goode* High Court, unrep 13 June 1997 where the distinction between "use" and "works" is considered in the context of proceedings under s 27 of LG(PD)A 1976. See also *Irish Wild Bird Conservancy v Clonakilty Golf and Country Club* High Court, unrep, 23 July 1993 where works for the reclamation of marshland were held not to be exempted development as they were in the nature of works and therefore the exemption in s 4(1) of LG(PD)A 1963 could not be relied on.

e   See *McMahon v Dublin Corporation* [1997] 1 ILRM 227 where it was held that the short term letting of houses as holiday homes in a development designed for normal domestic residences constituted a change of use.

4 Commentary

Section 3 contains the basis of the Planning Acts. Planning permission is required for development, ie for the carrying out of any works or for the making of any material change in the use of any structure or other land. "Works" is very broadly defined and includes "any" act, construction, excavation, demolition, extension, alteration, repair or renewal. A change in the use of a structure must amount to a material change in the use in order to constitute development and whether a change of use is material is a question of fact to be determined by An Bord Pleanála or ultimately by the High Court on appeal where an issue arises in this regard. A change of use may arise from the intensification of an existing use or where a use which was previously abandoned is subsequently reactivated. The strictness of the provisions of s 3 is mitigated by s 4 which provides that certain works and uses which otherwise would be deemed development are specified as being exempted from the provisions of the Acts and are thereby deemed exempted development.

4. Exempted development

(1) The following shall be exempted developments for the purposes of this Act:

(a) development consisting of the use of any land for the purposes of agriculture or forestry (including afforestation), and development consisting of the use for any of those purposes of any building occupied together with land so used;[3a]

(b) development by the council of a county in the county health district;[3b]

(c) development by the corporation of a county or other borough in such borough;

(d) development by the council of an urban district in such district;

(e) development consisting of the carrying out by the corporation of a county or other borough or the council of a county or an urban district of any works required for the construction of a new road or the maintenance or improvement of a road;[2a]

(f) development consisting of the carrying out by any local authority or statutory undertaker of any works for the purpose of inspecting, repairing, renewing, altering or removing any sewers, mains, pipes, cables, overhead wires, or other apparatus, including the breaking open of any street or other land for that purpose;

(g) development consisting of the carrying out of works for the maintenance, improvement or other alteration of any structure, being works which affect only the interior of the structure or which do not materially affect the external appearance of the structure so as to render such appearance inconsistent with the character of the structure or of neighbouring structures;[3c]

(h) development consisting of the use of any structure or other land within the curtilage of a dwellinghouse for any purpose incidental to the enjoyment of the dwellinghouse as such;

[(i) development consisting of the use of land for the purposes of a casual trading area (within the meaning of the Casual Trading Act, 1980);][1a]

[(j) development consisting of the carrying out of any of the works referred to in the Land Reclamation Act, 1949, [not being works comprised in the fencing or enclosure of land which has been open to or used by the public within the ten years preceding the date on which the works are commenced;]][1b, 3d]

(1A) ... [1c]

(2) (a) The Minister may by regulations provide for any class of development being exempted development for the purposes of this Act and such provision may be either without conditions or subject to conditions and either general or confined to a particular area or place.

(b) Regulations[3e] under this subsection may, in particular and without prejudice to the generality of the foregoing paragraph, provide, in the case of structures or other land used for a purpose of any specified class, for the use thereof for any other purpose being exempted development for the purposes of this Act. [2b]

(3) References in this Act to exempted development shall be construed as references to development which is –

(a) any of the developments specified in subsection (1) of this section, or

(b) development which, having regard to any regulations under subsection (2) of this section, is exempted development for the purposes of this Act.

[(4) (a) The Minister may, in connection with the Council Directive, prescribe development or classes of development for the purposes of this subsection.[2c]

(b) Notwithstanding paragraph (a) of subsection (1) of this section, development which is prescribed for the purposes of this subsection shall not be exempted development.][1d]   **[4]**

---

1 Amendments

a   Subsection (1)(i) was inserted by the Casual Trading Act 1980, s 7(3).

b   The words in square brackets were inserted by LG(PD)A 1976, s 43(1)(b).

c   Subsection (1A) was repealed by LG(PD)A 1999, s 32, which will come into operation on 1 January 2000.

d   The words in square brackets were inserted by EC(EIA)R 1989, art 6 (SI 349/1989). Prescribed developments are set out in LG(PD)R 1994 (SI 86/1994).

2 Cross References

a   See now the Roads Act 1993 generally in this regard.

b   See s 19(3) of the Roads Act 1993 which provides that the construction and maintenance of roads is an exempted development.

c   See LG(PD)R 1994, art 13.

3 Notes

a   See now however EC(EIA)R 1989 which modifies this concept and note this exemption only applies to use, and agricultural works are confined to those referred to in LG(PD)R 1994. See the decision of Costello P in *Irish Wild Bird Conservancy v Clonakilty Golf and Country Club* High Court, unrep, 23 July 1993 where works for the reclamation of marshland were held not to be exempted development as they were in the nature of works.

b   See LG(PD)R 1994 which sets out the procedures to be followed for certain local authority developments which is similar to that for planning applications but provides for no appeal mechanism against the ultimate decision.

c   See *Cork Corporation v O'Connell* [1982] ILRM 505, *Dublin Corporation v Langan* High Court, unrep, 14 May 1982 and *Cairnduff v O'Connell* [1986] IR 73. Reconstruction of a public house extensively damaged by fire but with sound structure was exempted development according to Blayney J in *Westmeath County Council v Moriarty* High Court, unrep, 30 July 1991. See also *Dublin Corporation v Bentham* High Court, unrep, 22 July 1992; *Carroll v Brushfield Ltd* High Court, unrep, 9 October 1992 and *McGoldrick v An Bord Pleanála* [1997] IR 497.

d   See *Tralee UDC v Stack* High Court, unrep, 13 January 1984.

e   On the interpretation of such regulations, see *Dillon v Irish Cement Ltd* Supreme Court, unrep, 26 November 1986, which requires that these regulations be strictly construed. See also *Murray v Buckley* High Court, unrep, 5 December 1990. Note however that the exempted development referred to here has now been modified.

4 Commentary

Certain developments which would otherwise require to be authorised by a grant of planning permission are exempted from such controls by virtue of s 4. These are developments by local authorities within their own areas, road construction works carried out by local authorities, alterations to a structure that does not materially change its appearance and the use of the structures within the curtilage of a dwelling house for the purposes of the enjoyment of that dwelling house. There are other exempted developments provided for under the LG(PD)R 1994, but unlike the provisions of s 4, these are subject to certain restrictions and conditions which do not apply to the exemptions contained in s 4. Exempted developments are to be strictly construed and in order to claim that a development is exempted one must be able to show clearly and unambiguously that one falls within the particular exempted development specified.

5.   References to the Minister

(1) If any question arises as to what, in any particular case, is or is not development or exempted development, the question shall be referred to and decided by the Board.[1a, 3a]

(2) Where a decision is given under this section, an appeal to the High Court from the decision may be taken at any time within the period of three months after the giving of the decision or such longer period as the High Court may in any particular case allow.[3b]   **[5]**

1 Amendments

a   As amended by LG(PD)A 1976, s 14(9), (10) which transferred the Minister's jurisdiction under s 5 to An Bord Pleanála.

3 Notes

a   See *Dublin Corporation v McGrath* High Court, unrep, 17 November 1978; *Stafford v Roadstone Ltd* [1980] ILRM 1 and *Carrickhall Holdings Ltd v Dublin Corporation* [1983] ILRM 268 where the scope and function of s 5, particularly in relation to a defence of exempted developments, was considered. See also the comments of Costello J in *Dublin County Council v Tallaght Block Co Ltd* [1982] ILRM 534. Furthermore, as Scannell points out in *Environmental and Planning Law* (Round Hall, 1995) comments to the contrary in *Readymix (Eire) v Dublin County Council* Supreme Court, unrep, 30 July 1974 predate the enactment of s 27 of LG(PD)A 1976.

b   Note the difference in periods within which an appeal may be brought in s 82 of LG(PD)A 1963 where an issue of law arises from the reference where the prescribed period is two months as opposed to s 5(2) where the prescribed period is three months. For a consideration of some legal principles in a s 5 reference see *McGoldrick v An Bord Pleanála* [1997] IR 497 where Barron J quashed a decision of the Board made contrary to fair procedures.

4 Commentary

An Bord Pleanála is charged with determining questions pursuant to ss 3 and 4 as to whether in any case a particular act or operation or a particular change of use is or is not development and/or exempted development. The Board can be compelled in certain circumstances to decide on such questions (see *Palmerlane Ltd v An Bord Pleanála* High Court, unrep, 28 January 1999, McGuinness J). Such questions referred to the Board are known as references and are decided in a similar manner to an appeal made to the Board under s 26 of the LG(PD)A 1963. An appeal on the merits of a decision by the Board on a reference may be brought to the High Court within three months of the date of such a decision, an appeal on a legal issue must be brought within two months of such a decision.

6.   Power of examination, investigation and survey

(1) A planning authority shall have all such powers of examination, investigation and survey as may be necessary for the performance of their functions in relation to this Act

or to any other Act under which they have functions affected by the performance of their functions under this Act.

(2) In particular and without prejudice to the generality thereof, subsection (1) of this section shall be construed as conferring powers to make –

    (a) examinations of tourist potential, interest and need,

    (b) land use surveys,

    (c) traffic, sociological and demographic surveys.   **[6]**

---

4 Commentary

The general power of entry under s 6 is circumscribed by s 83 which sets out the procedure for such entry and by s 64 which provides for the payment of compensation to land owners for damage arising from such entry.

---

7. Service of notices, etc.

(1) Where a notice or copy of an order is required or authorised by this Act or any order or regulation made thereunder to be served on or given to a person, it shall be addressed to him and shall be served on or given to him in one of the following ways:[3a]

    (a) where it is addressed to him by name, by delivering it to him;

    (b) by leaving it at the address at which he ordinarily resides or, in a case in which an address for service has been furnished, at that address;

    (c) by sending it by post in a prepaid registered letter addressed to him at the address at which he ordinarily resides or, in a case in which an address for service has been furnished, at that address;

    (d) where the address at which he ordinarily resides cannot be ascertained by reasonable inquiry and the notice or copy is so required or authorised to be given or served in respect of any land or premises, by delivering it to some person over sixteen years of age resident or employed on such land or premises or by affixing it in a conspicuous position on or near such land or premises.

(2) Where a notice or copy of an order is required by this Act or any order or regulation made thereunder to be served on or given to the owner or to the occupier of any land or premises and the name of the owner or of the occupier (as the case may be) cannot be ascertained by reasonable inquiry, it may be addressed to "the owner" or "the occupier" (as the case may require) without naming him.

(3) For the purposes of this section, a company registered under the Companies Acts, 1908 to 1959, shall be deemed to be ordinarily resident at its registered office, and every other body corporate and every unincorporated body shall be deemed to be ordinarily resident at its principal office or place of business.

(4) Where a notice or copy of an order is served on or given to a person by affixing it under paragraph (d) of subsection (1) of this section, a copy of the notice or order shall, within two weeks thereafter, be published in at least one newspaper circulating in the area in which the person is last known to have resided.

(5) A person who, at any time during the period of three months after a notice is affixed under paragraph (d) of subsection (1) of this section, removes, damages or defaces the

notice without lawful authority shall be guilty of an offence and shall be liable on summary conviction thereof to a fine not exceeding ten pounds.

(6) Where the Minister[1a] is satisfied that reasonable grounds exist for dispensing with the serving or giving under this Act or under any order or regulation made thereunder of a notice or copy of an order and that dispensing with the serving or giving of the notice or copy will not cause injury or wrong, he may dispense with the serving or giving of the notice or copy and every such dispensation shall have effect according to the tenor thereof.

(7) A dispensation under the foregoing subsection may be given either before or after the time when the notice or copy would, but for the dispensation, be required to be served or given and either before or after the doing of any act to which the notice or copy would, but for the dispensation, be a condition precedent.[3b]   **[7]**

---

1 Amendments

a   See LG(PD)A 1976, s 43(2) which provides that the reference to the Minister in sub-s (6) includes a reference to the Board.

3 Notes

a   See *Freeney v Bray Urban District Council* [1982] ILRM 29. Compare LG(PD)A 1992, s 22 for posting appeals.

b   In view of the very strict time limits provided for under the Planning Acts, this section appears to allow some degree of flexibility for the service of such notices and where a difficulty arises it may not always be necessary to seek an order of substituted service. However, it might be unwise to rely on this section *vis-à-vis* s 82(3) of LG(PD)A 1963 as the wording of sub-s 3(b)(iii) would appear to limit such service to personal service. Although the position is somewhat unclear and the time limit under s 82 is very strict, see *KSK Enterprises v An Bord Pleanála* Supreme Court, unrep, 24 March 1994 and *Schwestermann v An Bord Pleanála* [1994] 3 IR 437. For a consideration of the requirements relating to service under s 82 of LG(PD)A 1963 see *Lancefort v An Bord Pleanála* [1998] 2 ILRM 401 where the issue of service generally under the Planning Acts was considered.

4 Commentary

This section generally applies where notice is required to be given by a planning authority under the Planning Acts. Generally, where notice of a decision is required to be given by a planning authority, it has been held that this is required to be served on the person and the planning authority's obligations in this regard are strictly construed as the High Court has held, when deciding whether a planning authority has given its decision on applications for planning permission within the appropriate period (See *Freeney v Bray UDC* [1982] ILRM 29 and *Flynn & O'Flaherty Properties v Dublin Corporation* High Court, unrep, 11 December 1996, Kelly J). A similar strict approach has been held to apply to s 22 of LG(PD)A 1992 for those persons wishing to lodge appeals against decisions of a planning authority to An Bord Pleanála.

---

8.   Register

(1) A planning authority shall keep a register[3a] (in this Act referred to as the register) for the purposes of this Act in respect of all land within their area affected by this Act, and shall make all such entries and corrections[3b] therein as may from time to time be appropriate in accordance with this Act and any regulations made thereunder.

(2) The register shall incorporate a map for enabling a person to trace any entry in the register.

(3) The register shall be kept at the offices of the planning authority and shall be available for inspection during office hours.

(4) (a) A document purporting to be a copy of an entry in the register and to be certified by an officer of the planning authority as a correct copy shall be *prima facie* evidence of the entry and it shall not be necessary to prove the signature of such officer or that he was in fact such officer.

　　(b) Evidence of an entry in the register may be given by production of a copy thereof certified pursuant to this subsection and it shall not be necessary to produce the register itself.

　　(c) Where application is made to a planning authority for a copy under this section, the copy shall be issued to the applicant on payment by him to the planning authority of the [prescribed fee][1a] in respect of each entry.   **[8]**

---

1 Amendments

a　The words "the prescribed fee" were substituted for "a fee for ten shillings" by LG(PD)A 1982, s 12. The current prescribed fee is £7.30. See Sixth Schedule to LG(PD)R 1994 (SI 86/1994) as amended.

3 Notes

a　The importance of the register in litigation was emphasised by Henchy J in *Readymix (Eire) Ltd v Dublin County Council* Supreme Court, unrep, 30 July 1974.

b　A correction of the register was ordered in *State (Toft) v Galway Corporation* [1981] ILRM 439.

4 Commentary

This section requires a planning authority to keep a register and decisions of planning authorities under ss 26, 27, 28, 29, 30, 31, 32, 33, 35, 36, 37, 38, 44, 45, 46, 47, 48, 50, 55, 59, 66 and 72 of the LG(PD)A 1963, ss 25, 26, 28 and 29 of the LG(PD)A 1976 and decisions sought to be relied on by the planning authority under the Town and Regional Planning Acts 1934 and 1939 must all be entered on the register. The Courts have on occasions required that the matters entered on the register should be amended as in the case of *The State (Toft) v Galway Corporation* [1981] ILRM 439 and *Blessington Heritage Trust Ltd v Wicklow County Council* High Court, unrep, 21 January 1998.

9.　Obligation to give information to planning authority

(1) A planning authority may, for any purpose arising in relation to their functions under this Act, by notice in writing require the occupier of any structure or other land or any person receiving, whether for himself or for another, rent out of any structure or other land to state in writing to such authority, within a specified time not less than fourteen days after being so required, particulars of the estate, interest, or right by virtue of which he occupies such structure or other land or receives such rent (as the case may be), and the name and address (so far as they are known to him) of every person who to his knowledge has any estate or interest in or right over or in respect of such structure or other land.

(2) Every person who is required under this section to state in writing any matter or thing to a planning authority and either fails so to state such matter or thing within the time appointed under this section or, when so stating any such matter or thing, makes any statement in writing which is to his knowledge false or misleading in a material respect, shall be guilty of an offence under this section and shall be liable on summary conviction to a fine not exceeding [£100].[1a]   **[9]**

---

1 Amendments

a   Fine increased from £20 to £100 by LG(PD)A 1982, s 8.

---

10. Regulations generally[2a]

(1) The Minister may make regulations for prescribing any matter referred to in this Act as prescribed or to be prescribed or in relation to any matter referrred to in this Act as the subject of regulations.

(2) Every regulation made under this Act shall be laid before each House of the Oireachtas as soon as may be after it is made and, if a resolution annulling the regulation is passed by either such House within the next twenty-one days on which that House has sat after the regulation is laid before it, the regulation shall be annulled accordingly but without prejudice to the validity of anything previously done thereunder.   **[10]**

---

2 Cross References

a   See LG(PD)R 1994 (SI 86/1994); LG(PD)R 1995 (SI 69/1995) and LG(PD)(No 2)R 1995 (SI 75/1995), LG(PD)R 1999, (SI 92/1999).

---

11. Repeals

(1) The enactments mentioned in the Second Schedule to this Act are hereby repealed to the extent specified in the third column of that Schedule.   **[11]**

Part II

FINANCIAL PROVISIONS

---

4 Commentary

Part II provides for the sharing of costs relating to the carrying out of planning functions between separate local authorities or the giving of financial assistance to particular groups and organisations. The power to make such decisions is generally a power reserved to the elected members.

---

12. Expenses of administration of Minister

The expenses incurred by the Minister in the administration of this Act shall, to such extent as may be sanctioned by the Minister for Finance, be defrayed out of moneys provided by the Oireachtas.   **[12]**

13. Charging of expenses of planning authority who are council of a county

Expenses under this Act of a planning authority who are the council of a county shall be charged on the county (exclusive of every borough and urban district therein).   **[13]**

14. Assistance by planning authority in certain cases

(1) A planning authority may assist any of the bodies and persons specified in subsection (2) of this section by helping the body or person in money or kind or by the provision of services or facilities (including the services of staff).

(2) The bodies and persons referred to in subsection (1) of this section are:

(a)   a local development association,

(b)   a company under the Companies Acts, 1908 to 1959, having as one of its objects the object of providing amenities and facilities at tourist resorts and developing tourist traffic at or to such resorts,

(c)   a body or person concerned, with respect to the area of the planning authority, in the preservation or development of amenities (including the preservation of flora and fauna and of buildings, caves, sites, features and objects of artistic, architectural, archaeological, geological or historical interest) or in the carrying out of works of local improvement (including parking places) or maintenance of amenities,

[(cc)   a body or person providing homes or shelters for stray or unwanted dogs and cats,][1a]

(d)   in case the planning authority are the council of a county, the commissioners of a town in the county having commissioners.

(3) Assisting under this section shall be a reserved function.   **[14]**

---

1 Amendments

a   Subsection (2)(cc) was inserted by LG(PD)A 1976, s 43(1)(d).

---

15. Contribution towards training and research

(1) A planning authority may, within such limits and on such conditions as may be fixed by the Minister from time to time, contribute to the funds of any body which provides for training and research in relation to town and regional planning.[3a]

(2) Contributing under this section shall be a reserved function.   **[15]**

---

3 Notes

a   Article 4, Part I of Local Government Act 1991 (Removal of Controls) Regulations 1993 (SI 172/1993) provides that ministerial control in relation to s 15(1) shall be removed. Those regulations came into effect on 6 September 1993.

---

16. Apportionment of joint expenses

(1) Two or more planning authorities may make and carry out an agreement for sharing the cost of performing all or any of their functions under this Act and, where an agreement has been made under this subsection, the planning authorities concerned may terminate it at any time if they so agree.

(2) Where the Minister is satisfied that a planning authority propose to perform in their area a function under this Act wholly or partially in the interests of the area of, or at the request of, another planning authority (being a planning authority whose area is contiguous with the area of the first-mentioned planning authority), the other planning

authority shall defray the cost of the performance of the function to such extent as may be agreed upon between the authorities or, in default of agreement, as may be determined by the Minister.

(3) The making of an agreement under this section shall be reserved function.   **[16]**

17. Power to set off

Where a sum is due under this Act to any person by a planning authority and, at the same time, another sum under this Act is due by that person to that authority, the former sum may be set off against the latter either, as may be appropriate, in whole or in part.   **[17]**

18. [Payment of sum to or by appellant][1a]

[18]

---

1 Amendments

a   Section 18 was repealed by the BCA 1990, s 24.

Part III

DEVELOPMENT PLANS

19. Obligation to make development plan and contents of plan

(1) Every planning authority shall, within the period of three years beginning on the appointed day (or such longer period as the Minister may in any particular case allow), make a plan indicating development objectives[3a] for their area.

(2) A development plan[3b] shall consist of a written statement and a plan indicating the development objectives for the area in question, including objectives[3c] –

- (a) with respect to county boroughs, boroughs, urban districts and scheduled towns –
    - (i) for the use solely or primarily (as may be indicated in the development plan) of particular areas for particular purposes[3d] (whether residential, commercial, industrial, agricultural or otherwise),[3e]
    - (ii) for securing the greater convenience and safety of road users and pedestrians by the provision of parking places or road improvements or otherwise,
    - (iii) for development and renewal of obsolete areas,
    - (iv) for preserving, improving and extending amenities,
    - [(v) for the conservation and protection of European sites in the area to which the development plan relates,][1a]
    - [(vii) for protecting structures within the meaning of the Local Government (Planning and Development) Act, 1999, or parts of such structures, which are of special architectural, historical, archaeological, artistic, cultural, scientific, social or technical interest,
    - (viii) for preserving the character of architectural conservation areas.][1b]
- (b) with respect to other areas –
    - (i) for development and renewal of obsolete areas,
    - (ii) for preserving, improving and extending amenities,

21

(iii) for the provision of new water supplies and sewerage services and the extension of existing such supplies and services,

[(iv) for the conservation and protection of European sites in the area to which the development plan relates.]¹ᶜ

[(vi) for protecting structures (within the meaning of the Local Government (Planning and Development) Act, 1999), or parts of such structures, which are of special architectural, historical, archaeological, artistic, cultural, scientific, social or technical interest,

(vii) for preserving the character of architectural conservation areas.]¹ᵈ

(3) Without prejudice to the foregoing subsection and subsection (5) of this section, a development plan may indicate the objectives for any of the purposes mentioned in the Third Schedule to this Act and, with respect to areas other than county boroughs, boroughs, urban districts and scheduled towns, objectives for the use solely or primarily (as may be indicated in the development plan) of particular areas for particular purposes (whether residential, commercial, industrial, agricultural or otherwise).

(4) Where a planning authority propose to include in a development plan any development objective the responsibility for the effecting of which would fall on another local authority, the planning authority shall not include that objective in the plan save after consultation with the other local authority.

(5) A planning authority may make either –

(a) one development plan, being a plan in relation to the whole of their area and all the sub-paragraphs in paragraph (a) and, where appropriate, paragraph (b) of subsection (2) of this section, or

(b) two or more development plans, each plan being a plan in relation to the whole of their area and some one or more of those sub-paragraphs or to a part of their area and all or some one or more of those sub-paragraphs.

(6) (a) The making of an application to the Minister for the allowance of such a longer period as is referred to in subsection (1) of this section shall be a reserved function.

(b) Where a planning authority have applied to the Minister for the allowance of such a longer period as is referred to in subsection (1) of this section, they shall cause notice of the application to be published in at least one newspaper circulating in their area and in the *Iris Oifigiúil*.

(c) A notice under the foregoing paragraph –

(i) shall specify the longer period applied for, and

(ii) shall state that objections with respect to the application made to the Minister within a specified period of not less than one month will be taken into consideration before the grant of the application (and such objections shall be taken into consideration accordingly).

(7) The making of a development plan or any variations of any such plan shall be a reserved function.

(8) Regulations may make provision with respect to the making available for purchase by the public of printed copies of development plans and extracts therefrom.

(9) (a) Any reference in this Act to a development plan shall be construed as a reference to a plan under subsection (1) of this section (subject to any variations thereof).

(b) In this Act "**the development plan**" means the plan or plans under subsection (1) of this section of the relevant planning authority (subject to any variations thereof).   **[19]**

1 Amendments

a   Paragraph (a)(v) was inserted by the EC(NH)R 1997 (SI 94/1997), art 26(b).

b   Paragraph (b)(iv) was inserted by the EC(NH)R 1997 (SI 94/1997), art 26(b).

c   Paragraphs (a)(vii) and (a)(viii) were inserted by LG(PD)A 1999, s 33 which will come into operation on 1 January 2000.

d   Paragraphs (b)(vi) and (b)(vii) were inserted by LG(PD)A 1999, s 33 which will come into operation on 1 January 2000.

3 Notes

a   See *Glencar Exporations plc v Mayo County Council* [1993] 2 IR 237 for a discussion on the interpretation of the words "development objectives". See also *Keogh v Galway Corporation* High Court, unrep, 3 March 1995, *McCann v Galway Corporation* High Court, unrep, 15 November 1994 and *O'Connor v Clare County Council* High Court, unrep, 11 February 1994.

b   See *Tennyson v Dun Laoghaire Corporation* [1991] 2 IR 527 on the definition of a development plan and the interpretation of the provisions of such plans. See also *Huntsgrove Developments v Meath County Council* [1994] 2 ILRM 36.

c   See judgment of Kenny J in *Central Dublin Development Association v Attorney General* 109 ILTR 69, which is effectively the only case which considered in detail the constitutional implications of such plans and found, although on rather suspect grounds, that such plans were consistent with the Constitution and were, in particular, not inconsistent with property rights protected under Article 40.3.

d   See judgment of McMahon J (High Court) in *Shortt v Dublin County Council* [1983] ILRM 377. "Particular purpose" in this sub-section does not have the same meaning as in Rule 11(a) of the rules for assessing compensation.

e   The word "zoning" is not used anywhere in the Planning Acts. This sub-paragraph is the legal basis for zoning. There is a mandatory obligation on planning authorities to indicate zoning objectives in urban areas, but not in rural areas. Many plans leave large areas in agricultural use unzoned, even for agriculture. This is known to planners as "white land", another term which does not appear in the statutes. See the comments of Murphy J in *O'Connor v Clare County Council* High Court, unrep, 11 February 1994.

4 Commentary

The Planning Acts are structured on the basis that the elected members set out the context for the development and the control of development within the functional areas in their development plan and all decisions made on planning applications by the County Manager must be consistent with the provisions of the development plan. The development plan is crucial therefore as it sets the agenda for all local authority developments and provides a framework for the assessing of all planning applications. The plan must be reviewed at least once every five years but it would appear that this section envisages its review on a much more frequent basis. The making of a development plan is a reserved function and once adopted has been held to be in the nature of a contract between the local authority, developers and the public generally that they will not effect any development which will materially contravene the plan. The interpretation of the development plan is a matter of law and will be construed as it would by an ordinary person with no particular expertise in law or town planning.

20. Obligation to review development plan and variations of plan

(1) Where a planning authority have made a development plan, they shall, from time to time as occasion may require and at least once in every five years after the date of making of the plan, review the plan and make in it any variations (whether by way of alteration, addition or deletion) which they consider proper, [or make a new development plan].[1a]

[(1A) The Minister may extend (either in relation to planning authorities generally or in a particular case) the period during which a planning authority may comply with the requirements of subsection (1) of this section.][1b, 3b]

(2) Where a planning authority have completed the discharge of their obligations under section 19 of this Act by making two or more plans as provided for by paragraph (b) of subsection (5) of that section, the periods of five years referred to in subsection (1) of this section shall run from the date of making the last of such plans.   [20]

1 Amendments

a   The words in square brackets were inserted by LG(PD)A 1976, s 43(1)(e).

b   Subsection (1A) was inserted by LG(PD)A 1976, s 43(1)(f).

3 Notes

a   In *The State (Abenglen Property Ltd) v Dublin Corporation* [1984] IR 381; [1982] ILRM 590, D'Arcy J held that the then current development plan for Dublin was a new plan, and not a review of the earlier one. He said "The 1980 plan was a complete plan in itself". On this basis, most current development plans are new plans rather than reviews. See also *Huntsgrove Developments Ltd v Meath County Council* [1994] 2 ILRM 36. In *Ferris v Dublin County Council* High Court, unrep, 12 October 1990; Supreme Court, unrep, 7 November 1990 it was held that a development plan could not be amended by a simple resolution.

b   See *Blessington Heritage Trust Ltd v Wicklow County Council* High Court, unrep, 21 January 1998 where it was held that the provisions of s 20 are mandatory and a decision of the planning authority to adopt the plan outside the period prescribed in s 20(1)(a) was null and void.

4 Commentary

The review of a development plan is crucial to the proper functioning of the Planning Acts in that a planning authority may either vary the plan or make a new plan. It is very difficult to see the difference between a variation of a plan and the making of a new plan. The planning authority may have regard to a draft plan in dealing with a planning application having regard to s 2. A development plan must be reviewed at least once every five years, but the Minister may extend the period for such review to take place. However, if a development is adopted outside the period prescribed then such adoption will be void but the original plan continues until a new plan is adopted.

21. Publication of notices with respect to plans, etc.

(1) Where a planning authority have prepared a draft of a proposed development plan or of proposed variations of a development plan –

(a) they shall send copies of the prescribed documents to the prescribed authorities,[2a]

(b) they shall cause notice of the preparation of the draft to be published in the *Iris Oifigiúil* and in at least one newspaper circulating in their area,

[(c) where the draft includes any provision relating to any addition to or deletion from the record of protected structures, they shall -

    (i) serve notice of the preparation of the draft on the owner and on the occupier of the proposed protected structure or the protected structure, as the case may be, and

    (ii) incorporate in the notice particulars of the provision, including whether the addition or deletion was recommended by the Minister for Arts, Heritage, Gaeltacht and the Islands,][1a]

(d) where the draft includes any provision relating to the preservation of a public right of way, they shall serve notice (which shall incorporate particulars of the provision and a map indicating the right of way) of the preparation of the draft on the owner and on the occupier of the land.

(2) A notice under the foregoing subsection shall state –

    (a) that a copy of the draft may be inspected at a stated place and at stated times during a stated period of not less than three months (and the copy shall be kept available for inspection accordingly),

and

    (b) that objections or representations[3a] with respect to the draft made to the planning authority within the said period will be taken into consideration before the making of the plan or variations (and any such objections or representations shall be taken into consideration accordingly), and

    [(bb) that if any objections or representations are made within the said period to the planning authority with respect to a proposed addition to or deletion from the record of protected structures and if the addition or deletion was recommended by the Minister for Arts, Heritage, Gaeltacht and the Islands, the planning authority shall forward a copy of them to that Minister for that Minister's observations, and

    (bbb) that when objections or representations are considered under paragraph (b) of this subsection, any observations received from the Minister for Arts, Heritage, Gaeltacht and the Islands within one month after the receipt by that Minister of the objections or representations will also be taken into consideration, (and any such observations shall be taken into consideration accordingly), and][1b]

    (c) that any ratepayer making objection with respect to the draft may include in his objection a request to be afforded an opportunity to state his case before a person or persons appointed by the planning authority (and such opportunity shall be afforded to such objector and his statement shall be considered together with his objection),

and, in the case of a notice served pursuant to paragraph (d) of subsection (1) of this section, the notice shall also state that the draft includes provision relating to the preservation of the public right of way and that there is a right of appeal to the Circuit Court in relation to such provision.

(3) Any person may, before the expiration of the twenty-one days next following the period stated pursuant to paragraph (a) of subsection (2) of this section, appeal to the Circuit Court against the inclusion in the proposed plan or variations of any such provision as is referred to in paragraph (d) of subsection (1) of this section, and the Court, if satisfied that no public right of way subsists, shall so declare and the provision shall accordingly not be included.

(4) Where a planning authority make a development plan or variations of any such plan, they shall cause a notice of the making to be published in the *Iris Oifigiúil* and in at least one newspaper circulating in their area.

(5) A notice under the foregoing subsection shall state that a copy of the plan or variations is available for inspection at a stated place and at stated times (and the copy shall be kept available for inspection accordingly).

(6) (a) A document purporting to be a copy of the development plan or of a part thereof and to be certified by an officer of a planning authority as a correct copy shall be *prima facie* evidence of the plan or part, and it shall not be necessary to prove the signature of such officer or that he was in fact such officer.

(b) Evidence of a development plan or any part thereof may be given by production of a copy thereof certified pursuant to this subsection and it shall not be necessary to produce the plan itself.

(c) Where application is made to a planning authority for a copy under this section, the copy shall be issued to the applicant on payment by him to the planning authority of such fee as they may fix not exceeding the reasonable cost of making the copy.[3b]   **[21]**

---

1 Amendments

a   Subsection (1)(c) was substituted by LG(PD)A 1999, s 34 which will come into operation on 1 January 2000.

b   Paragraphs (2)(bb) and (2)(bbb) were inserted by LG(PD)A 1999, s 34 which will come into operation on 1 January 2000.

2 Cross References

a   See LG(PD)R 1994 (SI 86/1994), art 6 for the prescribed documents.

3 Notes

a   See *Finn v Bray UDC* [1969] IR 169.

b   See *MacPharthalain v Commissioners of Public Works* Supreme Court, unrep, 4 May 1993 on the necessity of adopting proper procedures in the preparation of plans which affect property rights. Is it permissible, eg, to preserve a view of lands which may significantly affect the development potential of such lands without informing the land owner of the proposal? See also *Malahide Community Council Ltd v Dublin County Council* High Court, unrep, 19 December 1994.

4 Commentary

This section provides that notice of the preservation of a building or a right of way is to be served but it is only in the latter case that there is a statutory right of appeal against such purported preservation to the Circuit Court. Representations may be made to the planning authority against any provision contained in the plan, but curiously the right to insist on an oral hearing is limited to ratepayers. The fact that this section appears arbitrarily to give a class of person a particular privilege denied to others may render this particular subsection open to question.

[21A. Amendment of draft development plan or draft variation[1a, 3a]

(1) Where a planning authority have prepared a draft of a proposed development plan or of proposed variations of a development plan and, after complying with the requirements of subsections (1) and (2) of section 21 of this Act, it appears to the authority that the draft should be amended, subject to subsection (2) of this section they may amend the draft and make the development plan or variations accordingly.

(2) In case the proposed amendment would, if made, be a material alteration of the draft concerned, the planning authority shall cause notice of the proposed amendment to be published in the *Iris Oifigiúil* and in at least one newspaper circulating in their area, and having complied with the requirements of subsection (3) and, where appropriate, a requirement of subsection (4) of this section, and having taken into account any representations, they may, as they shall think fit, make the proposed plan or proposed variation, as the case may be, with or without the proposed amendment or with such other amendment (not being an amendment providing for the preservation of a structure or public right of way) as, having regard to the particular circumstances, they consider appropriate.

(3) A notice under the foregoing subsection shall state that –

    (a) a copy of the proposed amendment of the draft may be inspected at a stated place and at stated times during a stated period of not less than one month (and the copy shall be kept available for inspection accordingly), and

    (b) written representations with respect to the proposed amendment of the draft made to the planning authority within the said period will be taken into consideration before the making of any amendment (and any such representations shall be taken into consideration accordingly), and

    [(c) if any written representations are made within the said period with respect to a proposed addition to or deletion from the record of protected structures and if the addition or deletion was recommended by the Minister for Arts, Heritage, Gaeltacht and the Islands, the planning authority shall forward a copy of the representations to that Minister for that Minister's observations, and

    (d) that when representations are considered under paragraph (b) of this subsection, any observations received from the Minister for Arts, Heritage. Gaeltacht and the Islands within one month after the receipt by that Minister of the representations will also be taken into consideration (and any such observations shall be taken into consideration accordingly),][1b]

    [(4) (a) Where the proposed amendment includes any provision to add to or delete from the record of protected structures, the planning authority shall, in addition to complying with the requirements of subsection (2) of this section, serve a copy of the notice incorporating particulars of the provision on the owner and on the occupier of the proposed protected structure or the protected structure, as the case may be.][1c]

    (b) Where the proposed amendment includes any provision to preserve a public right of way, the planning authority shall, in addition to complying with the requirements of the said subsection (2), serve a copy of the notice incorporating particulars of the provision and a map indicating the right of way on the owner and on the occupier of the land.

(5) Any person may, before the expiration of twenty-one days next following the period stated pursuant to paragraph (a) of subsection (3) of this section, appeal to the Circuit Court against the inclusion in the proposed amendment of any such provision as is referred to in subsection (4)(b) of this section, and the Court, if satisfied that no public right of way subsists, shall so declare and the provision shall accordingly not be included.] **[22]**

---

1 Amendments

a   Section 21A was inserted by LG(PD)A 1976, s 37.

b   Subparagraphs (c) and (d) were inserted by LG(PD)A 1999, s 34, which will come into operation on 1 January 2000.

c   Subsection (4)(a) was substituted by LG(PD)A 1999, s 34, which will come into operation on 1 January 2000.

3 Notes

a   This provision avoids the dilemma highlighted in *Finn v Bray UDC* [1969] IR 169. See *Huntsgrove Developments Ltd v Meath County Council* [1994] 2 ILRM 36. See also *Ferris v Dublin County Council* High Court, unrep, 12 October 1990; Supreme Court, unrep, 7 November 1990 where it was held that a plan could not be amended by a simple resolution. See also *Grange Developments Ltd v Dublin County Council* [1986] IR 246; [1987] ILRM 245 where it was held that members could not delegate to the County Manager the power to grant permission in contravention of the plan. However, a County Manager will have much greater discretion in granting a planning permission which may be in contravention of the development plan. See also the judgment of Kelly J in *Blessington & District Community Council v Wicklow County Council* High Court, unrep, 19 July 1996 regarding the duty of local authorities to have regard to their plan before making a decision on an application for permission.

4 Commentary

This section provides that a draft plan may be amended but if any major amendment is carried out to the draft, then the plan must go back on display for a further period of one month. After the expiration of this period then the members may either adopt either the first or the second draft but it would appear they are limited to either of these options.

---

22. General duty of planning authority[3a]

(1) It shall be the duty of a planning authority to take such steps as may be necessary for securing the objectives which are contained in the provisions of the development plan.

(2) The Minister may require the development plans of two or more planning authorities to be co-ordinated in respect of matters and in a manner specified by him and thereupon –

   (a) the authorities shall comply with the requisition, and

   (b) any dispute between them arising out of any matters inserted or to be inserted in a development plan shall be determined by the Minister.

(3) The Minister may require a planning authority to vary the development plan in respect of matters and in a manner specified by him and thereupon it shall be the duty of the authority to comply with the requisition.

(4) Subsection (3) of this section shall have effect subject to the proviso that where the planning authority, as a result of considering pursuant to paragraph (b) of subsection (2) of section 21 of this Act any objection or representation, decide, with the consent of the Minister, that the proposed variations should be altered in any respect, they may make the variations subject to that alteration.

[(5) Where under this section the Minister requires a planning authority to vary the development plan, pending compliance by them with the requisition it shall be the duty of the authority to have regard to the requisition in the performance of their function under this Act.]¹ᵃ   **[23]**

---

1 Amendments

a   Subsection (5) was inserted by LG(PD)A 76, s 43(1)(h).

3 Notes

a   See *An Taisce v Dublin Corporation* High Court, unrep, 31 January 1973; *AG (McGarry) v Sligo County Council* [1991] 1 IR 99 (HC, SC); [1989] ILRM 768 (SC); *O'Leary v Dublin County Council* [1988] IR 150; *Wilkinson v Dublin County Council* [1991] ILRM 605; *Ferris v Dublin County Council* High Court, unrep, 12 October 1990; Supreme Court, unrep, 7 November 1990; *Keogh v Galway Corporation* High Court, unrep, 3 March 1995; *McCann v Galway Corporation* High Court, unrep, 15 November 1994; *Tennyson v Dun Laoghaire Corporation* [1991] 2 IR 527; *Healy v Dublin County Council* High Court, unrep, 29 April 1993. See also the decision of Barron J in *Roughan v Clare County Council* High Court, unrep, 18 December 1996 where a development proposed in an area of special control but not within an area formally zoned was held to be a material contravention of the development plan.

4 Commentary

This is an important provision as it provides that a planning authority may not effect any development which contravenes its plan and requires that any developments to be carried out must be consistent with the plan. It has furthermore been interpreted to require that any major developments contemplated by a local authority within its functional area must be provided for in the plan.

---

23. Preparation and publication of model forms of development plans

The Minister may, as and when he thinks fit, prepare and publish, for the use and guidance of planning authorities and other persons interested, general instructions in relation to the preparation of development plans, together with model forms of development plans and of provisions and clauses usually inserted in such plans.³ᵃ   **[24]**

---

3 Notes

a   Guidelines on the preparation of urban development plans (the Blue Book) have been prepared by the Department of the Environment.

Part IV

Control of Development and of Retention of Certain Structures, etc.

24. General obligation to obtain permissions

(1) Subject to the provisions of this Act, permission shall be required under this Part of this Act –

- (a) in respect of any development of land, being neither exempted development nor development commenced before the appointed day,[2a, 3a] and

- (b) in the case of a structure which existed immediately before the appointed day and is on the commencement of that day an unauthorised structure, for the retention of the structure.

(2) A person shall not carry out any development in respect of which permission is required by subsection (1) of this section save under and in accordance with a permission granted under this Part of this Act.

(3) Any person who contravenes subsection (2) of this section shall be guilty of an offence.[1a, 2b]

(4) In a prosecution for an offence under this section –

- (a) it shall not be necessary for the prosecution to show, and it shall be assumed until the contrary is shown by the defendant, that the development in question was neither exempted development nor development commenced before the appointed day.[2c]

- (b) ...[1b]   **[25]**

---

1 Amendments

a   By LG(PD)A 1982, s 15 all words after "offence" were repealed. These words had set fines for the offence and continuing offences which would be imposed on summary conviction.

b   Subsection 4(b) was repealed by LG(PD)A 1976, s 45.

2 Cross References

a   See now LG(PD)A 1993 which retrospectively authorises an unauthorised development carried out by the State.

b   By LG(PD)A 1982, ss 8, 9 this offence is punishable on indictment by a fine not exceeding £10,000 or two years' imprisonment or both and if tried summarily by a fine of £800 or six months' imprisonment or both.

c   See LG(PD)A 1992, s 20, for revised penalties for breaches of this section, which can be £1 million and/or imprisonment for two years on conviction on indictment and there is furthermore provision for prosecution for continuing offences.

3 Notes

a   LG(PD)A 1963, s 40. The appointed day was 1 October 1964. This section does not apply to the retention of a structure or continuance of a use. However, this section creates the general obligation to obtain planning permission. See *Howard v Commissioners of Public Works* High Court, unrep, 17 February 1993; Supreme Court, unrep, 26 May 1993; *Byrne v Commissioners of Public Works* High Court, unrep, 27 November 1992.

4 Commentary

This section provides that a breach of a requirement of the Planning Acts is a criminal offence which if prosecuted under s 24 is indictable but which may be tried summarily. Because such an offence is deemed indictable, there is no time limit within which such a prosecution may be brought and the general five year rule which applies to most prosecutions under the Planning Acts does not apply to prosecutions under s 4 on indictment. A breach of the Planning Acts will occur if development which is not an exempted development is carried out without the necessary authorisation under the Planning Acts which will generally be a grant of permission under s 26 of LG(PD)A 1963.

25. Permission regulations

(1) The Minister shall by regulations[2a] (in this Act referred to as permission regulations) provide for –

(a) the grant of permissions for the development of land, and

(b) the grant of permissions for the retention of structures which existed immediately before the appointed day and are on that day unauthorised structures,

and such permissions may be granted on an application in that behalf made to the planning authority in accordance with the provisions of the regulations[3a] and subject to any requirements of or made pursuant to the regulations being complied with by the applicant.

(2) Regulations under this section may, in particular and without prejudice to the generality of the foregoing subsection, make provision for –

(a) applications, expressed to be outline applications, for permissions for development subject to the subsequent approval[3b] of the planning authority,

(b) requiring any applicants to publish any specified notices with respect to their applications,

(c) requiring any applicants to furnish to the Minister and to any other specified persons any specified information with respect to their applications,

[(cc) in connection with the Council Directive[3c] –

(i) the submission to the planning authority, in the case of specified applications or classes of applications, of an environmental impact statement in respect of the development to which the application relates,

(ii) enabling planning authorities to require, in the case of specified applications or classes of applications, the submission by the applicant of an environmental impact statement in respect of the development to which the application relates,

(iii) the information to be contained in an environmental impact statement,

(iv) the determination by planning authorities, for the purposes of dealing with applications, of the adequacy of information contained in environmental impact statements,

(v) the making of submissions or observations to the planning authority by persons other than the applicant in relation to development in respect of which the authority has received an environmental impact statement,[2b]

(vi) the making available for purchase of copies of environmental impact statements or extracts from such statements,

    (vii) requiring the giving of notice by planning authorities of any application in respect of development which is likely to have significant effects on the environment in another Member State of the European Communities,][1a

  [(viii) matters of procedure in relation to the making of a request for and the giving of a written opinion pursuant to subsection (6) of this section.][1b

  (d)   requiring any applicants to submit further information relative to their applications (including any information as to any estate or interest in or right over land),

[(dd)   enabling planning authorities to invite an applicant to submit to them revised plans or other drawings modifying, or other particulars providing for the modification of, the development to which the application relates and, in case such plans, drawings, or particulars are submitted to a planning authority in response to such an invitation, enabling the authority in deciding the application to grant a permission or an approval for the relevant development as modified by all or any of such plans, drawings, or particulars,][3d

  (e)   requiring the production of any evidence to verify any particulars of information given by any applicants,

  (f)   requiring planning authorities to furnish to the Minister and to any other specified persons any specified information with respect to any applications and the manner in which they have been dealt with,

  (g)   requiring planning authorities to publish any specified notices with respect to any applications or decisions on applications.

[(3) (a) At the request of an applicant or of a person intending to apply for permission, the Minister may, subject to paragraph (c) of this subsection, by order, having afforded the planning authority concerned an opportunity to furnish observations on the request, and where he is satisfied that exceptional circumstances so warrant, grant in respect of proposed development an exemption from a requirement of or under regulations under this section to prepare an environmental impact statement.][1c

  [(b) The Minister shall, in granting an exemption under paragraph (a) of this subsection, consider whether –

    (i) the effects, if any, of the proposed development on the environment should be assessed in some other manner, and

    (ii) the information collected in the course of such assessment should be made available to members of the public,

and he may, by order, apply such requirements regarding these matters in relation to the application for permission as he considers necessary or appropriate.] [1d

  [(c) The Minister shall, as soon as may be –

    (i) notify the planning authority concerned of his decision on any request made to him under paragraph (a) of this subsection, and of any requirements applied under paragraph (b) of this subsection, and

    (ii) where the proposed development to which the request relates comprises or is for the purposes of an activity in relation to which a licence under Part IV of the Environmental Protection Agency Act, 1992 (No. 7 of 1992) is required, notify the Environmental Protection Agency of his decision on the request, and of any requirements applied under paragraph

(b) of this subsection which relate to the risk of environmental pollution from the activity.]^{1e}

[(d) Notice of any exemption granted under paragraph (a) of this subsection, of the reasons for granting such exemption, and of any requirements applied under paragraph (b) of this subsection shall, as soon as may be, -

    (i) be published in the *Iris Oifigiúil* and in at least one daily newspaper published in the State, and

    (ii) be given, together with a copy of the information, if any, made available to members of the public in accordance with the said paragraph (b), to the Commission of the European Communities.] ^{1f}

[(e) An exemption shall not be granted under paragraph (a) of this subsection in respect of proposed development if another Member State of the European Communities, having been informed about the proposed development and its likely effects on the environment in that State, has indicated that it intends to furnish views on the said effects.]^{1g}

[(4) (a) A person who makes a request to the Minister for an exemption under subsection (3) of this section shall, as soon as may be –

    (i) inform the planning authority concerned of the making of the request and the date on which it was made, and

    (ii) where the proposed development comprises or is for the purposes of an activity in relation to which a licence under Part IV of the Environmental Protection Agency Act, 1992 (No. 7 of 1992) is required, notify the Environmental Protection Agency of the making of the request and the date on which it was made.]^{1h}

(b) Notwithstanding subsection (4) of section 26 of this Act, the appropriate period referred to in that subsection shall not, in a case in which a request is made to the Minister under subsection (3) of this section, include the period beginning on the day of the making of the request and ending on the day of receipt by the planning authority concerned of notice of the Minister's decision on the request.

[(5) Where an applicant is required to submit an environmental impact statement in respect of proposed development and the development is likely to have significant effects on the environment in another Member State of the European Communities, the planning authority concerned may enter into consultations with such State regarding the effects of the development on the environment in that State.] ^{1i}

[(6) (a) If an applicant or a person intending to apply for permission, before submitting an environmental impact statement in accordance with a requirement of or under regulations under this section, so requests, the relevant planning authority shall give a written opinion on the information to be contained in such statement.

(b) The giving of a written opinion in accordance with paragraph (a) of this subsection shall not prejudice the exercise by the planning authority concerned of its powers pursuant to the Planning Acts, 1963 to 1998, or any regulations made thereunder, to require the person who made the request to submit further information relative to the application concerned.]^{1j} **[26]**

---

1 Amendments

a   Subsection (2)(cc) was substituted by EC(EIA)R 1989 (SI 349/1989), art 7(a).

b   Sub-paragraph (viii) was inserted by EC(EIA)(A)R 1999 (SI 93/1999), art 4(a).

c   Subsection (3)(a) was inserted by EC(EIA)(A)R 1999 (SI 93/1999), art 4(b).

d   Subsection (3)(b) was substituted by EC(EIA)(A)R 1998 (SI 351/1998), art 3.

e   Subsection (3)(c) was substituted by EC(EIA)(A)R 1994 (SI 84/1994), art 5(a).

f   Subsection (3)(d) was substituted by EC(EIA)(A)R 1998 (SI 351/1998), art 3.

g   Subsection (3)(e) was inserted by EC(EIA)(A)R 1999 (SI 93/1999), art 4(c).

h   Subsection (4)(d) was substituted by EC(EIA)(A)R 1994 (SI 84/1994), art 5(c).

i   Subsection (5) was inserted by EC(EIA)(A)R 1998 (SI 351/1998), art 3.

j   Subsection (5) was inserted by EC(EIA)(A)R 1999 (SI 93/1999), art 4(d).

2 Cross References

a   These are LG(PD)R 1994 (SI 86/1994), Part IV.

b   These are set out in LG(PD)R 1994 (SI 86/1994) Part IV, arts 24–28 which are closely linked with EC(EIA)R 1989 (SI 349/1989).

3 Notes

a   The consequences of non-compliance with the regulations may or may not be fatal; contrast *Monaghan UDC v Alf-a-Bet Ltd* [1980] ILRM 64 with *State (Elm Developments Ltd) v An Bord Pleanála* [1981] ILRM 108.

b   An approval does not extend the duration of the outline permission, but dies with it, see *Irish Asphalt Ltd v An Bord Pleanála* HC, unrep, 28 July 1995 on approvals generally.

c   Care must be taken in this regard, see *O'Connor Downtown Properties Ltd v Nenagh UCD* [1993] 1 IR 1; *State (Conlon Construction Ltd) v Cork County Council* High Court, unrep, 31 July 1975; *State (NEC Ltd) v Dublin County Council* [1979] ILRM 249.

d   In *State (Abenglen Properties Ltd) v Dublin Corporation* [1984] IR 381; [1982] ILRM 590 D'Arcy J held that this was an optional power only.

4 Commentary

Section 25 provides the framework for the making of applications for planning permission. The precise requirements in this regard are set out Part IV of the LG(PD)R 1994. The Regulations set out the details with regard to the type of public notices to be erected, the plans to be submitted, the information which is to be given with an application, the fees to be paid, and the obligations of a local authority on receipt of such an application. Application may be made for full permission, which authorises the carrying out of the works in their totality, or an application may be made for outline permission which combined with the subsequent approval together constitute a permission which is the equivalent of full permission.

The requirement to give public notice and comply with the provisions of the Acts and Regulations is strictly construed. The planning authority may make a request for further information, but this must be a *bona fide* request and must not be in the nature of a request to alter or modify the plan submitted. With regard to this latter provision there is a specific power given but unlike a request for further information this does not have the effect of extending the period given to the local authority for the consideration of the application.

26. Permission for development

(1) Where –

(a) application is made to a planning authority in accordance with permission regulations for permission for the development of land or for an approval required by such regulations, and

(b) any requirements relating to the application of or made under such regulations are complied with,

the authority may decide to grant the permission or approval subject to or without conditions or to refuse it; and dealing with any such application the planning authority shall be restricted to considering the proper planning and development of the area of the authority (including the preservation and improvement of the amenities thereof), regard being had to the provisions of the development plan, the provisions of any special amenity area order relating to the said area and the matters referred to in subsection (2) of this section.[3a]

[(1A)(a) Without prejudice to subsection (1) of this section, and subject to paragraph (b) of this subsection, a planning authority shall, in dealing with an application for permission for the development of land in respect of which an environmental impact statement was submitted to them in accordance with a requirement of or under regulations under section 25 (as amended by the European Communities (Environmental Impact Assessment) Regulations, 1989 and 1994) of this Act, have regard to –

(i) the said statement,

(ii) any supplementary information relating to the said statement furnished to them by the applicant in accordance with a requirement under regulations under the said section 25,

(iii) any submissions or observations concerning the effects on the environment of the proposed development made to them by persons other than the applicant in accordance with regulations under the said section 25, and

(iv) where appropriate, the views of other Member States of the European Communities in relation to the effects on the environment of the proposed development.

(b) Notwithstanding paragraph (a) of this subsection, a planning authority shall, in dealing with an application for permission for the development of land where the development comprises or is for the purposes of an activity to which a licence under Part IV of the Environmental Protection Agency Act, 1992 (No. 7 of 1992) is required, have regard to the matters referred to in the said paragraph

(c) only in so far as those matters do not relate to the risk of environmental pollution from the activity.][1a]

(2) Conditions[3b] under subsection (1) of this section may, without prejudice to the generality[3c] of that subsection, include all or any of the following conditions:

(a) conditions for regulating the development or use of any land which adjoins, abuts or is adjacent to the land to be developed and which is under the control of the applicant, so far as appears to the planning authority to be expedient for the purposes of or in connection with the development authorised by the permission,

(b)   conditions for requiring the carrying out of works (including the provision of car parks) which the planning authority consider are required for the purposes of the development authorised by the permission,

[(bb)   conditions for requiring the taking of measures to reduce or prevent –

(i)   the emission of any noise or vibration from any structure comprised in the development authorised by the permission which might give reasonable cause for annoyance either to persons in any premises in the neighbourhood of the development or to persons lawfully using any public place in that neighbourhood, or

(ii)   the intrusion of any noise or vibration which might give reasonable cause for annoyance to any person lawfully occupying any such structure,][1b, 2a]

(c)   conditions for requiring provision of open spaces,

[(cc)   conditions for requiring in any case in which the development authorised by the permission would remove or alter any protected structure or any element of a protected structure which contributes to its special architectural, historical, archaeological, artistic, cultural, scientific, social or technical interest -

(i)   the preservation by record of that structure or element before the development authorised by the permission takes place, and

(ii)   where appropriate. the architectural salvaging of any such element,][1c]

(d)   conditions for requiring the planting of trees, shrubs or other plants or the landscaping of structures or other land,

(e)   conditions for requiring the giving of security for satisfactory completion of the proposed development (including maintenance until taken in charge by the local authority concerned of roads, open spaces, car parks, sewers, watermains or drains),

(f)   conditions for requiring roads, open spaces, car parks, sewers, watermains or drains in excess of the immediate[3d] needs of the proposed development,

(g)   conditions for requiring contribution[3e] (either in one sum or by instalments) towards and expenditure (including expenditure on the acquisition of land and expenditure consisting of a payment under subsection (7) of this section) that was incurred by any local authority in respect of works (including the provision of open spaces) which have facilitated the proposed development, being works commenced neither earlier than the 1st day of August, 1962, nor earlier than seven years before the grant of permission for the development,

(h)   conditions for requiring contribution (either in one sum or by instalments) towards any expenditure (including expenditure on the acquisition of land) that is proposed to be incurred by any local authority in respect of works (including the provision of open spaces) facilitating the proposed development, subject to stipulations[3f] providing for –

(i)   where the proposed works are, within a specified period, not commenced, the return of the contribution or the instalments thereof paid during that period (as may be appropriate),

(ii) where the proposed works are, within the said period, carried out in part only or in such manner as to facilitate the proposed development to a lesser extent, the return of a proportionate part of the contribution or the instalments thereof paid during that period (as may be appropriate), and

(iii) payment of interest on the contribution or any instalments thereof that have been paid (as may be appropriate) so long and in so far as it is or they are retained unexpended by the local authority,

(i) conditions for requiring compliance in respect of the land with any rules made by the planning authority under subsection (6) of this section,

(j) conditions for requiring the removal of any structures authorised by the permission, or the discontinuance of any use of the land so authorised, at the expiration of a specified period,[3g] and the carrying out of any works required for the reinstatement of land at the expiration of that period.

[(3)(a) In a case in which the development concerned would contravene materially the development plan or any special amenity order, a planning authority may, notwithstanding any other provision of this Act, decide to grant permission under this section, provided that the following requirements are complied with before the decision is made, namely,

(i) notice in the prescribed form of the intention of the planning authority to consider deciding to grant the permission shall be published in at least one daily newspaper circulating in their area,

(ii) copies of the notice shall be given to the applicant and to any person who has submitted an objection in writing to the development to which the application relates,

(iii) any objection or representation as regards the making of a decision to grant permission and which is received by the planning authority not later than twenty-one days after the first publication of the notice shall be duly considered by the authority, and

(iv) a resolution shall be passed by the authority requiring that a decision to grant permission be made.

(b) It shall be necessary for the passing of a resolution referred to in paragraph (a) of this subsection that the number of the members of the planning authority voting in favour of the resolution [is not less than three-quarters of the total number of the members of the planning authority (fractions being disregarded)][1d], and the requirement of this paragraph is in addition to and not in substitution for any other requirement applying in relation to such a resolution.

(c) Where notice is given pursuant to section 4 of the City and County Management (Amendment) Act, 1955, of intention to propose a resolution which, if passed, would require the manager to decide to grant a permission under this section, then if the manager is of opinion that the development concerned would contravene materially the development plan or any special amenity area order, he shall within seven days of the receipt by him of the notice make an order (a copy of which shall be furnished by him to each of the signatories to the notice) requiring that the provisions of sub-paragraphs (i), (ii) and (iii) of paragraph (a) of this subsection shall be complied with in

37

the particular case and the order, when made, shall operate to cause the relevant notice given pursuant to the said section 4 to be of no further effect.[3h]

(d)   If a resolution referred to in paragraph (a)(iv) of this subsection is duly passed, the manager shall decide[3i] to grant the relevant permission.][1e]

(4) (a)   Where –

   (i) an application is made to a planning authority in accordance with permission regulations for permission under this section or for an approval required by such regulations,

   (ii) any requirements relating to the application of or made under such regulations are complied with, and

   (iii) the planning authority do not give notice[3j] to the applicant of their decision within the appropriate period,

   a decision by the planning authority to grant the permission or approval shall be regarded as having been given on the last day of that period.[3k]

(b) In paragraph (a) of this subsection "**the appropriate period**" means –

   (i) in case any notice or notices requiring the applicant to publish any notice, to give further information[3l] or to produce evidence in respect of the application has or have been served by the planning authority pursuant to permission regulations within the period of two months beginning on the day of receipt by the planning authority of the application – within the period of two months beginning on the day on which the notice or notices has or have been complied with,

   [(ii) in case a notice referred to in subsection (3) of this section is published in relation to the application, within the period of two months beginning on the day on which the notice is first published,][1f]

   [(iiA) where an applicant is required to submit an environmental impact statement in respect of proposed development and the development is likely to have significant effects on the environment in another Member State of the European Communities, within –

   (I)   the period of two months beginning on the day on which submissions or observations in relation to the development have been made by such State and related consultations (if any) have been completed, or

   (II)   the period within the meaning of sub-paragraphs (i) or (ii) above, whichever period ends the later;] [1g]

   (iii) in any other case – within the period of two months beginning on the day of receipt[3m] by the planning authority of the application.

[(4A) If, but only if, before the expiration of the appropriate period within the meaning of subsection (4)(a) of this section the applicant for a permission under this section gives to the planning authority in writing his consent to the extension by them of that period, the planning authority may extend the period and in case, pursuant to the foregoing, a planning authority make an extension, subsection (4)(b) of this section shall, as regards the particular case to which the extension relates, be construed and have effect in accordance with the extension.][1h, 3n]

(4AA)...[1i]

[(5) (a)   Any person may, at any time before the expiration of the appropriate period,³⁰ appeal to the Board against a decision of a planning authority under this section.

(b)   Subject to the following provisions of this subsection, where an appeal is brought from a decision of a planning authority and is not withdrawn, the Board shall determine the application as if it had been made to the Board in the first instance and the decision of the Board shall operate to annul the decision of the planning authority as from the time when it was given; and the provisions of subsections (1) and (2) of this section shall apply, subject to any necessary modifications, in relation to the determination of an application by the Board on appeal under this subsection as they apply in relation to the determination under this section of an application by a planning authority.

(c)   Notwithstanding any other provision of this section, the Board in determining an appeal under this subsection shall, where it considers it appropriate, have regard to either or both of the following, namely –

(i)   the probable effect which a particular decision by it on the matter would have on any place or area which is outside the area of the relevant planning authority, and

(ii)   any other consideration relating to development outside the area of that authority.³ᵖ

(d)   Without prejudice to paragraph (b) of this subsection, the Board shall, in determining on appeal an application in respect of which an environmental impact statement was submitted by the applicant in accordance with a requirement of or under regulations under the Acts (whether at the instance of the Board or otherwise), have regard to that statement, to such supplementary information (if any) relating to the statement as may have been furnished to the Board or to the planning authority by the applicant in accordance with a requirement under such regulations, and to other submissions or observations (if any) made to the Board in accordance with the Acts or regulations under the Acts in relation to the effects on the environment of the development to which the application relates.]¹ʲ

[(dd)   Notwithstanding paragraph (d) of this subsection, the Board shall, in determining on appeal an application for permission for the development of land where the development comprises or is for the purposes of an activity in relation to which a licence under Part IV of the Environmental Protection Agency Act, 1992 (No. 7 of 1992) is required, have regard to the matters referred to in the said paragraph (d) only in so far as those matters do not relate to the risk of environmental pollution from the activity.]¹ᵏ

[(e)   Paragraph (b) of this subsection shall be construed and have effect subject to sections 11, 14 and 15 of the Local Government (Planning and Development) Act, 1992.

(f)   In paragraph (a) of this subsection **"the appropriate period"** means the period of one month beginning on the day of the giving of the decision of the planning authority.]¹ˡ

(6) A planning authority may make rules for regulating the manner in which advertisement structures are to be affixed to structures or other land.

(7) In a case in which a condition referred to in paragraph (f) of subsection (2) of this section is attached to any permission or approval granted under this section, a contribution towards such of the relevant roads, open spaces, car parks, sewers, watermains or drains as are constructed shall be made by the local authority[3q] who will be responsible for their maintenance, and the contribution shall be such as may be agreed upon between that local authority and the person carrying out the works or, in default of agreement, as may be determined by the Minister.

[(8) A decision given under this section and the notification of such decision shall –

    (a) in case the decision is made by a planning authority and is one by which any permission or approval is refused or is granted subject to conditions, comprise ·a statement specifying the reasons for the refusal or the imposition of conditions, and

    (b) in case the decision is made on appeal, comprise a statement specifying the reasons for the decision,

provided that where a condition imposed is a condition described in paragraph (a) or any subsequent paragraph of subsection (2) of this section, a reference to the paragraph of the said subsection (2) in which the condition is described shall be sufficient to meet the requirements of this subsection.][1m]

(9) (a)   Where the planning authority decide under this section to grant a permission or approval –

        (i) in case no appeal is taken against the decision, they shall make the grant[3r] as soon as may be after the expiration of the period for the taking by the applicant of an appeal or, in a case to which subsection (4) of this section applies, of the period for the taking of an appeal[3s] otherwise than by the applicant,

      [(ii) in case an appeal or appeals is or are taken against the decision, they shall not make the grant unless as regards the appeal, or as may be appropriate, each of the appeals –

            (I)   it is withdrawn, or

            (II)   it is dismissed by the Board pursuant to section 11 or 14 of the Local Government (Planning and Development) Act, 1992, or

            (III) in relation to it a direction is given to the authority by the Board pursuant to section 15 of the said Act,

        and, in the case of the withdrawal or dismissal of an appeal or of all such appeals, as may be appropriate, they shall make the grant as soon as may be after such withdrawal or dismissal and, in the case of such a direction, they shall make the grant, in accordance with the direction, as soon as may be after the giving by the Board of the direction.][1n]

    (b) Where the Minister decides on appeal under this section to grant a permission or approval, he shall make the grant as soon as may be after the decision.

(10)(a)   Where a permission or approval is granted under this section subject to any one or more of the conditions referred to in paragraphs (e), (g) and (h) of subsection (2) of this section, the permission or approval shall be of no effect and shall be disregarded until the condition or conditions has or have been complied with.

(b) Paragraph (a) of this subsection shall not apply where a condition referred to in paragraph (g) or (h) of subsection (2) of this section requires a contribution by instalments except in respect of development which is the subject of the permission or approval and is carried out after default in paying an instalment of the contribution.

(11) A person shall not be entitled solely by reason of a permission or approval under this section to carry out any development.[3t] **[27]**

---

1 Amendments

a   Subsection (1A) was inserted by EC(EIA)(A)R 1994 (SI 84/1994), art 6; see also the Roads Act 1993, s 51(8) which provides that the EC(EIA)R 1989 no longer apply to proposed road development.

b   Subsection 2(bb) was inserted by LG(PD)A 1976, s 39(c).

c   Subsection (2)(cc) was inserted by LG(PD)A 1999, s 35 which will come into operation on 1 January 2000.

d   Subsection 3 was substituted by LG(PD)A 1976, s 39(d).

e   Subsection 3(b) was amended by LGA 1991, s 45.

f   Subsection 4(b)(ii) was substituted by LG(PD)A 1976, s 39(e).

g   Sub-paragraph (iiA) was inserted into sub-s (4)(b) by EC(EIA)(A)R 1998, (SI 351/1998), art 4.

h   Subsection (4A) was inserted by LG(PD)A 1976, s 39(f).

i   Subsection (4AA) was deleted by EC(EIA)(A)R 1998 (SI 351/1998), art 4.

j   Subsection (5) was substituted by LG(PD)A 1992, s 3.

k   Subsection (5)(dd) was inserted by art 6 EC(EIA)(A)(R) 1994 (SI 84/1994).

l   Subsection (5)(e) and (f) was inserted by LG(PD)A 1992, s 3.

m   Subsection (8) was substituted by LG(PD)A 1976, s 39(g).

n   Subsection (9)(a)(ii) was substituted by LG(PD)A 1992, s 3.

2 Cross References

a   See LG(PD)A 1976, s 25 for enforcement of such conditions.

3 Notes

a   Consideration of irrelevant material was fatal to the validity of a "section 4" direction in *Flanagan v Galway and City County Manager* [1980] 2 IR 66, see also *Child v Wicklow County Council* High Court, unrep, 20 January 1995 and the cases referred to therein. For a consideration of the requirements relating to development plans see *Blessington & District Community Council Ltd v Wicklow County Council* High Court, unrep, 19 July 1996 where a mere averment in an affidavit was held to satisfy the requirements where there was no reference by the planning authority to the development plan on the planning file. On the issue of the interpretation of planning permissions, see *State (Aprile) v Naas UDC* [1985] ILRM 510; *James Barrett (Builders) v Dublin County Council* Supreme Court, unrep, 28 July 1983; *Coffey v Hebron Homes Ltd* High Court, unrep, 27 July 1984; *Dun Laoghaire Corporation v Frascati Estates Ltd* [1982] ILRM 469; *Horne v Freeney* High Court, unrep, 7 July 1982; *Kelly v An Bord Pleanála* High Court,, unrep 19 November 1993; *O'Donoghue v An Bord Pleanála* [1991] ILRM 750; *Readymix (Eire) Ltd v Dublin County Council* High Court, unrep, 12 August 1970; Supreme Court, unrep, 30 July 1974; *State (Kenny and Hussey) v An Bord Pleanála* High Court, unrep, 23 February 1984; Supreme Court, unrep, 20 December 1984;

State (McCoy) v Dun Laoghaire Corporation High Court, unrep, 1 June 1984; *State (Sweeney) v Minister for the Environment* [1979] ILRM 35; *XJS Investments Ltd v Dun Laoghaire Corporation* [1986] IR 750; [1987] ILRM 659. See also the decision in *MCD Management Services Ltd v Kildare County Council* [1995] 2 ILRM 532 which considered what documents could be taken into account in a decision determined on appeal by An Bord Pleanála.

b   See *Boland v An Bord Pleanála* Supreme Court, unrep, 21 March 1996 on the extent to which An Bord Pleanála may impose conditions; see also *Keleghan v Corby and Dublin Corporation* 111 ILTR 144, *State (Finglas Industrial Estates Ltd) v Dublin County Council* High Court, unrep 18 July 1981; Supreme Court, unrep, 17 February 1983, *Bord na Mona v An Bord Pleanála and Galway County Council* [1985] IR 205, *Houlihan v An Bord Pleanála* High Court, unrep, 4 October 1993 and *State (Sweeney) v Minister for the Environment* [1979] ILRM 35 on reasons for conditions. The Supreme Court in *Boland* has now definitely determined the extent to which the Board can by condition leave matters to be agreed between the planning authority and the applicant and contains a definitive statement of the law in this regard. For an interesting discussion on the construction of a condition see *Gregory v Dun Laoghaire-Rathdown County Council* Supreme Court, unrep, 28 July 1997.

c   Whilst the jurisdiction to attach conditions to the grant of a planning permission is undoubtedly general and not limited to those set out in sub-s (2), all conditions must be fairly related to planning and development. See *Dunne v Dublin County Council* [1974] IR 45. See also *Drogheda Port Company v Louth County Council* High Court, unrep, 11 April 1997 where the Court considered and rejected an argument that a planning authority was obliged to consult with the applicant before imposing a condition requiring a financial contribution, and where the general power to impose conditions is considered.

d   See also s 26(7) and LG(PD)R 1994, art 32. See *McDonagh v Galway County Council* Supreme Court, unrep, 17 May 1993.

e   An order for payment of the outstanding balance of a contribution was made by Finlay P on the application of Athlone UDC under LG(PD)A 1976, s 27(2). See also *Bord na Mona v Galway County Council* [1985] IR 205; *State (FHP Ltd) v An Bord Pleanála* [1989] ILRM 98; [1987] IR 698 and *Thomas McDonagh & Son Ltd v Galway Corporation* Supreme Court, unrep, 17 May 1993.

f   The power to attach such conditions is clearly subject to the itemised stipulations. It is not stated that the stipulations should be written into the conditions; a reference to the subparagraph would however, seem essential – see LG(PD)A 1976, s 26(8). See Keane J in *Bord na Móna v An Bord Pleanála* [1985] IR 205.

g   Not affected by the "withering" provisions of LG(PD)A 1982, s 2(2)(a)(ii).

h   This subsection was analysed in the Supreme Court judgment of Finlay CJ in *P & F Sharpe Ltd v Dublin City and County Manager* [1989] IR 701; [1989] ILRM 565.

i   It is straining language to provide that a manager "shall decide". See discussion in Keane, *The Law of Local Government in the Republic of Ireland* (ILSI, 1982) pp 180 *et seq*. It has been established however, in *Sharpe* that "section 4" motions do apply in planning cases and can be effective provided the elected members act judicially and in accordance with LG(PD)A 1963, s 26. See also *Flanagan v Galway City and County Manager* [1980] 2 IR 66.

j   See also *Freeney v Bray UDC* [1982] ILRM 29. If an *ultra vires* decision is notified within time there will not be a default permission. See *State (Abenglen Properties Ltd) v Dublin Corporation* [1984] IR 381 and *Creedon v Dublin Corporation* [1984] IR 428; [1983] ILRM 339. The "appropriate period" for sub-s (4)(a) (ie two months, or two months extended by consent) should not be confused with either "the appropriate period" for sub-s (5)(a) (ie one month) or "the appropriate period" for LG(PD)A 1982, ss 2, 4 (ie the several specified periods during which different categories of planning permission continue to have effect). This "appropriate period" commences to run only when any fees payable under LG(PD)A 1982, s 10 are received (see LG(PD)A 1982, s 10(2)(b)).

k   For an example of where the court held a default permission was deemed to have been given see *Dunne v Dublin County Council* [1974] IR 45; *Burke v Drogheda Corporation* High Court, unrep, 11 June 1982; *Molloy & Walsh v Dublin County Council* [1990] IR 90; [1990] ILRM 633 and *O'Connor Downtown Properties v Nenagh UDC* [1993] 1 IR 1. There cannot be a default permission for a development which would materially contravene the development plan. See *P & F Sharpe Ltd v Dublin City and County Manager* [1989] IR 701 and *Dublin County Council v Marren* [1985] ILRM 593. See also *Flynn and O'Flaherty Properties v Dublin Corporation* High Court, unrep, 11 December 1996 where an application was determined within the appropriate period but which decision was not communicated until the expiry gave rise to a default planning permission, being granted on the last day of the appropriate period.

l   However it must be a genuine request for further information. See *State (Conlon Construction Ltd) v Cork County Council* High Court, unrep, 31 July 1975; *O'Connor's Downtown Properties Ltd v Nenagh UDC* High Court, unrep, 22 September 1992.

m   Finlay P held in *State (Genport Ltd) v Dublin Corporation* [1983] ILRM 12 that an application which was made in several stages was received on the day it was finally submitted.

n   For a consideration of this issue in the context of default permissions, see *Flynn and O'Flaherty Properties v Dublin Corporation* High Court, unrep, 11 December 1996.

o   This period is strict and may not be extended (see O'Hanlon J in *Freeney v Bray UDC* [1982] ILRM 29. However, appeals posted within the time stipulated may reach An Bord Pleanála "not later than the third day after that period" (LG(PD)A 1976, s 22(2)). The period for the lodging of an appeal is one month from when the decision is given. Eg, if a decision is given on 10 June then the appeal must be lodged on or before 9 July. In this regard see *McCann v An Bord Pleanála* High Court, unrep, 20 June 1996.

p   See *Keane v An Bord Pleanála* [1998] 2 ILRM 241 where the court held that the Board was entitled to consider the effect of a development outside its functional area, if appropriate and indeed outside the territorial limits of the State. The effect on persons as well as the physical environment could be taken into account, as could the common good.

q   See *Killiney and Ballybrack Development Association Ltd v Minister for Local Government* [1978] ILRM 78.

r   If a planning authority refuses to make the grant the applicant should seek an order of *mandamus*: such application is not caught by the two-month time limit laid down in LG(PD)A 1963, s 82(3): see Barrington J in *State (Pine Valley Development Ltd) v Dublin County Council* [1984] IR 407 but see also *Colgan v Dublin Corporation* High Court, unrep, 19 March 1991. If the planning authority fails to make the grant it may be liable in damages; see *O'Neill v Clare County Council* [1983] ILRM 141. However it is safer if the decision is made but has not been communicated within the appropriate period to seek not only declaratory orders but also *certiorari* and this would bring such an application within s 82.

s   The right of a third party to appeal a default permission is preserved though the time limit for the making of such an approval may have expired if it is necessary to seek a declaratory order as to the existence of such permission. However see *Nolan v An Bord Pleanála* High Court, unrep, 19 July 1989 where it was held that failure to notify an objection nullified the permission granted.

t   See, eg, *O'Callaghan v The Commissioners of Public Works in Ireland* [1985] ILRM 364 and *Doolan v Murray* High Court, unrep 21 December 1993. See the judgment of Keane J in *Convery v Dublin County Council* Supreme Court, unrep, 12 November 1996 where it was held that the grant of planning permission cannot authorise an unlawful activity and by inference cannot justify a nuisance. See also the judgment of the Supreme Court in *Keane v An Bord Pleanála* [1998] 2 ILRM 241.

4 Commentary

A planning authority may, having considered the proper planning and development of the area, the provisions of the development plan, any EIS submitted, and the conditions which they are entitled to impose, decide to grant, subject to conditions, or refuse an application for planning permission. The permission granted may be subject to conditions, some of which are provided for in sub-s (2), but the matters therein referred to are by no means exhaustive. Despite the general language of s 26(2) a planning authority is not free to impose whatever conditions it wishes. Any conditions imposed must fairly and reasonably relate to the proposed development, conditions which seek to achieve the objectives of a separate statutory code would, it is submitted, be *ultra vires* the powers of the planning authority, and any conditions imposed must be clear, unambiguous and capable of being implemented by the applicant. A condition imposed which requires the consent of a third party would be invalid. Conditions attached to a planning permission will be strictly construed and it is necessary not just to look at the condition but at the reason for its imposition.

A planning authority may not grant a permission which is a material contravention of the development plan without publishing the requisite notices in local newspapers, allowing the public an opportunity to make submissions and representations with regard to the proposed development, and the submission of the proposal to the elected members who by resolution will authorise the proposed development by not less than three quarters of the members of the local authority voting in favour of the particular development. Where such a resolution is passed the Manager has no discretion but to grant permission, where such a resolution is not passed then the application must be refused. The decision whether to institute material contravention procedure is an executive decision but it is not clear the status of a resolution on the development plan, or An Bord Pleanala in any subsequent appeal, or the extent of the power of the Manager to subsequently modify the proposed development following the resolution of the elected members. An application which is a material contravention of the plan can never be granted planning permission by default.

The members may direct the Manager to grant planning permission pursuant to s 4 of the County Management (Amendment) Act 1955 and the Manager must comply with such a direction. However the courts have always held that it is virtually impossible for the elected members to comply with their obligations under the Planning Acts and to give a valid direction to the Manager under s 4 to grant the permission.

The planning authority must give notice of its decision within two months of the receipt of a valid application or from the receipt of a response to a further information request. An application can be made in writing to extend the period for the consideration of the application but such an extension of time is at the discretion of the local authority. Where notice of the determination of the decision is not delivered to the applicant within the two month period prescribed, then planning permission by default is deemed to have been given on the last day of the appropriate period. This allows an applicant to carry out the development proposed subject to the plans and particulars lodged. However such a decision effectively removes the third party right of appeal.

Any person has a right to lodge an appeal to An Bord Pleanála against the decision of a planning authority. Such an appeal must be lodged within one month from the date of the giving of the decision. It is not immediately clear when a decision is given for the purposes of this section but the safe approach is to deem the decision given when the order is signed by the County Manager despite the unfairness to which such an interpretation obviously gives rise. The one month period prescribed will be strictly construed as will the requirements for the lodging of a valid appeal and even minor infractions of the requirements of the regulations will invalidate an appeal lodged.

27. Permission for retention of structures

(1) Where, with respect to a structure which existed immediately before the appointed day and which is on the commencement of that day an unauthorised structure, –

    (a) application is made to the planning authority in accordance with permission regulations for permission for the retention[2a] of the structure, and

    (b) any requirements relating to the application of or made under such regulations are complied with,

the authority may decide to grant the permission subject to or without conditions or to refuse it; and in dealing with any such application the planning authority shall be restricted to considering the proper planning and development of the area of the authority (including the preservation and improvement of the amenities thereof), regard being had to the provisions of the development plan and the provisions of any special amenity area order relating to the said area.

(2) Conditions under subsection (1) of this section may, without prejudice to the generality of that subsection, include all or any of the following conditions:

    (a) conditions for regulating the development or use of any land which adjoins, abuts or is adjacent to the structure and which is under the control of the applicant, so far as appears to the planning authority to be expedient for the purposes of or in connection with the retention of the structure,

    (b) conditions for requiring the carrying out of works (including the provision of car parks) which the planning authority consider are required if the retention of the structure is to be permitted,

    (c) conditions for requiring provision of space around the structure,

    (d) conditions for requiring the planting of trees, shrubs or other plants or the landscaping of the structure or other land,

    (e) conditions for requiring compliance in respect of the structure with any rules made by the planning authority under subsection (6) of section 26 of this Act,

    (f) conditions for requiring the removal[2b] of the structure at the expiration of a specified period, and the carrying out of any works required for the reinstatement of land at the expiration of that period.

(3) (a)   Where –

      (i) an application is made to a planning authority in accordance with permission regulations for permission under this section,

      (ii) any requirements relating to the application of or made under such regulations are complied with, and

      (iii) the planning authority do not give notice to the applicant of their decision within the appropriate period,[2c]

    a decision by the planning authority to grant the permission shall be regarded as having been given on the last day of that period.

    (b)   In paragraph (a) of this subsection **"the appropriate period"** means –

      (i) in case any notice or notices requiring the applicant to publish any notice, to give further information or to produce evidence in respect of the application has or have been served by the planning authority pursuant to permission regulations within the period of two months beginning on the

45

day of receipt by the planning authority of the application – within the period of two months beginning on the day on which the notice or notices has or have been complied with,

(ii) in any other case, within the period of two months beginning on the day of receipt by the planning authority of the application.

(4) (a) Any person may, at any time before the expiration of the appropriate period, appeal to the [Board][1a] against a decision of a planning authority under this section.

(b) Where an appeal is brought under this subsection from a decision of a planning authority and is not withdrawn, the [Board][1a] shall determine the application as if it had been made to him in the first instance and his decision shall operate to annul the decision of the planning authority as from the time when it was given; and the provisions of subsections (1) and (2) of this section shall apply, subject to any necessary modifications, in relation to the determination of an application by the [Board][1a] on appeal under this subsection as they apply in relation to the determination under this section of an application by a planning authority.

(c) In paragraph (a) of this subsection **"the appropriate period"**[2d] means –

(i) in case the appellant is the applicant – the period of one month beginning on the day of receipt by him of the decision,

(ii) in any other case – the period of twenty-one days beginning on the day of the giving of the decision.

(5) A decision given under this section (whether on the original application or on appeal) by which permission is refused or is granted subject to conditions, and the notification of such decision, shall comprise a statement of the reasons[3a] for the refusal or the imposition of conditions.

(6) (a) Where the planning authority decide under this section to grant a permission –

(i) in case no appeal is taken against the decision, they shall make the grant[3b] as soon as may be after the expiration of the period for the taking by the applicant of an appeal or, in a case to which subsection (3) of this section applies, of the period for the taking of an appeal[3c] otherwise than by the applicant,

(ii) in case an appeal or appeals is or are taken against the decision, they shall not make the grant unless the appeal or appeals is or are withdrawn and, in that case, they shall make the grant as soon as may be after the withdrawal.

(b) Where the [Board][1a] decides on appeal under this section to grant a permission, it shall make the grant as soon as may be after the decision.

(7) A person shall not be entitled solely by reason of a permission under this section to retain any structure.[3d] **[28]**

---

1 Amendments

a   References to the Minister are to be construed as the Board: LG(PD)A 1976, s 14(9), (10).

2 Cross References

a   Retention permission is excluded from the "withering" provisions of LG(PD)A 1982, s 2(2)(a)(i). The power to grant permission includes power to retain an unauthorised use: see LG(PD)A 1963, s 28(i). Retention permission may take effect from the date of construction or commencement of use: see LG(PD)A 1963, s 28(2). One cannot make an outline application for retention. See also *The State (Fitzgerald) v An Bord Pleanála* [1985] ILRM 117 which deals with the principles governing the determination of an application for retention of an unauthorised structure.

b   Not affected by the "withering" provisions of LG(PD)A 1982, s 2(2)(a)(ii).

c   Not to be confused with "the appropriate period" for sub-s (4)(a) or ss 2 and 4 of LG(PD)A 1982. The appropriate period will commence to run only when the planning authority is in receipt of any fee payable under LG(PD)A 1982, s 10(2)(b).

d   Not to be confused with "the appropriate period" for sub-s (3)(a) or ss 2 and 4 of LG(PD)A 1982.

4 Commentary

Section 27 applies to those areas to which the Town and Regional Planning Acts 1934 or 1939 formerly applied and by virtue of this provision, and by virtue of the lapse of time it is unlikely that this section has any great relevance, over 35 years after the coming into force of the Planning Acts.

---

28. Supplemental provisions as to grant of permission[3a]

(1) The power to grant permission to develop land under this Part of this Act shall include power to grant permission for the retention on land of any structures constructed, erected or made on, in, or under the land on or after the appointed day and before the date of application, or for the continuance of any use of land instituted on or after the appointed day and before the date of the application (whether without permission granted under this Part of this Act or in accordance with permission so granted for a limited period only); and references in this Part of this Act ot permission to develop land or to carry out any development of land, and to applications for such permission, shall be construed accordingly.

(2) Any such permission as is mentioned in subsection (1) of this section may be granted so as to take effect from the date on which the structures were constructed, erected or made, or the use was instituted, or from the expiration of the said period, as the case may be.

(3) Where permission has been granted by virtue of subsection (1) of this section for the retention on land of any structures, or for the continuance of the use of land, subject to any condition, the references in subsections (1) and (3) of section 31 of this Act to any conditions subject to which permission was granted in respect of any development include references to any such condition.

(4) The power conferred by subsection (1) of this section is exercisable not only where development has been carried out without permission or where previous permission has been granted for a limited period only, but also so as to permit the retention of structures or the continuance of any use of land without complying with some condition subject to which a previous permission under this Part of this Act was granted.

(5) Where permission to develop land or for the retention of a structure is granted under this Part of this Act, then, except as may be otherwise provided by the permission, the

grant of permission shall enure for the benefit of the land or structure[1] and of all persons for the time being interested therein, but without prejudice to the provisions of this Part of this Act with respect to the revocation and modification of permissions granted thereunder.

(6) Where permission is granted under this Part of this Act for the construction, erection or making of a structure, the grant of permission may specify the purposes for which the structure may [or may not be used, and in case such grant specifies use as a dwelling as a purpose for which the structure may be used, the permission may also be granted subject to a condition specifying that the use as a dwelling shall be restricted to use by persons of a particular class[3b] or description and that provision to that effect shall be embodied in an agreement pursuant to section 38 of this Act][1a] and if no purpose is so specified, the permission shall be construed as including permission to use the structure for the purpose for which it is designed.[3c]

(7) (a) Where permission to develop land is granted under this Part of this Act for a limited period only, nothing in this Part of this Act shall be construed as requiring permission to be obtained thereunder for the resumption,[3d] at the expiration of that period, of the use of the land for the purpose for which it was normally used before the permission was granted.

(b) In determining for the purposes of this subsection the purposes for which land was normally used before the grant of permission, no account shall be taken of any use of the land begun in contravention of the provisions of this Part of this Act. **[29]**

---

1 Amendments

a   The words in square brackets were inserted by LG(PD)A 1976, s 39(h).

3 Notes

a   Henchy J described planning permission as an "appendage to the title to the property" in *Readymix (Eire) Ltd v Dublin County Council* Supreme Court, unrep, 30 July 1974: planning permission is to be construed by reference to objective documentary materials. See also the Supreme Court decision in *Keane v An Bord Pleanála* [1998] 2 ILRM 241 where the provisions of s 28(5) were considered, particularly in the context of an application where the developer did not have a sufficient interest to carry out the development, and where the case of *Frescati Estates Ltd v Walker* [1975] IR 177 was distinguished.

b   Most typically by restricting occupancy of a rural dwelling to the applicant and members of his family. See *Fawcett Properties Ltd v Buckingham County Council* [1961] AC 636.

c   See Barrington J's reasoning in *Galway Corporation v Connaught Protein Ltd* High Court, unrep, 28 March 1980 and the *Readymix* case for a discussion of the "purpose" for which a structure is designed.

d   However for this provision the position would be doubtful, See *Hartley v Minister of Housing and Local Government* [1970] 1 QB 413 where cessation of use amounted to abandonment of the earlier use so that resumption constituted a material change. See *Meath County Council v Daly* [1987] IR 391; [1988] ILRM 274; *Cork County Council v Ardfert Quarry Products Ltd* High Court, unrep, 7 December 1982 and *Dublin County Council v Tallaght Block Co Ltd* [1982] ILRM 534.

---

29. Obligation to purchase land on refusal of permission in certain cases

(1) Where, in a case determined on an appeal under this Part of this Act, permission to develop any land has been refused or has been granted subject to conditions, then, if the owner of the land claims –

(a) that the land has become incapable of reasonably beneficial use[3a] in its existing state, and

(b) that the land cannot be rendered capable of reasonably beneficial use by the carrying out of any other development for which permission has been granted under this Part of this Act,[1a]

(c) in a case where permission to develop the land was granted as aforesaid subject to conditions, that the land cannot be rendered capable of reasonably beneficial use by the carrying out of the permitted development in accordance with those conditions,

he may, at any time within the period of six months after the decision (or such longer period as the [Board][1b] may allow), serve on the planning authority a notice (hereafter in this section referred to as a purchase notice) requiring the planning authority to purchase his interest in the land in accordance with the provisions of this section.[3b]

(2) The planning authority on whom a purchase notice is served under this section shall, before the end of the period of three months beginning with the date of the service of that notice, serve on the owner by whom the purchase notice was served a notice stating either –

(a) that the authority are willing to comply with the purchase notice, or

(b) that, for reasons specified in the notice under this subsection, the authority are not willing to comply with the purchase notice and that they have transmitted a copy of the purchase notice and a copy of the notice under this subsection to the [Board].[1b]

(3) Where the planning authority upon whom a purchase notice is served under this section have served on the owner by whom the purchase notice was served a notice in accordance with paragraph (a) of subsection (2) of this section, it shall be the duty of the authority to acquire the interest of the owner and, for that purpose, the latter notice shall have the like effect as if it were a compulsory purchase order in respect of that interest which, consequent upon a decision made by the planning authority pursuant to subsection (1) of section 10 of the Local Government (No. 2) Act, 1960, had been duly made and confirmed.[3c]

(4) Where a purchase notice is served on a planning authority under this section and the authority propose to serve on the owner a notice in accordance with paragraph (b) of subsection (2) of this section, they shall transmit a copy of that notice and copy of the purchase notice to the [Board],[1b] and subject to the following provisions of this section the [Board][1b] shall, if it is satisfied[3d] that the conditions specified in paragraphs (a) to (c) or paragraphs (a) and (b) (as may be appropriate) of subsection (1) of this section are fulfilled, confirm the purchase notice, and thereupon it shall be the duty of the planning authority to acquire the interest of the owner, and for that purpose, –

(a) the planning authority shall serve on the owner a notice stating that they propose to comply with the purchase notice,

(b) the notice so served shall have the like effect as if it were a compulsory purchase order in respect of that interest which, consequent upon a decision by the planning authority pursuant to subsection (1) of section 10 of the Local Government (No. 2) Act, 1960, had been duly made and confirmed:

Provided that –

    (i) if it appears to the [Board][1b] to be expedient so to do, it may, in lieu of confirming the purchase notice, grant permission for the development in respect of which the application was made or, where permission for that development was granted subject to conditions, revoke or amend the conditions so far as appears to it to be required in order to enable the land to be rendered capable of reasonably beneficial use by the carrying out of that development;

    (ii) if it appears to the [Board],[1b] that the land, or any part of the land, could be rendered capable of reasonably beneficial use within a reasonable time by the carrying out of any other development for which permission ought to be granted, it may, in lieu of confirming the notice, or in lieu of confirming it so far as it relates to that part of the land, as the case may be, direct that such permission shall, subject to the provisions of this Act, be granted in the event of an application being made in that behalf.

(5) If within the period of six months from the end of the period specified in subsection (2) of this section, or the date on which a copy of the purchase notice is transmitted to the [Board],[1b] whichever is the earlier, the [Board][1b] has neither confirmed the notice nor taken any such other action as is mentioned in paragraph (i) or paragraph (ii) of the proviso to subsection (4) of this section, nor notified the owner by whom the notice was served that it does not propose to confirm the notice, the notice shall be deemed to be confirmed at the expiration of that period, and it shall be the duty of the planning authority on whom the notice was served to acquire the interest of the owner and, for that purpose –

(a) the planning authority shall serve on the owner a notice stating that they propose to comply with the purchase notice,

(b) the notice so served shall have the like effect as if it were a compulsory purchase order in respect of that interest which, consequent upon a decision made by the planning authority pursuant to subsection (1) of section 10 of the Local Government (No. 2) Act, 1960, had been duly made and confirmed.

(6) Where, for the purpose of determining whether the conditions specified in paragraphs (a) to (c) or paragraphs (a) and (b) (as may be appropriate) of subsection (1) of this section are fulfilled in relation to any land, any question arises as to what is or would in any particular circumstances be a reasonably beneficial use of that land, then, in determining that question for that purpose, no account shall be taken of any prospective use of that land which would involve the carrying out of development of any class which is not exempted development.   **[30]**

---

1 Amendments

a   The subsequent words were deleted by LG(PD)A 1990, s 13(7).

b All functions of the Minister were transferred to the Board by LG(PD)A 1976, s 14(5) and all former references to the Minister are now construed as to the Board.

3 Notes

a The concept of "reasonable beneficial use" is vague and it is difficult to conceive of a provision which provides for a procedure for the purchase of land yet only applies to land of effectively no value. There are English cases on this issue, see *R v Minister for Housing and Local Government* [1960] 1 WLR 587 and *General Estates Co Ltd v Minister for Housing and Local Government* [1967] 194 EG 201. See also Keane, *The Law of Local Government in the Republic of Ireland* (ILSI, 1982), p 136 and *Portland Estates v Limerick Corporation* [1980] ILRM 77.

b The right to serve the notice is not precluded by s 56.

c In *Portland Estates Ltd v Limerick Corporation* [1980] ILRM 77 the Supreme Court ruled that a planning authority is obliged to serve a Notice to Treat in such cases.

d There are no regulations governing the determination of this matter by the Board, yet the outcome will be of crucial importance to the owner. The words of McWilliam J in *O'Callaghan v The Commissioners of Public Works in Ireland* [1983] ILRM 391 (HC) are relevant: "... In the latter case it would be the responsibility of the body effecting the interference to ensure that procedures were adopted which conformed to the principles of natural justice, and, if they did not, the validity of the interference, but not of the statute, could be challenged in the Courts." At the very least the owner should be given a copy of all relevant documentation including any submissions made by them to the Board supporting their decision to refuse to purchase and the owner should also be given an opportunity of making his own submissions. See also *Nolan v Irish Land Commission* [1981] IR 23.

4 Commentary

This provision provides that where by virtue of a decision made under the Planning Acts land has become incapable of any reasonably beneficial use that a local authority may be compelled to acquire such land. The section is open to all manner of difficulties particularly the interpretation of "reasonably beneficial use" as it has been held that small areas of land can be used for agricultural purposes and that this is a reasonably beneficial use, and secondly the condition precedent in s 29(1)(a) would suggest that the level of compensation paid even in such circumstances will be derisory. Where such a notice is successful, the land is acquired by the local authority in the same manner as if it were required to be compulsorily acquired and the level of compensation determined by an arbitrator appointed in the same way as under a normal compulsory acquisition.

30. Revocation and modification of permission[3a]

(1) Subject to the provisions of this section, if the planning authority decide that it is expedient that any permission to develop land granted under this Part of this Act should be revoked or modified, they may, by notice served on the owner and on the occupier of the land affected and on any other person who in their opinion will be affected by the revocation or modification, revoke or modify the permission.[3b]

(2) In deciding, pursuant to this section, whether it is expedient to serve a notice under this section, the planning authority shall be restricted to considering the proper planning and development of the area of the authority (including the preservation and improvement of the amenities thereof), regard being had to the provisions of the development plan and the provisions of any special amenity area order relating to the said area.

[(2A) A planning authority shall neither revoke nor modify a permission under this section unless there has been a change in circumstances relating to the proper planning and development of the area concerned and such change in circumstances has occurred,

    (a) in case a notice relating to the permission is served under this section and is annulled, since the annulment of the notice,

    (b) in case no notice is so served, since the granting of the permission.

(2B) In case a planning authority pursuant in this section revoke or modify a permission, they shall specify in their decision the change in circumstances which warranted the revocation or modification.][1a]

(3) Any person on whom a notice under this section is served may, at any time before the day (not being earlier than one month after such service) specified in that behalf in the notice, appeal to the [Board][1b] against the notice.

(4) Where an appeal is brought under this section against a notice, the [Board][1b] may confirm the notice with or without modifications or annul the notice, and the provisions of subsection (2) of this section shall apply, subject to any necessary modifications, in relation to the deciding of an appeal under this subsection by the [Board][1b] as they apply in relation to the making of a decision by a planning authority.

(5) The power conferred by this section to revoke or modify permission to develop land may be exercised –

    (a) where the permission relates to the carrying out of works, at any time before those works have been commenced or, in the case of works which have been commenced and which, consequent on the making of a variation in the development plan, will contravene such plan, at any time before those works have been completed,

    (b) where the permission relates to a change of the use of any land, at any time before the change has taken place,

but the revocation or modification of permission for the carrying out of works shall not affect so much of the works as has been previously carried out.

(6) The provisions of section 29 of this Act shall apply in relation to a notice under this section revoking permission to develop land or modifying any such permission by the imposition of conditions and which is confirmed on appeal (whether with or without modification), as they apply in relation to the refusal of an application for such permission or the grant of such an application subject to conditions, and in any such case the said section 29 shall have effect subject to the following modifications:

    (i) in paragraph (c) of subsection (1), for "in a case where permission to develop the land was granted as aforesaid subject to conditions" there shall be substituted "in a case where the permission was modified by the imposition of conditions";

    (ii) for paragraph (i) of the proviso to subsection (4) there shall be substituted the following paragraph:

        "(i) if it appears to the [Board][1b] to be expedient so to do he may, in lieu of confirming the purchase notice, cancel the notice revoking the permission or, where the notice modified the permission by the imposition of conditions, revoke or amend those conditions so far as appears to him to be required in order to enable the land to be rendered capable of reasonably beneficial use by the carrying out of the development in respect of which the permission was granted."

(7) A notice under this section shall state the reasons for which it is given and particulars of it shall be entered in the register.

(8) The revocation or modification under this section of a permission shall be a reserved function.   **[31]**

---

1 Amendments

a   Subsections (2A) and (2B) were inserted by LG(PD)A 1976, s 39(i).

b   Former references to the Minister are now construed as to the Board: LG(PD)A 1976, s 14(9), (10).

3 Notes

a   See *Irish Asphalt Ltd v An Bord Pleanála* [1997] 1 ILRM 81 which appears to allow substantial modification of an outline planning permission and perhaps in exceptional circumstances a refusal, where circumstances change.

b   There is no power to revoke or modify an approval: see *State (Cogley) v Dublin Corporation* [1970] IR 244. However, since an approval dies with the relevant outline permission, revocation of the latter renders the former ineffective.

4 Commentary

This provides for the revocation of a permission where there has been a change in circumstances relating to the proper planning and development of the area, and where the permission relates to the carrying out of works where no such works have been carried out. An appeal against such a revocation lies to An Bord Pleanála and the period of appeal specified in the notice must not be less than one month. The decision to revoke a permission is a reserved function and the reasons for the revocation must be specified in the notice.

---

31. Enforcement of planning control (development)

(1) (a) Where any development of land, being neither exempted development nor development commenced before the appointed day, has been carried out after the appointed day[3a] without the grant of permission required in that behalf under this Part of this Act, or any condition subject to which such permission was granted in respect of any development has not been complied with, the planning authority within five years of such development being carried out, or, in case of non-compliance with a condition, within five years after the appropriate date, may, if they decide that it is expedient so to do, and shall, if they are directed by the Minister so to do serve on the owner and on the occupier of the land a notice under this section.

(b) In the foregoing paragraph "**the appropriate date**" means, in relation to a condition, the date specified in the condition (or in default of being specified in the condition, specified by notice served by the planning authority on the owner and on the occupier of the land) as the latest date for compliance with the condition.

[(c) A notice referred to in paragraph (b) of this subsection shall not be served after

—

(i) if the permission to which the condition is attached is a permission other than of the kind referred to in sub-paragraph (ii) of this paragraph, the date of the expiration, as respects the permission, of the appropriate period (within the meaning of section 2 of the Local Government (Planning and Development) Act, 1982) or, as the case may be, of the said period as extended under section 4 of the said Act,

(ii) if the permission to which the condition is attached is a permission for the retention on land of any structure, the expiration of a period of five years beginning on the day of the grant of the permission.][1a]

(2) The planning authority, in deciding whether it is expedient to serve a notice under paragraph (a) of subsection (1) of this section, and the Minister, in deciding whether he will direct the planning authority to serve such a notice, shall be restricted to considering the proper planning and development of the area of the authority (including the preservation and improvement of the amenities thereof), regard being had to the provisions of the development plan, the provisions of any special amenity area order relating to the said area and, in a case of non-compliance with a condition, the terms of the permission.[3b]

(3) Any notice served under paragraph (a) of subsection (1) of this section (hereafter in this section, referred to as an enforcement notice) shall specify the development which is alleged to have been carried out without the grant of such permission as aforesaid or, as the case may be, the matters in respect of which it is alleged that any such condition as aforesaid has not been complied with, and may require such steps as may be specified in the notice to be taken within such period as may be so specified for restoring the land to its condition before the development took place, or for securing compliance with the condition, as the case may be; and, in particular, any such notice may, for the purpose aforesaid, require the removal or alteration of any structures, the discontinuance of any use of land, or the carrying out on land of any works.

(4) An enforcement notice shall take effect at the expiration of such period (not being less than one month after the service thereof) as may be specified therein.

(5) If within the period specified in an enforcement notice, or within such extended period as the planning authority may allow, any steps required by the notice to be taken (other than the discontinuance of any use of land) have not been taken, the planning authority may enter on the land[2a] and take such steps, and may recover as a simple contract debt in any court of competent jurisdiction from the person who is then the owner of the land any expenses reasonably incurred by them in that behalf.

(6) Any expenses incurred by the owner or occupier of any land for the purpose of complying with an enforcement notice in respect of any development, and any sums paid by the owner of any land under the foregoing subsection in respect of the expenses of the planning authority in taking steps required to be taken by such a notice, shall be deemed to be incurred or paid for the use and at the request of the person by whom the development was carried out.

(7) An enforcement notice may be served whether or not there has been a prosecution under section 24 of this Act in relation to the relevant development.

(8) Where, by virtue of an enforcement notice, any use of land is required to be discontinued, or any condition is required to be complied with in respect of any use of

land or in respect of the carrying out of any works thereon, then, if any person, without the grant of permission in that behalf under this Part of this Act, uses the land or causes or permits the land to be used, or carries out or causes or permits to be carried out those works, in contravention of the notice, he shall be guilty of an offence and liable on summary conviction to a fine not exceeding [eight hundred pounds],[1b] and if the use or carrying out of works in contravention of the notice is continued after the conviction, he shall be guilty of a further offence and liable on summary conviction to a fine [(not exceeding in all [£800])[1c] not exceeding £150] for each day on which such use or carrying out of works is so continued.

(9) Nothing in this Part of this Act shall be construed as requiring permission to be obtained thereunder for the use of any land for the purpose for which it could lawfully have been used under this Part of this Act if the development in respect of which an enforcement notice is served had not been carried out.

(10) Particulars of an enforcement notice shall be entered in the register.[2b]   **[32]**

---

1 Amendments

a   Subsection (1)(c) was inserted by LG(PD)A 1992, s 19(1)(a).

b   LG(PD)A 1982, s 8 substituted £800 for £100. See now LG(PD)A 1992 which provides for fines of £1000 and £200 a day for continuing offences.

c   LG(PD)A 1982, s 8 substituted this fine for £800 per day. It also substituted £150 for £20 per day.

2 Cross References

a   See LG(PD)A 1963, s 81 in relation to entry onto the land by the planning authority.

b   See LG(PD)A 1976, s 28 in respect of the withdrawal of the notice and the cancellation of entries on the register.

3 Notes

a   The appointed day is 1 October 1964.

b   The planning authority and the Minister may also consider the matters set out in LG(PD)A 1976, s 24 and LG(PD)A 1982, s 7. See *O'Connor v Kerry County Council* [1988] ILRM 660; *Dublin Corporation v Mulligan* High Court, unrep, 6 May 1980.

4 Commentary

Section 31 provides a mechanism similar to ss 32 and 35 whereby a planning authority can serve a notice on the owner or occupier of land requiring that certain specified steps be taken in order to comply with the Planning Acts. The notice may be served if a development is being carried out without planning permission or where a development is being carried out other than in accordance with the permission and the notice will specify the steps to be taken in order to regularise the unauthorised development. The notice must be served within five years of the commencement of the unauthorised development and must provide a period which should not be less than one month for compliance with the requirements of the notice. The failure to comply with the notice within the required period is a criminal offence and can be prosecuted summarily in the District Court.

---

32. Enforcement of planning control (retention of structure)

(1) (a) Where any condition subject to which a permission for the retention of a structure was granted under this Part of this Act has not been complied with, the planning authority may within five years after the appropriate date, if they

decide that it is expedient so to do, serve on the owner and on the occupier of the structure a notice under this section.

(b) In the foregoing paragraph **"the appropriate date"** means, in relation to a condition, the date specified in the condition (or, in default of being specified in the condition, specified by notice served by the planning authority on the owner and on the occupier of the structure) as the latest date for compliance with the condition.

[(c) A notice referred to in paragraph (b) of this subsection shall not be served after the expiration of a period of five years beginning on the day of the grant of the permission referred to in paragraph (a) of this subsection.][1a]

(2) In deciding, pursuant to this section, whether it is expedient to serve a notice under paragraph (a) of subsection (1) of this section, the planning authority shall be restricted to considering the proper planning and development of the area of the authority (including the preservation and improvement of the amenities thereof), regard being had to the provisions of the development plan, the provisions of any special amenity area order relating to the said area and the terms of any permission granted.[2a]

(3) Any notice served under paragraph (a) of subsection (1) of this section (hereafter in this section referred to as an enforcement notice) shall specify the matters in respect of which it is alleged that any such condition as aforesaid had not been complied with, and may require such steps as may be specified in the notice to be taken within such period as may be so specified for compliance with the condition; and, in particular, any such notice may, for the purpose aforesaid, require the removal of the structure or require all or any of the following:

(a) the alteration of the structure,

(b) the carrying out of works (including the provision of car parks) which the planning authority consider are required if the retention of the structure is to be permitted.

(c) the provision of space around the structure,

(d) the planting of trees, shrubs or other plants or the landscaping of the structure or other land.

(4) An enforcement notice shall take effect at the expiration of such period (not being less than one month after the service thereof) as may be specified therein.

(5) If within the period specified in an enforcement notice, or within such extended period as the planning authority may allow, any steps required by the notice to be taken have not been taken, the planning authority may enter on the structure and take those steps, and may recover as a simple contract debt in any court of competent jurisdiction from the person who is then the owner of the structure any expenses reasonably incurred by them in that behalf.

(6) Particulars of an enforcement notice shall be entered in the register.[2b]   **[33]**

---

1 Amendments

a   Subsection (1)(c) was inserted by LG(PD)A 1992, s 19(1)(b).

2 Cross References

a   The planning authority may also consider the notice set out in LG(PD)A 1976, s 24 and LG(PD)A 1982, s 7.

b   See LG(PD)A 1976, s 28 in respect of the withdrawal of the notice and the cancellation of entries on the register.

4 Commentary

This is similar to the provisions of s 31 except that it applies to a limited class of development: those developments which were granted a retention permission pursuant to s 28 of LG(PD)A 1963. For those developments the appropriate notice is a notice under s 32 and it is submitted that a notice under ss 31 or 35 of LG(PD)A 1963 would be inappropriate in such circumstances.

33. [Enforcement of planning control (structure which is unauthorised structure on commencement of appointed day)]

[34]

4 Commentary

Section 33 relates to those structures which were unauthorised on 1 December, 1964 and the time limit for the service of notices under this section expired in 1969.

34. Liability of owner of land for failure to comply with requirements of enforcement notice other than discontinuance of use of land

(1) Subject to the provisions of this section, where an enforcement notice (other than a notice which has been annulled) has been served under any of the last three preceding sections on the person who was, when the notice was served on him, the owner of the land to which the enforcement notice relates and within the period specified in the enforcement notice, or within such extended period as the planning authority may allow, any steps required by the enforcement notice to be taken (other than the discontinuance of any use of land) have not been taken, that person shall be guilty of an offence and shall be liable on summary conviction to a fine not exceeding [£800.][1a]

(2) If a person against whom proceedings are brought under this section has at some time before the end of the said period specified in the enforcement notice for compliance with the notice (or of such extended period as the planning authority may allow for compliance with the notice) ceased to be the owner of the land, he shall, upon complaint duly made by him and on giving to the prosecution not less than three clear days' notice of his intention, be entitled to have the person who then became the owner of the land brought before the court in the proceedings.

(3) If, after it has been proved that any steps required by the enforcement notice have not been taken as aforesaid, the original defendant proves that the failure to take the steps was attributable in whole or in part to the default of the said other person, that other person may be convicted of the offence and, if the original defendant further proves that he took all reasonable steps to secure compliance with the enforcement notice, he shall be acquitted of the offence.

(4) For the purposes of subsection (1) and (2) of this section, a person who, apart from this subsection, would be the owner of land by reason of receiving rent shall, if he receives the rent as agent for another person, be regarded as not being such owner.

(5) If after a person is convicted under the foregoing provisions of this section he does not as soon as practicable do everything in his power to secure compliance with the enforcement notice, he shall be guilty of a further offence and shall be liable on

summary conviction to a fine [(not exceeding in all £800) not exceeding £150][1b] for each day following his first conviction on which any of the requirements of the enforcement notice (other than the discontinuance of any use of land) remain unfulfilled.

(6) If the owner of any land is obstructed or interfered with in taking steps required to be taken by an enforcement notice under any of the last three preceding sections,[3a] the person obstructing or interfering shall be guilty of an offence and shall be liable on summary conviction to a fine not exceeding [£800];[1c] and if in the case of a continuing offence the obstruction or interference is continued after conviction, he shall be guilty of a further offence and liable on summary conviction to a fine [(not exceeding in all £800) not exceeding £150][1d] for each day on which the obstruction or interference is so continued.[4]

(7) Subsection (6) of this section shall not apply where the person obstructing or interfering is the occupier of the land unless the owner has given to him not less than fourteen days' notice in writing of the intention to take steps.   [35]

---

1 Amendments

a   "£800" was substituted for "one hundred pounds" by LG(PD)A 1982, s 8.

b   The words in square brackets were inserted by LG(PD)A 1982, s 8.

c   "£800" substituted for "one hundred pounds" by LG(PD)A 1982, s 8.

d   The words in square brackets were inserted by LG(PD)A 1982, s 8. See now LG(PD)A 1992, s 20 which provides for fines of £1000 and £200 for each day of a continuing offence.

3 Notes

a   See *Dublin Corporation v Flynn* [1980] IR 357.

4 Commentary

Section 34 imposes liability on the owner of land who fails to comply with enforcement notices served under ss 31, 32 or 33 of LG(PD)A 1963. There is provision for continuing offences but all the elements of the original charge must be prosecuted in such cases.

---

35. Enforcement of planning control (development commenced and carried out in conformity with permission)

(1) Where any development authorised by a permission granted under this Part of this Act has been commenced but has not been or is not being carried out in conformity with such permission, the planning authority may, if they consider it expedient so to do, and shall, if they are directed so to do by the Minister, serve a notice under this section.

(2) The planning authority, in deciding whether it is expedient to serve a notice under this section, and the Minister, in deciding whether he will direct the planning authority to serve such a notice, shall be restricted to considering the proper planning and development of the area of the authority (including the provision and improvement of the amenities thereof), regard being had to the provisions of the development plan, the provisions of any special amenity area order relating to the said area[2a] and the terms of any permission granted.

(3) A notice under this section may be served on –

    (a) the person who commenced the development, or

(b) any other person who has carried out or is carrying out development authorised by the permission,

as the planning authority may decide.

(4) Any notice served under this section (hereafter in this section referred to as an enforcement notice) may require such steps as may be specified in the notice to be taken within such period as may be so specified for securing the carrying out of the development in conformity with the permission and, in particular, any such notice may, for the purpose aforesaid, require the removal or alteration of any structures, the discontinuance of any use of land or the carrying out on land of any works.

(5) An enforcement notice shall take effect at the expiration of such period (not being less than one month after the service thereof) as may be specified therein.

(6) If within the period specified in an enforcement notice, or within such extended period as the planning authority may allow, any steps required by the notice to be taken have not been taken, the planning authority may enter on the land and take such steps[2b] and may recover as a simple contract debt in any court of competent jurisdiction from the person on whom the notice was served any expenses reasonably incurred by them in that behalf.

(7) Where an enforcement notice has been served on a person and within the period specified therein, or within such extended period as the planning authority may allow, any steps required by the notice to be taken have not been taken, that person shall be guilty of an offence and shall be liable on summary conviction to a fine not exceeding [£800].[1a]

(8) If after a person is convicted under this section he does not as soon as practicable do everything in his power to secure compliance with the enforcement notice, he shall be guilty of a further offence and shall be liable on summary conviction to a fine [(not exceeding in all £800) not exceeding £150][1b] for each day following his first conviction on which any of the requirements of the enforcement notice remain unfulfilled.

(9) Particulars of an enforcement notice shall be entered in the register.[2c]

[(10) An enforcement notice shall not be served in relation to any development authorised by a permission granted under this Part of this Act which has been commenced but has not been carried out in conformity with such permission after the expiration of a period of five years beginning on the expiration, as respects such permission, of the appropriate period (within the meaning of section 2 of the Local Government (Planning and Development) Act, 1982) or, as the case may be, of the said period as extended under section 4 of the said Act.][1c, 3a]   **[36]**

---

1 Amendments

a   £800 inserted by LG(PD)A 1982, s 8(1). See now LG(PD)A 1992, s 20 which provides for increased fines, £1000 and £200 for each day of a continuing offence.

b   As amended by LG(PD)A 1982, s 8.

c   Subsection (10) was inserted by LG(PD)A 1992, s 19(2)(a).

2 Cross References

a   See LG(PD)A 1976, s 24 for additional matters which the planning authority may consider. The essential difference between s 31 and s 35 is the class of persons on whom the notice can be served.

b   See LG(PD)A 1963, s 81 in respect of the powers of the planning authority to enter onto land.

c   See LG(PD)A 1976, s 28 in respect of the withdrawal of notices and the cancellation of entries in the register.

3 Notes

a   See *Dublin County Council v Hill* [1992] ILRM 397.

4 Commentary

Section 35 is broadly similar to s 31 except that this section is limited to those developments being carried out on foot of a planning permission and may be served on the person who commenced the development or any other person who has carried out or is carrying out a development authorised by the permission. Such a notice will generally be served in cases where a developer has commenced but has failed to complete a development and may have left the site. In those circumstances a notice under s 31 would be of little use and it is particularly appropriate for unfinished housing estates or partly completed developments of this nature. There is now a five year limitation period for the service of such notices and a breach of the notice is a criminal office which is triable summarily in the District Court. It is important that the breach identified in the planning code elicits the correct notice and failure to serve the correct notice may invalidate the procedure adopted.

---

36. Requiring removal or alteration of structure

(1) If the planning authority decide that any structure should be removed or altered, the planning authority may serve a notice, requiring the carrying out of such removal or alteration and, in the case of a removal, any replacement appearing to the planning authority to be suitable, on the owner and on the occupier of the structure and on any other person who in their opinion will be affected by the notice.

(2) Subsection (1) of this section shall not apply in relation to an unauthorised structure unless –

   (a)   it is a structure which existed immediately before the appointed day and was on the commencement of that day an unauthorised structure and the notice under this section is served after the expiration of five years from the appointed day, or

   (b)   it is a structure constructed, erected or made on or after the appointed day and the notice under this section is served after the expiration of five years from its having been constructed, erected or made.[3a]

(3) In deciding pursuant to this section that a structure should be removed or altered, the planning authority shall be restricted to considering the proper planning and development of the area of the authority (including the preservation and improvement of the amenities thereof), regard being had to the provisions of the development plan and the provisions of any special amenity area order relating to the said area.[2a]

(4) Where a notice is served under this section, any person may, at any time before the day (not being earlier than one month after such service) specified in that behalf in the notice, appeal to the Board against the notice.

(5) Where an appeal is brought under this section against a notice, the Board may confirm the notice with or without modifications or annul the notice, and the provisions of subsection (3) of this section shall apply, subject to any necessary modifications, in relation to the deciding of an appeal under this subsection by the Board as they apply in relation to the making of a decision by the planning authority.[1a]

(6) A notice under this section (other than a notice which is annulled) shall take effect –

    (a) in case no appeal against it is taken or every appeal against it is withdrawn before the expiration of the period for taking an appeal – on the expiration of the period for taking an appeal,

    (b) in case an appeal or appeals is or are taken against it and the appeal or appeals is or are not withdrawn during the period for taking an appeal – when every appeal not so withdrawn has been either withdrawn or determined.

(7) If within the period specified in a notice under this section, or within such extended period as the planning authority may allow, the removal or alteration required by the notice has not been effected, the planning authority may enter on the structure and may effect such removal or alteration and any replacement specified in the notice.[2b]

(8) Where a notice under this section is complied with, the planning authority shall pay to the person complying with the notice the expenses reasonably incurred by him in carrying out the removal or alteration and any replacement specified in the notice, less the value of any salvageable materials.[2c]

(9) The provisions of section 29 of this Act shall apply in relation to a notice which is served under this section and which is confirmed on appeal (whether with or without modification) as they apply in relation to the refusal of an application for permission to develop land, in any such case the said section 29 shall have effect subject to the following modifications:

    (i) paragraph (c) of subsection (1) shall be disregarded;

    (ii) for paragraph (i) of the proviso to subsection (4) there shall be substituted the following paragraph:

        "(i) if it appears to the Minister to be expedient so to do he may, in lieu of conforming the purchase notice, cancel the notice requiring removal or alteration."

(10) Particulars of a notice served under this section shall be entered in the register.[2d] **[37]**

---

1 Amendments

a   Section 14 of LG(PD)A 1976 transferred the Minister's powers to the Board.

2 Cross References

a   See LG(PD)A 1976, s 24 for additional matters which the planning authority may consider.

b   See LG(PD)A 1963, s 81 in respect of the planning authority's power of entry onto the land.

c   See LG(PD)A 1963, s 60 in respect of compensation which may be payable.

d   See LG(PD)A 1976, s 28 in respect of the withdrawal of notices and the cancellation of entries on the register. See LG(PD)A 1990, s 18 for provisions relating to compensation where notices are served under this section.

3 Notes

a   The appointed day was 1 October 1964.

4 Commentary

Section 36 provides a power for planning authorities to alter or remove a structure. This would generally be an authorised structure or an unauthorised structure which has remained in existence for a period in excess of five years. The enforcement of such a notice would require the planning authority to compensate the land owner pursuant to s 60 of LG(PD)A 1963. An appeal against such a notice would lie to An Bord Pleanála. This is an alternative given to a local authority who wishes to alter or remove a structure to the compulsorily acquisition of the property, which is the normal route chosen in such cases.

---

37. Requiring discontinuance of use

(1) If the planning authority decide, as respects any use of land, that –

    (a) the use should be discontinued, or

    (b) any conditions should be imposed on the continuance thereof,

the planning authority may serve a notice, requiring discontinuance of that use or imposing those conditions, on the owner and on the occupier of the land and on any other person who in their opinion will be affected by the notice.

(2) Subsection (1) of this section shall not apply in relation to an unauthorised use unless it is a use commenced on or after the appointed day and the notice under this section is served after the expiration of five years from its having been commenced.

(3) In deciding, pursuant to this section, that any use should be discontinued or any conditions should be imposed, the planning authority shall be restricted to considering the proper planning and development of the area of the authority (including the preservation and improvement of the amenities thereof), regard being had to the provisions of the development plan and the provisions of any special amenity area order relating to the said area.[2a]

(4) Where a notice is served under this section, any person may, at any time before the day (not being earlier than one month after such service) specified in that behalf in the notice, appeal to the Board against the notice.

(5) Where an appeal is brought under this section against a notice, the Board may confirm the notice with or without modifications or annul the notice, and the provisions of subsection (3) of this section shall apply, subject to any necessary modifications, in relation to the deciding of an appeal under this subsection by the Board as they apply in relation to the making of a decision by the planning authority.[1a]

(6) A notice under this section (other than a notice which is annulled) shall take effect –

    (a) in case no appeal against it is taken or every appeal against it is withdrawn before the expiration of the period for taking an appeal – on the expiration of the period for taking an appeal,

    (b) in case an appeal or appeals is or are taken against it and the appeal or appeals is or are not withdrawn during the period for taking an appeal – when every appeal not so withdrawn has been either withdrawn or determined.

(7) Where, by virtue of a notice under this section, the use of land for any purpose is required to be discontinued, or any conditions are imposed on the continuance thereof, then, if any person uses the land for that purpose or, as the case may be, uses the land for

that purpose in contravention of those conditions, or causes or permits the land to be so used, he shall be guilty of an offence and liable on summary conviction to a fine not exceeding eight hundred pounds, and if such use is continued after the conviction, he shall be guilty of a further offence and liable on summary conviction to a fine [(not exceeding in all £800) not exceeding £150][1b] for each day on which such use is so continued.

(8) The provisions of section 29 of this Act shall apply in relation to a notice which is served under this section requiring discontinuance of use of land, or imposing conditions on such use, which is confirmed on appeal (whether with or without modifications), as they apply in relation to the refusal of an application for permission to use land or the grant of such an application subject to conditions, and in any such case the said section 29 shall have effect subject to the following modifications:

   (i) for paragraph (a) of subsection (1) there shall be substituted the following paragraph:

       "(a) that the land has become incapable of reasonably beneficial use on account of the required discontinuance or the imposed conditions (as the case may be)";

   (ii) paragraph (c) of subsection (1) shall be disregarded;

   (iii) for paragraph (i) of the proviso to subsection (4) there shall be substituted the following paragraph:

       "(i) if it appears to the Minister to be expedient so to do he may, in lieu of confirming the purchase notice, cancel the notice requiring the discontinuance or imposing conditions."[1c]

(9) Particulars of a notice served under this section shall be entered in the register.[2b] **[38]**

---

1 Amendments

a   LG(PD)A 1976, s 14 transferred the Minister's appellate functions under this section to the Board.

b   As amended by LG(PD)A 1982, s 8(1). See now LG(PD)A 1992, s 20 for increased fines £1000 and £200 for each day of a continuing offence.

c   Now the Board rather than the Minister: see LG(PD)A 1976, s 14.

2 Cross References

a   See LG(PD)A 1976, s 24 for additional matters which the planning authority may consider.

b   See LG(PD)A 1976, s 28 Act in respect of the withdrawal of notices and the cancellation of entries on the register. See LG(PD)A 1990, s 19 for provisions relating to compensation where notices are served under this section.

4 Commentary

Section 37 is similar to s 36 but notices served under this section may prohibit the use of land or may impose conditions on the use of land. Again, the use of the land would generally be authorised for the purposes of the Planning Acts and it is necessary, if such a notice is served, to pay compensation. An appeal lies against such a notice to An Bord Pleanála and particulars of the notice must be entered on the planning register.

---

38. Agreements regulating development or use of land

(1) A planning authority may enter into an agreement with any person interested in land in their area for the purpose of restricting or regulating the development or use of the land, either permanently or during such period as may be specified by the agreement, and any such agreement may contain such incidental and consequential provisions (including provisions of a financial character) as appear to the planning authority to be necessary or expedient for the purposes of the agreement.

[(1A) A planning authority entering into an agreement under this section may join with any body which is a prescribed authority for the purposes of section 21 of this Act.][1a

(2) An agreement made under this section with any person interested in land may be enforced by [the planning authority or any body joined with them][1b against persons deriving title under that person in respect of that land as if [the planning authority or such body, as may be appropriate,][1b were possessed of adjacent land and as if the agreement had been expressed to be made for the benefit of that land.

(3) Nothing in this section or in any agreement made thereunder shall be construed as restricting the exercise, in relation to land which is the subject of any such agreement, of any powers exercisable by the Minister, [the Board][1c or the planning authority under this Act so long as those powers are not exercised so as to contravene materially the provisions of the development plan, or as requiring the exercise of any such powers so as to contravene materially those provisions.

(4) Particulars of an agreement made under this section shall be entered in the register.   [39]

---

1 Amendments

a   Subsection (1A) was inserted by LG(PD)A 1976, s 39(j).

b   The words in square brackets were inserted by LG(PD)A 1976, s 39(k).

c   The words in square brackets were inserted by LG(PD)A 1976, s 39(l).

4 Commentary

Section 38 empowers a planning authority to enter into an agreement with any person for the purpose of restricting or regulating the development or the use of the land in question. These notices may be permanent or may be for a specified period. The requirement to enter such an agreement often arises from the condition of a permission but such a condition is questionable having regard to the equivalent English authorities and to the fact that such an agreement appears to envisaged in s 38 as being a voluntary agreement and not one imposed arising from a condition of a permission.

Generally such conditions in a planning permission restrict the use of the land to particular classes of person or sterilise the remainder of the land but a condition of a planning permission will achieve precisely the same result and will equally bind successors in title which appears to be the main object of requiring a land owner to enter into such a condition. A land owner who voluntarily undertakes to enter into such an arrangement is in a different position and such an agreement is legal.

---

39. Restrictions on certain local authorities[3a]

(1) The council of a county shall not effect any development in their county health district which contravenes materially the development plan.

(2) The corporation of a county or other borough shall not effect any development in such borough which contravenes materially the development plan.

(3) The council of an urban district shall not effect any development in such district which contravenes materially the development plan.   **[40]**

---

3 Notes

a   See *O'Leary v Dublin County Council* [1988] IR 150 for a consideration of this section. See also *Keogh v Galway Corporation* High Court, unrep, 3 March 1995; *McCann v Galway Corporation* High Court, unrep, 15 November 1994; *McGarry v Sligo County Council* [1991] 1 IR 99; *An Taisce v Dublin Corporation* High Court, unrep, 31 January 1973; *Wilkinson v Dublin County Council* [1991] ILRM 605; *Ferris v Dublin County Council* Supreme Court, unrep, 7 November 1990; *Byrne v Wicklow County Council* High Court, unrep, 3 November 1994 which suggest that different standards will apply to decisions of the County Manager on the determination of planning applications. See also *Blessington & District Community Council Ltd v Wicklow County Council* High Court, unrep, 19 July 1996 where Kelly J followed this approach and held that the Council could permit the demolition of a building listed for protection in the plan, notwithstanding that the provisions of the plan in this regard were not referred to on the planning file. See also the judgment of Barron J in *Roughan v Clare County Council* High Court, unrep, 18 December 1996 which established that all major developments to be carried out by a local authority should be specified in the development plan in holding that a travellers' halting site development was *ultra vires* the powers of the local authority.

4 Commentary

This is an important section which prevents local authorities from carrying out any development in contravention of their development plan. The standards which the courts apply to the issue of a material contravention is not the same as that under s 26(3) and s 39, even where there is abundant evidence before the planning authority that the proposed development is not a material contravention, a court may deem the development to be such as to materially contravene the plan. Section 39 has now been extended to provide that all major local authority developments must be included within the plan as otherwise the provisions of s 39 could be circumvented by failing to include any significant development objectives in their plan and by relying on the fact that there was no specific objective to be contravened. It should be seen therefore that *Blessington and District Community Council Ltd v Wicklow County Council* High Court, 19 July 1996, is different from the other cases referred to above at Note 3a, in that that case referred to a decision under s 26(3) whereas the remainder of the cases, with the exception of *Byrne v Wicklow County Council*, relate to decisions made under s 39.

---

40. Permission not required in certain cases

Notwithstanding anything in this Part of this Act, permission shall not be required under this Part of this Act –

   (a)   in the case of land which, on the appointed day, is being used temporarily for a purpose other than the purpose for which it is normally used, in respect of the resumption of the use of the land for the last-mentioned purpose;

   (b)   in the case of land which, on the appointed day, is normally used for one purpose and is also used on occasions, whether at regular intervals or not, for any other purpose, in respect of the use of the land for that other purpose on similar occasions after the appointed day;

(c) in respect of development required by a notice under section 31, 32, 33, 35 or 36 of this Act (disregarding development for which there is in fact permission under this Part of this Act). **[41]**

---

4 Commentary

Section 40 is now primarily important because of subpara (c) which provides that the carrying out of works pursuant to an enforcement notice under ss 31, 32 or 35 or a notice under s 33 and 36 of LG(PD)A 1963 and will not require permission and the carrying out of such works is essentially in the nature of an exempted development.

---

41. Registering of applications

(1) A planning authority shall enter in the register:

(a) particulars of any application made to them under this Part of this Act for permission for development or for retention of structures, including the name and address of the applicant, the date of receipt of the application and brief particulars of the development or retention forming the subject of the application,

[(aa) where an environmental impact statement was submitted in respect of an application, an indication of this fact,][1a]

[(aaa) where the development forming the subject of an application in respect of which an environmental impact statement was submitted comprises or is for the purposes of an activity in relation to which a licence under Part IV of the Environmental Protection Agency Act, 1992 (No. 7 of 1992) is required, an indication of this fact,][1b]

(b) particulars of any application made to them under this Part of this Act for approval required by permission regulations, including the name and address of the applicant, the date of receipt of the application and brief particulars of the matters forming the subject of the application,

(c) the decision of the planning authority in respect of any such application and the date of the decision,

(d) the date and effect of any decision on appeal of the Minister in respect of any such application,

(e) particulars of any application made by them under subsection (3) of section 26 of this Act, including the date of the sending of the application and brief particulars of the development concerned.

(2) Every such entry consisting of particulars of an application shall be made within the period of seven days beginning on the day of receipt of the application.

(3) Every such entry consisting of a decision on an application shall be made within the period of seven days beginning on the day of the decision.[3a] **[42]**

---

1 Amendments

a Section (1)(aa) was inserted by EC(EIA)(R) 1989 (SI 349/1989), art 9.

b Subsection (1)(aaa) was inserted by EC(EIA)(A)(R) 1994 (SI 84/1994), art 7.

3 Notes

a   See *State (Toft) v Galway Corporation* [1981] ILRM 439 for examples of where the register was amended subsequent to the decision.

4 Commentary

Section 41 does not contain an exhaustive list of the matters that must be entered on the Planning Register and in addition to those matters required by ss 26, 27 and 28 relating to applications for planning permission, notices served under ss 29, 30, 31, 32, 33, 35, 36, 37, 38, 44, 45, 46, 47, 48 and 50 of LG(PD)A 1963 are all required to be entered on the Planning Register as well as matters under s 25, 26, 28, 29 of LG(PD)A 1976.

It is desirable however that the details of the planning application, including all documentation accompanying the application should be retained having regard to the decision principally in *Readymix (Eire) Ltd v Dublin County Council* (SC, unrep, 30 July 1974) which provides that an applicant is bound not just by the conditions attached to the permission but by all plans and documentation lodged and consequently access to such documentation is important not least to ascertain the extent of compliance.

Part V

AMENITIES

42. Area of special amenity

[(1) When it appears to the planning authority that by reason of –

    (a) its outstanding natural beauty,

    (b) its special recreational value, or

    (c) a need for nature conservation,

an area should be declared under this section to be an area of special amenity, they may by order do so and the order may state the objective of the planning authority in relation to the preservation or enhancement of the character or special features of the area including objectives for the prevention or limitation of development in the area.[3a]

(1A) The Minister may, if he considers it necessary, direct a planning authority to make an order under this section in relation to an area specified in the direction and may, if he thinks fit, require that objectives specified in the direction be included by the planning authority in their order in respect of matters and in a manner so specified and in case the Minister gives a direction under this subsection the planning authority concerned shall comply with the direction and an order made pursuant to a direction under this subsection shall be revoked or varied only with the consent of the Minister.][1a]

(2) An order under this section shall come into operation on being confirmed, whether with or without modification, under the next section.

(3) Where the functional areas of two planning authorities are contiguous, either authority may, with the consent of the other, make an order under this section in respect of an area in or partly in the functional area of the other.

(4) Any order under this section for the time being in force may be revoked or varied by a subsequent order under this section.

(5) A planning authority shall, from time to time and at least once in every period of five years, review any order made by them under this section and for the time being in force (excepting any order merely revoking a previous order) for the purpose of deciding whether it is desirable to revoke or amend the order.

(6) The making of an order under this section shall be a reserved function.   **[43]**

---

1 Amendments

a   Subsections (1) and (1A) were substituted by LG(PD)A 1976, s 40(a).

3 Notes

a   A number of special amenity area orders have been made (eg, relating to Dublin Bay), but only two, affecting the Liffey Valley and North Bull Island have been confirmed. A refusal of permission for development in an area to which a special amenity area order relates cannot attract compensation: LG(PD)A 1990, Second Schedule, para 6.

4 Commentary

Section 42 enables the elected members of a planning authority to make a special amenity area order for particular areas, having regard to the natural beauty, the recreational value, or the need for nature conservation in that particular area. Such orders must be confirmed by the Minister and must be reviewed at least once in every period of five years so as to consider whether it is necessary to revoke or amend the order.

Such designation has a number of consequences, not least that those developments exempted under the various planning regulations lose their exempted status and in addition the compensation provisions of the LG(PD)A 1990 will not generally apply to refusals within such areas.

---

43. Confirmation of order under section 42 of this Act

(1) As soon as may be after they have made an order under section 42 of this Act, a planning authority shall publish in one or more newspapers circulating in the area to which the order relates a notice –

  (a) stating the fact of the order having been made and describing the area to which it relates,

  (b) naming a place where a copy of the order and of any map referred to therein may be seen during office hours,

  (c) specifying the period (not being less than one month) within and the manner in which objections to the order may be made to the planning authority,

  (d) specifying that the order requires confirmation by the Minister and that, where any objections are duly made to the order and are not withdrawn, a public local inquiry will be held and the objections will be considered before the order is confirmed.

(2) As soon as may be after the said period for making objections has expired, the planning authority may submit the order made under section 42 of this Act to the Minister for confirmation, and, when making any such submission, they shall also submit to the Minister any objections to the order which have been duly made and have not been withdrawn.

(3) If no such objection as aforesaid is duly made, or if all such objections so made are withdrawn, the Minister may by order confirm the order made under section 42 of this Act with or without modifications or refuse to confirm it; but in any other case he shall, before confirming, cause a public local inquiry to be held and shall consider any objections not withdrawn and the report of the person who held the inquiry, and may then by order confirm the order with or without modifications or refuse to confirm it.

(4) Every order made under this section by the Minister shall be laid before each House of the Oireachtas as soon as may be after it is made and, if a resolution annulling the order is passed by either such House within the next subsequent twenty-one days on which that House has sat after the order is laid before it, the order shall be annulled accordingly but without prejudice to the validity of anything previously done thereunder.

(5) Any reference in this Act to a special amenity area order shall be construed as a reference to an order confirmed under this section. **[44]**

---

4 Commentary

Section 43 specifies the procedures for the confirming of an order made under s 42 which procedure is similar to the making of a statutory instrument under the Planning Acts and reinforces the high status of such a designation and the significant consequences that flow from it.

---

44. Requiring removal or alteration of hedge

(1) If it appears to the planning authority that it is expedient in the interests of amenity that any hedge should be removed or altered, the planning authority may serve on the owner and on the occupier of the land on which the hedge is situate a notice requiring the carrying out of such removal or alteration and, in the case of a removal, any replacement appearing to the planning authority to be suitable.

(2) Where a notice is served under this section, any person may, at any time before the day (not being earlier than one month after such service) specified in that behalf in the notice, appeal to the [Board]¹ᵃ against the notice.

(3) Where an appeal is brought under this section from a notice, the [Board]¹ᵃ may confirm the notice with or without modifications or annul the notice.

(4) A notice under this section (other than a notice which is annulled) shall take effect –

    (a) in case no appeal against it is taken or every appeal against it is withdrawn before the expiration of the period for taking an appeal – on the expiration of the period for taking an appeal,

    (b) in case an appeal or appeals is or are taken against it and the appeal or appeals is or are not withdrawn during the period for taking an appeal – when every appeal not so withdrawn has been either withdrawn or determined.

(5) If within the period specified in a notice under this section, or within such extended period as the planning authority may allow, the removal or alteration required by the notice has not been effected, the planning authority may enter on the land on which the hedge is situate and may effect such removal or alteration and any replacement specified in the notice.

(6) Where a notice under this section is complied with, the planning authority shall pay to the person complying with the notice the expenses reasonably incurred by him in carrying out the removal or alteration and any replacement specified in the notice.

(7) Particulars of a notice served under this section shall be entered in the register.²ᵃ **[45]**

---

1 Amendments

a   Former references to the Minister are now construed as to the Board: LG(PD)A 1976, s 14(9), (10).

2 Cross References

a   See LG(PD)A 1990, s 20 on provisions relating to compensation for notices served with regard to this section.

4 Commentary

Section 44 allows a planning authority to serve a notice on any land owner with regard to a hedge that it considers should be removed or altered. An appeal against such a notice lies to An Bord Pleanála and the period prescribed in such a notice must not be less than one month. The term "hedge" is not defined in s 44 and whether a fence, wall or similar boundary is included within the section's ambit is not clear. If it is meant to apply to all such boundaries, then it is submitted that the section should be more clearly worded.

Compensation for the alteration or removal of a hedge under s 44 may be claimed under s 20 of the LG(PD)A 1990.

---

45. Tree preservation orders

(1) If it appears to the planning authority that it is expedient in the interests of amenity to make provision for the preservation of any tree, trees, group of trees or woodlands,[3a] they may for that purpose make an order with respect to any such tree, trees, group of trees or woodlands as may be specified in the order; and, in particular, provision may be made by any such order –

   (a) for prohibiting (subject to any exemptions for which provision may be made by the order) the cutting down, topping, lopping or wilful destruction of trees except with the consent of the planning authority, and for enabling that authority to give their consent subject to conditions;

   (b) for applying, in relation to any consent under the order, and to applications therefor, any of the provisions of Part IV of this Act relating to permission to develop land, and to applications for such permission, subject to such adaptations and modifications as may be specified in the order.

(2) ...[1a]

(3) Any order under this section may be revoked or varied by a subsequent order under this section.

(4) Where a planning authority make an order under this section, they shall serve a notice of the making of the order and a copy of the order on every person who is the owner or occupier of any land affected by the order, and on any other person then known to them to be entitled to fell any tree, trees, group of trees or woodlands to which the order relates.

(5) Any person on whom a notice and a copy of an order is served under this section may, at any time before the day specified in that behalf in the notice (not being earlier than one month after such service), appeal to the Minister against the order.

(6) Where an appeal is brought under this section against an order, the Minister may confirm the order with or without modifications or annul the order.[2a]

(7) Without prejudice to any other exemption for which provision may be made by an order under this section, no such order shall apply to the cutting down, topping or lopping of trees which are dying or dead or have become dangerous or the cutting down, topping or lopping of any trees in compliance with any obligation imposed by or under any statute or so far as may be necessary for the prevention of abatement of a nuisance.[3b]

(8) If any person contravenes the provisions of an order under this section (other than an order which has been annulled), he shall be guilty of an offence and shall be liable on summary conviction to a fine not exceeding two hundred pounds.[1b]

(9) Particulars of an order under this section shall be entered in the register.

(10) Any reference in this Act to a tree preservation order shall be construed as a reference to an order under this section (other than an order which has been annulled).[2b][3c]   **[46]**

---

1 Amendments

a   Subsection (2) was repealed by LG(PD)A 1990, s 3(1).

b   See now LG(PD)A 1992, s 20 for revised fines in this regard.

2 Cross References

a   Appeals under this section are now made to An Bord Pleanála; see LG(PD)A 1976, s 14.

b   See LG(PD)A 1990, s 21 for the provisions relating to compensation in this regard.

3 Notes

a   In the absence of definitions, the difference between a "group of trees" and "woodlands" is unclear. Where a planning authority wishes to preserve a number of trees without incurring exposure to a claim for damages suffered, it seems it may only have to make as many individual tree preservation orders as there are trees, no matter how many, to defeat such a claim. This was done, for example, by Dun Laoghaire Corporation in relation to the St Helen's Site at Booterstown, Co Dublin in 1988. See also *Wicklow County Council v An Bord Pleanála* High Court, unrep, 22 June 1989 which deals with tree preservation order appeals.

b   A notice may be served under the Roads Act 1993 requiring the cutting down or removal of trees, see *Boyne Grove Fruit Farms Ltd v J Murphy Developments Ltd* (Laffoy J *ex tempore*, 1996).

c   A felling licence is generally required under the Forestry Act 1946 for the removal of any tree over 10 years old in a rural area. See s 37(1) and s 37(2) of the 1946 Act for cases where such a felling licence is not required.

4 Commentary

Section 45 gives power to a planning authority to make tree preservation orders in respect of trees considered worthy of preservation. A tree preservation order is in the nature of a development plan specifying the trees that are to be retained and sub-s (1)(b) provides for the making of applications for consent to effectively modify the terms of the order. There is the right of appeal to the Board against such an order, and the time period prescribed in that notice must not be less than one month.

Compensation for orders made under s 45 can be claimed in appropriate circumstances pursuant to s 21 of LG(PD)A 1990.

---

46. Conservation orders

[(1) If it appears to the planning authority, after consultation with the prescribed authorities,[2a] that it is expedient in the interests of amenity to make provision to preserve from extinction or otherwise protect any flora or fauna in an area, or part of an area, to which a special amenity area order relates, being flora or fauna which are of special amenity value or special interest, they may make an order prohibiting (subject to any exemptions for which provision may be made by the order) the taking, killing or destroying of such flora or fauna.][1a]

(2) ...[1b]

(3) Any order under this section may be revoked or varied by a subsequent order under this section.

(4) Where a planning authority make an order under this section, they shall cause a notice stating the effect of the order and stating the right of appeal under the next subsection to be published in at least one newspaper circulating in the area to which the order relates.

(5) Any person may, at any time before the expiration of one month after the publication of a notice under the foregoing subsection, appeal to the [Board][1c] against the order to which the notice relates.

(6) Where an appeal is brought under this section against an order, the [Board][1c] may confirm the order with or without modifications or annul the order.

(7) ...[1d]

(8) If any person contravenes the provisions of an order under this section (other than an order which has been annulled), he shall be guilty of an offence and shall be liable on summary conviction to a fine not exceeding two hundred pounds.[1e]

(9) Particulars of an order under this section shall be entered in the register.

(10) ...[1f]

(11) Any reference in this Act to a conservation order shall be construed as a reference to an order under this section (other than an order which has been annulled).   **[47]**

---

1 Amendments

a   Subsection (1) was substituted by LG(PD)A 1976, s 40(b).

b   Subsection (2) was repealed by LG(PD)A 1976, s 45.

c   Former references to the Minister are construed as to the Board: LG(PD)A 1976, s 14(9), (10).

d   Subsection (7) was repealed by LG(PD)A 1976, s 45.

e   See now LG(PD)A 1992, s 20 for revised fines in regard. See LG(PD)A 1963, s 80 for provisions relating to the prosecution of offences under this Act.

f   Subsection (10) was repealed by LG(PD)A 1976, s 45.

2 Cross References

a   See LG(PD)R 1994 (SI 86/1994), art 163 for the prescribed authorities.

4 Commentary

Section 46 confers on planning authorities a power to make preservation orders with regard to flora or fauna within their functional area and provides that the breach of such an order is a criminal offence. There is provision for an appeal against such an order to An Bord Pleanála and again the time limit for such an appeal appears different than that under ss 44 and 45.

---

47. Creation of public rights of way pursuant to agreement

(1) A planning authority may enter into an agreement with any person having the necessary power in that behalf for the creation, by dedication by that person, of a public right of way over land.

(2) An agreement made under this section shall be on such terms as to payment or otherwise as may be specified in the agreement, and may, if it is so agreed, provide for limitations or conditions affecting the public right of way.

(3) Where an agreement has been made under this section, it shall be the duty of the planning authority to take all necessary steps for securing that the creation of the public right of way is effected in accordance with the agreement.

(4) Particulars of an agreement made under this section shall be entered in the register.   **[48]**

4. Commentary

Section 47 provides that a planning authority may create public rights of way by agreement with a land owner by the dedication by the land owner of the lands as a public right of way. It is submitted that the provisions of s 47 are superfluous because where a land owner dedicates lands as a public right of way then that is sufficient in itself to create a public right of way once the lands are used as such and it is unnecessary to enshrine such an agreement as a statutory provision in view of the common law.

What s 47 appears to do is to allow the local authority to carry out works and expend money on the public right of way rather than create the public right of way itself. For the compulsory creation of a public right of way see LG(PD)A 1963, s 48 and for supplemental provisions relating to public rights of way see LG(PD)A 1963, s 49. See also LG(PD)A 1963, s 21 for further references to rights of way which provides that where a draft development plan includes any provision relating to the preservation of a public right of way, then notice shall be served on the owner and on the occupier of such land.

48. Compulsory powers for creation of public rights of way

(1) Where it appears to the planning authority that there is need for a public right of way over any land, the planning authority may by order create a public right of way over the land.

(2) Where a planning authority make an order under this section, they shall serve a notice of the making of the order and a copy of the order on every person who is the owner or occupier of any land over which the order creates a public right of way and on any other person who in their opinion will be affected by the creation of the public right of way.

(3) Any person on whom a notice and a copy of an order is served under this section may, at any time before the day specified in that behalf in the notice (not being earlier than one month after such service), appeal to the [Board][1a] against the order.

(4) Where an appeal is brought under this section against an order, the [Board][1a] may confirm the order with or without modifications or annul the order.

(5) An order under this section (other than an order which is annulled) shall take effect –

    (a) in case no appeal against it is taken or every appeal against it is withdrawn before the expiration of the period for taking an appeal – on the expiration of the period for taking an appeal,

    (b) in case an appeal or appeals is or are taken against it and the appeal or appeals is or are not withdrawn during the period for taking an appeal – when every appeal not so withdrawn has been either withdrawn or determined.

(6) Particulars of a right of way created under this section shall be entered in the register.[2a]   **[49]**

---

1 Amendments

a   Former references to the Minister are now construed as to the Board: LG(PD)A 1976, s 14(9), (10).

2 Cross References

a   See LG(PD)A 1990, s 22 for provisions relating to compensation where an order is made under this section. See the Roads Act 1993 whereby a road may be deemed to be a public road where the local authority has constructed or otherwise provided it. This could allow a road funded indirectly by the waiving of contributions to be made to a public road if the local authority so decides. This is an executive, not a reserved, function.

4 Commentary

Section 48 confers upon planning authorities the power to compulsorily create public rights of way. They are required before the making of any such order to serve a notice on every person who is the owner or occupier of any land over which the public right of way is to be created and on any person who in their opinion will be affected by the creation of the public right of way.

There is provision for an appeal to An Bord Pleanála against any such notice which must give at least one month for the lodging of such an appeal.

Compensation for the compulsory creation of a public right of way may be claimed under s 22 of LG(PD)A 1990.

---

49. Supplemental provisions with respect to public rights of way

(1) Where a public right of way is created pursuant to this Act or a provision relating to its preservation is included in the development plan, the way shall be maintained by the planning authority.

(2) (a)   Where a right of way is required by this section to be maintained by the planning authority, a person shall not damage or obstruct the way, or hinder or interfere with the exercise of the right of way.

(b)   A person who contravenes this subsection shall be guilty of an offence and shall be liable on summary conviction to a fine not exceeding one hundred pounds; and if in the case of a continuing offence the contravention is continued after conviction, he shall be guilty of a further offence and liable on summary conviction to a fine not exceeding twenty pounds[1a] for each day on which the contravention is so continued.

(c)   In a prosecution for an offence under this subsection [or section 20(5) of the Local Government (Planning and Development) Act, 1992,][1b] in relation to a right of way with respect to which a provision for its preservation is included in the development plan, it shall not be necessary for the prosecution to show, and it shall be assumed until the contrary is shown by the defendant, that the right of way subsists.

(3) Where, in the case of a right of way required by this section to be maintained by the planning authority, the way is damaged or obstructed by any person, the planning authority maintaining the right of way may repair the damage or remove the obstruction, and the expenses incurred by them in the repair or removal shall be paid to them by the

said person and, in default of being so paid, shall be recoverable from him as a simple contract debt in any court of competent jurisdiction.

(4) A planning authority may, for the purpose of carrying out their duties under subsections (1) and (3) of this section, enter on land at all reasonable times.   **[50]**

---

1 Amendments

a   See now LG(PD)A 1992, s 20 for increased fines for contravention of this section.

b   The words in square brackets were inserted by LG(PD) 1992, s 20(6).

---

50. [Planting of trees, shrubs and other plants]¹ᵃ

[51]

---

1 Amendments

a   Section 50 was repealed by LGA 1994, s 4(1).

---

51. [Noise and vibration]¹ᵃ

[52]

---

1 Amendments

a   Section 51 was repealed by EPAA 1992, s 18.

---

52. [Litter] ¹ᵃ

[53]

---

1 Amendments

a   Section 52 was repealed by the Litter Act 1982, s 19.

---

53. [Exhibition of advertisements on certain structures etc.]¹ᵃ

[54]

---

1 Amendments

a   Section 53 was repealed by the Litter Act 1982, s 19.

---

54. Repairs and tidying of advertisement structures and advertisements

(1) If it appears to the planning authority that, having regard to the interests of public safety or amenity, an advertisement structure or advertisement in their area should be repaired or tidied, the planning authority may serve on the person having control of the advertisement structure or advertisement a notice requiring that person to repair or tidy the advertisement structure or advertisement within a specified period.

(2) If within the period specified in a notice under this section, the advertisement structure or advertisement is not repaired or tidied, the planning authority may enter on

the land on which the structure is situate or the advertisement is exhibited and repair or tidy the structure or advertisement and may recover as a simple contract debt in any court of competent jurisdiction from the person having control of the structure or advertisement any expenses reasonably incurred by them in that behalf.   **[55]**

4 Commentary

Section 54 enables a planning authority to serve notice on a person having control of an advertising structure requiring that person to repair the aforesaid structure and the notice must specify a specified period within which the works are to be carried out. In default of compliance with the notice, a planning authority can enter onto the lands (see the restrictions in this regard contained in s 81 of LG(PD)A 1963), carry out the works themselves and recover the costs as a simple contract debt.

In this regard therefore, s 54 is analogous to an enforcement notice under s 31 of LG(PD)A 1963.

[Part VI

Compensation][1A]

[56]

1 Amendments

a   Part VI (ss 55-73) was repealed by LG(PD)A 1990, s 3(1).

PART VII

Acquisition of Land, etc.

74. Appropriation of land to purposes and functions under this Act[3a]

(1) Where –

    (a)   land is vested in a planning authority otherwise than for the purposes of their functions under this Act, and

    (b)   the planning authority are satisfied that the land should be made available for those purposes,

the planning authority may, with the consent of the appropriate Minister, appropriate the land to any of those purposes.

(2) In subsection (1) of this section "**the appropriate Minister**" means –

    (a)   if the Ministerial functions relating to the land in question are vested in a single Minister other than the Minister – that Minister,

    (b)   if those functions are vested in two or more Ministers (neither or none of whom is the Minister) – such one of those Ministers as has, in relation to the land, the greater or greatest concern,

    (c)   in all other cases – the Minister.

(3) If, in relation to paragraph (b) of the foregoing subsection, any doubt as to which one of two or more Ministers has the greater or greatest concern, the doubt shall be determined by the Minister.   **[57]**

3 Notes

a   There is no power of compulsory acquisition in LG(PD)A 1963. See *Movie News Ltd v Galway County Council* High Court, unrep, 30 March 1975; Supreme Court, unrep, 15 July 1977 and *Leinster Importing Co Ltd v Dublin County Council* [1984] ILRM 605. However, there is a power under Local Government (Ireland) Act 1898 s 10, as extended by Local Government (No 2) Act 1960.

4 Commentary

The importance of s 74 has now been much reduced following the abolition of the ultra vires pursuant to LGA 1991.

75. Disposal of land by planning authority

(1) Any land acquired for the purposes of or appropriated under this Act by a planning authority may be sold, leased or exchanged subject to such conditions as they may consider necessary in order to secure the best use of that or other land, and any structures or works which have been, or are to be, constructed, erected, made or carried out on, in or under that or other land, or to secure the construction, erection, making or carrying out of any structures or works appearing to them to be needed for the proper planning and development of their area.

(2) The consent of the Minister shall be requisite for any sale, lease or exchange under subsection (1) of this section –

(a)   in case the price or rent, or what is obtained by the planning authority on the exchange, is not the best reasonably obtainable, or

(b)   in case the development proposed for the land would contravene materially the development plan,

but, save as aforesaid, shall not be requisite notwithstanding the provisions of any other enactment.

(3) Capital money arising from the disposal of land under subsection (1) of this section shall be applied for a capital purpose for which capital money may be properly applied.

(4) (a)   Where, as respects any land acquired for the purposes of or appropriated under this Act by a planning authority, the authority consider that they will not require the use of the land for any of their functions for a particular period, the authority may grant a lease of the land for that period or any less period and the lease shall be expressed as a lease granted for the purposes of this subsection.

(b)   Neither the Landlord and Tenant Acts, 1931 and 1958, nor the Rent Restrictions Act, 1960, shall apply in relation to a lease granted as aforesaid for the purposes of this subsection.   **[58]**

4 Commentary

Section 75 gives planning authorities wide powers to dispose of land in order to secure the best use of that land or adjoining lands. The provision appears to allow a local authority to provide for the building of structures on this land and dispose of that land thus possibly circumventing the controls under the Planning Acts.

Section 75 would be intended to secure appropriate inner city developments whereby suitable sites could be acquired and then disposed of to the private sector thereby facilitating the regeneration of such urban areas.

This section must now be read in conjunction with Part X of the LG(PD)R 1994 which require that a consultation process be entered into for certain developments to be carried out by the local authority, and for proposals for development in this regard to be laid before the elected members having first obtained the views of the public. The members, having been appraised of the proposals, can direct the Manager pursuant to s 3 of the City and County Management (Amendment) Act 1955 not to proceed with the development and regard should be had to s 2 of that Act which provides that the members have considerable powers to require additional information and be properly appraised of matters laid before them which require a resolution.

76. [Extinguishment of public right of way][1a]

[59]

1 Amendments

a   Section 76 was repealed by the Roads Act 1993, s 4.

77. Development by planning authority, etc.[3a]

(1) A planning authority may develop or secure the development of land and, in particular and without prejudice to the generality of the foregoing, may –

  (a) secure, facilitate and control the improvement of the frontage of any public road by widening, opening, enlarging or otherwise improving,

  (b) develop any land in the vicinity of any road or bridge which it is proposed to improve or construct,

  (c) provide areas with roads and such services and works as may be needed for development,

  (d) provide areas of convenient shape for development,

  (e) secure or carry out, as respects obsolete areas, the development or renewal thereof and the provision therein of open spaces,

  (f) secure the preservation of any view or prospect, any structure or natural physical feature, any trees subject to a tree preservation order, any site of geological, ecological or archaeological interest or any flora or fauna subject to a conservation order.

(2) A planning authority may provide –

  (a) sites for the establishment or relocation of industries, businesses (includes hotels, motels and guest-houses), dwellings, offices, shops, schools, churches and other community facilities and of such buildings, premises, dwellings, parks and structures as are referred to in paragraph (b) of this subsection,

  (b) factory buildings, office premises, shop premises, dwellings, amusement parks and structures for the purpose of entertainment, caravan parks, buildings for the purpose of providing accommodation, meals and refreshments, buildings for providing trade and professional services and advertisement structures, [buildings or structures for the purpose of providing homes or shelters for stray or unwanted dogs and cats,][1a]

  (c) any services which they consider ancillary to anything which is referred to in paragraphs (a) and (b) of this subsection and which they have provided, and may maintain and manage any such site, building, premises, dwelling, park, structure or service and may make any charges which they consider reasonable in relation to the provision, maintenance or management thereof.

(3) A planning authority may, in connection with any of their functions under this Act, make and carry out arrangements with any person or body for the development or management of land.

(4) For avoidance of doubt it is hereby declared that the powers which a planning authority may exercise pursuant to section 10 of the Local Government (No. 2) Act, 1960, with respect to compulsory acquisition for the purposes of any of their functions under this Act apply in relation to anything which is specified in subsection (1) of section 2 of this Act as being included in "**land**". **[60]**

---

1 Amendments

a   The words in square brackets were inserted by LG(PD)A 1976, s 43(1)(k).

3 Notes

a   The powers conferred on the planning authority by this section are wide-ranging. They enable it to enter into joint venture arrangements with other organisations (such as companies or statutory authorities), or to carry out, maintain and manage a wide variety of activities on its own, subject only to the most general stipulation (in relation to its functions) under the Planning Acts.

---

78. Public notice of development proposed to be carried out by certain local authorities

[(1) (a)   Regulations made in relation to any specified cases or classes of cases of development proposed to be carried out by local authorities who are planning authorities may provide for any or all of the following matters:

(i)   the publication by a local authority of any specified notice with respect to development that they propose to carry out (hereafter in this subsection referred to as "proposed development"),

(ii) the giving by a local authority to any specified persons of any specified notice, documents, particulars, plans or other information with respect to proposed development,

(iii) the making available for inspection by members of the public of any specified documents, particulars, plans or other information with respect to proposed development,

(iv) the making of submissions or observations to a local authority with respect to proposed development,

(v)   the preparation by a local authority of a report, dealing with any specified matters, with respect to proposed development, and the submission to the members of a local authority of such a report.

(b)   Regulations under this subsection may contain such incidental, supplemental and consequential provisions as appear to the Minister to be necessary or expedient.][1a]

[(2) For the purposes of the Council Directive, regulations made in relation to any specified cases or classes of cases of development proposed to be carried out by or on behalf of local authorities who are planning authorities may –

(a) require the authority to prepare an environmental impact statement in respect of specified proposed development,

(b) empower the Minister to require the authority to prepare an environmental impact statement in respect of other proposed development,

(c) require the authority to have, in respect of proposed development for which an environmental impact statement is required to be prepared, the certification of the Minister that the proposed development (or the proposed development as varied or modified by him) will not, in his opinion, have significant adverse effects on the environment, or will embody the best practicable means to prevent or limit such effects,

(d) require the Minister, before certifying proposed development, to have regard to an environmental impact statement prepared in respect of that development, to any submissions or observations made to him in accordance with regulations under this subsection, and to the views of other Member States of the European Communities arising from consultation, if any, in accordance with regulations under this subsection,

(e) enable the Minister, in relation to the certification referred to in paragraph (c) of this subsection, to vary or modify a proposed development in respect of which certification is sought,

(f) require the authority to give public notice in any specified form and manner, or to give notice to any specified persons, of applications for the certification referred to in paragraph (c) of this subsection,

[(g) require the availability for public inspection of environmental impact statements, the availability for purchase of copies of such statements or extracts therefrom and the furnishing of copies of such statements to the Minister and to any other specified persons,][1b]

(h) require the authority to furnish to the Minister further information in relation to proposed development in respect of which an environmental impact statement has been prepared,

(i) provide for the making of submissions or observations to the Minister in relation to the effects on the environment of proposed development in respect of which an environmental impact statement has been prepared,

(j) provide for consultation with other Member States of the European Communities in relation to proposed development,

(k) require the Minister to give notice of his decision in relation to proposed development for which certification is sought in accordance with regulations under this subsection,

(l) require a planning authority, in dealing with an application by a local authority for permission under Part IV of this Act for development outside the functional area of that local authority, to have regard to any certification of the development by the Minister under regulations in accordance with this subsection.

[(m) provide for matters of procedure in relation to the making of a request for and the giving of a written opinion pursuant to subsection (4) of this section.][1c]

(3) [(a)   The Minister may, subject to paragraph (d) of this subsection by order, where he is satisfied that exceptional circumstances so warrant grant an exemption in respect of proposed development from a requirement of regulations under subsection (2) of this section to prepare an environmental impact statement.]^{1d}

[(b)   The Minister shall, in granting an exemption under paragraph (a) of this subsection, consider whether –

(i) the effects, if any, of the proposed development on the environment should be assessed in some other manner, and

(ii) the information collected in the course of such assessment should be made available to members of the public,

and he may, by order, apply such requirements regarding these matters as he considers necessary or appropriate.

(c)   Notice of any exemption granted under paragraph (a) of this subsection, of the reasons for granting such exemption, and of any requirements applied under paragraph (b) of this subsection shall, as soon as may be, -

(i) be published in the *Iris Oifigiúil* and in at least one daily newspaper published in the State, and

(ii) be given, together with a copy of the information, if any, made available to members of the public in accordance with the said paragraph (b), to the Commission of the European Communities.]^{1c, 1e, 2a}

[(d) An exemption shall not be granted under paragraph (a) of this subsection in respect of proposed development if another Member State of the European Communities. having been informed about the proposed development and its likely effects on the environment in that State, has indicated that it intends to furnish views on the said effects.]^{1f}

[(4) (a) If a local authority, before preparing an environmental impact statement in accordance with regulations made under subsection (2) of this section, so requests, the Minister shall give a written opinion on the information to be contained in such statement.

(b) The giving of a written opinion in accordance with paragraph (a) of this subsection shall not prejudice the exercise by the Minister of his powers pursuant to the Planning Acts, 1963 to 1998, or any regulations made thereunder to require the local authority which made the request to furnish further information in relation to the application for certification of the proposed development concerned.]^{1g}   **[61]**

---

1 Amendments

a   Subsection (1) was substituted by LG(PD)A 1993, s 3.

b   Sub-paragraph (2)(g) was inserted by EC(EIA)(A)(R) 1994 (SI 184/1994), art 8.

c   Sub-paragraph (m) was inserted by EC(EIA)(A)R 1999 (SI 93/1999), art 5(a).

d   Subsection (3)(a) was substituted by EC(EIA)(A)R 1999 (SI 93/1999), art 5(b).

e   Subparagraphs (3b) and (c) were substituted by EC(EIA)(A)R 1998 (SI 351/1998), art 5.

f   Subsection (3)(d) was inserted by EC(EIA)(A)R 1999 (SI 93/1999), art 5(c).

g   Section (4) was inserted by EC(EIA)(A)R 1999 (SI 93/1999), art 5(d).

2 Cross References

a   See arts 130–149 of LG(PD)R 1994 for commentary on the new requirements.

4 Commentary

Section 78 provided that regulations may be made which specify that public notice must be given for certain development to be carried out by the local authority. These provisions were not enacted until arts 130-149 of the LG(PD)R 1994 were introduced and which lay down a procedure whereby notice of the intended development is published in the local papers, members of public are invited to make submissions, a report is prepared and this is laid before the elected members who may, by resolution pursuant to s 3 of the City and County Management (Amendment) Act 1955, direct the Manager not to proceed.

Section 2 of the City and County Management (Amendment) Act 1955 provides that the members have considerable power where such matters are placed before them and where they have power to make such resolutions.

---

79. Amendment of Landlord and Tenant Acts 1931 and 1958

(1) "business" in the Landlord and Tenant Act, 1931, shall include the carrying out by a planning authority of any of their functions.

(2) Subsection (1) of section 22 of the Landlord and Tenant Act, 1931, is hereby amended by the insertion after paragraph (b) of the following paragraph:

> (bb) that, such landlord being a planning authority within the meaning of the Local Government (Planning and Development) Act, 1963, such tenement or any part thereof is situate in an area in respect of which the development plan within the meaning of that Act indicates objectives for its development or renewal as being an obsolete area, or.[2a]

(3) Subsection (1) of section 15 of the Landlord and Tenant (Reversionary Leases) Act, 1958, is hereby amended by the addition of "or alternatively, being a planning authority within the meaning of the Local Government (Planning and Development) Act, 1963, satisfies the Court that, in case the reversionary lease would be a lease of the whole of the land, the land or any part of the land is situate in an area in respect of which the development plan within the meaning of that Act indicates objectives for its development or renewal as being an obsolete area or that, in case the reversionary lease would be a lease of part of the land, that part or any part of that part is situate in such an area".   **[62]**

---

2 Cross References

a   See now s 17(2)(a)(iii) of the Landlord and Tenant (Amendment) Act 1980.

4 Commentary

The Landlord and Tenant Acts 1931 and 1958 have been repealed but the definition of "business" has been included in s 79 of the Landlord and Tenant (Amendment) Act, 1980 and s 22(1) of the 1931 Act has been included in ss 17 and 33 of the 1980 Act.

PART VIII

MISCELLANEOUS

80. Prosecution of offences by planning authority

(1) An offence under this Act may be prosecuted [summarily][1a] by the planning authority in whose area the offence is committed.

(2) A planning authority shall not prosecute in a case in which an offence under section 53 of this Act is alleged to have been committed in relation to an advertisement unless the advertisement is exempted development and they have decided that the advertisement would injure the amenities of their area and, in the case of an advertisement advertising a public meeting, unless the advertisement has been in position for seven days or longer after the date of the meeting.

(3) Where –

    (a) an offence under section 46 or section 52 of this Act, or

    (b) an offence under section 53 of this Act[2a] consisting of defacing any structure, door, gate, window, tree or post,

is alleged to have been committed, any officer of the planning authority, duly authorised by them in writing and producing, if so required, his authority, may demand the name and address of any person whom he reasonably believes to be guilty of the offence.

(4) Any person whose name and address has been demanded under the foregoing subsection and who fails to comply with the demand shall be guilty of an offence and shall be liable on summary conviction to a fine not exceeding [£100.][1b]　　**[63]**

---

1 Amendments

a   "Summarily" was inserted by LG(PD)A 1982, s 13.

b   £100 was substituted for £5 by LG(PD)A 1982, s 8. See now LG(PD)A 1992, s 20 for revised penalties in this regard.

2 Cross References

a   Sections 52–53 were repealed by the Litter Act 1982, s 19.

4 Commentary

This gives a general power to planning authorities to prosecute summarily offences committed under the Planning Acts.

---

81. Restriction on exercise of power of entry of planning authority and obstruction of approved entry

(1) Where (in the case of occupied land) the occupier or (in the case of unoccupied land) the owner refuses to permit the exercise of a power of entry conferred by this Act on a planning authority, the authority shall not exercise the power save pursuant to an order of the District Court approving of the entry.

(2) The following provisions shall have effect in relation to an application for an order under this section:

    (a) the application shall be made, on notice to the person who refused to permit the exercise of the power of entry, to the justice of the District Court having jurisdiction in the district court district in which the land or part of the land is situate,

(b) the application shall be granted unless the proposed entry is to be made pursuant to section 31, 32 or 33 of this Act on a structure and the said person satisfies the court in a case of non-compliance with a condition, that the condition was complied with or, in any other case, that the structure is not an unauthorised structure,

(c) an order made on the application may require that entry shall not be effected during a specified period of one week or less commencing on the date of the order.

(3) Any person who, by act or omission, obstructs an entry approved of by order under this section shall be guilty of an offence and shall be liable on summary conviction to a fine not exceeding twenty-five pounds; and if in the case of a continuing offence the obstruction is continued after conviction, he shall be guilty of a further offence and liable on summary conviction to a fine not exceeding five pounds for each day on which the obstruction is so continued.[1a]   **[64]**

---

1 Amendments

a   See now LG(PD)A 1992, s 20 for revised penalties for breach of this section.

4 Commentary

Section 81 sets out the procedure for entry onto lands where the right of entry is opposed by the owner or occupier. In such circumstances the planning authority must obtain an order of the District Court approving entry.

---

82. Supplemental provisions relating to references and appeals

[(1) Regulations may provide for any matters of procedure in relation to any section 76 hearing.][1a, 3a]

(2) Regulations shall be made under this section providing –

(a)   ...[1b]

(b)   for any section 76 hearing being conducted by a person appointed for that purpose by the Minister.[1c]

(3) Where a question of law arises on any reference, appeal or section 76 hearing, the question may be referred to the High Court for decision by it by,

(a) in the case of a reference or appeal, the Board,[1d]

(b) in the case of a section 76 hearing, the Minister.[1e]

[(3A) A person shall not question the validity of –

(a) a decision of a planning authority on an application for a permission or approval under Part IV of this Act, or

(b) a decision of the Board on any appeal or on any reference,

(c) ...[1f]

otherwise than by way of an application for judicial review under Order 84 of the Rules of the Superior Courts (S.I. No. 15 of 1986) (hereafter in this section referred to as "the Order").

(3B)(a) An application for leave[3b] to apply for judicial review under the Order in respect of a decision referred to in subsection (3A) of this section shall –

  (i) be made within the period of two months commencing on the date on which the decision is given, and

  (ii) be made by motion on notice (grounded in the manner specified in the Order in respect of an *ex parte* motion for leave) to[2a] –

   (I) if the application relates to a decision referred to in subsection (3A)(a) of this section, the planning authority concerned and, where the applicant for leave is not the applicant for the permission or approval under Part IV of this Act, the applicant for such permission or approval,

   (II) if the application relates to a decision referred to in subsection (3A)(b) of this section, the Board and each party of each other party, as the case may be, to the appeal or reference,[3c]

   (III) any other person specified for that purpose by order of the High Court,

   and such leave shall not be granted unless the High Court is satisfied that there are substantial grounds for contending that the decision is invalid or ought to be quashed.[3d]

  (b)(i) The determination of the High Court of an application for leave to apply for judicial review as aforesaid or of an application for such judicial review shall be final and no appeal shall lie from the decision of the High Court to the Supreme Court in either case save with the leave of the High Court which leave shall only be granted where the High Court certifies that its decision involves a point of law of exceptional public importance and that it is desirable in the public interest that an appeal should be taken to the Supreme Court.

  (ii) This paragraph shall not apply to a determination of the High Court in so far as it involves a question as to the validity of any law having regard to the provisions of the Constitution.

  (c) References in subsection (3A) of this section and this subsection to the Order shall be construed as including references to the Order as amended or re-enacted (with or without modification) by rules of court.

  (d) The reference in paragraph (a)(ii)(II) of this subsection to a party to an appeal or reference shall be construed –

  (i) in the case of an appeal within the meaning of the Local Government (Planning and Development) Act, 1992, in accordance with that Act,

  (ii) in the case of an appeal (other than an appeal as aforesaid) or reference, in accordance with Article 35 of the Local Government (Planning and Development) Regulations, 1977 (S.I. No. 65 of 1977), or any regulations under section 18 of the Local Government (Planning and Development) Act, 1992, re-enacting, with or without modification, that Article.][1g]

(4) A person conducting an oral hearing of any reference or appeal may require any officer of a planning authority to give to him any information in relation to the reference or appeal which he reasonably requires for the purposes of the reference or appeal, and it shall be the duty of the officer to comply with the requirement.

(5) (a) A person conducting an oral hearing of any reference or appeal may visit and inspect any land to which the reference or appeal relates.

    (b) Any person who obstructs the exercise of the power conferred by this subsection shall be guilty of an offence and shall be liable on summary conviction to a fine not exceeding [£200.][1h]

(6) A person conducting an oral hearing of any reference or appeal may take evidence on oath and for that purpose may administer oaths, and a person giving evidence at any such hearing shall be entitled to the same immunities and privileges as if he were a witness before the High Court.

(7) (a) Subject to the following paragraph, a person conducting an oral hearing of any reference or appeal may, by giving notice in that behalf in writing to any person, require that person to attend at such time and place as is specified in the notice to give evidence in relation to any matter in question at the hearing or to produce any books, deeds, contracts, accounts, vouchers, maps, plans or other documents in his possession, custody or control which relate to any such matter.

    (b) The following provisions shall have effect for the purposes of the foregoing paragraph:

      (i) it shall not be necessary for a person to attend in compliance with a notice at a place more than ten miles from his ordinary place of residence unless such sum as will cover the reasonable and necessary expenses of the attendance have been paid or tendered to him;

      (ii) the planning authority shall, at the request of the person conducting the oral hearing, pay or tender to any person whose attendance is required such sum as the person conducting the hearing considers will cover the reasonable and necessary expenses of the attendance;

      (iii) any person who in compliance with a notice has attended at any place shall, save in so far as the reasonable and necessary expenses of the attendance have already been paid to him, be paid those expenses by the planning authority, and those expenses, save as aforesaid, shall, in default of being so paid, be recoverable as a simple contract debt in any court of competent jurisdiction;

      (iv) every person to whom a notice has been given who refuses or wilfully neglects to attend in accordance with the notice or who wilfully alters, suppresses, conceals or destroys any document to which the notice relates or who, having so attended, refuses to give evidence or refuses or wilfully fails to produce any document to which the notice relates shall be guilty of an offence and shall be liable on summary conviction to a fine not exceeding [£200.][1i]

[(8) Subsections (4) to (7) of this section shall apply, with any necessary modifications, in relation to a person conducting a section 76 hearing.

(9) In subsections (3) to (7) of this section —[1j]

"appeal", means an appeal to the Board;

"reference" means a reference under section 5 of this Act to the Board;

"**section 76 hearing**" means a hearing held pursuant to section 76 of this Act, as amended by section 43(1) of the Local Government (Planning and Development) Act, 1976.   **[65]**

---

1 Amendments

a   Subsection (1) was amended by LG(PD)A 1976, s 42 and by the BCA 1990, s 24.

b   Subsection (2)(a) was repealed by the BCA 1990, s 24.

c   Subsection (2)(b) was substituted by LG(PD)A 1976, s 42 and amended by the BCA 1990, s 24.

d   Subsection (3)(a) was amended by the BCA 1990, s 24.

e   Subsection (3)(b) was amended by the BCA 1990, s 24.

f   Subsection (3A)(c) was repealed by the BCA 1990, s 24.

g   Subsections (3A) and (3B) (inserted by LG(PD)A 1976, s 42) were substituted by LG(PD)A 1992, s 19.

h   A fine of £200 was substituted for £100 by LG(PD)A 1992, s 20.

i   A fine of £200 was substituted for £100 by LG(PD)A 1992, s 20.

j   Subsections (8) and (9) were substituted by LG(PD)A 1976, s 42 and subs (9) was amended by the BCA 1990, s 24.

2 Cross References

a   See LG(PD)A 1963, s 7 for the service of notices but note s 82(3B)(a)(ii) which suggests that such proceedings should be served personally on the parties. It is suggested that this is the safer approach in view of the very strict requirements of this section as set out in *KSK Enterprises Ltd v An Bord Pleanála* Supreme Court, unrep, 24 March 1994 where it was held that the two month time limit is strict and cannot be extended. In *Keane v An Bord Pleanála* [1998] 2 ILRM 241 it was held that grounds may not be amended after the expiry of this period.

3 Notes

a   Section 76 related to appeals arising from extinguishment of public rights of way and has been repealed by the Roads Act 1993, s 4, see now ss 4 and 5 of the BCA 1990 in relation to dispensations and relaxations of building control. For a consideration of *locus standi* to bring such proceedings see *Chambers v An Bord Pleanála* [1992] ILRM 296; *Lancefort Ltd v An Bord Pleanála* [1998] 2 ILRM 401 and *Malahide Community Council Ltd v Fingal County Council* Supreme Court, unrep, 14 May 1997.

b   For a discussion of these issues see *Byrne v Wicklow County Council* High Court, unrep, 3 November 1994; *Scott v An Bord Pleanála* [1995] 1 ILRM 424; *Arcon Mines & Ors* Supreme Court, 29 November 1994; *McNamara v An Bord Pleanála* [1996] 2 ILRM 339; *Max Developments Ltd v An Bord Pleanála* [1994] 2 IR 121. For the time periods within which such proceedings should be instituted, see *KSK Enterprises v An Bord Pleanála* Supreme Court, unrep, 24 March 1994; *McNamara v An Bord Pleanála* [1996] 2 ILRM 339; *Byrne v Wicklow County Council* (Keane J); *Keane v An Bord Pleanála* [1998] 2 ILRM 241. See also *Lancefort Ltd v An Bord Pleanála* [1998] ILRM 401 which considers the service of proceedings on the last day of the appropriate period and the position where one of the mandatory notice parties has not been served.

c   See however the judgment of Geoghegan J in *McCarthy v An Bord Pleanála* High Court, unrep, 15 May 1998 which held that "parties" should be interpreted as meaning relevant parties.

d   For discussion of substantial grounds, see *Scott v An Bord Pleanála* [1995] 1 ILRM 424 where substantial was defined as reasonable. See also a discussion of this issue in *McNamara v An Bord Pleanála* [1995] 2 ILRM 125 where this definition was elaborated on by Carroll J. *McNamara* was followed in *Mulhall v An Bord Pleanála* ILTR 10 June 1996 (McCracken J) and by Kelly J in *Blessington & District Community Council v Wicklow County Council* High Court, unrep, 19 July 1996 which contains an excellent summary of the law in this regard. See also *Lancefort Ltd v An Bord Pleanàla* [1998] 2 ILRM 401 McGuinness J on *locus standi*; see also *Blessington Heritage Trust Ltd v Wicklow County Council* High Court, unrep, 21 January 1998; *Wicklow Heritage Trust Ltd v Wicklow County Council* High Court, 5 February 1998 and *Irish Cement Ltd v An Bord Pleanála* High Court, unrep 24 Febrary 1998.

4 Commentary

Section 82 sets out the provisions for challenging by way of judicial review decisions on applications for planning permission, appeals to An Bord Pleanála, and references to the Board under s 5 of LG(PD)A 1963.

Where a challenge is made to a decision of a planning authority on a planning permission or the Board on an appeal or reference, the challenge can only be brought by way of judicial review. In those circumstances an application must first be brought for leave to apply for judicial review which must be on notice to all parties to the decision. All parties in this case includes, in the case of an appeal, the Board, the planning authority, the applicant for planning permission, and any other party to the appeal. Such proceedings, which must be grounded on a Notice of Motion together with a statement grounding the application for judicial review together with affidavits supporting whatever facts are relied upon must be served on all such parties within two months of the giving of the decision. This time period is strict and if all parties are not served within this period then the proceedings will be statute barred.

However, given the strictness of the time limit the actual period provided for is unclear, as the section does not make clear when a decision is "given" for the purposes of the commencement of time. It is the case that the Board and planning authorities take the date for the giving of the decision as the date of the Manager's order or the decision of the Board, but it would appear, having regard to the definition of "given" in the Interpretation Act 1937 that the period only begins to run from the date that notice is received of the decision.

In those circumstances therefore it can be argued that the two month period runs from the date on which notice of the decision on the planning application or notice of the determination of the appeal is received and this can often give a number of additional days within which to bring the proceedings.

However, in view of the strict time limits and the consequences of a failure to comply with those time limits, the prudent course of action is to serve the proceedings at the earlier dates simply for the purposes of certainty.

In such cases leave will only be granted where the court is satisfied that there are substantial grounds for the contention that the decision is invalid and ought to be quashed. This has been interpreted by the Supreme Court as being reasonable grounds but there are useful summaries of the law as to the required standard contained in *McNamara v An Bord Pleanála* [1995] 2 ILRM 125; *Scott v An Bord Pleanála* [1995] 1 ILRM 424 and *Blessington and District Community Council v Wicklow County Council* High Court, unrep, 19 July 1996.

If the court fails to certify that there are substantial grounds, then it must certify a point of law of exceptional public importance or public interest before any appeal can lie from such a decision to the Supreme Court. Unless such a point is certified then no appeal shall lie.

Section 82 also contains supplemental provisions relating to the conducting of oral hearings by An Bord Pleanála.

---

83. Power of authorised person to enter on land

(1) [A member of the Board or an authorised person][1a] may, subject to the provisions of this section, enter on any land at all reasonable times between the hours of 9 a.m. and 6 p.m. for any purpose connected with this Act.

(2) [A member of the Board or an authorised person]¹ᵃ entering on land under this section may do thereon all things reasonably necessary for the purpose for which the entry is made and, in particular, may survey, make plans, take levels, make excavations, and examine the depth and nature of the subsoil.

(3) Before [a member of the Board or an authorised person]¹ᵃ enters under this section on any land, the appropriate authority shall either obtain the consent (in the case of occupied land) of the occupier or (in the case of unoccupied land) the owner or shall give to the owner or occupier (as the case may be) not less than fourteen days' notice in writing of the intention to make the entry.

(4) A person to whom a notice of intention to enter on land has been given under this section by the appropriate authority may, not later than fourteen days after the giving of such notice, apply, on notice to such authority, to the justice of the District Court having jurisdiction in the district court district in which the land or part of the land is situate for an order prohibiting the entry, and, upon the hearing of the application, the justice may, if he so thinks proper, either wholly prohibit the entry or specify conditions to be observed by the person making the entry.

(5) Where a justice of the District Court prohibits under this section a proposed entry on land, it shall not be lawful for any person to enter under this section on the land, and where a justice of the District Court specifies under this section conditions to be observed by persons entering on land, every person who enters under this section on the land shall observe the conditions so specified.

(6) Subsections (3), (4) and (5) of this section shall not apply to entry for the purposes of Part IV of this Act and, in a case in which such entry is proposed, if the occupier (in the case of occupied land) or the owner (in the case of unoccupied land) refuses to permit the entry –

    (a) the entry shall not be effected unless it has been authorised by an order of the justice of the District Court having jurisdiction in the district court district in which the land or part of the land is situate and, in the case of occupied land, save after at least twenty-four hours' notice of the intended entry, and of the object thereof, has been given to the occupier,

    (b) an application for such an order shall be made on notice (in the case of occupied land) to the occupier or (in the case of unoccupied land) to the owner.

(7) Every person who, by act or omission, obstructs [a member of the Board or an authorised person]¹ᵃ in the lawful exercise of the powers conferred by this section shall be guilty of an offence and shall be liable on summary conviction to a fine not exceeding ten pounds; and if in the case of a continuing offence the obstruction is continued after conviction, he shall be guilty of a further offence and liable on summary conviction to a fine not exceeding five pounds for each day on which the obstruction is so continued.¹ᵇ

[(8) In this section –

"authorised person" means a person who is appointed by the planning authority, the Minister or the Board to be an authorised person for the purposes of this section;

"appropriate authority" means –

(a) in a case in which the authorised person was appointed by a planning authority – that authority,

(b) in a case in which the authorised person was appointed by the Minister – the Minister, and

(c) in a case in which the authorised person was appointed by the Board – the Board.][2a]   [66]

---

1 Amendments

a   Subsections (1), (2), (3) (7) and (8) were amended by LG(PD)A 1976, s 42(c).

b   See now LG(PD)A 1992, s 20 for revised penalty of £200.

2 Cross References

a   See LG(PD)A 1990, s 23 for compensation provisions where a person has suffered damage arising from any acts authorised under this section.

4 Commentary

Section 83 gives the right to members of An Bord Pleanála and persons appointed by planning authorities, the Minister or the Board to enter on lands and carry out certain studies related to their functions. Before such entry is effected, the Board, Minister or local authority, must obtain the consent of the occupier or the owner and give such person not less than 14 days' notice in writing of the intention to so enter. There is provision for an appeal to the District Court by a person so served wherein an order can be sought prohibiting the entry and the court can either prohibit the entry or impose conditions on such entry. It is not necessary where entry is required pursuant to an application for planning permission or for any other matter relating to Part IV of the LG(PD)A 1963. It is the case therefore that no notice is required where a member of the Board or an authorised person enters onto lands pursuant to an application for planning permission or arising from an appeal to the Board.

---

84. [Consultation by State authorities][1a]

[67]

---

1 Amendments

a   Section 84 was repealed by LG(PD)A 1993, s 5.

---

85. Cables, wires and pipelines

(1) A planning authority[3a] may, with the consent of the owner and of the occupier of any land not forming part of a public road, place, erect or construct cables, wires and pipelines (other than waterpipes, sewers and drains), and any apparatus incidental to such cables, wires and pipelines, on, under or over such land, and may from time to time inspect, repair, alter or renew, or may at any time remove, any cables, wires or pipelines placed, erected or constructed under this section.

(2) A planning authority may, with the consent of the owner and of the occupier of any structure, attach to such structure any bracket or other fixture required for the carrying or support of any cable, wire or pipeline placed, erected or constructed under this section.

(3) A planning authority may erect and maintain notices indicating the position of cables, wires or pipelines placed, erected or constructed under this section and may, with

the consent of the owner and of the occupier of any structure, affix such a notice to such structure.

(4) The foregoing subsections of this section shall have effect subject to the proviso that —

(a) a consent for the purposes of any of them shall not be unreasonably withheld,

(b) if the planning authority consider that such a consent has been unreasonably withheld, they may appeal to the [Board],[1a]

(c) if the [Board][1a] determines that such a consent was unreasonably withheld, it shall be treated as having been given.[3b]

(5) The planning authority may permit the use of any cables, wires or pipelines placed, erected or constructed under this section and of any apparatus incidental to such cables, wires or pipelines subject to such conditions and charges as they consider appropriate.[2a]   **[68]**

---

1 Amendments

a   Former references to the Minister are to be construed as the Board: LG(PD)A 1976, s 14(9), (10).

2 Cross References

a   See LG(PD)A 1990, s 24 for provisions relating to compensation arising from acts authorised under this section.

3 Notes

a   It should be noted that re LG(PD)A 1963, s 4, it would appear that only local authorities have the authority to lay pipes etc without planning permission as other authorities are only given a right of maintenance.

b   The cables, wires or pipelines can, therefore, be installed without the consent of the owner or occupier. Compensation in the case of damage by the depreciation of any interest in the level or structure affected can be claimed under LG(PD)A 1963, s 65.

4 Commentary

Section 85 confers the right on planning authorities to lay pipes, wires and cables across land so long as the consent of the owner and of the occupier is obtained. This consent cannot be unreasonably withheld and in such circumstances an appeal against a refusal will lie to An Bord Pleanála. It would appear from the terms of s 85 that such consent is not necessary where the local authorities seek to lay such pipes on lands forming part of the public road but it may be the case that this land may be in the ownership of the adjoining land owners and it is doubtful whether pipes can be laid on such private property without the consent of such land owners being obtained. This is particularly the case given the wider definition of what constitutes a public road pursuant to the Roads Act 1993.

---

86. [Building regulations][1a]

[69]

---

1 Amendments

1   Section 86 was repealed by the BCA 1990, s 24.

---

87. [Relaxation of building regulations][1a]

[70]

1 Amendments

1   Section 87 was repealed by the BCA 1990, s 24.

88. [Appeal against refusal by planning authority to relax building regulations][1a]

[71]

1 Amendments

1   Section 88 was repealed by the BCA 1990, s 24.

89. Petrol pumps, etc., on public roads[2a, 3a]

(1) The planning authority may grant to any person a licence to erect, construct, place, and maintain –

(a) a petrol pump, oil pump, air pump or other appliance for the servicing of vehicles,

(b) a vending machine,

(c) a town or landscape map for indicating directions or places,

(d) a hoarding, fence or scaffold,

(e) an advertisement structure,

(f) a cable, wire or pipeline,

(g) any other appliance or structure specified by the Minister by regulations as suitable for being licensed under this section,

on, under, over or along a public road.

(2) A person applying for a licence under this section shall furnish to the planning authority such plans and other information concerning the position, design and capacity of the appliance or structure as the authority may require.

(3) A licence may be granted under this section by the planning authority for such period and upon such conditions as the authority may specify, and where in the opinion of the planning authority by reason of the increase or alteration of traffic on the road or of the widening of the road or of any improvement of or relating to the road, the appliance or structure causes an obstruction or becomes dangerous, the authority may by notice in writing withdraw the licence and require the licensee to remove such appliance or structure at his own expense.

(4) (a) Any person may, in relation to the granting, refusing, withdrawing or continuing of a licence under this section or to the conditions specified by the planning authority for such a licence, appeal to the [Board].[1a]

(b) Where an appeal under this section is allowed, the [Board][1a] shall give such directions with respect to the withdrawing, granting or altering of a licence under this section as may be appropriate, and the planning authority shall comply therewith.[2a]

(5) (a) The [Board][1a] may make regulations prescribing the amount of the fee to be

paid to the planning authority for the grant of a licence under this section, and any such fees shall be applied by the planning authority in the manner directed by the regulations.

(b) Different fees may be prescribed under this subsection in respect of different appliances and structures.

(6) Nothing in this section shall be construed as affecting the application to petrol pumps of the regulations for the time being in force relating to the storage or sale of motor spirit or to authorise the use of a petrol pump otherwise than in accordance with those regulations.

(7) A person shall not be entitled solely by reason of a licence under this section to erect, construct, place or maintain on, under, over or along a public road any appliance or structure.

(8) Subject to subsection (9) of this section, any person who –

(a) erects, constructs, places or maintains an appliance or structure referred to in subsection (1) of this section on, under, over or along any public road without having a licence under this section so to do, or

(b) erects, constructs, places or maintains such an appliance or structure on, under, over or along any public road otherwise than in accordance with a licence under this section, or

(c) contravenes any condition subject to which a licence has been granted to him under this section,

shall be guilty of an offence and shall be liable on summary conviction to a fine not exceeding ten pounds;[1b] and if in the case of a continuing offence the contravention is continued after conviction, he shall be guilty of a further offence and shall be liable on summary conviction to a fine not exceeding two pounds[1c] for each day on which the contravention is so continued.

(9) (a) A planning authority may, by virtue of this subsection, themselves erect, construct, place or maintain, on, under, over or along a public road any appliance or structure referred to in subsection (1) of this section, and it shall not be necessary for them to have a licence under this section.

(b) Nothing in this subsection shall be taken as empowering a planning authority to hinder the reasonable use of a public road by the public or any person entitled to use it or as empowering a planning authority to create a nuisance to the owner or occupier of premises adjacent to the public road.

(10) Where a planning authority are not the road authority for the purposes of main roads in their area, they shall not, in pursuance of this section, grant a licence in respect of any appliance or structure on, under, over or along a main road or erect, construct or place any appliance or structure on, under, over or along a main road save after consultation with the authority who are the road authority for those purposes. **[72]**

---

1 Amendments

a Former references to the Minister are to be construed as the Board: LG(PD)A 1976, s 14(9), (10).

b See now LG(PD)A 1992, s 20 for revised penalty of £200.

c See now LG(PD)A 1992, s 20 for revised penalty of £200.

2 Cross References

a   See LG(PD)R 1994 (SI 86/1994), Part XII.

3 Notes

a   This section applies where a development is proposed to be constructed on or under a public road and a grant of planning permission is not appropriate in such circumstances. Note also that by s 42 of the Gas Act 1976 this section does not apply to the construction or maintenance of a pipeline by the Irish Gas Board (whether for use by itself or by another person) or for a pipeline required by the Minister for Transport and Power under s 40(2) of the same Act. See LG(PD)R 1994 class 23 Part I, Second Schedule.

4 Commentary

Section 89 provides that a planning authority may grant to a person a licence to construct and/or maintain certain structures on or under a public road. See also s 85 for the laying of pipes on lands not forming part of the public road. It is again doubtful whether in fact such a licence confers by itself the right to construct pipes or cables under a public road on land which is owned by the adjoining land owner and such a licence is best construed as a right to interfere with the public road which is always within the charge of the local authority but cannot of itself give the right to interfere with the property rights in the soil under the road where it is in the ownership of some other person.

90. Saving for national monuments

Nothing in this Act shall restrict, prejudice, or affect the functions of the Minister for Finance or the Commissioners of Public Works in Ireland under the National Monuments Acts, 1930 and 1954, in relation to national monuments as defined by those Acts or any particular such monuments.[3a]   [73]

3 Notes

a   See *O'Callaghan v The Commissioners of Public Works in Ireland* [1985] ILRM 364; [1983] ILRM 391.

4 Commentary

Section 90 makes clear that the Planning Acts do not apply to works carried out pursuant to the National Monuments Acts 1930 and 1954 and is the type of exemption that would have been necessary to all State activities before they could argue that they were not subject to the controls provided for under the Planning Acts.

91. [Amendment of section 42 of Public Health (Ireland) Act, 1878][1a]

[74]

1 Amendments

a   Section 91 was repealed by the BCA 1990, s 24.

92. Transitional

(1) An application for a special permission under the Act of 1934 which was under consideration by a planning authority immediately before the appointed day shall be treated for the purposes of this Act as an application for a permission under section 26 of this Act.

(2) A general or special permission granted under the Act of 1934 shall be treated for the purposes of this Act (including, in particular, sections 30, 31 and 35) as a permission granted under section 26 of this Act, and a record of such permission shall be included in the register.

(3) An appeal under section 59 of the Act of 1934 in relation to a grant or refusal of a special or general permission which was pending immediately before the appointed day shall be treated for the purposes of this Act as an appeal under section 26 of this Act, except that a direction shall not be given in relation to the appeal under paragraph (b) of subsection (1) of section 18 of this Act.

(4) In relation to an order made under section 14 of the Town and Regional Planning (Amendment) Act, 1939, before the appointed day, that Act and the Act of 1934 shall be treated as continuing in force for the purpose of enabling effect to be given in relation to the order to the provisions contained in the said section 14.

(5)...[1a]

(6) (a) A licence under section 137 of the Cork Improvement Act, 1868, section 47 of the Dublin Corporation Act, 1890, or section 35 of the Local Government Act, 1925,[2a] in force immediately before the appointed day shall be treated for the purposes of this Act as a licence under section 89 of this Act.

(b) An appeal under section 35 of the Local Government Act, 1925, pending immediately before the appointed day shall be treated for the purposes of this Act as an appeal under section 89 of this Act.

(c) Regulations in force immediately before the appointed day under section 35 of the Local Government Act, 1925, shall continue in force as if they were regulations under section 89 of this Act and may be amended or revoked accordingly.

(d) Subsection (8) of section 89 of this Act shall not have effect in relation to an appliance or structure referred to in subsection (1) of that section (other than a hoarding, fence or scaffold in the county borough of Dublin or in the county borough of Cork or a petrol pump) before the expiration of the period of six months beginning on the appointed day.   **[75]**

---

1 Amendments

a   Subsection (5) was repealed by the BCA 1990, s 24.

2 Cross References

a   Section 35 of the Local Government Act 1925 was repealed by the Roads Act 1993, s 4.

4 Commentary

Section 92 is an often overlooked provision which provides that a general or special permission granted under the Town and Regional Planning Act 1934 shall be treated as permission granted under the provisions of LG(PD)A 1963. In this sense therefore such permissions must be considered where certificates of compliance are issued and therefore the term of pre-1964 use is not necessarily indicative of a use which is authorised pursuant to the Planning Acts. If, for example, a permission was granted in 1959 under the old Acts and has not been complied with, then the use is technically unauthorised and while no prosecution may be brought on foot of such unauthorised use, the activity and/or structure remains unauthorised.

First Schedule   (Section 2)

TOWNS

Part I[3a]

Ardee
Balbriggan
Ballybay
Ballyshannon
Bandon
Bantry
Belturbet
Boyle
Callan
Cootehill
Droichead Nua
Edenderry
Fethard in the county of Tipperary South Riding
Gorey
Granard
Kilkee
Lismore
Loughrea
Mountmellick
Muinebeag
Mullingar
Newcastle West
Passage West
Portlaoighise
Rathkeale
Roscommon
Tramore
Tuam

Part II

Abbeyfeale
Abbeyleix
Athenry
Bailieborough
Ballaghaderreen
Ballinrobe
Ballybofey
Ballybunion
Ballyhaunis
Banagher
Blanchardstown
Blarney
Caher
Cahersiveen
Carndonagh
Carrick-on-Shannon
Castlecomer-Donaguile
Castleisland
Castlereagh
Celbridge
Clara
Claremorris

Clifden
Clondalkin
Dingle
Donegal
Dunmanway
Ennistimon
Gort
Graiguenamanagh-Tinnahinch
Greystones-Delgany
Kanturk
Kenmare
Kildare
Killorglin
Killybegs
Kilmallock
Lucan-Doddsborough
Malahide
Maynooth
Millstreet
Mitchelstown
Moate
Monasterevin
Mountrath
Moville
Portarlington
Portlaw
Rathdrum
Rathluirc
Roscrea
Rush
Skerries
Swineford
Swords
Tallaght
Thomastown
Tullow   **[76]**

---

3 Notes

a   "Scheduled town" is defined by LG(PD)A 1963, s 2 as any town in Part I and any non-municipal town in Part II of this Schedule.

"Non-municipal town" is defined by LG(PD)A 1963, s 2 by reference to the 1956 Census.

Under s 2(6) the area comprised in any town listed in Part II is determined by declaration of the relevant council.

Under s 2(8) the Minister may add to (or delete from) the list of towns. Notwithstanding the major changes in population that have occurred since this schedule was created, this list has not been modified or updated. It is ironic that towns the size of·Clondalkin or Tallaght are still specified in Part II, as are Swords, Skerries and Malahide, it is submitted that the list of towns needs to be urgently updated.

The importance of the status of scheduled town is that (in common with county boroughs, boroughs and urban districts) the development plan *must* provide for zoning and other matters referred to in LG(PD)A 1963, s 19(2)(a) in the case of a scheduled town. Such zoning etc is optional but not mandatory in the case of other areas – see LG(PD)A 1963, s 19(3).

Second Schedule   **(Section 11)**

REPEALS

Session and Chapter or Number and Year	Short Title	Extent of Repeal
10 & 11 Vic., c.34.	Towns Improvement Clauses Act, 1847	Sections 66 to 72 and 110 and 111.
14 & 15 Vic., c. 92.	Summary Jurisdiction (Ireland) Act, 1851.	Subsection (2) of section 9.
17 & 18 Vic., c. 103.	Towns Improvement (Ireland) Act, 1854.	In section 38 the words "and also so much thereof as relates to improving the line of the streets and removing obstructions"; section 44.
24 & 25 Vic., c. 26.	Dublin Improvement Act Amendment Act, 1861.	Section 9.
31 & 32 Vic., c. xxxiii.	Cork Improvement Act, 1868.	Sections 132 to 135 and 137 and 146.
41 & 42 Vic., c. 52.	Public Health (Ireland) Act, 1878.	Sections 39 and 40.
53 & 54 Vic., c. ccxlvi.	Dublin Corporation Act, 1890.	Sections 39, 47 and 48.
7 Edw. 7, c. 27.	Advertisements Regulation Act, 1907.	The whole Act.
7 Edw. 7, c. 53.	Public Health Acts Amendment Act, 1907.	Sections 27 and 91.
No. 5 of 1925.	Local Government Act, 1925.	Section 35.
No. 22 of 1934.	Town and Regional Planning Act, 1934.	The whole Act.
No. 11 of 1939.	Town and Regional Planning (Amendment) Act, 1939.	The whole Act.

[77]

Third Schedule   **(Section 19)**

PURPOSES FOR WHICH OBJECTIVES MAY BE INDICATED IN DEVELOPMENT PLAN[3A]

Part I

ROADS AND TRAFFIC

1. Securing the greater convenience and safety of road users and pedestrians.

2. Reservation of land for roads and parking places.

3. Establishment of public rights of way.

4. Construction of new roads and alteration of existing roads.

5. Closing or diverting of existing roads.

6. Extinguishment of public and private rights of way.

7. Establishing –

    (a) the line, width, level and construction of,

    (b) the means of access to and egress from, and

    (c) the general dimensions and character of, roads, whether new or existing.

8. Providing for works incidental to the making, improvement or landscaping of any road, including the erection of bridges, tunnels and subways and shelters, the provision of artificial lighting and seats and the planting or protecting of grass, trees and shrubs on or adjoining such road.

---

3 Notes

a   It will be recalled that LG(PD)A 1963, s 19(2) sets out objectives which *shall* be included in the development plan. Stated shortly these are concerned with (a) general zoning, road and parking improvements, (b) renewal of obsolete areas and amenities in urban areas and (c) in rural areas, renewal of obsolete areas, amenities and water and sewerage supplies. The development plan may include further objectives relating to any of the purposes set out in Schedule III.

Part II

STRUCTURES

1. Regulating and controlling, either generally or in particular areas, all or any of the following matters –

    (a) the size, height, floor area and character of structures;

    (b) building lines, coverage and the space about dwellings and other structures;

    (c) the extent of parking places required in, on or under structures of a particular class or size or services or facilities for the parking, loading, unloading or fuelling of vehicles;

    (d) the objects which may be affixed to structures;

    (e) the purposes for and the manner in which structures may be used or occupied, including, in the case of dwellings, the letting thereof in separate tenements.

2. Regulating and controlling the design, colour and materials of structures.

3. Reserving or allocating any particular land, or all land in any particular area, for structure of a specified class or classes, or prohibiting or restricting either permanently or temporarily, the erection, construction, or making of any particular class or classes of structures on any specified land.

4. Limiting the number of structures or the number of structures of a specified class which may be constructed, erected or made, on, in or under any area.

5. The removal or alteration of structures which are inconsistent with the development plan.

6. Regulating and controlling –

(a) the disposition or layout of structures or structures of any specified class (including the reservation of reasonable open space in relation to the number, class and character of structures in any particular development proposal);

(b) the manner in which any land is to be laid out for the purpose of development, including requirements as to road layout, landscaping, planting;

(c) the provision of water supplies, sewers, drains and public lighting;

(d) the provision of service roads and the location and design of means of access to roads;

(e) the provision of facilities for parking, unloading, loading and fuelling of vehicles on any land.

Part III

COMMUNITY PLANNING

1. Regulating the layout of areas, including density, spacing, grouping and orientation of structures in relation to roads, open spaces and other structures.

2. Determining the provision and siting of schools, churches, meeting halls and other community facilities.

3. Determining the provision and siting of sanitary services and recreational facilities.

Part IV

AMENITIES

1. Reserving of lands as –

(a) open spaces, whether public or private (other than open spaces reserved under Part II of this Schedule or under the next paragraph),

(b) caravan or camping sites.

2. Reserving, as a public park, public garden or public recreation space, land normally used as such.

3. Reserving of land for burial grounds.

4. Reserving of lands for game and bird sanctuaries.

5 ... [1a]

6. Preservation of caves, sites, features and other objects of archaeological, geological or historical interest.

7. Preservation of views and prospects and of amenities of places and features of natural beauty or interest.

8.   (a) Preservation and protection of woods.

     (b) Preservation and protection of trees, shrubs, plants and flowers.

[8A. Protection of features of the landscape which are of major importance for wild fauna and flora in accordance with the Habitats Directive.][1b]

9. Prohibiting, restricting or controlling, either generally or in particular places or within a specified distance of the centre line of all roads or any specified road, the erection of all or any particular forms of advertisement structure or the exhibition of all or any particular forms of advertisement.

10. Preventing, remedying or removing injury to amenities arising from the ruinous or neglected condition of any structure, or from the objectionable or neglected condition of any land attached to a structure or abutting on a public road or situate in a residential area.

11. Prohibiting, regulating or controlling the deposit or disposal of waste materials and refuse, the disposal of sewage and the pollution of rivers, lakes, ponds, gullies and the seashore.

12. Providing on derelict sites or other land facilities such as car parks, seating, playing facilities, tennis-courts, shelters, toilets and playgrounds.

13. Preservation of any existing public right of way giving access to seashore, mountain, lakeshore, riverbank, or other place of natural beauty or recreational utility.

14. Securing the reduction or prevention of noise.[1c]   **[78]**

---

1 Amendments

a   Paragraphs 5 and 5A were repealed by LG(PD)A 1999, s 36, which will come into operation on 1 January 2000.

b   Paragraph 8A was inserted by the EC(NH)R 1997 (SI 94/1997), art 26(c).

c   Paragraph 14 was inserted by EPAA 1992, s 106.

[Fourth Schedule   **(Section 69)][1a]**
[79]

---

1 Amendments

a   This schedule was repealed by LG(PD)A 1990, s 3.

[Fifth Schedule   **(Section 86)][1a]**
[80]

---

1 Amendments

a   This schedule was repealed by the BCA 1990, s 24.

LOCAL GOVERNMENT (PLANNING AND DEVELOPMENT) ACT, 1976

(No. 20 of 1976)

Schedule

AN BORD PLEANÁLA

An Act to make better provision, in the interests of the common good, in relation to the proper planning and development of cities, towns and other areas, whether urban or rural, and, for that purpose, to establish a body to be known as An Bord Pleanála and to define its functions and to amend and extend the Local Government (Planning and Development) Act, 1963, and to provide for other matters connected with the matters aforesaid. [5 July, 1976]

Be it enacted by the Oireachtas as follows:

1. Interpretation

In this Act –

"**the appropriate day**" means the day on which section 14 of this Act comes into operation;[3a]

"**the Board**" has the meaning assigned to it by section 3 of this Act;[3b]

"**company**" except in section 34(4), means a company within the meaning of section 2 of the Companies Act, 1963, or a company incorporated outside the State;[3c]

"**the establishment day**" means the day appointed to be the establishment day for the purposes of this Act by order of the Minister under section 2 of this Act;

"**judicial office**" means an office, being the office of Chief Justice, President of the High Court, ordinary judge of the Supreme Court or ordinary judge of the High Court;[3d]

"**manager**" means a manager within the meaning of section 1 of the City and County Management (Amendment) Act, 1955;

"**the Principal Act**" means the Local Government (Planning and Development) Act, 1963;

"**shares**" includes stock and "**share capital**" shall be construed accordingly.   **[81]**

---

3 Notes

a   The appropriate day referred to in s 1 was fixed as 5 March 1977.

b   The structure and activities of An Bord Pleanála are now generally regulated under the LG(PD)A 1983.

c   For the Companies Act 1963 read the Companies Acts, 1963 to 1990.

d   The judicial office no longer applies since the enactment of LG(PD)A 1983.

2.   Establishment day

The Minister may by order appoint a day to be the establishment day for the purposes of this Act.   **[82]**

3 Notes

a   The establishment day was fixed as 1 January 1977.

3.   Establishment of An Bord Pleanála

(1) On the establishment day there shall be established a body to be known as An Bord Pleanála (in this Act referred to as the Board) to perform the functions assigned to it by this Act.

(2) ....[1a]   **[83]**

1 Amendments

a   Subsection (2) was repealed by LG(PD)A 1983, s 25.

4 Commentary

An Bord Pleanála, established under LG(PD)A 1976 but much changed in subsequent legislation, replaced the Minister as the principal appellate body to hear and determine appeals made pursuant to the Planning Acts. The Board now hears appeals against decisions made by planning authorities under ss 26, 27, 30, 33, 36, 37, 44, 45, 46, 48, 85, and 89 of the LG(PD)A 1963 and the only matter which remains under the control of the Minister is the confirmation of the special amenity area order made pursuant to s 43 of LG(PD)A 1963. Those other appellate functions which remained with the Minister have now been superseded by virtue of other enactments and in particular ss 88, 76, 84, and 66 of the LG(PD)A 1963.

4.   [Chairman of the Board][1a]

[84]

1 Amendments

a   Section 4 was repealed by LG(PD)A 1983, s 25.

5.   Board to keep itself informed on certain policies and objectives

(1) The Board shall, so far as may in the opinion of the Board be necessary for the performance of its functions, keep itself informed of the policies and objectives for the time being of the Minister, planning authorities and any other body which is a public authority whose functions have, or may have, a bearing on the proper planning and development (including the preservation and development of amenities) of cities, towns or other areas, whether urban or rural.

(2) In this section **"public authority"** means any Minister of State not being the Minister, the Commissioners of Public Works in Ireland, the Irish Land Commission, a harbour authority within the meaning of section 2 of the Harbours Act, 1946, and any other body established by or under statute which is for the time being declared, by regulation made by the Minister, to be a public authority for the purposes of this section.[2a, 3a]   **[85]**

---

2 Cross References

a   See LG(PD)R 1994 (SI 86/1994), art 164 for bodies declared to be public authorities.

3 Notes

a   Failure to have regard to this section led to the decision of the Board being quashed in the *State (CIE) v An Bord Pleanála* Supreme Court, unrep, 12 December 1984 and it was held that while such policies are not binding on the Board they must have regard to them when deciding on appeals. See *Tennyson v Dun Laoghaire Corporation* [1991] 2 IR 527 on the interpretation of such documents.

4 Commentary

Section 5 provides that the Board shall keep itself informed of the policies and objectives of the Minister, planning authorities and any other body which is a public authority so defined in sub-s (2). It is interesting to note that the Board is not required to have regard to such policies but is merely required to keep itself informed and what its duty is with regard to such policies remains unclear. In *Keane v An Bord Pleanála* [1998] 2 ILRM 241 (SC) it was held that the Board must have regard to *all* the policies and objectives issued by the Minister and not just those issued pursuant to s 7 of LG(PD)A 1982. For the definition of the term "having regard to" see *Glencar Explorations plc v Mayo County Council* [1993] 2 IR 237. If *Keane* were to be applied broadly to the requirements of s 5, then the remit of the Board under this *section* would be very broad indeed and would be required to give effect to policies and objectives of the Minister, planning authorities, harbour authorities and other similar bodies and the full implications of this section on the discretion of the Board has yet to be fully considered.

---

6.   [General policy directives as to development][1a]

[86]

---

1 Amendments

a   Section 6 was repealed by LG(PD)A 1982, s 15.

---

7.   Grants to Board

There may, subject to such conditions, if any, as the Minister thinks proper, be paid to the Board in each financial year out of moneys provided by the Oireachtas a grant or grants of such amount or amounts as the Minister, with the consent of the Minister of Finance and after consultation with the Board in relation to its programme of expenditure for that year, may fix.   **[87]**

---

4 Commentary

Section 7 enables the Minister to control the expenditure of the Board on a yearly basis. It is questionable whether such close control by the Minister is appropriate for an independent appellate body which, it is respectfully submitted, should be seen to be independent from the Minister.

8.   Accounts and audits

(1) The Board shall keep in such form as may be approved by the Minister, after consultation with the Minister for Finance, all proper and usual accounts of all moneys received or expended by it.

(2) Accounts kept in pursuance of this section shall be submitted by the Board to the Comptroller and Auditor General for audit at such times as the Minister shall direct and, when audited by him, shall, together with the report of the Comptroller and Auditor General thereon, be presented to the Minister who shall cause copies to be laid before each House of the Oireachtas.   **[88]**

9.   Annual report and information to Minister

(1) The Board shall, not later than the 30th day of September in each year, make a report to the Minister of its proceedings during the preceding year and the Minister shall cause copies of the report to be laid before each House of the Oireachtas.

(2) The Board shall supply the Minister with such information relating to the performance of its functions as he shall from time to time request.   **[89]**

10. Employees of Board

(1) The Board shall appoint such and so many persons to be employees of the Board as the Board, subject to the approval of the Minister, [given with the consent of the Minister for the Public Service][1a] as to the number and kind of such employees, from time to time thinks proper.

(2) The Board may employ a person in a part-time capacity to be remunerated by the payment of fees of such amounts as the Board may, with the approval of the Minister given with the consent of the Minister for the Public Service, from time to time determine.

(3) An employee of the Board shall hold his employment on such terms and conditions as the Board, subject to the approval of the Minister, from time to time determines.

(4) There shall be paid by the Board to its employees out of moneys at its disposal such remuneration and allowances as the Board, subject to the approval of the Minister, with the consent of the Minister for the Public Service, from time to time determines.   **[90]**

---

1 Amendments

a   The words in square brackets were inserted by LG(PD)A 1983, s 21.

---

11. Superannuation of employees of Board[2a]

(1) As soon as conveniently may be after the establishment day, the Board shall prepare and submit to the Minister for his approval, a scheme or schemes for the granting of pensions, gratuities and other allowances on retirement or death to or in respect of such wholetime employees of the Board as it may think fit.

(2) The Board may at any time, prepare and submit to the Minister, a scheme amending a scheme under this section.

(3) Where a scheme is submitted to the Minister pursuant to this section, the Minister may, with the concurrence of the Minister for the Public Service, approve the scheme without modification or with such modification (whether by way of addition, omission or variation) as the Minister shall, with such concurrence, think proper.

(4) A scheme submitted to the Minister under this section shall, if approved of by the Minister with the concurrence of the Minister for the Public Service, be carried out by the Board in accordance with its terms.

(5) A scheme submitted and approved of under this section shall fix the time and conditions of retirement for all persons to or in respect of whom pensions, gratuities or other allowances are payable under the scheme, and different times and conditions may be fixed in respect of different classes of persons.

(6) If any dispute arises as to the claim of any person to, or the amount of, any pension, gratuity or other allowance payable in pursuance of a scheme under this section, such dispute shall be submitted to the Minister who shall refer it to the Minister for the Public Service, whose decision shall be final.

(7) Every scheme submitted and approved of under this section shall be laid before each House of the Oireachtas as soon as may be after it is approved of and if either House within the next twenty-one days on which that House has sat after the scheme is laid before it, passes a resolution annulling the scheme, the scheme shall be annulled accordingly, but without prejudice to the validity of anything previously done thereunder.   [91]

---

2 Cross References

a   See also LG(PD)A 1983, s 9 which deals with the superannuation of members of the Board.

---

12. Membership of either House of Oireachtas or of local authority of employees of Board[2a]

(1) Where a person who is an employee of the Board is nominated as a member of Seanad Éireann or for election to either House of the Oireachtas or becomes a member of a local authority, he shall stand seconded from employment by the Board and shall not be paid by, or be entitled to receive from, the Board any remuneration or allowances –

(a) in case he is nominated as a member of Seanad Éireann, in respect of the period commencing on his acceptance of the nomination and ending when he ceases to be a member of that House,

(b) in case he is nominated for election to either such House, in respect of the period commencing on his nomination and ending when he ceases to be a member of that House or fails to be elected or withdraws his candidature, as may be appropriate,

(c) in case he becomes a member of a local authority, in respect of the period commencing on his becoming a member of the local authority and ending when he ceases to be a member of that authority.

(2) A person who is for the time being entitled under the Standing Orders of either House of the Oireachtas to sit therein shall, while so entitled, be disqualified from becoming an employee of the Board.

(3) A person who is for the time being a member of a local authority shall, while holding office as such member, be disqualified from becoming an employee of the Board.   **[92]**

---

2 Cross References

a   See LG(PD)A 1983, s 5(10) and (13) which deal with membership of either House of the Oireachtas or of a local authority of the Chairman of the Board. LG(PD)A 1983, s 7(7) and (10) deal with membership of either House of the Oireachtas or of a local authority of an ordinary member of the Board.

---

13. Consultants and advisers

(1) The Board may from time to time engage such consultants or advisers as it may consider necessary for the discharge of its functions and any fees due to a consultant or adviser engaged pursuant to this section shall be paid by the Board out of moneys at its disposal.

(2) Any person may notify the Board in writing of his willingness to be engaged by the Board as a consultant or adviser pursuant to this section and such person when so notifying the Board shall give to the Board particulars of his qualifications and experience.

(3) The Board shall maintain a list of the persons who duly give to the Board a notification pursuant to subsection (2) of this section.

(4) The Board shall, in engaging a consultant or adviser under this section, have regard to the list maintained under subsection (3) of this section, but the foregoing provisions of this subsection shall not be construed as precluding the Board from engaging as a consultant or adviser a person whose name is not on the said list.

(5) The Board shall include in each report made under section 9 of this Act a statement of the names of the persons (if any) engaged pursuant to this section during the year to which the report relates.   **[93]**

---

4 Commentary

It is understood that a number of consultants are employed by the Board who carry out the duties of planning inspectors on particular appeals.

---

14. Certain appeals and other matters to be brought or referred to Board

(1) An appeal under a relevant section of the Principal Act shall, in lieu of being brought to the Minister, be brought to the Board and if it is not withdrawn, be decided by the Board, and –

  (a) in case the appeal relates to an application, notice or order, the application, notice or order shall be determined or confirmed or annulled (as the case may be) accordingly, and

(b) in case the appeal relates to a licence under section 89 of the Principal Act, such directions shall be given with respect to the withdrawing or granting or altering of the licence as may be appropriate.

(2) Any question as to what, in any particular case, is or is not development or exempted development shall, in lieu of being referred to and decided by the Minister under section 5(1) of the Principal Act, be referred to and be decided by the Board.

(3) In case a condition referred to in subsection (2)(f) of section 26 of the Principal Act is attached to a permission or approval granted under that section and there is not agreement in relation to the contribution required by subsection (7) of the said section 26 to be made by a local authority, the matter shall, in lieu of being determined by the Minister under the said subsection (7), be referred to the Board which shall determine the amount of the contribution.

(4) In case there is attached to a permission or approval granted under section 26 of the Principal Act a condition which provides that a contribution or other matter is to be agreed between the planning authority and the person to whom the permission or approval is granted and that in default of agreement the contribution or other matter is to be determined by the Minister, the condition shall be construed as providing that in default of agreement the contribution or other matter is to be determined by the Board.

(5) The functions of the Minister under section 29 of the Principal Act are hereby transferred to the Board and without prejudice to the generality of subsection (9) of this section the references in the said section 29 to the Minister shall each be construed as referring to the Board.

(6) Any question or dispute whether a new structure would or does replace substantially within the meaning of section 56 of the Principal Act a demolished or destroyed structure shall, in lieu of being determined by the Minister, be determined by the Board.

(7) For the purposes of the foregoing subsections of this section, the Principal Act (as amended by this Act) shall, with any necessary modifications, apply to the following, namely –

(a) the bringing of an appeal to the Board,

(b) the making of a reference to the Board,

(c) a decision of the Board on an appeal,

(d) the confirmation or annulment (as the case may be) by the Board of the notice or order to which an appeal relates,

(e) the determination of a question or dispute by the Board to which a reference under section 5(1) of the Principal Act relates,

(f) the determination by the Board of a disagreement, question or dispute to which section 26(7) or section 56(3) of the Principal Act relates,

(g) the confirmation of a purchase notice served on a planning authority under section 29 of the Principal Act,

(h) the compliance with directions given by the Board in relation to an appeal relating to a licence under section 89 of the Principal Act, and

(i) the determination by the Board of a contribution or other matter to be determined by the Board by virtue of subsection (4) of this section,

as, immediately before the appropriate day, it applied to whichever of the following is appropriate, namely, the bringing or making of a corresponding appeal or reference to the Minister under the Principal Act, a decision of the Minister on such an appeal, the confirmation or annulment or determination by the Minister of a notice, order, question or dispute relating to such an appeal or reference, the determination by the Minister of a disagreement, question or dispute to which the said section 26(7) or 56(3) relates, the confirmation by the Minister of a purchase notice, the compliance with directions given by the Minister in relation to an appeal relating to a licence under the said section 89 or the determination by the Minister of a contribution or other matter pursuant to a condition mentioned in the said subsection (4).

(8) The Board may in determining an appeal under section 26 or 27 of the Principal Act decide to grant a permission or approval even if the proposed development contravenes materially the development plan or any special amenity area order relating to the area of the planning authority to whose decision the appeal relates.[3a]

(9) Wherever the Principal Act refers to the Minister in relation to –

(a) an appeal under a relevant section,

(b) a reference under section 5(1) of the Principal Act,

(c) a determination of a disagreement, question or dispute to which section 26(7) or section 56(3) of the Principal Act relates,

(d) a decision on an appeal under a relevant section,

(e) a determination pursuant to section 85 of the Principal Act as to whether a consent was unreasonably withheld,

(f) a determination, confirmation or annulment (as the case may be) of the notice or order, question or dispute to which an appeal under a relevant section or a reference mentioned in paragraph (b) of this subsection relates,

(g) a requirement requiring applicants or planning authorities to furnish to the Minister any specified information, or

(h) any word cognate to appeal, reference, decision, determination, confirmation or annulment,

that Act,[1a] shall be construed as referring to the Board.

(10) In this section "a relevant section" means a section which is section 26, 27, 30, 33, 36, 37, 44, 45, 46, 48, 85 or 89 of the Principal Act.[2a]   **[94]**

---

1 Amendments

a   Section 14(9) was amended by the BCA 1990, s 24.

2 Cross References

a   Section 26 relates to appeals against the decision of the planning authority relating to applications for planning permission.

Section 27 relates to appeals against the decision of the planning authority relating to applications for retentions.

Section 30 relates to an appeal against a decision to revoke or modify a permission.

Section 33 relates to a notice served in respect of an unauthorised development existing immediately before the appointed day.

Section 36 relates to a notice served requiring the removal of a structure.

Section 37 relates to where the planning authority serves a notice requiring that a use be discontinued.

Section 44 relates to where a notice is served requiring the removal of a hedge.

Section 45 relates to where an appeal is made against a tree preservation order.

Section 46 relates to where an appeal is made against a conservation order.

Section 48 relates to the creation of a public right of way over lands by order.

Section 85 relates to consent being withheld unreasonable to the laying of cables, wires and pipelines.

Section 89 relates to appeals in relation to decisions on licences granted/refused.

3 Notes

a   In *Lancefort v An Bord Pleanála* High Court, unrep, 12 March 1998 the applicant sought to challenge the constitutionality of s 14(8) of LG(PD)A 1976 but it was held by McGuinness J that the applicant did not have sufficient interest to provide it with *locus standi* to challenge the sub-section.

4 Commentary

Section 14 transfers to the Board the duty of determining appeals and references made under the LG(PD)A 1963. All appeals of any substance with the exception of appeals against the making of a special amenity area order are now heard and determined by the Board. The Board also hears appeals pursuant to s 25 of LG(PD)A 1976 which allows a local authority to take an area of ground dedicated as open space without the payment of compensation. Section 88 of LG(PD)A 63 which concerned an appeal against a refusal to relax building regulations was repealed by the BCA 1990; s 76 of LG(PD)A 1963 on the extinguishment of a public right of way has now been repealed by the Roads Act 1990 and s 84 LG(PD)A 1963 with regard to consultation by State authorities was repealed by LG(PD)A 1993. Consequently the appellate function of the Minister except for special amenity area orders is now of little relevance.

15. £10 deposit to be lodged by appellants

(1) ...[1a]

(2) As soon as may be after an appeal to the Board is either withdrawn or determined, subject to section 18(3) of this Act, the Board shall return the deposit to the appellant.   [95]

1 Amendments

a   Section 15(1) was repealed by LG(PD)A 1982, s 15.

4 Commentary

There is now no provision under the Planning Acts for the lodging of a deposit with a planning appeal so this section is of no relevance to the actual operation of appeals lodged with the Board.

16. [Oral hearings][1a]

[96]

1 Amendments

a   Section 16 was repealed by LG(PD)A 1983, s 25.

17. [Matters other than those raised by parties may be taken into account in determining references or appeals][1a]

[97]

---

1 Amendments

a   Section 17 was repealed by LG(PD)A 1992, s 22.

---

18. Power of Board as regards vexatious references or appeals, etc

(1) ...[1a]

(2) ...[1b]

(3) In case the Board in determining an appeal is of opinion that the appeal is vexatious, the Board may direct that the deposit lodged in relation to the appeal shall be forfeited to the Board.[3a]   **[98]**

---

1 Amendments

a   Subsection (1) was repealed by LG(PD)A 1983, s 25.

b   Subsection (2) was repealed by LG(PD)A 1983, s 25.

4 Commentary

This section is no longer of relevance as non-returnable fees have replaced deposits.

---

19. Expenses of appeal

(1) Where there is an appeal to the Board against a decision of a planning authority —[1a]

   (a) the Board, if it so thinks proper and irrespective of the result of the appeal, may direct the planning authority to pay —

      (i)   to the appellant, such sum as the Board, in its absolute discretion, specifies as compensation to the appellant for the expense occasioned to him in relation to the appeal,

      (ii) to the Board, such sum as the Board, in its absolute discretion, specifies as compensation to the Board towards the expense incurred by the Board in relation to the hearing of the appeal,

   (b) in case the decision of the planning authority is confirmed on appeal, or where the decision is varied on appeal, if the Board in determining the appeal does not accede in substance to the appellant's grounds of appeal, the Board, if it so thinks proper, may direct the appellant to pay —

      (i)   to the planning authority, such sum as the Board, in its absolute discretion, specifies as compensation to the planning authority for the expense occasioned to them in relation to the appeal,

      (ii) to any of the other parties to the appeal, such sum as the Board, in its absolute discretion, specifies as compensation to the party for the expense occasioned to him in relation to the appeal,

      (iii) to the Board, such sum as the Board, in its absolute discretion, specifies as compensation to the Board towards the expense incurred by the Board in relation to the hearing of the appeal.

(2) ...[1b]

(3) Any sum directed under this section to be paid shall, in default of being paid, be recoverable as a simple contract debt in any court of competent jurisdiction.   **[99]**

---

1 Amendments

a   Subsection (1) was amended by LG(PD)A 1992, s 19(4)(a).

b   Subsection (2) was repealed by LG(PD)A 1992, s 22.

4 Commentary

Section 19 provides that the Board, where it considers it appropriate, can direct an appellant to pay the costs or a proportion of the costs of the Board, the planning authority or any other party to an appeal. This section surprisingly has never been used by the Board and there must be instances where either a developer or third parties or indeed the planning authority has been put to unnecessary or unreasonable expense in the conducting of an appeal where such an order might be appropriate and would be an effective method of discouraging frivolous and vexatious submissions. See also s 16 of LG(PD)A 1983 which allows the Board to dismiss an appeal where it considers it vexatious, frivolous or without substance or foundation.

---

20. [Supplemental provisions relating to references and appeals][1a]

[100]

---

1 Amendments

a   Section 20 was repealed by LG(PD)A 1992, s 22.

---

21. Transitional

(1) In case immediately before the appropriate day an appeal, contribution, question or dispute referred to in section 14 of this Act or an appeal pursuant to section 25 of this Act was being considered by the Minister, the said section 14 and sections 16, 17, 18, 19 and 20 of this Act shall apply in relation to the appeal, contribution, question or dispute which, in lieu of being further considered by the Minister under the Principal Act, shall unless it is withdrawn, be decided or determined by the Board as if it had been originally brought or referred to the Board under this Act.

(2) In case before the appropriate day a purchase notice within the meaning of section 29 of the Principal Act has been served on a planning authority and the authority have not served before that day a notice in relation thereto under subsection (2) of that section stating that they are willing to comply with the purchase notice, the following provisions shall have effect:

    (a)   in case the planning authority propose to serve on the relevant owner a notice in accordance with paragraph (b) of the said subsection (2) and the authority have not before the said day transmitted to the Minister copies of the notices referred to in subsection (4) of the said section 29, for the avoidance of doubt it is hereby declared that section 14(5) of this Act shall apply in relation to the notice,

    (b)   in case the planning authority have before the appropriate day transmitted to the Minister the copies of the notices referred to in the said subsection (4) but the Minister before the appropriate day has neither confirmed the purchase notice nor taken any such other action as is mentioned in paragraph (i) or paragraph (ii) of the proviso to the said subsection (4), nor notified the owner by whom the notice was served that he does not propose to confirm the notice, the notice in lieu of being further considered by the Minister shall be considered by the Board as if the copy of it had been transmitted by the Board on the appropriate day, and the said subsection (4) and subsection (5) of the said section 29, as amended by this Act, shall with the necessary modifications apply in relation to the notice, and

(c) in either case, notwithstanding section 14(9) of this Act, the said subsection (2) shall have effect in relation to the notice required to be served by that subsection as if "the Minister or the Board, as may be appropriate" were therein substituted for "the Minister".

(3) For the purpose of enabling the Board to perform its function on and from the appropriate day, the Board may, as an interim measure, make arrangements for the supply to the Board by the Minister of any services required by the Board pending the making by the Board of sufficient appointments pursuant to section 10 of this Act and the Minister may supply and the Board may avail of services for which arrangements are made under this subsection.   **[101]**

---

4 Commentary

Section 21 provides for the transitional period between the transfer of the powers of the Minister to deal with appeals to the Board and is now of little relevance.

---

22. [Time for appeals generally][1a]

[102]

---

1 Amendments

a   Section 22 was repealed by LG(PD)A 1992, s 22.

---

23. Reports of inspections, etc.

Where in connection with either the performance by the Minister of any of the functions assigned to him under the Local Government (Planning and Development) Acts, 1963 and 1976, or the performance by the Board of its functions an inspection is carried out or an oral hearing is conducted on behalf of the Minister or the Board, as the case may be, by a person appointed for the purpose by the Minister or the Board, the person so appointed shall make to the Minister or the Board, as may be appropriate, a written report on the inspection or hearing, as the case may be, and shall include in his report a recommendation relating to the matter with which the inspection or hearing was concerned, and the Minister or the Board, as may be appropriate, shall, before determining the matter in relation to which the inspection was carried out or the hearing was conducted, consider the report (including any recommendation contained therein).[3a]

[103]

3 Notes

a   See *Killiney and Ballybrack Development Association v The Minister for Local Government* [1978] ILRM 78. See also *Simunovich v An Bord Pleanála* High Court, unrep, 23 April 1993, Lardner J and *Max Developments v An Bord Pleanála* [1994] 2 IR 121. In *Knock Shrine Association v An Bord Pleanála* (*ex tempore*, 1996) it was held that an error in law in an inspector's report, whose recommendation the Board had adopted, did not invalidate the decision. The chairman gave oral evidence that though the decision was the same, it had been arrived at by a different route and no reliance was placed on the inspector's report. The Court refused to quash the decision. See also *Lancefort Ltd v An Bord Pleanála* High Court, unrep, 12 March 1998 where McGuinness J held that there was no duty on an inspector to submit a report of a site inspection to the Board or to include materials from the inspection in the report of the oral hearing.

4 Commentary

The reports of the inspector are now made pursuant to the LG(PD)(No 2)R (SI 75/1995) which provides for the making available for public inspection documents relating to planning appeals and other matters determined by An Bord Pleanála in any case received by it after 10 April 1995. The Regulations became operative on 6 April 1995. For the role of an inspector in the conduct of oral hearings see LG(PD)A 1963, s 82.

---

24. Additional matters to which planning authority or Board may have regard in considering certain applications, etc. and certain appeals[2a]

(1) Notwithstanding anything contained in the Principal Act, a planning authority in considering,

   (a) an application for a permission under section 26 or 27 of that Act,

   (b) whether or not it is expedient to serve a notice under section 30, 31, 32, 33 or 35 of that Act,

   (c) whether or not to serve a notice under section 36 or 37 of that Act,

shall, where they consider it appropriate, have regard to either or both of the following, namely,

   (i)   the probable effect which a particular decision by them on the matter would have on any place which is not within, or on any area which is outside, their area, and

   (ii) any other consideration relating to development outside their area.

(2) Notwithstanding anything contained in the Principal Act, the Board in considering an appeal brought under section 27, 30, 33, 36 or 37 of that Act[1a] shall, where it considers it appropriate, have regard to either or both of the following namely,

   (a) the probable effect which a particular decision by it on the matter would have on any place which is not within, or on any area which is outside, the area of the relevant planning authority, and

   (b) any other consideration relating to development outside the area of that authority.   **[104]**

---

1 Amendments

a   Subsection (2) was amended by LG(PD)A 1992, s 19(4)(b).

2 Cross References

a   See also LG(PD)A 1992, s 3(c) for a similar provision in relation to appeals under s 26. This section enables a planning authority to consider, eg, the national or regional employment implications of a large development. See *Keane v An Bord Pleanála & Commissioners of Irish Lights* [1997] ILRM 508 for a discussion of this issue regarding a development designed to aid navigation on the open seas.

---

25. Enforcement of planning control (open spaces)[3a]

(1) Where –

    (a) development is being or has been carried out pursuant to a permission under section 26 of the Principal Act, and

    (b) (i) a condition requiring the provision or maintenance of land as open space, being open space to which this section applies, was attached to the permission, or

        (ii) it was either explicit or implicit in the application for the said permission that land would be provided or maintained as such open space, and

    (c) the planning authority have served on the owner of the land a written request that, within a period specified in the request (being a period of not less than two months commencing on the date of the request), he will provide, level, plant or otherwise adapt or maintain such land in a manner so specified, being a manner which in their opinion would make it suitable for the purpose for which the open space was to be provided, and

    (d) the owner fails to comply or to secure compliance with such request within the period so specified,

the planning authority may, if they think fit, publish in a newspaper circulating in the district a notice (subsequently in this section referred to as an acquisition notice) of their intention to acquire the land by order under this section and the acquisition notice shall specify a period (being a period of not less than two months commencing on the date on which the notice is published) within which an appeal may be made under this section.

(2) Where a planning authority publish an acquisition notice, they shall serve a copy of the notice on the owner of the land to which the notice relates not later than ten days after the date of the publication.

(3) Any person for the time being having an interest in the land to which an acquisition notice relates may within the period specified in the notice appeal -

    (a) in case the appeal is made before the appropriate day, to the Minister,

    (b) in case the appeal is made on or after the appropriate day, to the Board.

(4) Where an appeal is brought under this section, the Minister or the Board, as may be appropriate, may –

    (a) annul the acquisition notice to which the appeal relates, or

    (b) confirm the acquisition notice, with or without modification, in respect of all or such part of the relevant land as the Minister or the Board considers reasonable.

(5) In case a planning authority publish an acquisition notice and either –

    (a) the period for appealing against the notice has expired and no appeal has been taken, or

(b) an appeal has been taken against the notice and the appeal has been withdrawn or the notice has been confirmed whether unconditionally or subject to modifications,

the planning authority may make an order in the prescribed form[2a] which order shall be expressed and shall operate to vest the land to which the acquisition notice, or, where appropriate, the acquisition notice as confirmed, relates in the planning authority on a specified date for all the estate, term or interest for which immediately before the date of the order the said land was held by the owner together with all rights and liabilities which, immediately before the said date, were enjoyed or incurred in connection therewith by the owner together with an obligation to comply with the request made under paragraph (c) of subsection (1) of this section.

(6) Where a planning authority have acquired by an order under this section land which is subject, either alone or in conjunction with other land, to a purchase annuity, payment in lieu of rent, or other annual sum (not being merely a rent under a contract of tenancy) payable to the Irish Land Commission or to the Commissioners of Public Works in Ireland, the authority shall become and be liable, as from the date on which the land is vested in them by the vesting order, for the payment to the Irish Land Commission or to the Commissioners of Public Works in Ireland, as the case may be, of the annual sum or such portion thereof as shall be apportioned by the Irish Land Commission or by the Commissioners of Public Works in Ireland, as the case may be, on the land as if the land had been transferred to the authority by the owner thereof on that date.

(7) When a planning authority make an order under this section in relation to any land, they shall send the order to the registering authority under the Registration of Title Act, 1964, and thereupon the registering authority shall cause the planning authority to be registered as owner of the land in accordance with the order.

(8) Where a claim is made for compensation in respect of land to which an order under this section relates, [the claim shall, in default of agreement, be determined by arbitration under the Acquisition of Land (Assessment of Compensation) Act, 1919, in the like manner in all respects as if such claim arose in relation to the compulsory acquisition of land, but subject to the proviso that the arbitrator shall have jurisdiction to make a nil award and to the following provisions:][1a]

(a) unless it is shown by or on behalf of the owner that an amount equal to the value of the land to which the relevant permission under section 26 of the Principal Act relates, being that value at the time when the application for the permission was made, as a result of the development has not been recovered and as a further such result will not in future be recoverable by disposing of the land which is land to which the permission relates and which is not land to which the order relates, the arbitrator shall make a nil award, and

(b) in the assessment of the value of the land to which the order relates, no regard shall be had to its value for use other than as open space and a deduction shall be made in respect of the cost of carrying out such works as may be necessary to comply with the request made pursuant to paragraph (c) of subsection (1) of this section.

(9) A planning authority shall enter in the register –

(a) particulars of any acquisition notice published by them,

(b) the date and effect of any decision on appeal in relation to such notice,

(c) particulars of any order made under this section,

and every such entry shall be made within the period of seven days commencing on the day of publication, receipt of notification of the decision or the making of the order, as may be appropriate.

(10) This section applies to any form of open space (whether referred to as open space or by any other description in the relevant application for a permission or in a condition attached to the relevant permission) being land which is not described in the said application or condition either as private open space or in terms indicating that it is not intended that members of the public are to have resort thereto without restriction. **[105]**

---

1 Amendments

a   Subsection (8) was amended by LG(PD)A 1990, s 33.

2 Cross References

a   See LG(PD)R 1994 (SI 86/1994), art 165.

3 Notes

a   This section does not apply to developments which were complete prior to the coming into effect of the section. See *Dublin County Council v Grealy* [1990] 1 IR 177 and *Dublin County Council v Brennan and McGowan Ltd* High Court, unrep, 7 February 1983, Barron J.

4 Commentary

Section 25 gives a planning authority power to acquire at no cost land designated as open space pursuant to a planning permission. In such circumstances the planning authority is entitled to acquire the land at no cost but an appeal against such an acquisition lies to An Bord Pleanála. It would appear that the concept of taking in charge applies only to roads and consequently this is the mechanism whereby open space can become vested in a planning authority. In those circumstances it is submitted that until such an order is served, the open space remains within the ownership of the landowner and this could give rise to difficulties especially where a housing development is located within a rural area where the provisions of the LG(PD)R 1994 could apply. This section can only become operative when the open space has not been laid and properly developed as an open space pursuant to the grant of planning permission. This section has never been effectively tested and whether in fact it grants the power to a local authority to take the land without the payment of compensation in such circumstances must be questionable and indeed the definition of open space which the section applies in sub-ss (1) and (10) is vague and capable of a degree of confusion.

---

26. Warning notice

(1) Where it appears to a planning authority that –

(a) land is being or is likely to be developed in contravention of section 24 of the Principal Act, or

(b) any unauthorised use is being [or is likely to be][1a] made of land, or

(c) any tree or other feature (whether structural or natural) or any other thing the preservation of which is required by a condition subject to which a permission for the development of any land was granted, may be removed or damaged,

the planning authority may serve on the owner of the land a notice (in this section subsequently referred to as a warning notice) and may give a copy of the said notice to any other person who in their opinion may be concerned with the matters to which the notice relates.

(2) A warning notice shall refer to the land concerned and –

    (a) in relation to any land being developed or likely to be developed, require that development thereof in contravention of section 24 of the Principal Act shall not be commenced or, if such development has been commenced, that it shall be discontinued forthwith,

    [(b) in relation to any unauthorised use being or likely to be made of land, require that the unauthorised use shall be discontinued forthwith or shall not be commenced, as the case may be,][1b]

    (c) in relation to a condition requiring the preservation of any tree, other feature or thing, require that the tree, other feature or thing, as may be appropriate, shall neither be removed nor damaged and that any reasonable steps necessary for its preservation shall be taken by the owner of the land,

and such notice shall also require the owner of the land to take adequate steps to ensure compliance with the notice and shall contain a warning that proceedings under this section may be brought by the relevant planning authority against him and any other person who fails to comply with the requirements of the notice or who assists or permits any development or use of land or the doing of any other thing in contravention thereof.

(3) In case a warning notice has been served in relation to a breach of the condition mentioned in paragraph (c) of subsection (2) of this section, anything done in relation to the tree, other feature or thing to which the notice relates shall if it is done with the consent in writing of the planning authority by whom the notice was served not be an offence under this section.

[(3A) A warning notice in relation to any unauthorised use of land shall not be served after the expiration of a period of five years beginning on the day on which such unauthorised use first commenced.][1c, 3a]

(4) Any person who –

    (a) knowingly fails to comply with the requirements of a warning notice, or

    (b) knowingly assists or permits,

        (i) the carrying out by another of any development required by a warning notice not to be commenced or to be discontinued, or

        [(ii) the commencement or continuance by another of a use required by a warning notice not to be commenced or to be discontinued, or][1d]

        (iii) the doing by another of any other thing in contravention of a warning notice, or

    (c) otherwise damages or removes any tree, other feature or thing to which a warning notice relates,

shall be guilty of an offence. [1e, 2a]

(5) …[1f]

(6) An enforcement notice within the meaning of section 31, 32 or 35 of the Principal Act may be served whether or not there has been a prosecution under this section. [3b]

(7) The following provisions shall apply in relation to proceedings under this section in which the offence alleged is the removal of or damage to a tree, other feature or thing to which a warning notice relates, namely –

    (a) in case the defendant is the owner of the land to which the warning notice relates,

        (i) it shall be sufficient for the prosecution to prove the fact that the tree, other feature or thing, as may be appropriate, was removed or damaged, and

        (ii) without prejudice to any other defence which may be open to him, it shall be a good defence if the defendant proves that he took, or caused to be taken, reasonable steps to secure compliance with the requirements of the warning notice and that he acted at all times in good faith in relation to the notice,

    (b) in any other case if, but only if, the prosecution proves that –

        (i) after the service of the warning notice steps were taken to inform persons of the existence of the notice, or to protect from damage or to preserve the tree, other feature or thing, as the case may be, with which the alleged offence is concerned, and

        (ii) the alleged removal or damage by the defendant occurred after the steps referred to in subparagraph (i) of this paragraph were taken,

    it shall be assumed, until the contrary is shown by the defendant, that the tree, other feature or thing was knowingly removed or damaged, as may be appropriate, by the defendant.

(8) In a prosecution for an offence under this section it shall not be necessary for the prosecution to show, and it shall be assumed until the contrary is shown by the defendant, that the development (if any) in question was neither exempted development nor development commenced before the appointed day.

(9) For the purposes of this section, a tree shall be regarded as being removed if it is cut down or otherwise wilfully destroyed.

(10) Where a warning notice is served under this section by a planning authority, particulars of the notice shall be entered by the authority in the register. **[106]**

---

1 Amendments

a   Subsection (1)(b) was amended by LG(PD)A 1992, s 19(4)(c).

b   Subsection (2)(b) was amended by LG(PD)A 1992, s 19(4)(d).

c   Subsection (3A) was inserted by LG(PD)A 1992, s 19(4)(e).

d   Subsection (4)(b)(ii) was substituted by LG(PD)A 1992, s 19(4)(f).

e   Subsection (4) was amended by LG(PD)A 1982, s 15(2)(c).

f   Subsection (5) was repealed by LG(PD)A 1982, s 15(2)(a).

2 Cross References

a   See LG(PD)A 1992, s 20 which provides for fines of up to £1 million and/or two years' imprisonment and/or £10,000 and/or two years' imprisonment for repeat offences under this section.

3 Notes

a   Subsection (3A) shall have effect as respects an unauthorised use of land commenced before or after the commencement of the subsection. For a consideration of time limits with regard to s 26 enforcement proceedings, see *Mountcharles (Earl of) v Meath County Council* [1997] ILRM 446.

b   See *Dublin County Council v Balfe Ltd* High Court, unrep, 3 November 1995 on the time limits applicable where summary proceedings are instituted.

4 Commentary

Section 26 prosecutions are not subject to a five year limitation period. The planning authority may serve a warning notice on the owner of the land if it appears to it that the land is being or is likely to be developed in contravention of s 24 of LG(PD)A 1963 or unauthorised use is to be made of the land or if it appears to the planning authority that an unauthorised is likely to occur.

It was stated in the judgment of the Supreme Court in *Mahon & Ors v IRFU* [1997] ILRM 446 that the relief provided for in s 26 encompasses the species of *quia timet* relief. In addition to the service of the notice on the owner of the land, the planning authority may give a copy of the notice to any person who may be concerned with matters to which the warning notice relates. The contents of such notices are set out in subs-s (2). It is an offence if any person knowingly fails to comply with the terms of the warning or knowingly assists or permits another to contravene the warning notice. The onus of proof in relation to the knowledge of the defendant rests with the prosecution except in the case of offences which consist of the removal of or damage to a tree or other feature or thing. In such cases if the defendant is the owner of the land it is sufficient for the prosecution to prove the fact of the removal or damage to the tree and effectively the onus then shifts to the defendant. It is a good defence for the owner to show that he took all reasonable steps to secure compliance with the warning notice and that he at all material times acted in good faith in relation to the notice.

Where the offence concerns a development, the prosecution needs to show that the development concerned is not an exempted development and was not commenced before the appointed day. Where a person has been convicted of an offence under s 26(7) and continues the offence after conviction he will be guilty of a further offence; see s 20(4) of LG(PD)A 1992. In light of the provision of a daily fine it appears that the offence is of a continuing nature and that there may be repeated prosecutions. Particulars of the warning notice must be entered on the planning register maintained by the planning authority.

---

27. [High Court or Circuit Court may prohibit unauthorised development or use of land[1a, 3a]

(1) Where –

    (a) development of land, being development for which a permission is required under Part IV of the Principal Act, has been carried out, or is being carried out, without such permission, or

    (b) an unauthorised use is being made of land,

the High Court or the Circuit Court may, on the application of a planning authority or any other person, whether or not the person has an interest in the land, by order require any person to do or not to do, or to cease to do, as the case may be, anything that the court considers necessary and specifies in the order to ensure, as appropriate –

    (i)   that the development or unauthorised use is not continued,

    (ii) in so far as is practicable, that the land is restored to its condition prior to the commencement of the development or unauthorised use.

(2) Where any development authorised by a permission granted under Part IV of the Principal Act has been commenced but has not been, or is not being, carried out in

conformity with the permission because of non-compliance with the requirements of a condition attached to the permission or for any other reason, the High Court or the Circuit Court may, on the application of a planning authority or any other person, whether or not that person has an interest in the land, by order require any person to do or not to do, or to cease to do, as the case may be, anything that the Court considers necessary and specifies in the order to ensure that the development is carried out in conformity with the permission.

(3) An application to the High Court or the Circuit Court for an order under this section shall be by motion and the Court when considering the matter may make such interim or interlocutory order (if any) as it considers appropriate. The order by which an application under this section is determined may contain such terms and conditions (if any) as to the payment of costs as the Court considers appropriate.

(4) Rules of court may provide for an order under this section to be made against a person whose identity is unknown.

(5) An application under this section to the Circuit Court shall be made to the judge of the Circuit Court for the circuit in which the land the subject of the application is situated.

(6) (a)   (i) Subsection (1)(a) of this section shall not apply to development of land carried out before the appropriate day.

(ii) An application to the High Court or the Circuit Court for an order under this section in relation to development to which subsection (1)(a) of this section applies shall not be made after the expiration of a period of five years beginning on the day on which the development was substantially completed.

(b) An application to the High Court or the Circuit Court for an order under this section –

(i) in relation to an unauthorised use of land (whether commenced before or after the appropriate day) shall not be made after the expiration of a period of five years beginning on the day on which such use first commenced;

(ii) in relation to development to which subsection (2) of this section applies (whether carried out before or after the appropriate day) shall not be made after the expiration of a period of five years beginning on the expiration, as respects the permission authorising the development, of the appropriate period (within the meaning of section 2 of the Local Government (Planning and Development) Act, 1982) or, as the case may be, of the said period ad extended under section 4 of the said Act.

(c) In this subsection "**appropriate day**" means the day, as respects the paragraph in which the said expression occurs, on which paragraph (g) of section 19(4) of the Local Government (Planning and Development) Act, 1992, comes into operation.] [2a, 3b]   **[107]**

---

1 Amendments

a   Section 27 was substituted by LG(PD)A 1992, s 19(4)(g).

2 Cross References

a   See also the Circuit Court Rules (No 1) 1995 (SI 215/1995) which set out the procedure for bringing such cases in the Circuit Court.

3 Notes

a   Section 27 is now the most widely used and effective enforcement mechanism, see *Morris v Garvey* [1983] IR 319; *Dublin Corporation v Maiden Poster Sites* [1983] ILRM 48; *Stafford v Roadstone Ltd* [1980] ILRM 1; *Avenue Properties Ltd v Farrell Homes Ltd* [1982] ILRM 21; *Dublin County Council v Sellwood Quarries Ltd* [1981] ILRM 23; *Dublin Corporation v Kevins* High Court, unrep, 14 July 1980, Finlay P; *Dublin County Council v Tallaght Block Co Ltd* [1982] ILRM 534; *Westmeath County Council v Moriarty* High Court, unrep, 30 July 1991; *Cork Corporation v O'Connell* [1982] ILRM 505; *Carroll v Brushfield Ltd* High Court, unrep, 9 October 1992; *Dublin County Council v Macken* High Court, unrep, 13 May 1994; *Leech v Reilly* High Court, unrep, 26 April 1983; *Marry v Connaughton* High Court, unrep, 25 January 1984; *Dublin Corporation v Sullivan* High Court, unrep, 21 December 1984, Finlay P; *Ellis v Nolan* High Court, unrep, 6 May 1983; *Coffey v Hebron Homes Ltd* High Court, unrep, 27 July 1984; *Dublin County Council v Matra Investments Ltd* (1980) 114 ILTR 102; *Dublin Corporation v Garland* [1982] ILRM 104; *Dublin County Council v Kirby* [1985] ILRM 325; *Dublin County Council v O'Riordan* [1986] ILRM 104. See also *South Dublin County Council v Balfe* High Court, unrep, 3 November 1995 where it was held that in order to rely on a defence under s 27 proceedings it must be referred to in the replying affidavit and cannot be raised in the closing submissions; see also *MCD Management Services Ltd v Kildare County Council* [1995] 2 ILRM 532.

b   For a discussion on the time limits for the bringing of s 27 proceedings, see *Kildare County Council v Goode* High Court, unrep, 13 June 1997. See further *Dublin Corporation v O'Dwyer Brothers (Mount Street) Ltd* High Court, unrep, 2 May 1997 where this issue was also considered and where the court refused a stay in order to allow the respondents time to lodge an application for retention. See also *South Dublin County Council v Balfe* High Court, unrep, 3 November 1995. For consideration of the issue of whether a *qua timet* injunction can be brought to restrain an anticipated breach of the Planning Acts under s 27, see *Mahon & Ors v IRFU* [1997] ILRM 446 where the Supreme Court reversed Costello P in the High Court and held that such proceedings could not be brought. Section 27 refers only to events occurring in the present or which have occurred in the past and there is no reference to future events. With regard to the general equitable jurisdiction of the courts under s 27 see *MMDS Television Ltd v South East Community Deflector Association Ltd* High Court, unrep, 8 April 1997 and *Fusco v Aprile* High Court, unrep, 6 June 1997.

4 Commentary

Section 27 provides for the enforcement of planning control by the making of orders in the nature of injunctions by the High Court and the Circuit Court. Where a development requiring planning permission has been or is being carried out without permission or where an unauthorised use of being made of land then an order may be made under s 27(1). Such an order may require a person to do, refrain from doing or cease doing anything which the court considers necessary to ensure that the development or unauthorised use is discontinued and, so far as it is practicable, to ensure that the land is restored to its condition prior to the commencement of the development or the unauthorised use.

Where any development authorised by a planning permission has been commenced but has not been or is not being carried out in conformity with the terms of the permission, the High Court or Circuit Court may, on the application of the planning authority or any other person (whether or not they have any interest in the land concerned), make an order directing a person to do or refrain from doing whatever the court considers necessary to ensure that the development is carried out in compliance with the planning permission. The applicant does not need to show that he has suffered any personal damage by reason of the breach (see *Stafford v Roadstone Ltd* [1980] ILRM 1).

28. Withdrawal by planning authority of certain notices and cancellations of relevant entries in register

(1) Where a planning authority serve a notice mentioned in section 30, 31, 32, 35, 36, 37 or 44 of the Principal Act they may by notice in writing withdraw the notice.

(2) Where a notice is withdrawn pursuant to this section by a planning authority, the fact that the notice was withdrawn shall be recorded by the authority in the register.   **[108]**

4 Commentary

The provisions relating to a planning register are found at LG(PD)A 1963, s 8. It would equally seem to follow that until the notice is withdrawn it remains on the planning register and it would be prudent where, for example, a prosecution is brought on foot of such a notice and fails that the court would make an order requiring the planning authority to withdraw the notice from the register. See generally *Hughes v An Bord Pleanala* High Court, unrep, July 1999, Geoghegan J.

29. Limit of duration of planning permission

(1)-(4) ... [1a, 3a]

(5) Any person who is aggrieved by the decision of a planning authority on an application for a waiver notice may appeal to the Board within the period of twenty-one days, beginning on the date on which the planning authority notify the applicant of their decision.

(6) Where an appeal is brought under subsection (5) of this section, the Board may –

    (a) in case a waiver notice has been issued by a planning authority, confirm or annul the notice, or

    (b) in case a waiver notice has not been so issued, confirm the decision of the planning authority or issue a waiver notice.

(7) ... [1b]

(8) In any legal proceedings a development certificate shall be *prima facie* evidence of the facts thereby certified, and any document purporting to be a development certificate shall be admitted as evidence without proof of the signature of the person purporting to sign the certificate or that the person was an officer of the relevant planning authority, until the contrary is shown.

(9) ... [1c]

(10) When a planning authority grant an extension or further extension, or issue a development certificate, particulars thereof shall be recorded on the relevant entry in the register.

(11) Any person who is aggrieved by a decision of a planning authority on an application for a development certificate may appeal to the Circuit Court within six months of the date of such decision.

(12) Where an appeal is brought under subsection (11) of this section, the Court, if satisfied that the case comes within paragraph (a) of subsection (7) of this section and

that a dispute mentioned in paragraph (b) of the said subsection (7) has arisen, may decide accordingly and, as may be appropriate, determine either or both of the following, the extent to which the relevant development was completed before the relevant permission under Part IV of the Principal Act ceased to have effect, or whether or not the part in dispute of the relevant development consists of the provision of things mentioned in sub-paragraph (ii) of the said paragraph (b), inform the appropriate planning authority of its decision and direct the authority to issue forthwith, if they have not already done so, an appropriate development certificate or, if a development certificate has been issued which is inappropriate having regard to the decision of the Court, transmit such certificate to the authority and direct that in lieu thereof an appropriate development certificate be issued by the authority forthwith.

(13) Where on an application by a person, the Circuit Court is satisfied that there has been unreasonable delay by a planning authority in dealing with an application for a development certificate and the Court is also satisfied in both of the respects mentioned in subsection (12) of this section, the Court may decide accordingly and make the determination mentioned in the said subsection (12) which is appropriate, inform the authority of its decision and direct the authority to issue forthwith an appropriate development certificate.   **[109]**

---

1 Amendments

a   Subsections (1)-(4) were repealed by LG(PD)A 1982, s 15(2)(b).

b   Subsection (7) was repealed by LG(PD)A 1982, s 15(2)(b).

c   Subsection (9) was repealed by LG(PD)A 1982, s 15(2)(b).

3 Notes

a   The repealed subsections (1), (2), (3), (4), (7) and (9) provided for "withering", waiver notices (which waived compliance with a condition in a planning permission) and development certificates (which certified how much of a development was complete at the date the relevant planning permission ceased to have effect). The effect of the repeal is to abolish waiver notices and development certificates subject to current appeals which remain effective. Duration of planning permissions is now governed by LG(PD)A 1982, ss 2, 3.

4 Commentary

The remaining provisions of s 29 apply only to those provisions which were originally subject to this section.

---

30. Summary proceedings[3a]

(1) Subject to subsection (2) of this section, summary proceedings to which this section applies may be commenced –

(a) at any time within six months from the date on which the offence was committed, or

(b) at any time within three months from the date on which evidence sufficient, in the opinion of the person by whom the proceedings are instituted, to justify proceedings comes to such person's knowledge,

whichever is the later.

(2) Summary proceedings mentioned in subsection (1) of this section shall not be instituted later than five years from the date on which the offence was committed.

(3) For the purposes of this section, a certificate signed by or on behalf of the person instituting the proceedings as to the date on which evidence described in subsection (1) of this section came to the knowledge of such person shall be *prima facie* evidence thereof and in any legal proceedings a document purporting to be a certificate issued for the purposes of this section and to be so signed shall be deemed to be so signed and shall be admitted as evidence without proof of the signature of the person purporting to sign the certificate, unless the contrary is shown.

(4) Subsection (1) of this section shall have effect notwithstanding section 10(4) of the Petty Sessions (Ireland) Act, 1851.

(5) This section applies to the following summary proceedings, namely:

* (a) summary proceedings pursuant to section 26 of this Act or in respect of a contravention of section 24(2) of the Principal Act and which are instituted by the planning authority in whose area the offence is alleged to have been committed,

(b) summary proceedings pursuant to section 32 or 33 of this Act. **[110]**

3 Notes

a   It would appear that proceedings under this section should be deferred on the basis of the 3 months or 6 months limits referred to at s 55(1) and that the 5 year limit specified is a maximum limit. The issue of when a planning authority generally will be deemed to have notice of an unauthorised development is unclear, particularly where officers generally have knowledge of the unauthorised development but choose not to take proceedings. Keane in the *Law of Local Government in the Republic of Ireland* (1982, ILSI) suggests that proceedings may be taken anytime within the 5 years so long as a person with no knowledge of the unauthorised development can be produced.

4 Commentary

The date of the offence for the purposes of s 30 is, in the case of s 26 of LG(PD)A 1976, the date of non-compliance with the notice served, in the case of an offence under s 24(2) of LG(PD)A 1963 it is the date of the carrying out of the unauthorised development, in the case of proceedings under ss 32 or 33 of LG(PD)A 1963, it is the date of non-compliance with the notice.

31. [Submissions and consultations][1a]

[111]

1 Amendments

a   Section 31 was repealed by LG(PD)A 1983, s 25.

32. Declaration by members and employees of Board, and members and officers of planning authorities of certain interests[2a]

(1) It shall be the duty of a person to whom this section applies to give to the relevant body a declaration in the prescribed form,[2b] signed by him and containing particulars of every interest of his which is an interest to which this section applies and for so long as he continues to be a person to whom this section applies it shall be his duty where there is a change regarding an interest particulars of which are contained in the declaration or

where he acquires any other interest to which this section applies, to give to the relevant body a fresh such declaration.

(2) (a) This section applies to the following persons, namely:

      (i) a member of the Board,

      (ii) a member of a planning authority,

      (iii) an employee of the Board or any other person,

          (I) whose services are availed of by the Board, and

          (II) who is of a class, description or grade prescribed for the purposes of this section,

      (iv) an officer of a planning authority who is the holder of an office which is of a class, description or grade so prescribed.

(b) This section applies to the following interests, namely:

      (i) any estate or interest which a person to whom this section applies has, in case the person is a member or officer of a planning authority, in land situated in the area of the relevant authority, and in any other case, in any land,

      (ii) any business of dealing in or developing land in which such a person is engaged or employed and any such business carried on by a company or other body of which he, or any nominee of his, is a member,

      (iii) any profession, business or occupation in which such a person is engaged, whether on his own behalf or otherwise, and which relates to dealing in or developing land.

(3) A person to whom this section applies and who has an interest to which this section applies shall be regarded as complying with the requirements of subsection (1) of this section if, and only if, he gives to the relevant body a declaration mentioned in that subsection within the period of twenty-eight days beginning –

(a) in case the person is such a person on the commencement of this section, on such commencement,

(b) in case the person becomes such a person after the commencement of this section, on the day on which he becomes such a person,

(c) in case there is a change regarding an interest particulars of which are contained in a declaration already given by the person or where the person acquires any other interest to which this section applies, on the day on which the change occurs or the other such interest is acquired.

(4) For the purposes of this section, a person to whom this section applies shall be regarded as having an estate or interest in land if he, or any nominee of his, is a member of a company or other body which has an estate or interest in the land.

(5) For the purposes of this section, a person shall not be regarded as having an interest to which this section applies if the interest is so remote or insignificant that it cannot reasonably be regarded as likely to influence a person in considering or discussing, or in voting on, any question with respect to any matter arising or coming before the Board or authority, as may be appropriate, or in performing any function in relation to any such matter.

(6) Where a person to whom this section applies has an interest to which this section applies by reason only of the beneficial ownership of shares in a company or other body

by him or by his nominee and the total nominal value of those shares does not exceed the lesser of –

    (a) five hundred pounds, or

    (b) one-hundredth part of the total nominal value of either the issued share capital of the company or body or, where that capital is issued in shares of more than one class, the issued share capital of the class or classes of shares in which he has an interest,

subsection (1) of this section shall not have effect in relation to that interest.

(7) The Board and each planning authority shall for the purposes of this section keep a register (which register is in this section referred to as the register of interests) and shall enter therein the particulars contained in declarations given to the Board or the authority, as the case may be, pursuant to this section. The register of interests shall be kept at the offices of the Board or the planning authority, as the case may be, and shall be available for public inspection during office hours.

(8) Where a person ceases to be a person to whom this section applies, any particulars entered in the register of interests as a result of a declaration being given by the person to the relevant body pursuant to this section shall be removed, as soon as may be after the expiration of the period of five years beginning on the day on which the person ceases to be such a person, from the said register by that body.

(9) Subject to subsection (10) of this section, a person who fails to comply with subsection (1) of this section or who, when purporting to comply with the requirements of the said subsection (1), gives particulars which are false or which to his knowledge are misleading in a material respect, shall be guilty of an offence and shall be liable on summary conviction to a fine not exceeding [£1000][1a] or at the discretion of the court, to imprisonment for a term not exceeding six months, or to both the fine and the imprisonment.

(10) In any proceedings for an offence under this section it shall be a defence for the defendant to prove that at the relevant time he believed, in good faith and upon reasonable grounds, that –

    (a) the relevant particulars were true,

    (b) there was no matter as regards which he was then required to make a declaration under subsection (1) of this section, or

    (c) that the matter in relation to which the offence is alleged was not one as regards which he was so required to make such declaration.

(11)(a) For the purposes of this section and section 33 of this Act,

      (i) a manager shall be deemed to be an officer of every planning authority for which he is manager,

      (ii) an assistant county manager for a county shall be deemed to be an officer of every planning authority in the county, and

      (iii) an officer of a planning authority who, by virtue of an arrangement or agreement entered into under any enactment, is performing duties under another planning authority, shall be deemed to be also an officer of the other authority.

    (b) In this section the **"relevant body"** means,

    (i) in case a person to whom this section applies is either a member or employee of the Board, or other person whose services are availed of by the Board, the Board, and

    (ii) in case such a person is either a member or officer of a planning authority, the authority.   **[112]**

1 Amendments

a   Fines were increased to £1000 by LG(PD)A 1992, s 20(1).

2 Cross References

a   See now LG(PD)R 1994 (SI 86/1994), art 166 which prescribes the persons to whom s 32 applies.

b   See LG(PD)R 1994 (SI 86/1994), art 167 for the form of declaration.

4 Commentary

Section 32 requires members and employees of the Board and members and officers of the planning authorities to give a schedule of their interests, although this provision appears only to apply to the officers and members themselves and not to their spouses and members of their family and this provision can be compared with s 33 which is more restrictive in this regard.

33. Requirements affecting members and employees of Board, members and certain officers of planning authorities and certain other persons who have certain beneficial interests

(1) Where a member of the Board has a pecuniary or other beneficial interest in, or which is material to, any appeal, contribution, question or dispute which falls to be decided or determined by the Board, he shall comply with the following requirements:

    (a) he shall disclose to the Board the nature of his interest,

    (b) he shall take no part in the discussion or consideration of the matter,

    (c) he shall not vote or otherwise act as a member of the Board in relation to the matter, and

    (d) he shall neither influence nor seek to influence a decision of the Board as regards the matter.

(2) Where, at a meeting of a planning authority or of any committee of a planning authority, a resolution, motion, question or other matter is proposed or otherwise arises either pursuant to, or as regards the performance by the authority of a function under, the Local Government (Planning and Development) Acts, 1963 and 1976, or in relation to the acquisition or disposal by the authority of land under or for the purposes of those Acts or any other enactment, a member of the authority or committee present at the meeting shall, if he had a pecuniary or other beneficial interest in, or which is material to, the matter –

    (a) at the meeting, and before discussion or consideration of the matter commences, disclose the nature of his interest,

    (b) withdraw from the meeting for so long as the matter is being discussed or considered,

and accordingly, he shall take no part in the discussion or consideration of the matter and shall refrain from voting in relation to it.

(3) A member of a planning authority or of any committee of a planning authority who has a pecuniary or other beneficial interest in, or which is material to, a matter arising either pursuant to, or as regards the performance by the authority of a function under, the Local Government (Planning and Development) Acts, 1963 and 1976, or in relation to the acquisition or disposal by the authority of land under or for the purposes of those Acts or any other enactment, shall neither influence nor seek to influence a decision of the authority as regards the matter.

(4) Where the manager of a planning authority has a pecuniary or other beneficial interest in, or which is material to, any matter which arises or comes before the authority either pursuant to, or as regards the performance by the authority of a function under, the Local Government (Planning and Development) Acts, 1963 and 1976, or in relation to the acquisition or disposal by the authority of land under or for the purposes of those Acts or any other enactment, he shall, as soon as may be, disclose to the members of the planning authority the nature of his interest.

(5) (a) Where an employee of the Board or any other person whose services are availed of by the Board has a pecuniary or other beneficial interest in, or which is material to, any appeal, contribution, question or dispute which falls to be decided or determined by the Board, he shall comply with the following requirements:

    (i) he shall neither influence nor seek to influence a decision of the Board as regards the matter, and

    (ii) in case, as such employee or other person, he is concerned with the matter, he shall disclose to the Board the nature of his interest and comply with any directions the Board may give him in relation to the matter.

  (b) Where an officer of a planning authority, not being the manager, has a pecuniary or other beneficial interest in, or which is material to, any matter which arises or comes before the authority, either pursuant to, or as regards the performance by the authority of a function under, the Local Government (Planning and Development) Acts, 1963 and 1976, or in relation to the acquisition or disposal of land by the authority under or for the purposes of those Acts or any other enactment, he shall comply with the following requirements:

    (i) he shall neither influence nor seek to influence a decision of the authority as regards the matter, and

    (ii) in case, as such officer, he is concerned with the matter, he shall disclose to the manager of the authority the nature of his interest and comply with any directions the manager may give him in relation to the matter.

(6) For the purposes of this section but without prejudice to the generality of any of the foregoing subsections hereof, a person shall be regarded as having a beneficial interest if –

  (a) he or his spouse, or any nominee of his or of his spouse, is a member of a company or any other body which has a beneficial interest in, or which is material to, a resolution, motion, question or other matter mentioned in the foregoing subsections of this section,

(b) he or his spouse is in partnership with or is in the employment of a person who has a beneficial interest in, or which is material to, such a resolution, motion, question or other matter,

(c) he or his spouse is a party to any arrangement or agreement (whether or not enforceable) concerning land to which such a resolution, motion, question or other matter relates,

(d) his spouse has a beneficial interest in, or which is material to, such a resolution, motion, question or other matter.

(7) For the purposes of this section, a person shall not be regarded as having a beneficial interest in, or which is material to, any resolution, motion, question or other matter by reason only of an interest of his or of any company or of any other body or person mentioned in subsection (6) of this section which is so remote or insignificant that it cannot reasonably be regarded as likely to influence a person in considering or discussing, or in voting on, any question with respect to the matter, or in performing any function in relation to that matter.

(8) Where a person has a beneficial interest mentioned in subsections (1), (2), (3), (4) or (5) of this section by reason only of the beneficial ownership of shares in a company or other body by him or by his spouse and the total nominal value of those shares does not exceed the lesser of –

(a) five hundred pounds, or

(b) one-hundredth part of the total nominal value of either the issued share capital of the company or body or, where that capital is issued in shares of more than one class, the issued share capital of the class of shares in which he has an interest,

none of those subsections shall have effect in relation to that beneficial interest.

(9) Where at a meeting described in subsection (2) of this section a disclosure is made under that subsection, particulars of the disclosure and of any subsequent withdrawal from the meeting pursuant to the said subsection shall be recorded in the minutes of the meeting.

(10) Subject to subsection (11) of this section, a person who contravenes or fails to comply with a requirement of this section shall be guilty of an offence and shall be liable on summary conviction to a fine not exceeding [£1000][1a] or, at the discretion of the court, to imprisonment for a term not exceeding six months, or to both the fine and the imprisonment.

(11) In any proceedings for an offence under this section it shall be a defence for the defendant to prove that at the time of the alleged offence he did not known and had no reason to believe that a matter in which, or in relation to which, he had a beneficial interest had arisen or had come before, or was being considered by, the Board or the relevant planning authority or committee, as may be appropriate, or that the beneficial interest to which the alleged offence relates was one in relation to which a requirement of this section applied.   **[113]**

---

1 Amendments

a   As amended by LG(PD)A 1992, s 20(2).

4 Commentary

Section 33 requires that a member of the Board shall not participate in any matter in which he has an interest and similar provisions apply to members and officers of planning authorities. The general provisions relating to interests are contained in sub-s (6) and are framed in a very broad manner and can apply to other enactments as well as to the Planning Acts.

34. Supplemental provisions relating to sections 32 and 33[1a]

(1) Proceedings for an offence under section 32 or 33 of this Act shall not be instituted except by or with the consent of the Director of Public Prosecutions.

(2) Where a person is convicted of an offence under section 32 or 33 of this Act, the following provisions shall have effect:

    (a) the person shall be disqualified for being a member of the Board,

    (b) in case the person is a member of the Board, he shall on such conviction accordingly cease to be a member of the Board,

    (c) in case the person is a member of a planning authority or a member of any committee of a planning authority, he shall on such conviction cease to be a member of the authority or the committee, as may be appropriate,

    (d) in case the person is a member of both a planning authority and any one or more such committees, he shall so cease to be a member of both the authority and every such committee, and

    (e) in case the person by virtue of this subsection ceases to be a member of a planning authority or any such committee, he shall be disqualified for being a member of the authority or committee during the period which, but for the cessation of his membership of the authority or committee under this section, would be the remainder of his term.

(3) In case a person contravenes or fails to comply with a requirement of section 32 or 33 of this Act, or acts as a member of the Board, a planning authority or committee of a planning authority while disqualified for membership by virtue of this section, the fact of such contravention or failure or of his so acting, as the case may be, shall not invalidate any act or proceeding of the Board, authority or committee.

(4) Where any body which is a company within the meaning of section 155 of the Companies Act, 1963, is deemed under that section to be a subsidiary of another or to be another such company's holding company, a person who is a member of the first-mentioned such company shall, for the purposes of sections 32 and 33 of this Act be deemed also to be a member of the other company.   **[114]**

---

1 Amendments

a   See LG(PD)R 1994 (SI 86/1994), art 166 and Form No 3 of the Third Schedule.

4 Commentary

Section 34 provides that proceedings for failure to disclose an interest or for taking part in a decision-making process on a matter in which the person concerned had an interest can only be prosecuted with the consent of the Director of Public Prosecutions. Even if a person who had an interest in the lands was involved in the decision-making process, this would not of itself render the decision invalid. Subsection (2)(a) is no longer of any significance having regard to LG(PD)A

1982, s 15. Approval for sub-s (2)(b) is defined in LG(PD)R 1994, art 3 and generally under Part V.

35. Regulations

The Minister may make regulations,

(a) providing for,

    (i) the payment to planning authorities of prescribed fees by applicants for a waiver notice under section 29 of this Act,

    (ii) the publication by planning authorities of specified notices with respect to applications for permission under the Principal Act to develop land or for such a waiver notice,

(b) enabling an applicant to appeal to the Board against a refusal of an approval which is required to be obtained under a condition subject to which a permission or approval is granted under the Principal Act,

(c) making such incidental, consequential, transitional or supplementary provisions as may appear to him to be necessary or proper for any purpose of this Act or in consequence of, or to give full effect to, any of its provisions. **[115]**

36. Onus of proof

In any proceedings for an offence under this Act or under the Principal Act, it shall not be necessary to negative by evidence the existence of any permission granted under Part IV of the Principal Act and the onus of proving such permission shall be on the person seeking to avail himself thereof. **[116]**

---

4 Commentary

This is an exception to the general rule that in a criminal case the prosecution must prove all elements of the case and provides that where a planning permission is to be relied upon it is essentially a matter of defence.

---

37. Amendment of draft development or draft variation[3a]

[117]

---

3 Notes

a   Section 37 inserts a new s 21A into LG(PD)A 1963. See the amended Act.

---

38. [Certain fines which may be imposed under the Principal Act increased][1a]

[118]

---

1 Amendments

a   Section 38 was repealed by LG(PD)A 1982, s 15(2)(a).

---

39. Amendment of Part IV of Principal Act[3a]

[119]

3 Notes

a   Section 39 amends Part IV of LG(PD)A 1963. See the amended Act.

40. Amendment of Part V of Principal Act[3a]

[120]

3 Notes

a   Section 40 amends LG(PD)A 63, Part V. See the amended Act.

41. [Amendment of Part VI of Principal Act][3a]

[121]

3 Notes

a   Section 41 amends LG(PD)A 1963, Part VI which part was repealed in its entirety by LG(PD)A 1990. See the amended Act.

42. Amendment of Part VIII of Principal Act[3a]

[122]

3 Notes

a   Section 42 amends LG(PD)A 1963, s 82, which has since been extensively amended, mainly by LG(PD)A 1992. See the amended Act.

43. Miscellaneous amendments of Principal Act[3a]

[123]

3 Notes

a   Section 43 amends LG(PD) A 1963, s 2(6), s 4, s 14(2), s 20(1), s 21(1), s 22, s 76 (now repealed), s 77(2) and Third Schedule. See the amended Act.

44. [Amendment of section 42 of Public Health (Ireland) Act, 1878][1a]

[124]

1 Amendments

a   Section 44 was repealed by the BCA 1990, s 24.

45. Repeals[3a]

The following provisions of the Principal Act are hereby repealed, namely, paragraph (b) of section 24(4); subsection (2), (7) and (10) of section 46; section 55(5); in paragraph (h) of section 56(1) all the words from "by reference to" to the end of the paragraph.   **[125]**

---

3 Notes

a   Sections 55 and 56 of LG(PD)A 1963 have now been repealed in full: see LG(PD)A 1990, s 3(1).

---

46. Short title, collective citation, commencement and construction

(1) This Act may be cited as the Local Government (Planning and Development) Act, 1976.

(2) The Principal Act and this Act may be cited together as the Local Government (Planning and Development) Acts, 1963 and 1976.

(3) This Act shall come into operation on such day or days as may be fixed therefor by any order or orders of the Minister, either generally or with reference to any particular purpose or provision and different days may be so fixed for different purposes and different provisions of this Act.

(4) This Act and the Principal Act shall be construed together as one Act.   **[126]**

Schedule[1a]

[127]

---

1 Amendments

a   The Schedule was repealed by LG(PD)A 1983, s 25.

LOCAL GOVERNMENT (PLANNING AND DEVELOPMENT) ACT, 1982

(No. 21 of 1982)

ARRANGEMENT OF SECTIONS

Section

ACTS REFERRED TO

Criminal Procedure Act, 1967   1967, No. 12
Local Government (Planning and Development), Act 1976   1976, No. 20
Local Government (Planning and Development), Acts 1963 and 1976

An Act to amend and extend the Local Government (Planning and Development), Acts, 1963 and 1976. [28th July, 1982]

Be it enacted by the Oireachtas as follows:

1. Interpretation

(1) In this Act –

"the Act of 1976" means the Local Government (Planning and Development) Act, 1976;

"development certificate" means a certificate issued under section 29 of the Act of 1976;

"waiver notice" means a notice issued under section 29 of the Act of 1976.   **[128]**

---

4 Commentary

The purpose of LG(PD)A 1982 was to introduce a limitation on the duration of planning permissions which prior to the enactment of this legislation generally had no expiry date. This created difficulties for major infrastructural developments. Consequent upon the decision to limit the duration of most planning permissions to a five year period was the necessity to introduce legislation allowing this period to be extended where substantial works had been carried out. The legislation also provides that certain offences may be tried summarily, ie those offences which are indictable may, if the defendant, District Court judge and the prosecutor agree, be tried by the District Judge where it is considered that the offence is a minor one.

2. Limit of duration of planning permission

(1) Subject to subsection (2) of this section, a permission granted under Part IV of the Principal Act, whether before or after the passing of this Act, shall on the expiration of the appropriate period [3a] (but without prejudice to the validity of anything done pursuant thereto prior to the expiration of that period) cease to have effect[3b] as regards –

    (a) in case the development to which the permission relates is not commenced during that period, the entire development, and

    (b) in case such development is commenced during that period, so much thereof as is not completed within that period.

(2) (a)   Subsection (1) of this section shall not apply –

    (i) to any permission for the retention on land of any structure,

    (ii) to any permission granted either for a limited period only or subject to a condition which is of a kind described in section 26(2)(j) or 27(2)(f) of the Principal Act,

    (iii) to any permission which is of a class or description specified in regulations made by the Minister for the purposes of this section,

    (iv) in the case of a house, shop, office or other building which itself has been completed, in relation to the provision of any structure or works included in the relevant permission and which are either necessary for or ancillary or incidental to the use of the building in accordance with that permission,

    (v) in the case of a development comprising a number of buildings of which only some have been completed, in relation to the provision of roads, services and open spaces included in the relevant permission and which are necessary for or ancillary to such completed buildings.

    (b) Subsection (1) of this section shall not affect –

    (i) the continuance of any use, in accordance with a permission, of land,

    (ii) where a development has been completed (whether to an extent described in paragraph (a) of this subsection or otherwise), the obligation of any person to comply with any condition attached to the relevant permission whereby something is required either to be done or not to be done.

(3) (a) Where regulations[2a] under this section are proposed to be made, the Minister shall cause a draft thereof to be laid before both Houses of the Oireachtas and the regulations shall not be made until a resolution approving of the draft has been passed by each such House.

    (b) Section 10(2) of the Principal Act shall not apply in relation to regulations made under this section.

(4) This section shall be deemed to have come into operation on the 1st day of November, 1981.

(5) In this section and in section 4 of this Act, "**the appropriate period**" means -

(a) in relation to any permission which was granted before the 1st day of November, 1976, the period beginning on the date of such grant and ending on the 31st day of October, 1983,

(b) in relation to any permission which was or is granted not earlier than the 1st day of November, 1976, nor later than the 31st day of October, 1982 –

   (i) in case in relation to the permission a period is specified pursuant to section 3 of this Act, that period, and

   (ii) in any other case, the period ending on the day which is seven years after the date of such grant or the 31st day of October, 1987, whichever is the earlier,

(c) in relation to any permission which was or is granted on or after the 1st day of November, 1987 –

   (i) in case in relation to the permission a period is specified pursuant to section 3 of this Act, that period, and

   (ii) in any other case, the period of five years beginning on the date of such grant:

Provided that where a planning authority have, before the commencement of this section, made an order under section 29(9) of the Act of 1976 and by virtue of the order the permission to which the order relates would, if this section had not been enacted, cease to have effect on a date which is later than that on which it would, apart from this proviso, cease to have effect, then, notwithstanding the foregoing provisions of this section and section 15 of this Act, the appropriate period in relation to the permission shall end on such later date.

(6) A planning authority in exercising, in relation to a permission referred to in subsection (5)(b) of this section, the power conferred on them by section 3 of this Act shall not exercise the power so as to specify a period which is shorter than that which, by virtue of the said subsection (5)(b), would apply in relation to the permission if the power were not so exercised. **[129]**

---

2 Cross References

a   These are set out in LG(PD)R 1994 (SI 86/1994), Part VI.

3 Notes

a   Not to be confused with "the appropriate period" for LG(PD)A 1963, s 26(4)(a)(iii) (two months unless extended by consent); LG(PD)A 1963, s 26(5)(a) (one month); LG(PD)A 1963 s 27(3)(a)(iii) (two months unless extended by consent) or LG(PD)A 1963, s 27(4)(a) (one month).

b   This section, together with ss 3 and 4 replaces LG(PD)A 1976 s 29(1), (2), (9).

4 Commentary

Section 2 provides generally that a planning permission granted on or after 1 November 1981 will be limited to a period of five years unless the grant of permission expressly provides for a longer period. The permission will therefore cease to have effect five years from the date of the grant of permission (which normally issues one month after the date of the decision to grant permission). If within that five year period substantial works have not been carried out then the permission will cease to exist on the expiration of the period and it will be as if no permission was granted on the lands. Section 2 refers to different periods within which existing permissions will expire but this is no longer of relevance as all permissions granted prior to 1 November 1981 have expired since 1987. Once the time limit for the permission expires, it is not permissible to proceed with any further parts of the development unless a new permission is granted or unless the planning authority extends the life of the permission pursuant to LG(PD)A 1982, s 4.

3. Power to vary appropriate period

Without prejudice to the powers conferred on them by Part IV of the Principal Act to grant a permission to develop land for a limited period only, in deciding to grant a permission under section 26 of the Principal Act, a planning authority or the Board, as may be appropriate, may, having regard to the nature and extent of the relevant development and any other material consideration, specify the period, being a period of more than five years, during which the permission is to have effect,[3a] and in case the planning authority exercise, or refuse to exercise, the power conferred on them by this section, such exercise or refusal shall be regarded as forming part of the relevant decision of such authority under the said section 26.   **[130]**

3 Notes

a   Section 4 applications were considered by Gannon J in *The State (McCoy) v Corporation of Dun Laoghaire* High Court, unrep 1 June 1984.

4 Commentary

Generally the duration of a planning permission is five years. However, s 3 provides that a longer period may be specified if special considerations, such as the scale of the development, justifies such a decision.

4. Power to extend appropriate period [3a]

(1) On an application being made to them in that behalf, a planning authority shall, as regards a particular permission,[3b] extend the appropriate period, by such additional period as the authority consider requisite to enable the development to which the permission relates to be completed, if, and only if, each of the following requirements is complied with:

   (a) the application is in accordance with such regulations[2a] under this Act as apply to it,

   (b) any requirements of, or made under, such regulations are complied with as regards the application, and

   (c) the authority are satisfied in relation to the permission that –

       (i)   the development to which such permission relates commenced before the expiration of the appropriate period sought to be extended, and

       (ii) substantial works[3c] were carried out pursuant to such permission during such period, and

       (iii) the development will be completed within a reasonable time.

(2) Where –

   (a) an application is duly made under this section to a planning authority,

   (b) any requirements of, or made under, regulations under section 11 of this Act are complied with as regards the application, and

(c) the planning authority do not give notice to the applicant of their decision as regards the application within the period of two months beginning on –

    (i) in case all the aforesaid requirements referred to in paragraph (b) of this subsection are complied with on or before the day of receipt by the planning authority of the application, that day, and

    (ii) in any other case, the day on which all of the said requirements stand complied with,

subject to section 10(2) of this Act, a decision by the planning authority to extend, or to further extend, as may be appropriate, the period, which in relation to the relevant permission is the appropriate period, by such additional period as is specified in the application shall be regarded as having been given by the planning authority on the last day of the said two month period.

(3) (a) Where a decision to extend an appropriate period is given under subsection (1) of this section, or, pursuant to subsection (2) of this section, such a decision is to be regarded as having been given, the planning authority shall not further extend the appropriate period, unless each of the following requirements is complied with:

    (i) an application in that behalf is made to them in accordance with such regulations[2b] under this Act as apply to it,

    (ii) any requirements of, or made under, such regulations are complied with as regards the application, and

    (iii) the authority are satisfied that the relevant development has not been completed due to circumstances beyond the control of the person carrying out the development.

(b) An appropriate period shall be further extended under this subsection only for such period as the relevant planning authority consider requisite to enable the relevant development to be completed.

(4) Particulars of any application made to a planning authority under this section and of the decision of the planning authority in respect of such application shall be recorded on the relevant entry in the register.

(5) Where a decision to extend, or to further extend, is given under this section, or pursuant to subsection (2) of this section, such a decision is to be regarded as having been given, section 2 of this Act shall, in relation to the permission to which the decision relates, be construed and have effect subject to and in accordance with the terms of the decision.

(6) This section shall not be construed as precluding the extension, or the further extension, of an appropriate period by reason of the fact that the period has expired.   **[131]**

---

2 Cross References

a   These regulations are contained in LG(PD)R 1994 (SI 86/1994), Part VI.

b   These regulations are contained in LG(PD)R 1994 (SI 86/1994), Part VI.

3 Notes

a This is an important power which planning authorities might be advised by the Minister (under the power conferred on him by LG(PD)A 82, s 7(1)) to exercise in appropriate cases. Applications for large scale developments of an ongoing nature such as mining or quarrying are cases in point. It will usually be uneconomic for a quarry operator to borrow or provide the high level of capital needed if the life of the quarry is to be limited to 5 years. A finance house is unlikely to lend unless the planning permission clearly authorises the operation to continue for the necessary 15 or 20 years. An applicant should not be put to the expense, doubt or delay of an appeal if there is no good reason for limiting the grant to 5 years. The application should specify the desired period and support the period with reasons.

b In *Garden Village Construction Co Ltd v Wicklow County Council* Supreme Court, unrep, 28 July 1994 it was held that the works must be referrable to the permission sought to be extended, works necessary to facilitate the permission to be extended but not carried out pursuant to that permission could not amount to substantial works. See also *State (McCoy) v Dun Laoghaire Corporation* High Court, unrep, 1 June 1984.

c See *Frenchurch Properties Ltd v Wexford County Council* [1991] ILRM 769 for "substantial works", see also *Garden Village Construction Co Ltd v Wicklow County Council*, High Court unrep, 1 October 1993, and Supreme Court, unrep, 28 July 1994.

4 Commentary

The life of a permission can be extended if substantial works pursuant to that permission have been carried out within the life of the permission and the development will be completed within a reasonable time. The application for such an extension cannot be made earlier than one year before the permission expires but it would seem that an application can be made at any time after the expiry of the permission. The critical issue in s 4 is what will be considered "substantial works" for the purposes of the section. It has been held that a planning authority must use its own expertise and judgment to determine whether substantial works have been carried out pursuant to a particular permission. Substantial works should be given the meaning that it has in ordinary English, ie the opposite of insubstantial and it is wholly inappropriate to apply some mathematical formula to either the quality of work or expenditure.

Once a valid application is made the planning authority must determine it within a period of two months from that date and an extension of time will be deemed to be given by default in the event that a decision is not made within the appropriate period or is not communicated to the applicant within that period. There is no provision for an appeal against the decision of a planning authority to refuse to extend the period but such decisions are susceptible to judicial review and the leading cases on this section are *Frenchurch Properties Ltd v Wexford County Council* [1991] ILRM 769; *Garden Village Construction Co Ltd v Wicklow County Council* (HC, unrep, 1 October 1993, SC, unrep, 28 July 1994); *The State (McCoy) v Corporation of Dun Laoghaire* (HC, unrep 1 June 1984) and *Littondale Ltd v Wicklow County Council* [1996] 2 ILRM 519.

---

5. [Power to declare references, appeals and applications withdrawn]¹ᵃ

[132]

---

1 Amendments

a Section 5 was repealed by LG(PD)A 1992, s 22.

---

6. Validity of certain permissions and approvals ³ᵃ

(1) A permission or approval granted on appeal under Part IV of the Principal Act prior to the 15th day of March, 1977, shall not be, and shall not be regarded as ever having

been, invalid by reason only of the fact that the development concerned contravened, or would contravene, materially the development plan relating to the area of the planning authority to whose decision the appeal related.

(2) If, because of any or all of its provisions, subsection (1) of this section, would, but for this subsection, conflict with a constitutional right of any person, the provisions of that subsection shall be subject to such limitation as is necessary to secure that they do not so conflict but shall be otherwise of full force and effect.   **[133]**

---

3 Notes

a   Section 6 was enacted following the decision of the Supreme Court in *State (Pine Valley Developments) v Dublin County Council* [1984] IR 407, [1982] ILRM 169 which declared that the Minister did not have the power to grant planning permission for a development which contravened the development plan as it only applies to decisions made by the Minister in applications before 15 March 1977. The section is now of little relevance.

---

7.   General policy directives as to planning and development[3a]

(1) The Minister shall, from time to time, issue such general directives as to policy in relation to planning and development as he considers necessary.

(2) A planning authority and the Board shall in performing its functions have regard to any directive under this section.

(3) Nothing in this section shall be construed as enabling the Minister to exercise any power or control in relation to any particular case with which a planning authority or the Board is or may be concerned.

(4) Where the Minister gives a directive under this section, the following provisions shall apply:

  (a) as soon as may be the Minister shall cause a copy of the directive to be laid before each House of the Oireachtas,

  (b) the directive shall be published in the *Iris Oifigiúil*, and

  (c) the Minister shall cause a copy of the directive to be sent to each planning authority and to the Board.[2a]   **[134]**

---

2 Cross References

a   See now the Local Government (Planning and Development) General Policy Directive (Shopping) 1998 (SI 193/1998) which specifies the policy considerations to which planning authorities and An Bord Pleanála must have regard in performing their functions in relation to specified developments of supermarkets and other retail developments. This replaces a similar directive issued in 1982 and SI 193/1998 came into effect on 10 June 1998.

3 Notes

a   Section 7 replaces LG(PD)A 1976, s 6 (repealed by LG(PD)A 1982, s 15(2)(a)). The important change is that the Minister shall give directions to planning authorities as well as to the Board.

4 Commentary

This section provides that planning authorities and the Board must have regard to any directives issued by the Minister in relation to planning and development matters. It would appear that in any event such authorities must have regard to government policy even if it has not been issued pursuant to s 7, this is borne out in the judgment of the Supreme Court in *Keane v An Bord Pleanála* [1998] 2 ILRM 241 (SC). The phrase "have regard to" is not defined, but it is clear that while the planning authority or the Board would not be bound by the Directive, it could only depart from them where there are substantial grounds for doing so, in this regard see the decision of Blayney J in *Glencar Explorations plc v Mayo County Council* [1993] 2 IR 237.

8. [Alteration of certain penalties under Principal Act of 1976][1a]

[135]

1 Amendments

a   Section 8 was repealed by LG(PD)A 1992, s 22.

9. Certain offences may be tried summarily

(1) A Justice of the District Court shall have jurisdiction to try summarily an offence referred to in [section 20(3) of the Local Government (Planning and Development) Act, 1992, or an offence under the said section 20(3)][1a] if –

(a) the Justice is of opinion that the facts proved or alleged against a defendant charged with such an offence constitute a minor offence fit to be tried summarily,

(b) the Director of Public Prosecutions consents, and

(c) the defendant (on being informed by the Justice of his right to be tried by a jury) does not object to being tried summarily,

and, upon conviction under this subsection, the said defendant shall be liable -

(i) in case he is convicted of an offence so referred to, to a fine not exceeding [£1,000,][1b] or, at the discretion of the court, to imprisonment for a term not exceeding six months, or to both the fine and the imprisonment,

(ii) [in case he is convicted of an offence under the said section 20(3), to a fine not exceeding £200 or, at the discretion of the court, to imprisonment for a term not exceeding six months, or to both the fine and the imprisonment:

Provided that if a person is convicted in the same proceedings of two or more offences under the said section 20(3) the aggregate term of imprisonment to which he shall be liable shall not exceed six months.][1c]

(2) Section 13 of the Criminal Procedure Act, 1967,[2a] shall apply in relation to an offence referred to in subsection (1) of this section as if, in lieu of the penalties specified in subsection (3) of the said section 13, there were specified therein the penalty provided for by subsection (1) of this section in relation to the offence, and the reference in subsection (2)(a) of the said section 13 to the penalties provided for in the said subsection (3) shall be construed and have effect accordingly.   **[136]**

1 Amendments

a   The words in square brackets were inserted by LG(PD)A 1992, s 20(7)(a).

b   The words in square brackets were inserted by LG(PD)A 1992, s 20(7)(b).

c   The words in square brackets were inserted by LG(PD)A 1992, s 20(7)(c).

2 Cross References

a   Section 13 of the Criminal Procedure Act 1967 deals with the procedure to be followed where an accused pleads guilty to an indictable offence in the District Court.

4 Commentary

Section 9 confers on a District Court judge jurisdiction to try summarily those offences which are indictable under the Planning Acts. The normal rules in such cases apply, ie that it must be considered by the District Judge that the offence is a minor one, the Director of Public Prosecutions must consent and the defendant must not object to being tried summarily. In the event that any of these requirements are not complied with, the defendant has a right to proceed for trial by jury but if he choses this route he risks a higher fine and/or longer term of imprisonment.

---

10. Fees

(1) The Minister may, with the consent of the Minister for Finance, make regulations providing for –

    (a) the payment to planning authorities of prescribed fees in relation to applications for –

        (i)   permission under Part IV of the Principal Act,

        (ii) approvals required by permission regulations,

        (iii) approvals required to be obtained under a condition subject to which a permission or approval is granted under the Principal Act, or

        (iv) extensions or further extensions under section 4 of this Act,

    (b) the payment to the Board of prescribed fees in relation to appeals or references to, or determinations by, the Board,

and the regulations may provide for the payment of different fees in relation to cases of different classes or descriptions, for exemption from the payment of fees in specified circumstances, for the waiver, remission or refund (in whole or in part) of fees in specified circumstances and for the manner in which fees are to be disposed of. [2a]

(2) Where under regulations under this section a fee is payable to a planning authority by an applicant in respect of an application referred to in subsection (1)(a) of this section, the following provisions shall have effect:

    (a) the application shall not be decided by the authority unless the authority is in receipt of the fee, and

    (b) notwithstanding anything contained in section 26(4) or 27(3) of the Principal Act or in section 4(2) of this Act, a decision of a planning authority shall not be regarded, pursuant to any of those sections, as having been given on a day which is earlier than that which is two months after the day on which the authority is in receipt of the fee, and the said sections 26(4), 27(3) and 4(2) shall be construed subject to and in accordance with the provisions of this paragraph.

(3) ...[1a]

(4) Where under regulations under this section a fee is payable either to a planning authority or to the Board and the person by whom the fee is payable is not [2b] –

    (a) the applicant for a permission, approval or licence, or

(b) an appellant to the Board, or

(c) the person making a reference to, or a request for a determination by, the Board,

submissions or observations made, as regards the relevant application, appeal, reference or determination, by or on behalf of the person by whom such fee is payable, shall not be considered by the planning authority or the Board, as may be appropriate, if the fee has not been received by the authority or the Board.

(5) Where under regulations under this section a fee is payable to the Board by a person making a reference to, or a request for a determination by, the Board, the relevant question or matter shall not be decided or determined by the Board unless the fee is received by the Board.

(6) ...[1b]

(7) ...[1c]   **[137]**

---

1 Amendments

a   Subsection (3) was repealed by LG(PD)A 1992, s 22.

b   Subsection (6) was repealed by LG(PD)A 1992, s 22.

c   Subsection (7) was repealed by LG(PD)A 1992, s 22.

2 Cross References

a   See LG(PD)R 1994 (SI 86/1994).

b   For fees payable to the Board, see *Maher v An Bord Pleanála* High Court, unrep 10 April 1992.

4 Commentary

Section 10 provides that regulations may be made requiring the payment of fees to lodge planning applications or for the making of appeals to An Bord Pleanála. The fees payable are set out in the LG(PD)R 1994, Fourth Schedule. Section 10 provides that an application is not valid unless the correct fee is paid, the planning authority may not determine an application unless the correct fee is paid and no permission can be deemed to be granted by default until two months after the correct fee has been paid.

---

11. Regulations

(1) The Minister may make regulations[2a] providing for any matter of procedure in relation to applications under section 4 of this Act and making such incidental, consequential or supplementary provision as may appear to him to be necessary or proper to give full effect to any of the provisions of sections 2, 3 or 4 of this Act.

(2) In particular and without prejudice to the generality of subsection (1) of this section, regulations under this section may –

(a) specify the time at which applications under section 4 of this Act may be made, the manner in which such applications shall be made and the particulars they shall contain,

(b) require applicants to furnish to the planning authority any specified information with respect to their applications (including any information regarding any estate or interest in or right over land),

(c) require applicants to submit to a planning authority any further information relative to their applications (including any information as to any such estate, interest or right),

(d) require the production of any evidence to verify any particulars or information given by the applicant,

(e) require the notification (in a prescribed manner) by planning authorities of decisions on such applications.   **[138]**

2 Cross References

a   These are contained in LG(PD)R 1994 (SI 86/1994); the application may be brought within one year of the date of expiration of the "appropriate period" but not earlier and this has been clarified in art 80 of the Regulations.

12. Amendment of section 8 of Principal Act[3a]

[139]

3 Notes

a   Section 12 amends LG(PD)A 1963, s 8(4). See the amended Act.

13. Amendment of section 80 of Principal Act[3a]

[140]

3 Notes

a   Section 13 amends LG(PD)A 1963, s 80. See the amended Act.

14. Savers

(1) Neither section 15 nor the proviso to section 2(5) of this Act shall be construed as affecting the exercise by the Circuit Court or the Board, in relation to any application referred to in section 15(4)(b) of this Act, of any power conferred on it by section 29 of the Act of 1976.

(2) Where before the commencement of this section an application was made to a planning authority for a permission or for an approval, a decision of the authority as regards the application shall not, by reason only of the enactment of section 2 of this Act, be regarded, pursuant to section 26(4) or 27(3) of the Principal Act, as having been given.   **[141]**

15. Repeals

(1) In subsection (3) of section 24 of the Principal Act all the words between "guilty of an offence" and the end of the subsection are hereby repealed.

(2) Subject to subsection (3) of this section, the following provisions of the Act of 1976 are hereby repealed:

(a) sections 6, 15(1), 26(5) and 38,

(b) subsections (1), (2), (3), (4), (7) and (9) of section 29,

(c) "and shall be liable on summary conviction to a fine not exceeding two hundred and fifty pounds" in section 26(4).

(3) This section, in so far as it repeals section 15(1) of the Act of 1976, shall come into operation on such day as the Minister shall fix by order.

(4) Notwithstanding subsection (2) of this section –

(a) any waiver notice or any development certificate shall continue in force and to have effect,

(b) a planning authority may after the commencement of this section issue a waiver notice or a development certificate if, but only if, an application made to them in that behalf has been received by them before such commencement.   **[142]**

16. Short title, collective citation and construction

(1) This Act may be cited as the Local Government (Planning and Development) Act, 1982.

(2) The Local Government (Planning and Development) Acts, 1963 and 1976, and this Act may be cited together as the Local Government (Planning and Development) Acts, 1963 to 1982.

(3) This Act and the Local Government (Planning and Development) Acts, 1963 and 1976, shall be construed together as one Act.   **[143]**

LOCAL GOVERNMENT (PLANNING AND DEVELOPMENT) ACT, 1983

(No. 28 of 1983)

ACTS REFERRED TO

Civil Service Regulations Act, 1957	1956, No. 46
Local Government (Planning and Development) Act, 1963	1963, No. 28
Local Government (Planning and Development) Acts, 1963 to 1982	
Local Government (Planning and Development) Act, 1976	1976, No. 20
European Assembly Elections Act, 1977	1977, No. 30
Local Government (Planning and Development) Act, 1982	1982, No. 21

An Act to amend and extend the Local Government (Planning and Development) Acts, 1963 to 1982. [20 July, 1983]

Be it enacted by the Oireachtas as follows:

1. Definitions

In this Act –

"the Assembly" means the Assembly of the European Communities;

"**the Act of 1977**" means the European Assembly Elections Act, 1977;

"**chairman**" means, save where the context otherwise requires, the chairman of the Board and "**chairmanship**" shall be construed accordingly;

"**deputy chairman**", except in section 8(1) of this Act, means the deputy chairman of the Board and "**deputy chairmanship**" shall be construed accordingly;

"**ordinary member**" means a member of the Board other than the chairman.   **[144]**

2.   Board to continue to be body corporate, etc.

(1) The Board shall continue to be a body corporate with perpetual succession and a seal and power to sue and be sued in its corporate name and to acquire, hold and dispose of land.

(2) The seal of the Board shall be authenticated by the signature of the chairman or of some other member, or of an employee of the Board or of a person whose services are availed of by the Board by virtue of section 21(3) of the Act of 1976, authorised by the Board to act in that behalf.

(3) Judicial notice shall continue to be taken of the seal of the Board and every document purporting to be an instrument made by the Board and to be sealed with the seal (purporting to be authenticated in accordance with subsection (2) of this section) of the Board shall be received in evidence and be deemed to be such instrument without proof unless the contrary is shown.

(4) A person who immediately before the passing of this Act held the office either of chairman or of an ordinary member shall, subject to section 3(2) of the Act of 1976 and to section 10 of this Act, continue to hold that office.   **[145]**

---

4 Commentary

An Bord Pleanála was created by the LG(PD)A 1976 and this section effectively continues the existence of that legal entity.

---

3.   Board to consist of chairman and five other members[1a]

[(1) Subject to subsections (2) and (4) of this section, the Board shall consist of a chairman and five other members.

(2) The Minister may by order increase the number of ordinary members where he or she is of the opinion that the number of appeals, references or other matters with which the Board is concerned is at such a level so as to necessitate the appointment of an additional Board member or members to enable the Board to fulfil its duty and objective under section 2 of the Local Government (Planning and Development) Act, 1992.

(3) Where an order is proposed to be made under subsection (2) of this section, a draft of the order shall be laid before each House of the Oireachtas and the order shall not be made until a resolution approving of the draft has been passed by each such House.

(4) (a)   Notwithstanding subsection (2) of this section or subsection (2) of section 7 of this Act, where the Minister is of the opinion that one or more than one additional ordinary member should be appointed as a matter of urgency due to the number of appeals, references or other matters with which the Board is concerned, the Minister may, pending the making and approval of an order

under subsections (2) and (3) of this section, appoint one or more than one person from among the officers of the Minister who is an established civil servant for the purposes of the Civil Service Regulation Act, 1956 and the employees of the Board, on a temporary basis.

(b) A person shall not be appointed to be an ordinary member under this subsection for a term in excess of nine months.

(5) An order made under subsection (2) of this section shall have effect for such a period not exceeding five years as shall be specified therein.]   **[146]**

---

1 Amendments

a   Section 3 was substituted by LG(PD)A 1998, s 1.

4 Commentary

Section 3 provides that while the Board shall generally consist of a chairman and five other members, the number of Board members may be increased by the Minister from time to time, in particular where such an increase in membership is necessitated by the need to fufil the objectives of the Board to determine all appeals wherever possible within a four month statutory period.

---

4.   General duty of Board

(1) ...[1a, 2a]

(2) The Board may make submissions to the Minister as regards any matter pertaining to its functions.

(3) The Minister may consult with the Board as regards any matter pertaining to the performance of –

(a) the functions of the Board, or

(b) the functions assigned to the Minister by or under the Local Government (Planning and Development) Acts, 1963 to 1983, or by any other enactment or by an order, regulation or other instrument thereunder.

(4) (a) The provisions of subsection (1) of this section are without prejudice to the provisions specified in paragraph (b) of this subsection.

(b) The provisions referred to in paragraph (a) of this subsection are –

(i) the provisions of the Local Government (Planning and Development) Acts, 1963 to 1983, or of any regulations made thereunder which relate to the performance by the Board of its functions,

(ii) the provisions of any other enactment, order, regulation or other instrument thereunder which so relates.

[147]

---

1 Amendments

a   Subsection (1) was repealed by LG(PD)A 1992.

2 Cross references

a   The general duty of the Board with regard to the determination of appeals is now contained in LG(PD)A 1992, s 2.

4 Commentary

Section 4 provides that the Board may make submissions to the Minister with regard to matters pertaining to its functions and the Minister may similarly consult with the Board with regard to its functions but the Minister is precluded from making any direct representations to the Board on any particular matter; see LG(PD)A 1983, s 23.

---

5. Chairman[3a]

(1) The chairman shall be appointed by the Government.

(2) There shall be a committee (in this section subsequently referred to as "the committee") consisting of –

(a) the President of the High Court,

(b) the Chairman of the County Council's General Council,

(c) the Chief Engineering Adviser of the Department of the Environment,

(d) the Chairman of the Council of An Taisce – the National Trust for Ireland,

(e) the President of the Construction Industry Federation, and

(f) the President of the Executive Council of the Irish Congress of Trade Unions.

(3) Where –

(a) any of the persons aforesaid signifies at any time his unwillingness or inability to act for any period as a member of the committee, or

(b) any of the persons aforesaid is through ill-health or otherwise unable to act for any period,

the Minister may, when making a request under subsection (7) of this section, appoint another person to be a member of the committee in his place and such person shall remain a member of the committee until such time as the selection by the committee pursuant to the request is made.

(4) Where the Minister makes a request under subsection (7) of this section and at the time of making the request any of the offices aforesaid is vacant, the Minister may appoint a person to be a member of the committee and such person shall remain a member of the committee until such time as the selection by the committee pursuant to the request is made.

(5) Where pursuant to subsection (3) or (4) of this section the Minister appoints a person to be a member of the committee, he shall, as soon as may be, cause a notice of appointment to be published in the *Iris Oifigiúil*.

(6) (a) The Minister may by order amend subsection (2) of this section.

(b) The Minister may by order amend or revoke an order under this subsection (including an order under this paragraph).

(c) Where an order under this subsection is proposed to be made, the Minister shall cause a draft thereof to be laid before both Houses of the Oireachtas and the order shall not be made until a resolution approving of the draft has been passed by each such House.

(d) Where an order under this subsection is for the time being in force, subsection (2) of this section shall be construed and have effect subject to the terms of the order.

(7) (a) The committee shall, whenever so requested by the Minister, select three candidates, or if in the opinion of the committee there is not a sufficient number of suitable applicants, such lesser number of candidates as the committee shall determine, for appointment to be the chairman and shall inform the Minister of the names of the candidates, or, as may be appropriate, the name of the candidate, selected and of the reasons why, in the opinion of the committee, they are or he is suitable for such appointment.

(b) In selecting candidates the committee shall have regard to the special knowledge and experience and other qualifications or personal qualities which the committee consider appropriate to enable a person effectively to perform the functions of the chairman.

(8) Except in the case of a reappointment under subsection (12) of this section, the Government shall not appoint a person to be the chairman unless the person was amongst those, or, where appropriate, was the candidate, selected by the committee pursuant to a request under subsection (7) of this section in relation to that appointment but –

(a) if the committee is unable to select any suitable candidate pursuant to a particular request under the said subsection (7), or

(b) if the Government decide not to appoint to be chairman any of the candidates, or, where appropriate, the candidate, selected by the committee pursuant to a particular such request,

then either –

(c) the Government shall appoint a person to be the chairman who was amongst those, or, where appropriate, was the candidate, selected by the committee pursuant to a previous such request (if any) in relation to that appointment, or

(d) the Minister shall make a further such request to the committee and the Government shall appoint to be the chairman a person who was amongst those, or, where appropriate, was the candidate, selected by the committee pursuant to that request or pursuant to another such request made in relation to that appointment.

(9) The Minister may make regulations as regards –[2a]

(a) the publication of notice that a request has been received by the committee under subsection (7) of this section,

(b) applications for selection by the committee,

(c) any other matter which the Minister considers expedient for the purposes of this section,

(10) A person who is, for the time being –

(a) entitled under the Standing Orders of either House of the Oireachtas to sit therein,

(b) a representative in the Assembly,

(c) a member of a local authority,

shall be disqualified for being appointed as the chairman.

(11) The chairman shall be appointed in a wholetime capacity and shall not at any time during his term of office hold any other office or employment in respect of which emoluments are payable.

(12) Subject to the provisions of this section, the chairman shall hold office for a term of seven years and may be reappointed by the Government for a second or subsequent term of office: Provided that a person shall not be reappointed under this subsection unless, at the time of his reappointment, he is or was the outgoing chairman of the Board.

(13)(a) The chairman may resign his chairmanship by letter addressed to the Minister and the resignation shall take effect as on and from the date of the receipt of the letter by the Minister.

   (b) The chairman shall vacate the office of chairman on attaining the age of sixty-five years.

   (c) A person shall ceased to be the chairman if he –

   (i) is nominated either as a member of the Seanad Éireann or for election to either House of the Oireachtas,

   (ii) is either nominated for election to the Assembly or appointed under section 15 of the Act of 1977 to be a representative in the Assembly,

   (iii) becomes a member of a local authority.

(14)(a) There shall be paid by the Board to the chairman the same salary as is paid to a judge of the High Court.

   (b) Subject to the provisions of this section, the chairman shall hold office on such terms and conditions (including terms relating to allowances for expenses) as the Minister, with the consent of the Minister for the Public Service, determines.

(15) The chairman may be removed from office by the Government if he has become incapable through ill-health of effectively performing his duties, or if he has committed stated misbehaviour, or if his removal appears to the Government to be necessary for the effective performance by the Board of its functions, and in case the chairman is removed from office under this subsection, the Government shall cause to be laid before each House of the Oireachtas a statement in writing of the reasons for the removal.   **[148]**

---

2 Cross References

a   See LG(PD)R 1994 (SI 86/1994), arts 137–144.

3 Notes

a   See *Keane v An Bord Pleanála* High Court, unrep, 4 October 1995 (Murphy J) for a discussion of whether the former chairman of An Bord Pleanála was a competent witness at an oral hearing.

4 Commentary

The chairman of the Board exercises important functions with regard to the efficient discharge of the business of the Board and the dispersion of work among the Board members. A committee set up in accordance with sub-s (2) selects three candidates for the position, one of whom is then chosen by the government to be the chairman. The chairman can only be removed from office by the government in accordance with sub-s (15).

---

6.   Chairman to ensure efficient discharge of business of Board, etc.

(1) It shall be the function of the chairman, or where he is not available or where the office of chairman is vacant, of the deputy chairman –

   (a) to ensure the efficient discharge of the business of the Board, and

   (b) to arrange the distribution of the business of the Board among its members.

(2) Where the chairman is of opinion that the conduct of an ordinary member has been such as to bring the Board into disrepute or has been prejudicial to the effective performance by the Board of all or any one or more of its functions, he may in his absolute discretion –

  (a) require the member of the Board to attend for interview and there interview the member privately and inform him of such opinion, or

  (b) where he considers it appropriate to do so, otherwise investigate the matter and, if he considers it appropriate so to do, report to the Minister the result of the investigation.

[149]

---

4 Commentary

Section 6 sets out the functions of the chairman with regard to the Board.

---

7.   Ordinary members

(1) The Minister may prescribe –

  (a) for the purposes of paragraph (a) of subsection (2) of this section any two or more organisations which in his opinion are representative of persons whose professions or occupations relate to physical planning and development,

  (b) for the purposes of paragraph (b) of the said subsection (2) any two or more organisations which in his opinion are representative of persons concerned with the protection and preservation of the environment and of amenities,

  (c) for the purposes of paragraph (c) of the said subsection (2) any two or more organisations which in his opinion are concerned with the promotion of economic or other development or are representative of either or both of the following, namely, persons carrying on the business of developing land or persons employed or engaged in or otherwise connected with the construction industry,

  (d) for the purposes of paragraph (d) of the said subsection (2) any two or more organisations which in his opinion are, in relation to the community, concerned with the promotion of social, economic or general interests.

(2) Subject to section 12(4) of this Act, the ordinary members shall be appointed by the Minister as follows:

  (a) one shall be so appointed from among persons selected by organisations which for the time being stand prescribed for the purposes of this paragraph by the Minister;[2a]

  (b) one shall be so appointed from among persons selected by organisations which for the time being stand prescribed for the purposes of this paragraph by the Minister; [2b]

  (c) one shall be so appointed from among persons selected by organisations which for the time being stand prescribed for the purposes of this paragraph by the Minister; [2c]

(d) one shall be so appointed from among persons selected by organisations which for the time being stand prescribed for the purposes of this paragraph by the Minister; [2d]

(e) one shall be so appointed from among the officers of the Minister who are established civil servants for the purposes of the Civil Service Regulation Act, 1956.

[(2A) Where the Minister decides to appoint an additional member or members to the Board pursuant to an order under section 3(2) of this Act (as inserted by section 1 of the Local Government (Planning and Development) Act, 1998) that member or those members shall be appointed from among persons selected by the organisations which for the time being stand prescribed for the purposes of paragraphs (a), (b), (c) and (d) of subsection (2) of this section: provided that –

(a) where not more than four additional members are appointed pursuant to an order under section 3(2) of this Act, not more than one shall be appointed from among persons selected by organisations which for the time being stand prescribed for the purposes of a particular paragraph of subsection (2) of this section;

(b) where more than four but not more than eight additional members are appointed pursuant to an order under section 3(2) of this Act, not more than two shall be appointed from among persons selected by organisations which for the time being stand prescribed for the purposes of a particular paragraph of subsection (2) of this section.][1a]

(3) An organisation prescribed for the purposes of paragraph (a), (b), (c) or (d) of subsection (2) of this section shall, whenever so requested by the Minister, select such number of candidates (not being less than two) as the Minister may specify for appointment as an ordinary member and shall inform the minister of the names of the candidates selected and of the reasons why, in the opinion of the organisation, they are suitable for such appointment. [2e]

(4) Except in the case of an appointment pursuant to paragraph (e) of subsection (2) of this section or of a reappointment under subsection (9) of this section and subject to section 12(4) of this Act, the Minister shall not appoint a person to be an ordinary member unless the person was amongst those selected pursuant to a request under subsection (3) of this section in relation to that appointment, but –

(a) if all of the appropriate organisations refuse or fail to select any candidate pursuant to a particular request under the said subsection (3), or

(b) if the Minister decides not to appoint as an ordinary member any of the candidates selected by such organisations pursuant to a particular request under that subsection,

then either –

(c) the Minister shall appoint as an ordinary member a person who was amongst those selected by such an organisation pursuant to a previous request (if any) under that subsection in relation to that appointment, or

(d) the Minister shall make a further such request and shall appoint as an ordinary member a person who was amongst those selected pursuant to that request or pursuant to another such request made in relation to that appointment.

(5) Where a request is made pursuant to subsection (3) of this section, failure or refusal by the organisation of whom the request is made to select the number of candidates specified in the request shall not preclude the appointment as an ordinary member of a person who was selected in relation to that appointment either by the aforesaid organisation or by any other organisation.

(6) The Minister may make regulations as regards –

    (a) the period within which the Minister is to be informed in accordance with subsection (3) of this section,

    (b) any other matter which the Minister considers expedient for the purposes of this section.

(7) A person who is for the time being –

    (a) entitled under the Standing Orders of either House of the Oireachtas to sit therein,

    (b) a representative in the Assembly,

    (c) a member of a local authority,

shall be disqualified for being appointed to be an ordinary member.

(8) Each of the ordinary members shall be appointed in a wholetime capacity and shall not at any time during his term of office hold any other office or employment in respect of which emoluments are payable.

(9) Subject to the provisions of section 12(4)(b) of this Act, an ordinary member shall hold office for such term (not exceeding five years) as shall be specified by the Minister when appointing him to office and may be reappointed by the Minister for a second or subsequent term of office: Provided that a person shall not be reappointed under this subsection unless, at the time of his reappointment, he is or was an outgoing member of the Board.

(10)(a) An ordinary member may resign his membership by letter addressed to the Minister and the resignation shall take effect as on and from the date of the receipt of the letter by the Minister.

    (b) A person shall vacate the office of ordinary member on attaining the age of sixty-five years.

    (c) A person shall cease to be an ordinary member if he –

        (i) is nominated either as a member of Seanad Éireann or for election to either House of the Oireachtas,

        (ii) is either nominated for election to the Assembly or appointed under section 15 of the Act of 1977 to be a representative in the Assembly,

        (iii) becomes a member of a local authority.

(11)(a) There shall be paid by the Board to each ordinary member such remuneration and allowances for expenses as the Minister, with the consent of the Minister for the Public Service, determines.

    (b) Subject to the provisions of this section, an ordinary member shall hold office on such terms and conditions as the Minister, with the consent of the Minister for the Public Service, determines.

(12) An ordinary member may be removed from office by the Minister if he has become incapable through ill-health of effectively performing his duties, or if he has committed

stated misbehaviour, or if his removal appears to the Minister to be necessary for the effective performance by the Board of its functions, and in case an ordinary member is removed from office under this subsection, the Minister shall cause to be laid before each House of the Oireachtas a statement in writing of the reasons for the removal.**[150]**

---

1 Amendments

a   Subsection (2A) was inserted by LG(PD)A 1998, s 1.

2 Cross References

a   See LG(PD)R 1994 (SI 86/1994), art 145.

b   See LG(PD)R 1994 (SI 86/1994), art 146.

c   See LG(PD)R 1994 (SI 86/1994), art 147.

d   See LG(PD)R 1994 (SI 86/1994), art 148.

e   See LG(PD)R 1994, art 149.

4 Commentary

Section 7 sets out the qualifications and selection procedure for the other members of the Board. The particular organisations that may recommend members for appointment to the Board are set out in LG(PD)R 1994, arts 145-149 and relate to those organisations which are involved in construction activities, the protection of the environment or the design and supervision of building projects.

The position with regard to the deputy chairman of the Board is likely to be more significant having regard to the increase in the members of the Board provided for under the LG(PD)A 1998.

---

8.   Deputy chairman of Board

(1) The Minister shall appoint from amongst the ordinary members a person to be the deputy chairman of the Board and such appointment shall be for such period as shall be specified in the appointment.

(2) If at any time the deputy chairman ceases to be an ordinary member of the board, he shall thereupon cease to be deputy chairman.

(3) The deputy chairman shall, in addition to his remuneration as an ordinary member, be paid by the Board such additional remuneration (if any) as the Minister, with the consent of the Minister for the Public Service, determines.

(4) The deputy chairman may resign his deputy chairmanship by letter addressed to the Minister and the resignation shall take effect as on and from the date of the receipt of the letter by the Minister.   **[151]**

9.   Superannuation of members of Board[2a]

(1) The Minister may with the concurrence of the Minister of the Public Service –

   (a) make a scheme or schemes for the granting of pensions, gratuities or other allowances to or in respect of the chairman and ordinary members ceasing to hold office,

   (b) make a scheme or schemes for the granting of gratuities to or in respect of persons ceasing to hold office by virtue of section 10 of this Act.

(2) A scheme under this section may provide that the termination of the appointment of the chairman or of an ordinary member during that person's term of office shall not preclude the award to him under the scheme of a pension, gratuity or other allowance.

(3) The Minister may, with the concurrence of the Minister for the Public Service, amend a scheme made by him under this section.

(4) If any dispute arises as to the claim of any person to, or the amount of, any pension, gratuity, or allowance payable in pursuance of a scheme under this section, such dispute shall be submitted to the Minister who shall refer it to the Minister for the Public Service, whose decision shall be final.

(5) A scheme under this section shall be carried out by the Board in accordance with its terms.

(6) No pension, gratuity or other allowance shall be granted by the Board to or in respect of any person referred to in subsection (1) of this section ceasing to hold office otherwise than in accordance with a scheme under this section.

(7) Notwithstanding section 25 of this Act, the scheme made by the Minister under Article 28 of the Schedule to the Act of 1976, shall continue in force and may be amended as if made under this section.

(8) Every scheme made under this section shall be laid before each House of the Oireachtas as soon as may be after it is made and if either such House, within the next twenty-one days on which that House has sat after the scheme is laid before it, passes a resolution annulling the scheme, the scheme shall be annulled accordingly, but without prejudice to the validity of anything previously done thereunder.   **[152]**

---

2 Cross References

a   See also LG(PD)A 1976, s 11 in respect of superannuation of employees of the Board.

---

10. Cesser of office

(1) The person who, immediately before the commencement of this subsection, held the office of chairman of the Board, shall, on such commencement, cease to be chairman.

(2) Every person who, immediately before the commencement of this subsection was an ordinary member of the Board, shall, on such commencement, cease to be such ordinary member.   **[153]**

11. Meetings and procedure of Board

(1) The Board shall hold such and so many meetings as may be necessary for the performance of its functions.

(2) The chairman and each ordinary member at a meeting of the Board shall have a vote.

(3) At a meeting of the Board –

   (a)   the chairman shall, if present, be chairman of the meeting,

   (b)   if and for so long as the chairman is not present, or if the office of chairman is vacant, the deputy chairman shall, if present, be chairman of the meeting,

   (c)   if and for so long as neither the chairman nor the deputy chairman is present, or if the chairman is not present or if the office of chairman is vacant, and in either case, the office of deputy chairman is vacant, the ordinary members who are present shall choose one of their number to be chairman of the meeting.

(4) Every question at a meeting of the Board shall be determined by a majority of votes of the members present and, in the event that voting is equally divided, the person who is chairman of the meeting shall have a casting vote.

(5) (a) Subject to the Local Government (Planning and Development) Acts, 1963 to 1983, and to any regulations made thereunder, and subject also to any other enactment or order, regulation or other instrument thereunder, which regulates or otherwise affects the procedure of the Board, the Board shall regulate its own procedure and business.

(b) The Minister may require the Board to keep him informed of the arrangements made under this subsection for the regulation of its procedure and business.

(6) (a) Subject to paragraphs (b) and (c) of this subsection, the Board may perform or exercise any of its functions through or by any member of the Board or other person who, in either case, has been duly authorised by the Board in that behalf.

(b) Paragraph (a) of this subsection shall be construed as enabling a member of the Board finally to determine a particular case if, and only if, the case to which an authorisation under that paragraph relates has been considered at a meeting of the Board prior to the giving of the authorisation.

(c) Paragraph (a) of this subsection shall not be construed as enabling the Board to authorise a person who is not a member of the Board finally to determine any particular case with which the Board is concerned.   **[154]**

---

4 Commentary

Section 11 sets out the procedures for the determination of appeals. Generally it would appear that when an appeal is lodged the file is assigned to an inspector appointed by the Board who, having inspected the site, prepares a report and a recommendation for the Board. This file has been assigned to a particular Board member who reports to the Board which ultimately determines the matter. The Board is given a discretion as to how its business is to be regulated so that effectively the chairman of the Board determines procedures. The quorum for a meeting is three so that it is possible that with a nine member Board there could be three seperate Boards hearing and determining appeals at the same time. There is no requirement for the chairman or deputy chairman to be present as any three members of the Board who sit together can decide among themselves who will be chairman for the purposes of that meeting.

---

12. Board's quorum, vacancies, etc.

(1) The quorum for a meeting of the Board shall be three.

(2) Subject to subsection (1) of this section, the Board may act notwithstanding a vacancy in the chairmanship, the deputy chairmanship or among the ordinary members.

(3) Where a vacancy occurs in the chairmanship, deputy chairmanship or among the ordinary members, the Minister shall, as soon as may be, take steps to fill the vacancy.

(4) (a) Where, owing to the illness of the chairman or of an ordinary member, or for any other reason, a sufficient number of members of the Board is not available to enable the Board effectively to perform its functions, the Minister may, as an interim measure, appoint from among the officers referred to in section 7(2)(e) of this Act, one or more persons to be an ordinary member.

(b) A person shall not be appointed to be an ordinary member under this subsection for a term in excess of twelve months. **[155]**

13. Prohibition on disclosure of information

(1) No person shall, without the consent of the Board (which may be given to the person, subject to or without conditions, as regards any information, as regards particular information or as regards information of a particular class or description) disclose –

(a) any information obtained by him while serving as a member or employee of, or consultant or adviser to, the Board or as a person whose services are availed of by the Board by virtue of section 21(3) of the Act of 1976,

(b) any information so obtained relative to the business of the Board or to the performance of its functions.

(2) A person who contravenes subsection (1) of this section shall be guilty of an offence and shall be liable on summary conviction to a fine not exceeding [£1,000]. [1a]

(3) Nothing in subsection (1) of this section shall prevent –

(a) disclosure of information in a report made to the Board or in a report made by or on behalf of the Board to the Minister,

(b) disclosure of information by any person in the course of and in accordance with the duties of his office. **[156]**

---

1 Amendments

a "£1000" was substituted for "£800" by LG(PD)A 1992, s 20(8).

4 Commentary

This is a general restriction on information being given without the consent of the Board but this provision is somewhat limited in importance given the general requirements of access to information and access to environmental information which is now enshrined in European law and binds the Board as an emanation of the State.

---

14. Prohibition of certain communications in relation to appeals, etc.

(1) It shall not be lawful to communicate with the chairman or with an ordinary member for the purpose of influencing improperly his consideration of an appeal, reference, or other matter with which the Board is concerned or a decision of the Board as regards any such matter.

(2) If the chairman or an ordinary member becomes of opinion that a communication is in contravention of subsection (1) of this section, it shall be his duty not to entertain the communication further. **[157]**

15. [Oral hearings][1a]

[158]

---

1 Amendments

a Section 15 was repealed by LG(PD)A 1992, s 22.

---

16. [Board may dismiss appeals under section 26 of Principal Act if vexatious, etc.][1a]

[159]

1 Amendments

a   Section 16 was repealed by LG(PD)A 1992, s 22.

17. [Notice requiring statement of grounds of appeal][1a]

[160]

1 Amendments

a   Section 17 was repealed by LG(PD)A 1992, s 22.

18. [Power of Board regarding delays by parties etc., to appeals][1a]

[161]

1 Amendments

a   Section 18 was repealed by LG(PD)A 1992, s 22.

19. [Appeals against conditions[1a]]

[162]

1 Amendments

a   Section 19 was repealed by LG(PD)A 1992, s 22.

20. Amendment of section 26 of Principal Act[3a]

[163]

3 Notes

a   Section 20 was repealed by LG(PD)A 1992, s 22.

21. Amendment of sections 10 and 19 of Act of 1976[3a]

[164]

3 Notes

a   Section 21 amends LG(PD)A 1976, ss 10 and 19. Section 19 was repealed by LG(PD)A 1992, s 22. See the amended Act.

22. Construction

(1) Section 26(5)(b) of the Principal Act, as amended by section 14(9) of the Act of 1976, shall be construed and have effect subject to sections 16, 18 and 19 of this Act, and the provisions relating to appeals to the Board of the Local Government (Planning and Development) Acts, 1963 to 1982, shall be construed and have effect subject to section 17 of this Act.[3a]

(2) Nothing in section 17 or 18 of this Act shall be construed as affecting any power conferred on the Board by or under any enactment other than those sections.   **[165]**

---

3 Notes

a   Sections 16, 17, 18 and 19 of LG(PD)A 1963 to which this section refers have been repealed by LG(PD)A 1992, s 22.

---

23. Restriction

(1) Nothing in this Act shall be construed as enabling the Minister to exercise any power or control in relation to any particular case with which the Board is or may be concerned.

(2) The reference to this Act in subsection (1) of this section shall not be construed as including a reference to section 7 of the Local Government (Planning and Development) Act, 1982.[2a]   **[166]**

---

2 Cross References

a   Section 7 of LG(PD)A 1982 empowers the Minister to issue directives to which planning authorities and An Bord Pleanála are bound to have regard.

---

24. Saver

Nothing in this Act shall be construed as interrupting or otherwise affecting the continued existence of the Board or the performance by it of any of its functions.   **[167]**

25. Repeals

The following provisions of the Act of 1976 are hereby repealed, namely, s 3(2), 4, 16, 18(1), 18(2), 31 and the Schedule.   **[168]**

26. Short title, collective citation, commencement and construction

(1) This Act may be cited as the Local Government (Planning and Development) Act, 1983.

(2) The Local Government (Planning and Development) Acts, 1963 to 1982, and this Act may be cited together as the Local Government (Planning and Development) Acts, 1963 to 1983.

(3) This Act shall come into operation on such day or days as the Minister may fix by order, either generally or with reference to any particular purpose or provision, and different days may be so fixed for different purposes and different provisions of this Act.

(4) This Act and the Local Government (Planning and Development) Acts, 1963 to 1982, shall be construed together as one Act.   **[169]**

Local Government (Planning and Development) Act, 1990

(No. 11 of 1990)

Part I

Preliminary

Part II

Compensation Generally

Part III

Compensation in Relation to Decisions under Part IV of Principal Act

Part IV

Compensation in Relation to Sections 36, 37, 44, 45, 48, 83 and 85 of Principal Act

Part V

CONNECTION OF PREMISES TO PUBLIC SEWERS AND WATER SUPPLIES

First Schedule

RULES FOR THE DETERMINATION OF THE AMOUNT OF COMPENSATION

Second Schedule

DEVELOPMENT IN RESPECT OF WHICH A REFUSAL OF PERMISSION WILL NOT ATTRACT COMPENSATION

Third Schedule

REASONS FOR THE REFUSAL OF PERMISSION WHICH EXCLUDE COMPENSATION

Fourth Schedule

CONDITIONS WHICH MAY BE IMPOSED ON THE GRANTING OF PERMISSION TO DEVELOP LAND, WITHOUT COMPENSATION

ACTS REFERRED TO

Acquisition of Land (Assessment of Compensation) Act, 19191919, c. 57	
Companies Act, 1963	1963, No. 33
Harbours Act, 1946	1946, No. 9
Health Act, 1970	1970, No. 1
Housing of the Working Classes Act, 18901890, c. 70	
Lands Clauses Consolidation Act, 1845	1845, c.18
Local Government Act, 1941	1941, No. 23
Local Government (Planning and Development) Act, 1963	1963, No. 28
Local Government (Planning and Development) Act, 1976	1976, No. 20
Local Government (Roads and Motorways) Act, 1974	1974, No. 6
Local Government (Sanitary Services) Act, 1962	1962, No. 26
National Monuments (Amendment) Act, 1987	1987, No. 17
Public Health Acts Amendment Act, 1890	1890, c. 59
Public Health (Ireland) Act, 1878	1878, c. 52
Vocational Education Act, 1930	1930, No. 29
Waterworks Clauses Act, 1847	1847, c. 17

An Act to amend and extend the Local Government (Planning and Development) Acts, 1963 to 1983, and, for the purposes of those Acts, to amend certain provisions of the Waterworks Clauses Act, 1847, the Public Health (Ireland) Act, 1878 and related enactments.[10th June, 1990]

Be it enacted by the Oireachtas as follows:

Part I

PRELIMINARY

1. Short title, collective citation and construction

(1) This Act may be cited as the Local Government (Planning and Development) Act, 1990.[3a]

(2) The Local Government (Planning and Development) Acts, 1963 to 1983, and this Act may be cited together as the Local Government (Planning and Development) Acts, 1963 to 1990.

(3) This Act and the Local Government (Planning and Development) Acts, 1963 to 1983, shall be construed together as one Act.   **[170]**

---

4 Commentary

This Act repeals the previous provisions of the LG(PD)A 1963 which dealt with compensation. The Planning Acts limit how lands may be developed and inevitably such restrictions reduce the value of land as opposed to a system which does not provide for controls on how land might be developed. On the other hand, a grant of permission inevitably increases the value of land. The constitutionality of these provisions was considered in *Central Dublin Development Association v The Attorney General* 109 ILTR 69 and they were found to be constitutional. However the constitutionality of the Planning Acts has never been considered by the Supreme Court and it must be noted that the *Central Dublin Development Association* case dealt with the provisions of LG(PD)A 1963 which have been made considerably more restrictive by subsequent amendments, in particular by the provisions of LG(PD)A 1990 which relate to compensation.

Furthermore, it was a central finding of the *Central Dublin Development Association* decision that the Rent Restriction Acts were constitutional but subsequently the Supreme Court declared them not to be in accordance with the Constitution and this must leave at least some question mark over the constitutionality of the Planning Acts.

---

2. Interpretation

(1) In this Act –

"the Board" means An Bord Pleanála;

"habitable house" means a building or part of a building which –

    (a) is used as a dwelling, or

    (b) is not in use but when last used, disregarding any unauthorised use, as a dwelling, or

    (c) was provided for use as a dwelling but has not been occupied;

"the Minister" means the Minister for the Environment;

"the Principal Act" means the Local Government (Planning and Development) Act, 1963.

(2) In this Act unless otherwise indicated, a reference to a section, Schedule or Part is to a section, Schedule or Part of this Act and a reference to a subsection or paragraph is to the subsection or paragraph of the provision in which the reference occurs.

(3) A reference in this Act to any enactment shall be construed as a reference to that enactment as amended or adapted by or under any other enactment.   **[171]**

---

4 Commentary

LG(PD)A 1990 provides a statutory definition of "habitable house". The definition is very broad and would appear to include a derelict structure or indeed a structure long since abandoned for use as a dwelling house.

---

3. Repeals and saver

(1) The following provisions are hereby repealed: section 45(2) and Part VI of the Principal Act and section 24 of the Public Health (Ireland) Act, 1878.

(2) Section 2 of the Acquisition of Land (Assessment of Compensation) Act, 1919, as amended by section 69(1) of the Principal Act shall, notwithstanding the repeal of section 69 of the Principal Act by this Act, apply to every case, other than a case under this Act, where any compensation assessed will be payable by a planning authority or any other local authority.

(3) Section 25(8) of the Local Government (Planning and Development) Act, 1976, is hereby amended by the deletion of the words "and the matter falls to be determined by arbitration in pursuance of section 68 of the Principal Act, the following provisions shall apply:" and the substitution of ", the claim shall, in default of agreement, be determined by arbitration under the Acquisition of Land (Assessment of Compensation) Act, 1919, in the like manner in all respects as if such claim arose in relation to the compulsory acquisition of land, but subject to the proviso that the arbitrator shall have jurisdiction to make a nil award and to the following provisions:".   **[172]**

---

4 Commentary

LG(PD)A 1990 came into force on 10 June 1990. In *Wood v Wicklow County Council* High Court, unrep, 20 July 1994 it was held that the provisions of LG(PD)A 1990 applied even though the repealed provisions of the LG(PD)A 1963 applied when the application was made.

Part II

COMPENSATION GENERALLY

4. Compensation claims: time limits[3a]

A claim for compensation under this Act shall be made not later than six months after –

    (a) in the case of a claim under section 11, the notification of the decision of the planning authority or the Board, as the case may be,

    (b) in the case of a claim under section 17, the time when the notice takes effect,

    (c) in the case of a claim under section 18, the removal or alteration of the structure,

    (d) in the case of a claim under section 19, the discontinuance or compliance,

    (e) in the case of a claim under section 20, the removal or alteration of the hedge,

    (f) in the case of a claim under section 21, the date on which the consent is refused or is granted subject to conditions,

    (g) in the case of a claim under section 22, the time when the order creating the public right of way commences to have effect,

    (h) in the case of a claim under section 23, the time when the damage is suffered, and

    (i) in the case of a claim under section 24, the action of the planning authority.   **[173]**

3 Notes

a   See *Wood v Wicklow County Council* [1995] 1 ILRM 51; *McKone Estates v Kildare County Council* [1984] ILRM 313.

4 Commentary

A general time limit within which a claim must be made is six months from the date of the notification of the decision. The time limit would appear then to run from the date that the decision is received. In the case of s 17, the time limit runs from the date either that the appeal period expires or from the date of the decision of the Board on appeal to uphold the revocation. In the case of s 18, the claim time period runs from the date of the removal or alteration of the structure which would appear to mean from the date that the works are either commenced or completed and similarly the time limits in s 20 are not clear.

In any event, there is a period for this time limit to be extended and furthermore an invalid claim is not a bar to proceeding as the local authority is required to indicate any deficiencies in the notice and require a claimant to amend the claim accordingly.

5.   Determination of compensation claim

A claim for compensation under this Act shall, in default of agreement, be determined by arbitration under the Acquisition of Land (Assessment of Compensation) Act, 1919, but subject to –

(a)   the First Schedule in respect of a reduction in the value of an interest in land,

(b)   the proviso that the arbitrator shall have jurisdiction to make a nil award, and

(c)   the application of the First Schedule to a claim for compensation under Part IV for a reduction in the value of an interest as if a reference to "the relevant decision under Part IV of the Principal Act" or to the "said decision" was, in relation to each of the sections in that Part mentioned in Column A of the Table to this section, a reference to the matter set out in Column B of that Table opposite the reference in Column A thereof to that section.

Table

Column A Section	Column B
18	the removal or alteration of a structure consequent upon a notice under section 36 of the Principal Act.
19	the discontinuance, or the compliance with conditions on the continuance, of the use of land consequent upon a notice under section 37 of the Principal Act.
20	the removal or alteration of a hedge consequent upon a notice under section 44 of the Principal Act.
21	the refusal of consent required under an order under section 45 of the Principal Act, or the grant or such a consent subject to conditions.
22	the making by the planning authority of an order under section 48 of the Principal Act creating the public right of way.
24	the action of the planning authority pursuant to section 85 of the Principal Act.

[174]

4 Commentary

If, having made a claim for compensation, no agreement is forthcoming between the parties, the matter is then referred to an arbitrator under the Land (Assessment of Compensation) Act 1919. There are currently two arbitrators who can be nominated under this Act to hear and determine a claim. This hearing is subject to the application of the very technical rules contained in the First Schedule to LG(PD)A 1990 and no appeal lies from the decision of the arbitrator.

6. Regulations in relation to compensation

Regulations made by the Minister may provide for –

   (a) the form in which claims for compensation are to be made,

   (b) the provision by a claimant of evidence in support of his claim and information as to his interest in the land to which the claim relates,

   (c) a statement by a claimant of the names and addresses of all other persons (so far as they are known to him) having an interest in the land to which the claim relates and, unless the claim is withdrawn, the notification by the planning authority or the claimant of every other person (if any) appearing to them or him to have an interest in the land,

   (d) the information and documents to be submitted with an application for an order under section 14,

   (e) the information and documents to be submitted by the planning authority in relation to an application for an order under section 14.   **[175]**

4 Commentary

Regulations with regard to the making and determining of claims for compensation are now contained in Part VIII of the LG(PD)R 1994, arts 108-113.

7. Prohibition of double compensation

Where a person would, but for this section, be entitled to compensation under this Act in respect of any matter or thing and also to compensation under any other enactment in respect of the same matter or thing, he shall not be entitled to compensation in respect of such matter or thing both under this Act and under the other enactment, and shall not be entitled to any greater amount of compensation under this Act in respect of such matter or thing than the amount of the compensation to which he would be entitled under the other enactment in respect of such matter or thing.   **[176]**

4 Commentary

This section prevents the payment of double compensation, as for example, where permission has been revoked to facilitate a road construction project where compensation would in any event be paid to an equal value for the land acquired and this prevents claims being made both under the acquisition of the land and for the revocation of planning permission.

8. Recovery of compensation from planning authority

(1) All compensation payable under this Act by the planning authority shall, when the amount thereof has been determined by agreement or by arbitration in accordance with

this Act, be recoverable from that authority as a simple contract debt in any court of competent jurisdiction.

(2) All costs and expenses of parties to an arbitration to determine the amount of any compensation shall, in so far as such costs and expenses are payable by the planning authority, be recoverable from that authority as a simple contract debt in any court of competent jurisdiction.

(3) Sections 69 to 79 of the Lands Clauses Consolidation Act, 1845, as amended or adapted by or under the Second Schedule to the Housing of the Working Classes Act, 1890, or any other Act, shall apply in relation to moneys by this section made recoverable as a simple contract debt as if such moneys were a price or compensation under the said Act as so amended or adapted.

(4) Where money is paid into court under section 69 of the Lands Clauses Consolidation Act, 1845, as applied by this section, by the planning authority, no costs shall be payable by that authority to any person in respect of any proceedings for the investment, payment of income, or payment of capital of such money.   **[177]**

---

4 Commentary

Compensation can be recovered from a planning authority by a very simple procedure in a court of competent jurisdiction. It should be noted that interest will run at a high rate against the planning authority from the date that it entered onto the lands.

---

9.   Registration of compensation

(1) Where, on a claim for compensation under Part III, compensation has become payable of an amount exceeding one hundred pounds, the planning authority shall prepare and retain a statement of that fact, specifying the refusal of permission or grant of permission subject to conditions, or the revocation or modification of permission, the land to which the claim for compensation relates, and the amount of the compensation.

(2)   (a)   A planning authority shall enter in the register kept in pursuance of section 8 of the Principal Act particulars of the statements prepared by them under this section.

    (b)   Every such entry shall be made within the period of fourteen days beginning on the day of the preparation of the statement.   **[178]**

---

4 Commentary

There is a duty on planning authorities to enter onto the register compensation claims which are due to a value exceeding £100. This entry must be made within 14 days beginning on the day of the preparation of the statement.

---

10. Recovery by planning authority of compensation on subsequent development[3a]

(1) No person shall carry out any development to which this section applies, on land in respect of which a statement (in this section referred to as a compensation statement) stands registered (whether under section 72 of the Principal Act or section 9 of this Act) until such amount as is recoverable under this section in respect of the compensation

specified in the statement has been paid or secured to the satisfaction of the planning authority.

(2) This section applies to any development (other than exempted development), being development of a kind specified in section 13(2):

Provided that –

(i) this section shall not apply to any development by virtue of a permission to develop land under Part IV of the Principal Act referred to in section 13(5) where such permission was granted subject to conditions other than conditions of a class or description set out in the Fourth Schedule,

(ii) in a case where the compensation specified in the statement became payable in respect of the imposition of conditions on the granting of permission to develop land, this section shall not apply to the development for which that permission was granted.

(3) Subject to subsection (4), the amount recoverable under this section in respect of the compensation specified in a compensation statement –

(a) if the land on which the development is to be carried out (in this subsection referred to as the development area) is identical with, or includes (with other land) the whole of, the land comprised in the compensation statement, shall be the amount of compensation specified in that statement;

(b) if the development area forms part of the land comprised in the compensation statement, or includes part of that land together with other land not comprised in that statement, shall be so much of the amount of compensation specified in that statement as is attributable to land comprised in that statement and falling within the development area.

(4) For the purposes of paragraph (b) of subsection (3), the following provisions shall have effect:

(a) the planning authority shall (if it appears to them to be practicable to do so) apportion the amount of the compensation between the different parts of the land according to the way in which those parts appear to them to be differently affected by the refusal of permission or grant of permission subject to conditions;

(b) if no apportionment is made, the amount of the compensation shall be treated as distributed rateably according to area over the land to which the statement relates;

(c) if an apportionment is made, the compensation shall be treated as distributed in accordance with that apportionment as between the different parts of the land by reference to which the apportionment is made, and so much of the compensation as, in accordance with the apportionment, is attributed to a part of the land shall be treated as distributed rateably according to area over that part of the land;

(d) if any person disputes an apportionment under this subsection, the dispute shall be submitted to and decided by a property arbitrator.

(5) Where, in connection with the development of any land, an amount becomes recoverable under this section in respect of the compensation specified in a

compensation statement, then no amount shall be recoverable, in so far as it is attributable to that land, in connection with any subsequent development thereof.

(6) An amount recoverable under this section in respect of any compensation shall be payable to the planning authority, and –

(a) shall be so payable either as a single capital payment or as a series of instalments of capital and interest combined (the interest being determined at the same rate as for a judgment debt), or as a series of other annual or periodical payments, of such amounts, and payable at such times, as the planning authority may direct, after taking into account any representations made by the person by whom the development is to be carried out, and

(b) except where the amount is payable as a single capital payment, shall be secured by that person in such manner (whether by mortgage, covenant or otherwise) as the planning authority may direct.

(7) If any person initiates any development to which this section applies in contravention of subsection (1) of this section, the planning authority may serve a notice upon him specifying the amount appearing to them to be the amount recoverable under this section in respect of the compensation in question, and requiring him to pay that amount to them within such period, not being less than three months after the service of the notice, as may be specified in the notice, and, in default of the said amount being paid to the planning authority within the period specified in the notice, it shall be recoverable as a simple contract debt in any court of competent jurisdiction.   **[179]**

---

4 Commentary

Where compensation of an amount greater than £100 is paid, and that is entered on the planning register, a person may not carry out any subsequent development on the lands until the compensation recovered has been repaid. This section sets out how in particular circumstances compensation paid can be apportioned within particular parts of the land and effectively aims to prevent a person benefiting unjustly by allowing the lands for which compensation was paid to be subsequently developed. See comments in *Dublin Corporation v Building and Allied Trade Union* [1996] 2 ILRM 547 where the Supreme Court discussed a corresponding provision in LG(PD)A 1963 in the context of the decision made to make an award of compensation under the Acquisition of Land (Assessment of Compensation) Act 1919.

Part III

COMPENSATION IN RELATION TO DECISIONS UNDER PART IV OF PRINCIPAL ACT

11. Right to compensation[3a]

If, on a claim made to the planning authority, it is shown that, as a result of a decision under Part IV of the Principal Act involving a refusal of permission to develop land or a grant of such permission subject to conditions, the value of an interest of any person existing in the land to which the decision relates at the time of the decision is reduced, that person shall, subject to the provisions of this Part, be entitled to be paid by the planning authority by way of compensation –

(a) such amount, representing the reduction in value, as may be agreed,

(b) in the absence of agreement, the amount of such reduction in value, determined in accordance with the First Schedule, and

(c) in the case of the occupier of the land, the damage (if any) to his trade, business or profession carried out on the land.   **[180]**

---

3 Notes

a   See *Dublin Corporation v Smithwick* [1976] ILRM 280.

4 Commentary

Section 11 provides the basis for the making of a claim for compensation. It provides that if as a result of a decision made subsequent to the making of a planning application the value of an interest in any person has been reduced, then compensation must be paid by the planning authority amounting to the value of the reduction in the interest. However this is subject to the restrictions contained in s 12.

---

12. Restriction of compensation[3a]

(1) Compensation under section 11 shall not be payable in respect of the refusal of permission for any development –

   (a) of a class or description set out in the Second Schedule, or

   (b) if the reason or one of the reasons for the refusal is a reason set out in the Third Schedule.

(2) Compensation under section 11 shall not be payable in respect of the imposition, on the granting of permission to develop land, of any condition of a class or description set out in the Fourth Schedule.

(3) Compensation under section 11 shall not be payable in respect of the refusal of permission, or of the imposition of conditions on the granting of permission, for the retention on land of any structures to which section 28 of the Principal Act relates.

(4) Where, under section 29 of the Principal Act, it is the duty of a planning authority to acquire an interest in land, compensation under section 11 shall not be payable in relation to that interest.   **[181]**

---

3 Notes

a   See *O'Connor v Clare County Council* High Court, unrep, 11 February 1994.

4 Commentary

Section 12 effectively limits very severely the rights granted in s 11. If it is a class of development specified in the Second Schedule to LG(PD)A 1990 or permission has been refused for a reason set out in the Third Schedule then planning permission compensation is not payable. These reasons are very broad and it is difficult to find a decision which is not subject to at least one of the reasons contained in the Third Schedule. There is some argument that these reasons are so restrictive and prevent the obtaining of compensation that this section may be unconstitutional but having regard to the common good arguments, it might be difficult to succeed. In any event this matter has never been the subject of judicial determination by the Supreme Court. However, it is clear that reasons for refusal should accord as closely as possible to the reasons specified in the Third Schedule given that the Act provides for interference with the constitutional right to property.

---

13. Notice preventing compensation[3a]

(1) Where a claim for compensation is made under section 11, the planning authority concerned may, not later than three months after the claim is received and having regard to all the circumstances of the case, serve a notice in such form as may be prescribed[2a] on the person by whom or on behalf of whom the claim has been made stating that, notwithstanding the refusal of permission to develop land or the grant of such permission subject to conditions, the land in question is in their opinion capable of other development for which permission under Part IV of the Principal Act ought to be granted.

(2) For the purpose of subsection (1), other development means development of a residential, commercial or industrial character, consisting wholly or mainly of the construction of houses, flats, shops or office premises, hotels, garages and petrol filling stations, theatres or structures for the purpose of entertainment, or industrial buildings (including warehouses), or any combination thereof.

(3) A notice under subsection (1) shall continue in force for a period of five years commencing on the day of service of the notice unless before the expiration of that period –

   (a) the notice is withdrawn by the planning authority, or

   (b) a permission is granted under Part IV of the Principal Act to develop the land to which the notice relates in a manner consistent with the other development specified in the notice, subject to no conditions or to conditions of a class or description set out in the Fourth Schedule, or

   (c) the notice is annulled by virtue of subsection (5).

(4) Compensation shall not be payable on a claim made under section 11 where –

   (a) a notice under subsection (1) is in force in relation to that claim, or

   (b) a notice under subsection (1) was in force in relation to that claim but has ceased to be in force by reason of the expiration of the period mentioned in subsection (3) and an application for permission under Part IV of the Principal Act to develop the land to which the notice relates in a manner consistent with the other development specified in the notice has not been made within the said period, or

   (c) a notice under subsection (1) was in force in relation to the claim but has ceased to be in force by virtue of paragraph (b) of subsection (3).

(5) A notice under subsection (1) shall be annulled where, upon an application for permission under Part IV of the Principal Act to develop the land to which the notice relates in a manner consistent with the other development specified in the notice, such permission is refused or is granted subject to conditions other than conditions of a class or description set out in the Fourth Schedule.

(6) No claim for compensation under section 11 shall lie in relation to a decision under Part IV of the Principal Act referred to in subsection (5).

(7) Section 29(1)(b) of the Principal Act is hereby amended by the deletion after the word "Act", of the words "or for which the planning authority have undertaken to grant such permission,".   **[182]**

---

2 Cross References

a   See LG(PD)R 1994, art 113.

3 Notes

a   See *Grange Developments Ltd v Dublin County Council* [1986] IR 246; [1987] ILRM 245, and *Browne v Cashel UDC* High Court, unrep, 29 March 1993 whereby any notice served in this regard which contravenes the development plan will be invalid.

4 Commentary

This section provides that where a claim is made for compensation and the claim is likely to succeed, the planning authority may serve a notice specifying some other form of development and is effectively a grant of planning permission for that particular type of development specified in the notice. The notice lasts for five years. It is now well established that a notice served under s 13 which permits a development in contravention of the development plan will be invalid.

---

14. Restrictions on sections 12 and 13[2a]

(1) Where, in a case determined on an appeal under Part IV of the Principal Act, permission to develop any land has, save in a case referred to in subsection (2), been refused or has been granted subject to any condition relating to any of the matters set out in paragraphs 8 and 9 of the Fourth Schedule, nothing contained in section 12 shall prevent compensation being paid if, an application having been made in that behalf within two months after the notification of the decision by the Board, or within such longer period as the Minister may allow, the Minister makes an order declaring that he is satisfied that it would not be just and reasonable in the particular circumstances that payment of compensation should be prevented by the provisions of section 12.

(2) Subsection (1) does not apply –

   (a) where there has been a refusal of permission for the erection of any advertisement structure or for the use of any land for the exhibition of any advertisement,

   (b) where there has been a refusal of permission for development including any structure or any addition to or extension of a structure if the reason or one of the reasons for the refusal is that the structure, addition or extension –

      (i) would infringe an existing building line or, where none exists, a building line determined by the planning authority or by the Board;

      (ii) would be under a public road;

      (iii) would endanger the health or safety of persons occupying or employed in the structure or any adjoining structure; or

      (iv) would be prejudicial to public health, and

   (c) where a notice has been served under section 13(1).

(3) Where in a case in which a notice has been served under section 13(1), save in a case referred to in paragraphs (a) and (b) of subsection (2), upon a subsequent application for permission under Part IV of the Principal Act to develop the land to which the notice relates in a manner consistent with the other development specified in the notice, such permission is granted subject to any condition relating to any of the matters set out in paragraphs 8 and 9 of the Fourth Schedule, then nothing contained in section 12 or

section 13 shall prevent compensation being paid if, an application having been made in that behalf within (but not after) two months after the notification of the decision, the Minister makes an order declaring that he is satisfied that it would not be just and reasonable in the particular circumstances that payment of compensation should be prevented by the provisions of section 12 or section 13.   **[183]**

---

2 Cross References

a   See LG(PD)R 1994, art 112.

4 Commentary

Section 14 contains a saver clause which allows the Minister, notwithstanding the provisions of ss 12 and 13, to allow compensation to be paid where it is considered just and reasonable that it should be so paid. This again is subject to the limitations contained in sub-s (2) and to the provisions set out in sub-s (3).

---

15. Special provision for structures substantially replacing structures demolished or destroyed by fire

(1) Nothing in section 12 shall prevent compensation being paid –

   (a) in a case in which there has been a refusal of permission for the erection of a new structure substantially replacing a structure (other than an unauthorised structure) which has been demolished or destroyed by fire or otherwise within the two years preceding the date of application for permission or there has been imposed a condition in consequence of which such new structure may not be used for the purpose for which the demolished or destroyed structure was last used, or

   (b) in a case in which there has been imposed a condition in consequence of which the new structure referred to in paragraph (a) or the front thereof, or the front of an existing structure (other than an unauthorised structure) which has been taken down in order to be re-erected or altered, is set back or forward.

(2) Every dispute and question whether a new structure would or does replace substantially within the meaning of subsection (1) a demolished or destroyed structure shall be determined by the Board.   **[184]**

---

4 Commentary

This is ambiguously worded provision which allows compensation to be paid where permission is refused for the erection of a new structure substantially replacing a structure which has been demolished or destroyed by fire or otherwise within the two years preceding the date of the application for permission. It is not clear whether the word "or" in s 15(1)(a) is disjunctive or conjunctive, for if it is disjunctive then this is a very broad provision which has never been adequately utilised. It does not of course apply to an unauthorised structure and the ambiguity with regard to when a structure has been demolished or destroyed is ultimately a question that will be determined by An Bord Pleanála.

---

16. Restriction on assignment of compensation under section 11

A person shall not be entitled to assign to any other person all or any part of any prospective compensation under section 11, and every purported assignment or promise, express or implied, to pay any other person any money in respect of any such compensation is void. **[185]**

---

4 Commentary

A person may not assign any part of a prospective compensation under s 11 to any other person. Why such an assignment should be expressly prohibited is not altogether clear.

---

17. Compensation where permission is revoked or modified

(1) Where permission to develop land has been revoked or modified by a notice under section 30 of the Principal Act –

(a) if, on a claim made to the planning authority, it is shown that any person interested in the land has incurred expenditure in carrying out works which are rendered abortive by the revocation or modification, that authority shall pay to that person compensation in respect of that expenditure;

(b) the provisions of this Act shall apply in relation to the notice where it revoked the permission or modified it by the imposition of conditions –

(i) in case it revoked the permission, as they apply in relation to refusal of permission to develop land, and

(ii) in case it modified the permission by the imposition of conditions, as they apply in relation to a grant of permission to develop land subject to conditions,

subject to the modifications that a reference to the time when the notice takes effect shall be substituted for any reference to the time of a decision and, in section 12(4), the reference to section 29 of the Principal Act shall be construed as a reference to that section as applied by section 30 of that Act.

(2) For the purposes of this section, any expenditure reasonably incurred in the preparation of plans for the purposes of any works or upon other similar matters preparatory thereto shall be deemed to be included in the expenditure incurred in carrying out those works but, except as aforesaid, no compensation shall be paid by virtue of this section in respect of any works carried out before the grant of the permission which is revoked or modified, or in respect of any other loss or damage arising out of anything done or omitted to be done before the grant of that permission. **[186]**

---

4 Commentary

Section 17 provides for compensation where a planning permission is revoked. Compensation is payable where a person has incurred expenditure carrying out works which were rendered abortive but it should be noted that planning permission cannot be revoked where development has already commenced, and therefore it is not entirely clear as to how s 17 will apply. The carrying out of plans and other assessments including the preparation of an Environmental Impact Assessment is payable however under the definition of "works".

Part IV

COMPENSATION IN RELATION TO SECTIONS 36, 37, 44, 45, 48, 83 AND 85 OF PRINCIPAL ACT

18. Removal or alteration of structure (1963, section 36)

(1) If, on a claim made to the planning authority, it is shown that, as a result of the removal or alteration of any structure consequent upon a notice under section 36 of the Principal Act, the value of an interest of any person in the structure existing at the time of the notice is reduced, or that any person having an interest in the structure at that time has suffered damage by being disturbed in his enjoyment of the structure, such person shall, subject to the provisions of this Act, be entitled to be paid by the planning authority by way of compensation the amount of such reduction in value or the amount of such damage.

(2) Where, under section 29 of the Principal Act as applied by subsection (9) of section 36 of that Act, it is the duty of the planning authority to acquire an interest in land, compensation in relation to that interest shall not be payable pursuant to this section.   **[187]**

---

4 Commentary

Section 18 provides for compensation to be paid for the removal or alteration of a structure.

---

19. Discontinuance of use (1963, section 37)

(1) If, on a claim made to the planning authority, it is shown that, as a result of the discontinuance, or the compliance with conditions on the continuance, of any use of land consequent upon a notice under section 37 of the Principal Act, the value of an interest of any person in the land existing at the time of the notice is reduced, or that any person having an interest in the land at that time has suffered damage by being disturbed in his enjoyment of the land, such person shall, subject to the provisions of this Act, be entitled to be paid by the planning authority by way of compensation the amount of such reduction in value or the amount of such damage, provided that no compensation shall be paid under this section in relation to damage resulting from the imposition under section 37 of the Principal Act of conditions on the continuance of the use of land, being conditions imposed in order to avoid or reduce serious water pollution or the danger of such pollution.

(2) Subsection (1) shall not apply where the use of land is use for the exhibition of advertising unless at the time of such discontinuance or compliance, the land has been used for the exhibition of advertising for less than five years, whether such use was continuous or intermittent or whether or not, while the land was being so used, advertising was exhibited at the same place on the land.

(3) Where, under section 29 of the Principal Act as applied by subsection (8) of section 37 of that Act, it is the duty of the planning authority to acquire an interest in land, compensation in relation to that interest shall not be payable pursuant to this section.   **[188]**

4 Commentary

This section provides for payment of compensation where arising out of a notice to discontinue use the value of an interest in land has been reduced. Such a notice is served under LG(PD)A 1963, s 37 and is in the nature of an enforcement notice.

20. Removal or alteration of hedge (1963, section 44)

If, on a claim made to the planning authority, it is shown that, as a result of the removal or alteration of any hedge consequent upon a notice under section 44 of the Principal Act, the value of an interest of any person in the land existing at the time of the notice is reduced, or that any person having an interest in the land at that time has suffered damage by being disturbed in his enjoyment of such land, such person shall, subject to the provisions of this Act, be entitled to be paid by the planning authority by way of compensation the amount of such reduction in value or such damage.   **[189]**

4 Commentary

This section provides for the payment of compensation where a notice requiring the removal/ alteration of a structure is served under LG(PD)A 1963, s 44.

21. Tree preservation orders (1963, section 45)

If, on a claim made to the planning authority, it is shown that, as a result of any decision of the authority [or the Board]¹ᵃ to refuse a consent required under an order under section 45 of the Principal Act, or to grant any such consent subject to conditions, the value of an interest of any person in the land to which such decision relates existing at the time of the decision is reduced, or that any person having an interest in the land at that time has suffered damage by being disturbed in his enjoyment of the land, such person shall, subject to the provisions of this Act, be entitled to be paid by the planning authority by way of compensation the amount of such reduction in value or the amount of such damage, but –

(a) where the order declares that, as respects any tree, trees or group of trees not comprised in woodlands, the tree, trees or group is or are of special amenity value or special interest no compensation shall be payable in relation to the tree, trees or group;

(b) where the order declares that, as respects any trees comprised in woodlands, a condition comprising a requirement to replant is an essential condition for attachment in the interests of amenity to any consent given under the order no compensation shall be payable in relation to such a condition attached to any such consent;

(c) where the order declares that, as respects any trees comprised in woodlands, a condition comprising a requirement to preserve a specified proportion of the trees, not being greater than twenty per cent, is an essential condition for attachment, because of special amenity value or of special interest, to any consent given under the order, no compensation shall be payable in relation to such a condition attached to any consent;

(d) where the order declares that, as respects any trees comprised in woodlands, a condition comprising a requirement to phase the felling or extraction of trees over a period of up to 20 years in such manner as may be specified in the order, is an essential condition for attachment, because of special amenity value or of special interest, to any consent given under the order, no compensation shall be payable in relation to such a condition attached to any consent.   **[190]**

---

1 Amendments

a   The words in square brackets were inserted by LG(PD)A 1992, s 21.

4 Commentary

Section 21 provides for the payment of compensation where the planning authority or the Board refuse a consent to fell trees arising from the making of a tree preservation order. However, subparas (a) to (d) severely limit the instances where compensation can be paid. Indeed, it is difficult to see how this provision confers any substantive right to compensation and again the constitutional implications of this section have never been questioned. Generally speaking, no planning permission is necessary to fell a tree except where an order is made under LG(PD)A 1963, s 45.

---

22. Creation of public rights of way (1963, section 48)

If, on a claim made to the planning authority, it is shown that the value of an interest of any person in land, being land over which a public right of way has been created by an order under section 48 of the Principal Act made by that authority, is reduced, or that any person having an interest in such land has suffered damage by being disturbed in his enjoyment of the land, in consequence of the creation of the public right of way, such person shall, subject to the provisions of this Act, be entitled to be paid by the planning authority by way of compensation the amount of such reduction in value or the amount of such damage.   **[191]**

---

4 Commentary

Section 22 relates to compensation payable when public rights of way are created by virtue of LG(PD)A 1963, s 48.

---

23. Entry on land (1963, section 83)

If, on a claim made to the planning authority, it is shown that, as a result of anything done under section 83 of the Principal Act, any person has suffered damage, such person shall, subject to the provisions of this Act, be entitled to be paid by the planning authority by way of compensation the amount of such damage.   **[192]**

---

4 Commentary

Section 23 relates to the compensation payable where the planning authority enters onto lands pursuant to LG(PD)A 1963, s 83. Section 83 is a general enabling power which allows a member of the Board, or any authorised person, to enter onto lands and do all things reasonably necessary for the purposes of such entry and make plans, take levels or make excavations or examine the depth and nature of the subsoil with regard to such entry.

---

24. Cables, wires and pipelines (1963, section 85)

If, on a claim made to the planning authority, it is shown that, as a result of the action of such authority pursuant to section 85 of the Principal Act in placing, renewing or removing any cable, wire or pipeline, attaching any bracket or fixture or affixing any notice, the value of an interest of any person in the land or structure existing at the time of the action of the planning authority is reduced, or that any person having an interest in the land or structure at that time has suffered damage by being disturbed in his enjoyment of such land or structure, such person shall, subject to the provisions of this Act, be entitled to be paid by the planning authority by way of compensation the amount of such reduction in value or the amount of the damage.   **[193]**

4 Commentary

Section 24 provides for compensation to be paid where a planning authority, pursuant to LG(PD)A 1963, s 85, places cables, pipes or wires on land.

Part V

CONNECTION OF PREMISES TO PUBLIC SEWERS AND WATER SUPPLIES

25. Connection to sanitary authority sewers[3a]

(1) This section shall apply to any structure which, at the commencement of this section –

    (a) is an unauthorised structure or a structure the use of which constitutes an unauthorised use, or

    (b) is not connected to a sewer of a sanitary authority,

or to any structure which is constructed, erected or made on or after the commencement of this section.

(2) Section 27 of the Public Health (Ireland) Act, 1878, shall not apply in relation to a structure to which this section applies.

(3) Notwithstanding section 23 of the Public Health (Ireland) Act, 1878, or any other enactment, the owner or occupier of a structure to which this section applies shall not be entitled to connect his drains to any sewer of the sanitary authority in whose functional area the premises is situated except with the consent of the sanitary authority, which may be given subject to such conditions as the sanitary authority consider reasonable.

(4) Any person who connects a drain or causes it to be connected to a sewer of a sanitary authority in contravention of subsection (3) shall be guilty of an offence and shall be liable on summary conviction to a fine not exceeding £1,000.

(5) The sanitary authority may close any connection between a drain and sewer made in contravention of subsection (3) and may recover from the person who made the connection or who caused the connection to be made any expenses incurred by them under this subsection and in default of the said amount being paid to the authority, it shall be recoverable as a simple contract debt in any court of competent jurisdiction.

(6) Where a notice under section 8(1) of the Local Government (Sanitary Services) Act, 1962 takes effect in relation to any premises, a consent of the sanitary authority by

whom the notice has been served shall not be required under subsection (3) for the connection of the said premises to the appropriate sewer of the sanitary authority.

(7) Unless otherwise indicated, the grant of a permission under Part IV of the Principal Act, or of approval under bye-laws made under section 41 of the Public Health (Ireland) Act, 1878, or section 23 of the Public Health Acts Amendment Act, 1890, or regulations made under section 86 of the Principal Act in relation to a structure to which this section applies shall be taken to include the consent of the sanitary authority under subsection (3) to the connection of that structure to the appropriate sewer of the sanitary authority.

(8) In considering whether to give consent under subsection (3), a sanitary authority shall be entitled to have regard to the constraints described at paragraph 1 of the Third Schedule in so far as these may apply to the provision of sewerage facilities by them.

(9) In this section, each of the terms **"drain"**, **"sanitary authority"** and **"sewer"** has the meaning assigned to it in the Local Government (Sanitary Services) Acts, 1878 to 1964.[3b] **[194]**

3 Notes

a   For the position prior to the enactment of this section, see *Ballybay Meat Exporters Ltd v Monaghan County Council* [1990] ILRM 864.

b   The legal distinction between a drain (generally privately owned) and a sewer, which is by definition always vested in the local authority (the sanitary authority), is not clear and this area of law needs to be clarified, see generally Keane, *The Law of Local Government in the Republic of Ireland* (ILSI, 1982).

4 Commentary

Section 25 removes the right which had existed previously of any person to connect to the sewers or drains of a sanitary authority. Following the enactment of s 25 the consent of the local authority is required before connection is made. However the grant of a planning permission is deemed to be an express permission to connect to such sewers or drains unless a contrary intention appears in the grant of permission. The section also contains ancillary provisions which allow for an unauthorised connection to be the subject matter of a criminal offence, the planning authority can recover costs in the event of an unauthorised connection, and the position whereby a notice is served under the Local Government (Sanitary Services) Act 1962 requiring the connection of any premises to the adjoining sewer.

26. Limitation of section 53 of the Waterworks Clauses Act, 1847

(1) Section 53 of the Waterworks Clauses Act, 1847, and any other enactment which confers a right to a supply of water for domestic purposes shall not apply in relation to a dwelling house which is an unauthorised structure or the use of which constitutes an unauthorised use.

(2) Nothing in this section shall restrict the operation of section 8(2) of the Local Government (Sanitary Services) Act, 1962. **[195]**

First Schedule

RULES FOR THE DETERMINATION OF THE AMOUNT OF COMPENSATION

1. The reduction in value shall, subject to the provisions of this Schedule, be determined by reference to the difference between the antecedent and subsequent values of the land, where –

   (a) the antecedent value of the land is the amount which the land, if sold in the open market by a willing seller immediately prior to the relevant decision under Part IV of the Principal Act (and assuming that the relevant application for permission had not been made), might have been expected to realise, and

   (b) the subsequent value of the land is the amount which the land, if sold in the open market by a willing seller immediately after the said decision, might be expected to realise.

2. In determining the antecedent value and subsequent value of the land for the purposes of Rule 1 –

   (a) regard shall be had to –

      (i) any contribution which a planning authority might have required or might require as a condition precedent to development of the land,

      (ii) any restriction on the development of the land which, without conferring a right to compensation, could have been or could be imposed under any Act or under any order, regulations, rule or bye-law made under any Act,

      (iii) the fact that exempted development might have been or may be carried out on the land, and

      (iv) the open market value of comparable land, if any, in the vicinity of the land whose values are being determined;

   (b) no account shall be taken of –

      (i) any part of the value of the land attributable to subsidies or grants available from public moneys, or to any tax or rating allowances in respect of development, from which development of the land might benefit,

      (ii) the special suitability or adaptability of the land for any purpose if that purpose is a purpose to which it could be applied only in pursuance of statutory powers, or for which there is no market apart from the special needs of a particular purchaser or the requirements of any statutory body as defined in Rule 5; provided that any *bona fide* offer for the purchase of the land which may be brought to the notice of the arbitrator shall be taken into consideration,

      (iii) any increase in the value of land attributable to the use thereof or of any structure thereon in a manner which could be restrained by any court, or is contrary to law, or detrimental to the health of the inmates of the structure or to public health or safety or to the environment,

      (iv) any depreciation or increase in value attributable to the land, or any land in the vicinity, being reserved for a particular purpose in a development plan,

      (v) any value attributable to any unauthorised structure or unauthorised use,

(vi) (I)   the existence of proposals for development of the land or any other land by a statutory body, or

     (II) the possibility or probability of the land or other land becoming subject to a scheme of development undertaken by such statutory body, and

(c) all returns and assessments of capital value for taxation made or acquiesced in by the claimant may be considered.

3.(1) In assessing the possibilities, if any, for developing the land, for the purposes of determining its antecedent value, regard shall be had only to such reasonable possibilities as, having regard to all material considerations, could be judged to have existed immediately prior to the relevant decision under Part IV of the Principal Act.

(2) Material considerations for the purposes of the foregoing sub-rule shall, without prejudice to the generality thereof, include –

(a) the nature and location of the land,

(b) the likelihood or unlikelihood, as the case may be, of obtaining permission, or further permission, to develop the land in the light of the provisions of the development plan,

(c) the assumption that, if any permission to develop the land were to be granted, any conditions which might reasonably be imposed in relation to matters referred to in the Fourth Schedule (but no other conditions) would be imposed, and

(d) any permission to develop the land, not being permission for development of a kind specified in section 13(2), already existing at the time of the relevant decision under Part IV of the Principal Act.

4.(1) In determining the subsequent value of the land in a case in which there has been a refusal of permission –

(a) it shall be assumed, subject to sub-rule (2), that, after the refusal, permission under Part IV of the Principal Act would not be granted for any development of a kind specified in section 13(2),

(b) regard shall be had to any conditions in relation to matters referred to in the Fourth Schedule (but no other conditions) which might reasonably be imposed in the granting of permission to develop the land.

(2) In a case in which there has been a refusal of permission in relation to land in respect of which there is in force an undertaking under Part VI of the Principal Act, it shall be assumed in determining the subsequent value of the land that, after the refusal, permission under Part IV of the Principal Act would not be granted for any development other than development to which the said undertaking relates.

5. (1) In Rule 2, "**statutory body**" means:

(a) a Minister of the Government

(b) the Commissioners of Public Works in Ireland,

(c) a local authority within the meaning of the local Government Act, 1941,

(d) a harbour authority within the meaning of the Harbours Act, 1946,

(e) a health board established under the Health Act, 1970,

(f) a vocational education committee within the meaning of the Vocational Education Act, 1930,

(g) a board or other body established by or under statute,

(h) a company in which all the shares are held by, or on behalf of, or by directors appointed by, a Minister of the Government, or

(i) a company in which all the shares are held by a board, company, or other body referred to in paragraph (g) or (h).

(2) In sub-rule (1)(h) and (i), "**company**" means a company within the meaning of section 2 of the Companies Act, 1963.   **[196]**

Second Schedule

DEVELOPMENT IN RESPECT OF WHICH A REFUSAL OF PERMISSION WILL NOT ATTRACT COMPENSATION

1.   Any development that consists of or includes the making of any material change in the use of any structures or other land.[3a]

2.   The demolition of a habitable house.

[3. Any development which would materially affect a protected structure or proposed protected structure within the meaning of the Local Government (Planning and Development) Act, 1999.][1a]

4.   The erection of any advertisement structure.

5.   The use of land for the exhibition of any advertisement.

6.   Development in an area to which a special amenity area order relates.

7.   Any development on land with respect to which there is available (notwithstanding the refusal of permission) a grant of permission under Part IV of the Principal Act for any development of a residential, commercial or industrial character, if the development consists wholly or mainly of the construction of houses, flats, shops or office premises, hotels, garages and petrol filling stations, theatres or structures for the purpose of entertainment, or industrial buildings (including warehouses), or any combination thereof, subject to no conditions other than conditions of the kind referred to in the Fourth Schedule.

8.   Any development on land with respect to which compensation has already been paid under section 11, or under section 55 of the Principal Act, by reference to a previous decision under Part IV of that Act involving a refusal of permission.

[197]

Amendments

a   Paragraph 3 was substituted by LG(PD)A 1999, s 37 which will come into operation on 1 January 2000.

3 Notes

a   See *Viscount Securities Ltd v Dublin County Council* 112 ILTR 17.

Third Schedule

REASONS FOR THE REFUSAL OF PERMISSION WHICH EXCLUDE COMPENSATION[3a]

1. Development of the kind proposed on the land would be premature[3b] by reference to any one or combination of the following constraints and the period within which the constraints involved may reasonably be expected to cease –

(a) any existing deficiency in the provision of water supplies or sewerage facilities,

(b) the capacity of existing or prospective water supplies or sewerage facilities being required for prospective development as regards which a grant of a permission under Part IV of the Principal Act, an undertaking under Part VI of that Act or a notice under section 13 exists,

(c) the capacity of existing or prospective water supplies or sewerage facilities being required for the prospective development of another part of the functional area of the planning authority, as indicated in the development plan,

(d) the capacity of existing or prospective water supplies or sewerage facilities being required for any other prospective development or for any development objective, as indicated in the development plan,

(e) any existing deficiency in the road network serving the area of the proposed development, including considerations of capacity, width, alignment, or the surface or structural condition of the pavement, which would render that network, or any part of it, unsuitable to carry the increased road traffic likely to result from the development,

(f) any prospective deficiency (including the considerations specified in sub-paragraph (e)) in the road network serving the area of the proposed development which –

    (i) would arise because of the increased road traffic likely to result from that development and from prospective development as regards which a grant of permission under Part IV of the Principal Act, an undertaking under Part VI of that Act or a notice under section 13 exists, or

    (ii) would arise because of the increased road traffic likely to result from that development and from any other prospective development or from any development objective, as indicated in the development plan, and

    (iii) would render that road network, or any part of it, unsuitable to carry the increased road traffic likely to result from the proposed development.

2. Development of the kind proposed would be premature pending the determination by the planning authority or the road authority of a road layout for the area or any part thereof.

3. Development of the kind proposed would be premature by reference to the order of priority, if any, for development indicated in the development plan. [3c]

4. The proposed development would endanger public safety by reason of traffic hazard or obstruction of road users or otherwise.

5. The proposed development, by itself or by the precedent which the grant of permission for it would set for other relevant development, would adversely affect the use of a national road or other major road by traffic.

6. The proposed development would interfere with a view or prospect of special amenity value or special interest which it is necessary to preserve. [3d]

7. The proposed development would cause serious air pollution, water pollution, noise pollution or vibration or pollution connected with the disposal of waste.

8. In the case of development including any structure or any addition[3e] to or extension of a structure, the structure, addition or extension would –

   (i)   infringe an existing building line or, where none exists, a building line determined by the planning authority or by the Board,

   (ii)   be under a public road,

  (iii)   seriously injure the amenities, or depreciate the value, of property in the vicinity,

  (iv)   tend to create any serious traffic congestion,

   (v)   endanger or interfere with the safety of aircraft or the safe and efficient navigation thereof,

  (vi)   endanger the health or safety of persons occupying or employed in the structure or any adjoining structure, or

 (vii)   be prejudicial to public health.

9. The development would contravene materially a condition attached to an existing permission for development.

10. The proposed development would injure or interfere with a historic monument which stands registered in the Register of Historic Monuments under section 5 of the National Monuments (Amendment) Act, 1987, or which is situated in an archaeological area so registered.

11. The development would contravene materially a development objective indicated in the development plan for the use solely or primarily (as may be indicated in the development plan) of particular areas for particular purposes (whether residential, commercial, industrial, agricultural or otherwise). [3f]

12. Paragraph 11 shall, subject to paragraph 13, not apply in a case where a development objective for the use specified in paragraph 11 applied to the land at any time within the five years immediately prior to the date on which the relevant application was made for permission under Part IV of the Principal Act to develop the land, and the development would not have contravened materially that development objective.

13. Paragraph 12 shall not apply in a case where a person acquired his interest in the land –

  (a) after the development objective referred to in paragraph 11 has come into operation, or

  (b) after notice has been published,

     (i) in accordance with section 21 of the Principal Act, of a proposed new development plan or of proposed variations of a development plan, or

    (ii) in accordance with section 21A of the Principal Act, of a material alteration of the draft concerned,

indicating in draft the development objective referred to in paragraph 11.

14. For the purposes of paragraph 13, the onus shall be on a person to prove all relevant facts relating to his interest in the land to the satisfaction of the planning authority.

15. In this Schedule, each of the terms "road authority" and "national road" has the meaning assigned to it in the Local Government (Roads and Motorways) Act, 1974.

[198]

3 Notes

a   The courts have stressed generally the need to use the exact wording of the Act. See *XJS Ltd v Dun Laoghaire Corporation* [1986] IR 750; [1987] ILRM 659. But see also *Eighty Five Developments Ltd v Dublin County Council* High Court, unrep, 31 January 1992 and *J Wood & Co Ltd v Wicklow County Council* [1995] 1 ILRM 51.

b   Compare *Shortt v Dublin County Council* [1983] ILRM 377.

c   See *O'Connor v Clare County Council* High Court, unrep, 11 February 1994.

d   Gannon J in *Eighty Five Developments Limited v Dublin County Council* High Court, unrep, 31 January 1992 emphasised the requirement to use the full version as set out in the Act. In the Supreme Court it was emphasised that reasons excluding compensation should accord as closely as possible to the relevant excluding compensation.

e   See *Dunbur Ltd v Wicklow County Council* High Court, unrep, 6 July 1989 which was decided under LG(PD)A 1963 and this paragraph reflects the decision in that case.

f   See *O'Connor v Clare County Council* High Court, unrep, 11 February 1994.

Fourth Schedule

CONDITIONS WHICH MAY BE IMPOSED, ON THE GRANTING OF PERMISSION TO DEVELOP LAND, WITHOUT COMPENSATION

1. A condition, under section 26(2)(e) of the Principal Act, requiring the giving of security for satisfactory completion of the proposed development (including maintenance until taken in charge by the local authority concerned of roads, open spaces, car-parks, sewers, watermains or drains).

2. A condition, under section 26(2)(g) of the Principal Act, requiring a contribution towards expenditure incurred by any local authority in respect of works (including the provision of open spaces) which have facilitated the proposed development.

3. A condition, under section 26(2)(h) of the Principal Act, requiring a contribution towards expenditure (including expenditure on the acquisition of land) that is proposed to be incurred by any local authority in respect of works facilitating the proposed development.

4. A condition, under section 26(2)(j) of the Principal Act, requiring the removal of an advertisement structure.

5. Any condition under section 26(2)(j) of the Principal Act in a case in which the relevant application for permission relates to a temporary structure.

6. Any condition relating to all or any of the following matters –

   (a) the size, height, floor area and character of structures;

   (b) building lines, site coverage and the space about dwellings and other structures;

   (c) the extent of parking places required in, on or under structures of a particular class or size or services or facilities for the parking, loading, unloading or fuelling of vehicles;

   (d) the objects which may be affixed to structures;

   (e) the purposes for and the manner in which structures may be used or occupied, including, in the case of dwellings, the letting thereof in separate tenements.

7. Any condition relating to the design, colour and materials of structures.

8. Any conditions reserving or allocating specified land for structures of a specified class or classes, or prohibiting or restricting either permanently or temporarily, the erection, construction or making of any particular class or classes of structures on any specified land.

9. Any condition limiting the number of structures of a particular class which may be constructed, erected or made, on, in or under any specified land.

10. Any condition relating to –

(a) the disposition or layout of structures or structures of any specified class (including the reservation of reasonable open space in relation to the number, class and character of structures in any particular development proposal);

(b) the manner in which any land is to be laid out for the purpose of development, including requirements as to road layout, landscaping, planting;

(c) the provision of water supplies, sewers, drains and public lighting;

(d) the provision of service roads and the location and design of means of access to roads;

(e) the provision of facilities for parking, unloading, loading and fuelling of vehicles on any land.

11. Any condition relating to the alteration or removal of unauthorised structures.

12. Any condition relating to the layout of the proposed development, including density, spacing, grouping and orientation of structures in relation to roads, open spaces, and other structures.

13. Any condition relating to the provision and siting of sanitary services and recreational facilities.

14. Any condition reserving, as a public park, public garden or public recreation space, land normally used as such.

[15. Any conditions relating to the protection of a protected structure or proposed protected structure within the meaning of the Local Government (Planning and Development) Act, 1999.][1a]

16 ...

17. Any condition relating to the preservation of caves, sites, features and other objects of archaeological, geological or historical interest.

18. Any condition relating to the preservation of views and prospects and of amenities of places and features of natural beauty or interest.

19. Any condition relating to the preservation and protection of trees, shrubs, plants and flowers.

20. Any condition prohibiting, restricting or controlling, either generally or within a specified distance of the centre line of any specified road, the erection of all or any particular forms of advertisement structure or the exhibition of all or any particular forms of advertisement.

21. Any condition preventing, remedying or removing injury to amenities arising from the ruinous or neglected condition of any structure, or from the objectionable or

neglected condition of any land attached to a structure or abutting on a public road or situate in a residential area.

22. Any condition prohibiting, regulating or controlling the deposit or disposal of waste materials and refuse, the disposal of sewage and the pollution of rivers, lakes, ponds, gullies and the seashore.

23. Any condition for preserving any existing public right of way giving access to seashore, mountain, lakeshore, riverbank, or other place of natural beauty or recreational utility.

24. Any condition relating to a matter in respect of which a requirement could have been imposed under any other Act, or under any order, regulation, rule or bye-law made under any other Act, without liability for compensation.

25. Any condition relating to measures to reduce or prevent the emission or the intrusion of noise or vibration.

26. Any condition prohibiting the demolition of a habitable house.

27. Any condition relating to the filling of land.

28. Any condition in the interest of ensuring the safety of aircraft or the safe and efficient navigation thereof.

29. Any condition determining the sequence in which works shall be carried out or specifying a period within which works shall be completed.

30. Any condition restricting the occupation of any structure included in a development until the completion of other works included in the development or until any other specified condition is complied with or until the planning authority consents to such occupation. **[199]**

Amendments

a   Paragraphs 15 and 16 were substituted by LG(PD)A 1999, s 37 which will come into force on 1 January 2000.

LOCAL GOVERNMENT (PLANNING AND DEVELOPMENT) ACT, 1992

(No. 14 of 1992)

ARRANGEMENT OF SECTIONS

Section

Schedule

ENACTMENTS REPEALED

ACTS REFERRED TO

An Act to amend and extend the Local Government (Planning and Development) Acts, 1963 to 1991, in relation to appeals and other matters with which An Bord Pleanála is concerned and in relation to legal proceedings concerned with matters arising under or connected with the said Acts and to provide for related matters. [16 July, 1992]

Be it enacted by the Oireachtas as follows:

1. Interpretation

(1) In this Act, except where the context otherwise requires –

"**the Act of 1976**" means the Local Government (Planning and Development) Act, 1976;

"**the Act of 1982**" means the Local Government (Planning and Development) Act, 1982;

"**the Act of 1983**" means the Local Government (Planning and Development) Act, 1983;

"**the Act of 1990**" means the Local Government (Planning and Development) Act, 1990;

"**the Acts**" means the Local Government (Planning and Development) Acts, 1963 to 1992;

"**appeal**" means an appeal to the Board under section 26(5) of the Principal Act;

"**appellant**" means the person by whom an appeal is made;

"**other matter with which the Board is concerned**" means –

    (a) an appeal to the Board under the Acts or any order or regulations made under the Acts, other than an appeal under section 26(5) of the Principal Act,

    (b) a reference under section 5 of the Principal Act,

    (c) a request for a determination of a disagreement, question or dispute to which section 26(7) of the Principal Act or section 15(2) of the Act of 1990 relates,

    (d) a purchase notice transmitted to the Board pursuant to section 29(4) of the Principal Act, or

    (e) a request for a determination of a contribution or other matter which, pursuant to a condition attached to a permission or approval granted under section 26 of the Principal Act, is to be agreed between the planning authority and the person to whom the permission or approval is granted and in default of agreement is to be determined by the Board;

"**party to an appeal**" means any of the following persons, namely –

    (a) the appellant,

    (b) the planning authority against whose decision an appeal is made,

    (c) the applicant for any permission or approval in relation to which an appeal is made by another person (other than a person acting on behalf of the appellant),

and "**party**" shall be construed accordingly;

"**planning application**" means an application to a planning authority in accordance with permission regulations for permission for the development of land or for an approval required by such regulations;

"**prescribe**" means prescribe by regulations;

"**the Principal Act**" means the Local Government (Planning and Development) Act, 1963.

(2) In this Act –

    (a) a reference to a section is to a section of this Act, unless it is indicated that reference to some other enactment is intended, and

    (b) a reference to a subsection, paragraph or sub-paragraph is to the subsection, paragraph or sub-paragraph of the provision in which the reference occurs, unless it is indicated that reference to some other provision is intended.

(3) In this Act a reference to any enactment shall, unless the context otherwise requires, be construed as a reference to that enactment as amended, adapted or extended by or under any subsequent enactment (including this Act).   **[200]**

---

4 Commentary

This Act came into force on 16 July 1992.

---

2. Duty and objective of Board

(1) It shall be the duty of the Board to ensure that appeals and other matters with which it is concerned are disposed of as expeditiously as may be and, for that purpose, to take all such steps as are open to it to ensure that, in so far as is practicable, there are no avoidable delays at any stage in the determination of appeals and other matters.

(2) In particular, and without prejudice to the generality of subsection (1) and subject to subsections (3), (4) and (7), it shall be the objective of the Board to ensure that every appeal or other matter is determined within –

    (a) a period of four months beginning on the date of receipt by the Board of the appeal or other matter, or

    (b) such other period as the Minister may prescribe, either generally or in respect of a particular class or classes of appeals or other matters.

(3) (a)   Where it appears to the Board that it would not be possible or appropriate, because of the particular circumstances of an appeal or other matter with which the Board is concerned, to determine the appeal or other matter within the period referred to in paragraph (a) or (b) of subsection (2) (as the case may be) the Board shall, by notice in writing served on the parties to the appeal or other matter before the expiration of that period, inform those parties of the reasons why it would not be possible or appropriate (as the case may be) to determine the appeal or other matter within that period and shall specify the date before which the Board intends that the appeal or other matter shall be determined.

    (b) Where a notice has been served under paragraph (a), the Board shall take all such steps as are open to it to ensure that the appeal or other matter is determined before the date specified in the notice.

(4) The Minister may by regulations –

    (a) provide that subsection (2) shall not have effect for such period as is specified in the regulations, or

    (b) vary a period mentioned in that subsection,

either generally or in respect of a particular class or classes of appeals or other matters with which the Board is concerned where it appears to him to be necessary, by virtue of exceptional circumstances, to do so and for so long as such regulations are in force this section shall be construed and have effect in accordance therewith.

(5) The Board shall include in each report made under section 9 of the Act of 1976 a statement of the number of appeals and other matters with which the Board is concerned that it has determined within a period referred to in paragraph (a) or (b) of subsection (2) and such other information as to the time taken to determine appeals and other matters as the Minister may direct.

(6) Subsections (2) to (5) shall apply in relation to appeals and other matters with which the Board is concerned that are received by the Board on or after the date which is six months after the date of the passing of this Act.

(7) This section shall not apply in relation to purchase notices transmitted to the Board pursuant to section 29(4) of the Principal Act.   **[201]**

---

4 Commentary

This section introduces a general duty on the Board to determine appeals within a four month period. Up until this date the Board had no specific time limit within which to determine an appeal but it should be noted that this is not the entire limit which should be compared to that imposed on planning authorities pursuant to LG(PD)A 1963, s 26. The duty on the Board is to dispose of appeals as expeditiously as possible and the four month time limit is a guide rather than a mandatory statutory duty. Where the four month period cannot be complied with, the Board should specify a date within which the appeal will be determined. At present most appeals are not determined within the four month period. The default provisions of s 26 will not apply where the time limit provided for under s 2 is not complied with.

---

3.   Amendment of section 26 of Principal Act[3a]

[202]

---

3 Notes

a   This section amends LG(PD) 1963, s 26. See the amended section.

---

4.   Provisions as to making of appeals [2a]

(1) An appeal shall –

    (a) be made in writing,

    (b) state the name and address of the appellant,

    (c) state the subject matter of the appeal,

    (d) state in full the grounds of appeal and the reasons, considerations and arguments on which they are based, and

    (e) be accompanied by such fee (if any) as may be payable in respect of such appeal in accordance with regulations under section 10 of the Act of 1982.

(2) (a)   An appeal which does not comply with the requirements of subsection (1) shall be invalid.

    (b) The requirement of subsection (1)(d) shall apply whether or not the appellant requests, or proposes to request, in accordance with section 12, an oral hearing of the appeal.

(3) Without prejudice to section 9, an appellant shall not be entitled to elaborate in writing upon, or make further submissions in writing in relation to, the grounds of appeal stated in the appeal or to submit further grounds of appeal and any such elaboration, submissions or further grounds of appeal that is or are received by the Board shall not be considered by it. [3a]

(4) (a) An appeal shall be accompanied by such documents, particulars or other information relating to the appeal as the appellant considers necessary or appropriate.

   (b) Without prejudice to section 10, the Board shall not consider any documents, particulars or other information submitted by an appellant other than the documents, particulars or other information which accompanied the appeal.

(5) An appeal shall be made –

   (a) by sending the appeal by prepaid post to the Board, or

   (b) by leaving the appeal with an employee of the Board at the offices of the Board during office hours, or[3b]

   (c) by such other means as may be prescribed. **[203]**

---

2 Cross References

a   See LG(PD)R 1994 (SI 86/1994), art 48(1) which provides that this section shall apply to appeals under LG(PD)A 1963, s 27(4). See also art 53 in relation to references. Section 4 is also referred to in art 6(2).

3 Notes

a   It is now the practice of the Board not to consider any additional submissions made after an initial submission unless so requested by the Board.

b   See *Graves v An Bord Pleanála* High Court, unrep, 17 June 1997 where it was held that these provisions are mandatory and must be strictly complied with. An appeal left at the Board's offices but outside office hours and not with an employee of the Board was not lodged within the appropriate period notwithstanding that it was so delivered within the appropriate period.

4 Commentary

Section 4 provides statutory guidance as to how an appeal is to be made and the provisions should be strictly complied with. Therefore if an appeal is not made in writing, does not state the name and address of the appellant or the subject matter of the appeal, the appeal will be invalid. Furthermore, the full grounds of appeal must be set out and it is not permissible to elaborate subsequently on the grounds of appeal once they are lodged, even if the elaboration occurs within the statutory time limit provided for the making of the appeal. The provisions of s 4 have been strictly interpreted by the Board and the courts have upheld this interpretation.

---

5. Availability of documents

(1) Where a planning authority give their decision in respect of a planning application after the commencement of this section, the documents concerned mentioned in section 6 shall be made available for inspection by members of the public during office hours at the offices of the authority for a period of one month beginning on the day of the giving of the decision or, if an appeal or appeals is or are taken against the decision, until as regards the appeal or, as may be appropriate, each of the appeals –

   (a) it is withdrawn, or

(b) it is determined by the Board or dismissed by it pursuant to section 11 or 14, or

(c) in relation to it a direction is given to the authority by the Board pursuant to section 15.

(2) The Minister may prescribe additional requirements in relation to the availability for inspection by members of the public of documents relating to planning applications, including requirements in relation to such availability before the commencement, or after the expiration, of the period mentioned in subsection (1).

(3) In this section "**planning application**" includes –

(a) an application for a permission under section 27 of the Principal Act for retention of a structure, and

(b) an application for an approval that is required to be obtained under a condition subject to which a permission or an approval is granted under the Acts.   **[204]**

---

4 Commentary

Section 5 provides that certain documents will be made available for inspection from the date of the making of an appeal to An Bord Pleanála until the appeal is determined. Thereafter the range of documents is more limited for a period of five years from the date of the decision and subsequently such documents may only be made available at the discretion of the planning authority.

---

6.   Submission of documents, etc. to Board by planning authorities[2a]

Where an appeal is made to the Board the planning authority concerned shall, within a period of fourteen days beginning on the day on which a copy of the appeal is sent to them by the Board, submit to the Board –

(a) a copy of the planning application concerned and of any drawings, maps, particulars, evidence, environmental impact statement, other written study or further information received or obtained by them from the applicant in accordance with regulations under the Acts,

(b) a copy of any report prepared by or for the planning authority in relation to the planning application, and

(c) a copy of the decision of the planning authority in respect of the planning application and a copy of the notification of the decision given to the applicant.**[205]**

---

2 Cross References

a   By virtue of LG(PD)R 1994 (SI 86/1994), art 48(2), s 6 shall apply to appeals under LG(PD)A 1963, s 27 and a reference to a planning application under this section shall be construed as a reference to an application for permission under LG(PD)A 1963, s 27.

4 Commentary

Section 6 provides for the duties on planning authorities to make documentation available to the Board once notice of an appeal is given. This is necessary in order for the four month time limit provided for under s 2 to be complied with.

---

7.   Submissions or observations by other parties [2a]

(1) The Board shall, as soon as may be after receipt of an appeal, give a copy thereof to each other party.

(2) (a)   Each other party may make submissions or observations in writing to the Board in relation to the appeal within a period of one month beginning on the day on which a copy of the appeal is sent to that party by the Board.

  (b) Any submissions or observations received by the Board after the expiration of the period mentioned in paragraph (a) shall not be considered by the Board.

(3) Where no submissions or observations have been received from a party within the period mentioned in subsection (2), the Board may without further notice to that party determine the appeal.

(4) Without prejudice to section 9, a party shall not be entitled to elaborate in writing upon any submissions or observations made in accordance with subsection (2) or make any further submissions or observations in writing in relation to the appeal and any such elaboration, submissions or observations that is or are received by the Board shall not be considered by it.   **[206]**

---

2 Cross References

a   See LG(PD)R 1994 (SI 86/1994), art 48(1) which provides that this section shall apply to appeals under LG(PD)A 1963, s 27(4); see also art 53 which relates to references.

4 Commentary

Section 7 provides for the communication of submissions to the Board to each party to the appeal. Again there are strict time limits imposed for the making of such submissions and these time limits are strictly enforced by the Board.

7A(1) If an applicant, before submitting an environmental impact statement to the Board in accordance with a requirement of or under regulations under this Act, so requests, the Board shall give a written opinion on the information to be contained in such statement.

(2) The giving of a written opinion in accordance with paragraph (a) of this section shall not prejudice the exercise by the Board of its powers pursuant to this Act or any regulations made thereunder to require the applicant to submit specified information in relation to the appeal.

(3) The Minister may by regulations provide for matters of procedure in relation to the making of a request for and the giving of a written opinion pursuant to this section.[1a]**[207]**

---

1 Amendments

a   Section 7A was inserted by EC(EIA)(A)R 1999, (SI 93/1999), art 6.

---

8.   Submissions or observations by persons other than parties[2a]

(1) (a)   Any person other than a party may make submissions or observations in writing to the Board in relation to an appeal.

  (b) Without prejudice to subsection (3),[1a] submissions or observations as aforesaid <u>may be made within the period mentioned in subsection (2)</u> and any submissions or observations received by the Board after the expiration of that period shall not be considered by the Board.

(2)[1b] The period referred to in subsection (1)(b) is −

(a) where notice of receipt of an environmental impact statement is published in accordance with regulations under section 18, the period of one month beginning on the day of publication of the notice, or

(b) in any other case, the period of one month beginning on the day of receipt of the appeal by the Board or, where there is more than one appeal against the decision of the planning authority, on the day on which the Board last receives an appeal.

(3) The provisions of subsection (1)(b) shall not apply to submissions or observations made by a Member State of the European Communities (within the meaning of the European Communities Act, 1972) arising from consultation in accordance with the Council Directive in relation to the effects on the environment of the development to which the appeal relates.

(4) Without prejudice to section 9, a person who makes submissions or observations to the Board in accordance with this section shall not be entitled to elaborate in writing upon the submissions or observations or make further submissions or observations in writing in relation to the appeal and any such elaboration, submissions or observations that is or are received by the Board shall not be considered by it.   **[208]**

---

1 Amendments

a LG(PD)R 1994 (SI 86/1994), art 49(3) amends s 8 in so far as it relates to appeals governed by that article by the deletion of "Without prejudice to sub-s (3)" in s 8(1)(b) and by the deletion of s 8(3) and the substitution of a new subs 8(2) to read as follows:

"(2) The period referred to in subsection (1)(b) is the period of one month beginning on the day of receipt of the appeal by the Board or, where there is more than one appeal to the Board, on the day on which the Board last receives an appeal."

The appeals to which art 49 applies are any appeals to the Board under LG(PD)A 1963 except ss 26(5), 27(b), or 85(4)(b) LG(PD)A 1976.

b LG(PD)R 1994 (SI 86/1994), art 53(3) provides that s 8 shall apply to a reference subject to the deletion from s 8(1)(b) of the words "Without prejudice to subsection (3)", and the deletion of s 8(3) and the substitution for s 8(2) of the following subs:

"(2) The period referred to in subsection (1)(b) is the period of one month beginning on the day of receipt by the Board of the reference."

2 Cross References

a LG(PD)R 1994 (SI 86/1994), art 48(1) provides that s 8 shall now apply to appeals under LG(PD)A 1963, s 27(4). See also art 53 which relates to references.

4 Commentary

Section 8 provides that observations may be made by persons other than parties to the appeal. It is difficult to see the distinction between submissions made by parties to the appeal and by observers as it would appear that in the case of an oral hearing all the parties would have equal rights. However it may be the case that observers to an appeal are not entitled to cross-examine and are limited only to the making of statements at an oral hearing whereas the parties would appear to have the right to call witnesses and cross-examine. However, given that an oral hearing is informal in nature, it would appear that these distinctions may be more apparent than real.

9.   Power of Board to request submissions or observations [2a]

Where the Board is of opinion that, in the particular circumstances of an appeal, it is appropriate in the interests of justice to request any party or any person who has made submissions or observations to the Board in relation to the appeal to make submissions or observations in relation to any matter which has arisen in relation to the appeal, the Board may, in its discretion, notwithstanding section 4(3), 7(4), 8(4) or 13(3)(b), serve on any such person a notice under this section –

   (a)   requesting that person, within a period specified in the notice (not being less than fourteen or more than twenty-eight days beginning on the date of service of the notice) to submit to the Board submissions or observations in relation to the matter in question, and

   (b)   stating that, if submissions or observations are not received before the expiration of the period specified in the notice, the Board will, after the expiration of that period and without further notice to the person, pursuant to section 11 determine the appeal.   **[209]**

---

2 Cross References

a   LG(PD)R 1994 (SI 86/1994), art 48(1) provides that this section shall apply to appeals under LG(PD)A 1963, s 27(4); see also art 53 which relates to references.

4 Commentary

Section 9 gives the Board a power to introduce flexibility to the appeal by allowing any party to make further submissions where it considers that such submissions are necessary in the interests of justice. This is a broad discretion but the only person who can initiate such submissions is the Board itself.

---

10.   Power of Board to require submission of documents, etc.[2a]

(1) Where the Board is of opinion that any document, particulars or other information is or are necessary for the purpose of enabling it to determine an appeal, the Board may serve on any party, or on any person who has made submissions or observations to the Board in relation to the appeal, a notice under this section –

   (a)   requiring that person, within a period specified in the notice (being a period of not less than fourteen days beginning on the date of service of the notice) to submit to the Board such document, particulars or other information (which document, particulars or other information shall be specified in the notice), and

   (b)   stating that, in default of compliance with the requirements of the notice, the Board will, after the expiration of the period so specified and without further notice to the person, pursuant to section 11 dismiss or otherwise determine the appeal.

(2) Nothing in this section shall be construed as affecting any power conferred on the Board by or under any other enactment.   **[210]**

---

2 Cross References

a   LG(PD)R 1994 (SI 86/1994), art 48(1) provides that this section shall apply to appeals under LG(PD)A 1963, s 27(4); see also art 53 which relates to references.

4 Commentary

Section 10 gives the power to the Board to require the submission of documents or other particulars which it considers necessary in order to determine its appeal. However it does not appear to give to the Board discretion to serve it on persons who are not either parties or observers in the appeal and this is a weakness as it might be necessary for the Board to receive documentation from other persons who are not parties to the appeal.

11. Powers of Board where notice served under section 9 or 10[2a]

Where a notice has been served under section 9 or 10, the Board, at any time after the expiration of the period specified in the notice, may, having considered any submissions or observations or document, particulars or other information (as the case may be) submitted by the person on whom the notice has been served, without further notice to that person determine or, in the case of a notice served under section 10, dismiss the appeal.   **[211]**

2 Cross References

a   LG(PD)R 1994 (SI 86/1994), art 48(1) provides that this section shall apply to appeals under LG(PD)A 1963, s 27(4); see also art 53 which relates to references.

4 Commentary

Section 11 simply provides a guillotine procedure where the documentation required has not been submitted.

12. Oral hearings [2a, 3a]

(1) The Board shall have an absolute discretion to hold an oral hearing of any appeal.

(2) (a)   A party to an appeal may request an oral hearing of the appeal.

    (b) (i)   A request for an oral hearing of an appeal shall be made in writing to the Board and shall be accompanied by such fee (if any) as may be payable in respect of such request in accordance with regulations under section 10 of the Act of 1982.

        (ii)   A request for an oral hearing of an appeal which is not accompanied by such fee (if any) as may be payable in respect of such request shall not be considered by the Board.

    (c)   A request by an appellant for an oral hearing of an appeal shall be made within the appropriate period mentioned in section 26(5) of the Principal Act and any request received by the Board after the expiration of that period shall not be considered by the Board.[1a, 1b, 1c]

    (d)   A request by a party to an appeal other than the appellant for an oral hearing of an appeal shall be made within the period mentioned in section 7(2)(a) within which that party may make submissions or observations to the Board in relation to the appeal, and any such request received by the Board after the expiration of that period shall not be considered by the Board.

(3) Where the Board is requested to hold an oral hearing of an appeal and decides to determine the appeal without an oral hearing, the Board shall serve notice of its decision on the person who requested the hearing and on each other party to the appeal.[4]   **[212]**

1 Amendments

a   LG(PD)R 1994 (SI 86/1994), art 49(4)(a) substitutes a new s 12(2)(c) in so far as this section relates to appeals under LG(PD)A 1963, s 89(4) which section deals with the licensing of structures on or adjacent to the public road. The revised wording for s 12(2)(c) would read as follows:

> "(c) A request by an appellant for an oral hearing of an appeal shall accompany the appeal and any request for an oral hearing received by the Board other than a request which accompanies the appeal shall not be considered by the Board."

b   LG(PD)R 1994 (SI 86/1994), art 49(4)(b) substitutes a new s 12(2)(c) in so far as it relates to the classes of appeals specified in art 49(1). The various sections relating to appeals are set out in LG(PD)A 1976, s 14. The wording of art 49(1) excludes appeals under LG(PD)A 1963, ss 26(5), 27(4) and 85(4)(b) from its provisions. The new s 12(2)(c) would read as follows:

> "(c) Where a provision of the Principal Act or of the Act of 1976 authorising an appeal to the Board enables the appeal only to be made within, or before the expiration of, a specified period or before a specified day, a request by an appellant for an oral hearing of an appeal may only be made within, or before the expiration of, the specified period or before the specified day and any request for an oral hearing not so received by the Board shall not be considered by the Board."

c   LG(PD)R 1994 (SI 86/1994), art 53(4) provides that s 12 shall apply to a reference subject to the substitution for s 12(2)(c) of the following paragraph:

> "(c) A request by a person making a reference for an oral hearing of the reference shall accompany the reference and any request for an oral hearing received by the Board other than a request which accompanies the reference shall not be considered by the Board."

2 Cross References

a   LG(PD)R 1994 (SI 86/1994), art 48(3) provides that s 12 may now apply to appeals under LG(PD)A 1963, s 27(4) subject to the substitution of s 27(4) for s 26(5) in subs 12(2)(c); see also art 53 which applies to references.

3 Notes

a   See *Max Developments v An Bord Pleanála* [1994] 2 IR 121 as to how an estoppel can arise when an issue is raised at an oral hearing and thereafter at judicial review proceedings. On oral hearings generally, see *Simunovich v An Bord Pleanála* High Court, unrep, 23 April 1993; *Geraghty v Minister of Local Government* [1976] IR 153 and *Keane v An Bord Pleanála* High Court, unrep, 4 October 1995.

4 Commentary

Section 12 provides that the Board has a discretion to hold an oral hearing. This is usually conducted by an inspector appointed by the Board and is informal in nature. Generally the inspector sets out the procedure to be followed and will determine which party will go first. It is open to each party to call witnesses and to cross-examine at such a hearing. Observers are afforded the right to make submissions at the oral hearing and the inspector prepares a report which is submitted to the Board. This report includes a recommendation but the Board has a discretion either to accept or reject or modify this recommendation. It is also open for the Board to take matters into account which have not been raised at the oral hearing when coming to their decision.

13. Matters other than those raised by parties or other persons may be taken into account in determining appeals

(1) The Board in determining an appeal may take into account matters other than those raised by the parties or by any person who has made submissions or observations to the Board in relation to the appeal if the matters are matters to which, by virtue of section 26(5) of the Principal Act, the Board may have regard. [1a, 1b, 1c]

(2) The Board shall give notice in writing to each of the parties and to each of the persons who have made submissions or observations in relation to the appeal of the matters that it proposes to take into account under subsection (1) and shall indicate in that notice:

(a) in a case where the Board proposes to hold an oral hearing of the appeal, or where an oral hearing of the appeal has been concluded and the Board considers it expedient to re-open the hearing, that submissions in relation to the said matters may be made to the person conducting the hearing, or

(b) in a case where the Board does not propose to hold an oral hearing of the appeal, or where an oral hearing of the appeal has been concluded and the Board does not consider it expedient to re-open the hearing, that submissions or observations in relation to the said matters may be made to the Board in writing within a period specified in the notice (being a period of not less than fourteen or more than twenty-eight days beginning on the date of service of the notice).

(3) (a) Submissions or observations as aforesaid that are received by the Board after the expiration of the period mentioned in subsection (2)(b) shall not be considered by the Board.

(b) Without prejudice to section 9, where a party or a person referred to in subsection (1) makes submissions or observations to the Board in accordance with subsection (2)(b), that party or person shall not be entitled to elaborate in writing upon those submissions or observations or make further submissions or observations in writing in relation to the matters referred to in subsection (1) and any such elaboration, submissions or observations that is or are received by the Board shall not be considered by it.[3]   **[213]**

---

1 Amendments

a LG(PD)R 1994 (SI 86/1994), art 48(4) substitutes a new s 13(1) for appeals under LG(PD)A 1963, s 27(4) which subsection reads as follows:

"(1) The Board in determining an appeal may take into account matters other than those raised by the parties or by any person who has made submissions or observations to the Board in relation to the appeal if the matters either relate to the proper planning and development of the area of the relevant planning authority or are matters to which by virtue of section 24(2) of the Act of 1976 the Board may have regard."

b LG(PD)R 1994 (SI 86/1994), art 49(5) substitutes a new s 13(1) in relation to all appeals except those under LG(PD)A 1963, ss 26(5), 27(4) and 85(4)(b), the new s 13(1) to read as follows:

"(1) The Board in determining an appeal may take into account matters other than those raised by the parties or by any person who has made submissions or observations to the Board in relation to the appeal if the matters either relate to the proper planning and development of the area of the relevant planning authority or are matters to which by virtue of section 24(2) of the Act of 1976 the Board may have regard."

The appeals to which these sections relate are set out in LG(PD)A 1976, s 14.

c   See also LG(PD)R 1994 (SI 86/1994), art 53(4) which provides that this section shall also apply to references and in this regard a new subs 13(1) has been substituted which reads as follows:

"(1) The Board in determining a reference may take into account matters other than those raised by the parties or by any person who has made submissions or observations to the Board in relation to the reference."

4 Commentary

Section 13 allows the Board to take into account matters other than matters which were raised by parties or observers to the appeal. To that extent the Board has its own investigative powers and therefore the limitations contained in s 10 are all the more surprising in that regard. However, the decision of the Board may be open to review where it takes into account certain matters and does not allow a party to make comments on those matters which it has considered before making its determination, particularly where those matters are central to its decision-making function.

---

14. Board may dismiss appeals if vexatious, etc. [2a]

(1) Subject to subsection (2), the Board shall in the following circumstances have an absolute discretion to dismiss an appeal –

(a)   where, having considered the grounds of appeal, the Board is of opinion that the appeal is vexatious, frivolous or without substance or foundation, or

(b)   where, having regard to –

(i)   the nature of the appeal (including any question which in the Board's opinion is raised by the appeal), and

(ii)   any previous permission or approval which in its opinion is relevant,

the Board is satisfied that in the particular circumstances the appeal should not be further considered by it.

(2) The exercise by the Board of the power conferred on it by subsection (1) shall be subject to the restriction imposed on the Board by section 26(5) of the Principal Act.**[214]**

---

2 Cross References

a   See also LG(PD)A 1976, s 19(1).

4 Commentary

Section 14 gives the Board the power to dismiss an appeal where it is vexatious or frivolous but this power has rarely, if ever, been used by the Board. The Board may also dismiss the appeal if the matter has previously been considered by the Board and in those circumstances it can dismiss the appeal in a summary fashion.

---

15. Appeals against conditions [3a]

(1) Where –

(a)   an appeal is brought from a decision of a planning authority to grant a permission or approval, and

(b) the appeal relates only to a condition or conditions that the said decision provides that the permission or approval shall be subject to, and

(c) the Board is satisfied, having regard to the nature of the condition or conditions, that the determination by the Board of the relevant application as if it had been made to it in the first instance would not be warranted,

then, subject to a compliance by the Board with subsection (2), the Board may, in its absolute discretion, give to the relevant planning authority such directions as it considers appropriate relating to the attachment, amendment or removal by that authority either of the condition or conditions to which the appeal relates or of other conditions.

(2) In exercising the power conferred on it by subsection (1), apart from considering the condition or conditions to which the relevant appeal relates, the Board shall be restricted to considering –

(a) the matters which by virtue of section 26(5) of the Principal Act the Board would be restricted to considering were it determining the relevant application as if it had been made to it in the first instance, and

(b) the terms of any previous permission or approval considered by the Board to be relevant. **[215]**

---

3 Notes

a   Scannell, *Environmental and Planning Law* (Roundhall, Sweet & Maxwell 1995) suggests on the authority of *Bord Na Mona v An Bord Pleanála* [1985] IR 205 that where a decision of the Board is declared invalid under s 15 the matter would be remitted to the planning authority. In practice however, it is submitted with respect that as the respondent would be present and the local authority would be a notice party, it is more likely that such matter would be remitted to the Board for its determination. For consideration of an appeal determined under this provision see *MCD Management Services Ltd v Kildare County Council* [1995] 2 ILRM 532 where it was held that documents submitted by the applicant could not be called in aid when considering the terms of the permission granted.

4 Commentary

Section 15 provides that an appeal can be made against conditions only. This allows an appeal purely against a single condition but in those circumstances the Board has discretion to re-open the entirety of the appeal. It is normal for the Board in those circumstances to indicate its intention to re-open the entire matter and an applicant will have an opportunity to withdraw the appeal, thus allowing the decision of the planning authority to stand. It is necessary in those circumstances to carefully consider whether in fact to appeal against a condition or whether to take the permission as it stands and make a subsequent application to modify the condition. This would overcome a developer's concern that the entirety of the permission might be overruled by the Board. It is difficult to see, where there is appeal against a condition only, that the Board can review the entirety of the decision and it is respectfully submitted that it should only be in cases where the condition appealed against is strictly bound up with the overall permission and cannot be separated from it that the Board should be allowed to re-open the entirety of the appeal.

---

16. Power of Board to declare appeals and applications withdrawn [1a, 2a]

(1) Where the Board is of opinion that an appeal, or a planning application to which an appeal relates, has been abandoned, the Board may serve on the person who made the appeal or application, as may be appropriate, a notice stating that fact and requiring that person, within a period specified in the notice (being a period of not less than fourteen

or more than twenty-eight days beginning on the date of service of the notice) to make to the Board a submission in writing as to why the appeal or application, as the case may be, should not be regarded as having been withdrawn.

(2) Where a notice has been served under subsection (1) the Board may, at any time after the expiration of the period specified in the notice, and after considering the submission (if any) made to the Board pursuant to the notice, declare –

    (a) in case the notice refers to a planning application, that the application shall be regarded as having been withdrawn, and

    (b) in case the notice refers to an appeal, that the appeal shall be regarded as having been withdrawn.

(3) Where pursuant to this section the Board declares that a planning application is to be regarded as having been withdrawn, the following provisions shall apply as regards the application:

    (a) any appeal in relation to the application shall be regarded as having been withdrawn and accordingly shall not be determined by the Board, and

    (b) notwithstanding any previous decision under section 26 of the Principal Act by a planning authority as regards the application, no permission or approval shall be granted under that section by the authority on foot of the application. **[216]**

---

1 Amendments

a   LG(PD)R 1994 (SI 86/1994), art 53 provides that s 16 shall apply to a reference subject to the modifications contained in that section.

2 Cross References

a   By virtue of LG(PD)R 1994 (SI 86/1994), art 48(2) s 16 shall now apply to appeals under LG(PD)A 1963, s 27(4) and in this context a reference to a planning application shall be construed as a reference to an application for permission under LG(PD)A 1963, s 27.

4 Commentary

Section 16 gives the power to the Board to declare appeals and applications withdrawn where it is considered that the appeal has been abandoned. The effect of such a determination is that the application is withdrawn and that no decision on the application will have been deemed to have been made not just by the Board but also by the planning authority so that effectively the decision that gave rise to the appeal is revoked.

---

17. Time for appeals, etc. [3a]

(1) (a) Subject to paragraph (b), the provisions of section 26(5) of the Principal Act authorising appeals to be made before the expiration of the appropriate period within the meaning of that subsection shall be construed as including a provision that an appeal received by the Board after the expiration of the appropriate period shall be invalid as not having been made in time.[1a]

      (b) Where the last day of the appropriate period within the meaning of the said section 26(5) is a Saturday, a Sunday, a public holiday (within the meaning of the Holidays (Employees) Act, 1973) or any other day on which the offices of the Board are closed, an appeal shall, notwithstanding paragraph (a), be valid as having been made in time if received by the Board on the next following day on which the offices of the Board are open.[3b]

(2) Where a requirement of or under this Act requires submissions, observations or a request to be made, or documents, particulars or other information to be submitted, to the Board within a specified period and the last day of that period is a Saturday, a Sunday, a public holiday (within the meaning of the Holidays (Employees) Act, 1973) or any other day on which the offices of the Board are closed, the submissions, observations or request, or documents, particulars or other information (as the case may be) shall be regarded as having been received before the expiration of that period if received by the Board on the next following day on which the offices of the Board are open.   **[217]**

1 Amendments

a   LG(PD)R 1994 (SI 86/1994), art 48(5) provides that s 17 shall apply to appeals under LG(PD)A 1963, s 27(4) subject to the substitution of "27(4)" for "26(5)" in subsections 1(a) and (1)(b).

3 Notes

a   For a discussion of what constitutes a "month" see *McCann v An Bord Pleanála* High Court, unrep, 20 June 1996.

b   For consideration of an appeal lodged which relied on this provision, see *Graves v An Bord Pleanála* High Court unrep, 17 June 1997.

4 Commentary

Section 17 provides for the time limits within which an appeal must be made to the Board. The time period specified is one month from the date of the giving of the decision. The word "given" has now been defined as one month from the date of the order being signed and therefore it is the date of the manager's order that the appeal period runs from. There are special provisions where the last day falls on a Saturday or Sunday and generally the appeal must be lodged in the next working day. It is important to note that it is within two months that the appeal must be filed and therefore effectively a person has one month and 30 days within which to lodge the appeal. A month means a calendar month.

18. Regulations

(1) The Minister may by regulations –

   (a) provide for such additional, incidental, consequential or supplemental matters as regards procedure in respect of appeals as appear to the Minister to be necessary or expedient,

   (b) make such provision as regards procedure in respect of other matters with which the Board is concerned as appear to the Minister to be necessary or expedient, including provision for the application of one or more of the provisions of this Act (with or without modifications or adaptations) to such matters.

(2) In particular, and without prejudice to the generality of subsection (1), regulations under this section may –

   (a) provide for any oral hearing by the Board being conducted by a person appointed for that purpose by the Board,

   (b) for the purposes of the Council Directive, enable the Board –

      (i)   when considering an appeal to require the submission to the Board by the applicant of an environmental impact statement in respect of the development to which the appeal relates,

     (ii)   to determine the adequacy for the purposes of its determination of an appeal of the information contained in an environmental impact statement (whether submitted at the instance of the Board or otherwise),

 [(iii)   to require the submission to the Board by the applicant of additional information in relation to the development to which the appeal relates, and][1a]

  (c) enable the Board where it is determining an appeal under section 26(5) or 27(4) of the Principal Act to invite an applicant and enable an applicant so invited to submit to the Board revised plans or other drawings modifying, or other particulars providing for the modification of, the development to which the appeal relates.

(3) Where plans, drawings or particulars mentioned in subsection (2)(c) are submitted to the Board in accordance with regulations under this section, the Board may in determining the appeal grant a permission or an approval for the relevant development as modified by all or any of such plans, drawings or particulars.   **[218]**

---

1 Amendments

a   Sub-paragraph (b)(iii) was inserted by EC(EIA)(A)R 1994 (SI 84/1994), art 9.

4 Commentary

Regulations have now been made with regard to the making of appeals and these are contained in Part V of the LG(PD)R 1994.

---

19. Amendment of Principal Act and Act of 1976[3a]

[219]

---

3 Notes

a   Section 19 amends LG(PD)A 1963, ss 31, 32 35 and 82, and LG(PD)A 1976, ss 19, 24, 26 and 27. See the amended Acts.

4 Commentary

Section 19 makes major amendments to a number of sections in the 1963 Act. It generally introduces a five year limitation period for the bringing of proceedings under ss 31, 32 and 35 of LG(PD)A 1963 and for proceedings under s 27 of the LG(PD)A 1976. It furthermore introduces a new procedure for the judicial review of planning decisions which provides that such proceedings must be brought on notice to all parties to the appeal and must be brought within two months of the giving of the decision. The decision is given from the date that the manager's order is signed or from the date that the decision of the Board is signed.

---

20. Alteration of certain penalties under the Acts

(1) A person convicted by the District Court of an offence for which a penalty is provided in any section of the Principal Act specified in column (2) of the Table to this section at any reference number (not being an offence referred to in the section as a further offence) shall, in lieu of the penalty so provided, be liable to the penalty specified in column (3) of the said Table at that reference number, and that section shall be construed and have effect accordingly.

(2) (a) A person convicted of an offence under subsection (9) of section 32 of the Act of 1976 shall, in lieu of so much of the penalty specified in that subsection as consists of a fine, be liable to a fine not exceeding £1,000, and the said subsection (9) shall be construed and have effect accordingly.

(b) A person convicted of an offence under subsection (10) of section 33 of the Act of 1976 shall, in lieu of so much of the penalty specified in that subsection as consists of a fine, be liable to a fine not exceeding £1,000, and the said subsection (10) shall be construed and have effect accordingly.

(3) A person who is guilty of an offence under section 24(3) of the Principal Act or section 26(4) of the Act of 1976 shall be liable on conviction on indictment to a fine not exceeding £1,000,000 or to imprisonment for a term not exceeding two years, or to both such fine and imprisonment and if the contravention in respect of which he is convicted of an offence under either of the said provisions is continued after the conviction, he shall be guilty of a further offence on every day on which the contravention continues and for each such offence he shall be liable on conviction on indictment to a fine not exceeding £10,000, or to imprisonment for a term not exceeding two years, or to both such fine and imprisonment:

Provided that if a person is convicted in the same proceedings of two or more such further offences the aggregate term of imprisonment to which he shall be liable shall not exceed two years.

(4) Subsection (4) of section 24 of the Principal Act or subsections (7) and (8) of section 26 of the Act of 1976 (as appropriate) shall apply to proceedings for a further offence referred to in subsection (3) as that subsection or those subsections applies or apply to proceedings for an offence under subsection (3) of the said section 24 or subsection (4) of the said section 26 (as appropriate).

(5) (a) So much of each section of the Principal Act specified in paragraph (b) that makes provision in relation to an offence referred to in the section as a further offence shall cease to have effect and, in lieu thereof, it is hereby provided that if the contravention in respect of which a person is convicted of an offence under an aforesaid section is continued after the conviction, that person shall be guilty of a further offence on every day on which the contravention continues and for each such offence he shall be liable on summary conviction to a fine not exceeding –

(i) if the section under which he is convicted of the first offence is a section referred to in paragraph (b)(i), £200, and

(ii) if the section under which he is convicted of the first offence is a section referred to in paragraph (b)(ii), £50.

(b) The sections of the Principal Act referred to in paragraph (a) are –

(i) sections 31(8), 34, 35, 37(7) and 49(2)(b), and

(ii) sections 81(3), 83(7) and 89(8).

(6) Sections 49(2)(c) of the Principal Act is hereby amended by the insertion after "under this subsection" of "or section 20(5) of the Local Government (Planning and Development) Act, 1992,".

(7) Section 9(1) of the Act of 1982 is hereby amended –

(a) by the substitution for "section 8(3) of this Act, or an offence under section 8(4) of this Act" of "section 20(3) of the Local Government (Planning and Development) Act, 1992, or an offence under the said section 20(3)",

(b) by the substitution in paragraph (i) for "£800" of "£1,000", and

(c) by the substitution for paragraph (ii) of the following paragraph:

> "(ii) in case he is convicted of an offence under the said section 20(3), to a fine not exceeding £200 or, at the discretion of the court, to imprisonment for a term not exceeding six months, or to both the fine and the imprisonment:
>
> Provided that if a person is convicted in the same proceedings of two or more offences under the said section 20(3) the aggregate term of imprisonment to which he shall be liable shall not exceed six months.".

(8) Section 13(2) of the Act of 1983 is hereby amended by the substitution for "£800" of "£1,000".

(9) This section shall have effect as respects offences committed after the commencement of this section.

TABLE

Ref. No. (1)	Section of Principal Act (2)	Penalty (3)
1.	7(5), 9(2), 80(4), 81(3), 82(5)(b), 82(7)(b)(iv), 83(7) and 89(8)	£200
2.	31(8), 34(1), 34(6), 35(7), 37(7), 45(8), 46(8), and 49(2)(b)	£1,000

[220]

---

4 Commentary

Section 20 provides for a range of penalties to be imposed where a person is convicted of an offence under the various provisions of the Planning Acts. Criminal prosecutions under the Planning Acts can sometimes be brought summarily but generally they are indictable offences which may be prosecuted summarily. The range of offences for each particular breach of sections are set out in the Table to the Act.

---

21. Amendment of Act of 1990

The Act of 1990 is hereby amended by the insertion in section 21 after "any decision of the authority" of "or the Board". **[221]**

22. Repeals and revocations

(1) The enactments mentioned in the Schedule to this Act are hereby repealed to the extent specified in the third column of that Schedule.

(2) Paragraph (c) of Article 8 and Article 11 of the European Communities (Environmental Impact Assessment) Regulations, 1989 (S.I. No. 349 of 1989), are hereby revoked. **[222]**

23. Transitional provisions

(1) In the case of –

(a) an appeal that is received by the Board before the commencement of a provision of this Act, or

    (b) any other matter with which the Board is concerned that is received by the Board before the commencement of regulations under section 18,

the following provisions shall apply –

        (i)   the provision concerned or the said regulations (as the case may be) shall not apply or have effect in relation to the said appeal or other matter, and

        (ii)   the provisions of the Local Government (Planning and Development) Acts, 1963 to 1991, and regulations made thereunder that were in force immediately before the commencement of the provision concerned or the said regulations (as the case may be) shall, notwithstanding section 22, continue in force and have effect in relation to the said appeal or other matter.

(2) This section shall not prejudice the operation of section 2(6).   **[223]**

24. Short title, collective citation, commencement and construction

(1) This Act may be cited as the Local Government (Planning and Development) Act, 1992.

(2) The Local Government (Planning and Development) Acts, 1963 to 1991, and this Act may be cited together as the Local Government (Planning and Development) Acts, 1963 to 1992.

(3) (a)   This Act shall come into operation on such day or days as may be fixed therefor by order or orders of the Minister, either generally or with reference to any particular purpose or provision, and different days may be so fixed for different purposes and different provisions of this Act.

    (b)   Without prejudice to the generality of paragraph (a), an order under this subsection may fix different days for the coming into operation of paragraph (g) of section 19(4) as respects different provisions of subsection (6) of the section inserted in the Act of 1976 by that paragraph.

(4) This Act and the Local Government (Planning and Development) Acts, 1963 to 1991, shall be construed together as one Act.   **[224]**

Schedule   **(Section 22)**

ENACTMENTS REPEALED

Number and Year	Short Title	Extent of Repeal
No. 28 of 1963	Local Government (Planning and Development) Act, 1963	Subsections (5) and (5A) of section 26.
No. 20 of 1976	Local Government (Planning and Development) Act, 1976	Section 17, subsection (2) of section 19 and sections 20 and 22.
No. 21 of 1982	Local Government (Planning and Development) Act, 1982	Sections 5 and 8 and subsections (3), (6), and (7) of section 10.
No. 28 of 1983	Local Government (Planning and Development) Act, 1983	Paragraph (a) of section 4(1), sections 15 to 20, subsection (2) of section 21, paragraph 2 of the Table to section 21 and section 22.

[225]

LOCAL GOVERNMENT (PLANNING AND DEVELOPMENT) ACT, 1993

(No. 12 of 1993)

ARRANGEMENT OF SECTIONS

ACTS REFERRED TO

An Act to amend and extend the Local Government (Planning and Development) Acts, 1963 to 1992. [14th June, 1993]

Be it enacted by the Oireachtas as follows:

1. Interpretation

(1) In this Act –

"the Acts" means the Local Government (Planning and Development) Acts, 1963 to 1992, and any instrument made thereunder;

"the Commissioners" means the Commissioners of Public Works in Ireland;

"the Principal Act" means the Local Government (Planning and Development) Act, 1963;

"State authority" means any authority being –

    (a) a Minister of the Government, or

    (b) the Commissioners.

(2) In this Act a reference to the carrying out of development on behalf of a State authority shall, where that authority is a Minister of the Government, be construed as including a reference to the carrying out of development by the Commissioners on his behalf.

(3) In this Act –

    (a) a reference to a section is a reference to a section of this Act, unless it is indicated that reference to some other enactment is intended,

    (b) a reference to a subsection or paragraph is a reference to the subsection or paragraph of the provision in which the reference occurs, unless it is indicated that reference to some other provision is intended.

(4) In this Act a reference to any other enactment shall, unless the context otherwise requires, be construed as a reference to that enactment as amended, adapted or extended by or under any subsequent enactment (including this Act). **[226]**

4 Commentary

LG(PD)A 1993 arose from the decision of *Howard v Commissioners of Public Works* Supreme Court, unrep, 26 May 1993 which held that State authorities were not exempt from the necessity to obtain planning permission. This Act provides for how the controls under the Planning Acts are to apply to such authorities.

2. Development by State authorities

(1) (a) Without prejudice to section 4 of the Principal Act, the Minister may, by regulations, provide that the Acts shall not apply to any specified class or classes of development by or on behalf of a State authority where –

    (i) such development is, in the opinion of the Minister, in connection with or for the purposes of public safety or order, the administration of justice or national security or defence; [2a] or

    (ii) the carrying out of such development requires to be authorised by or under any enactment (whether such authorisation takes the form of the grant of a licence, consent, approval or any other type of authorisation), [2b]

and for so long as such regulations are in force the Acts shall not apply to the said class or classes of development.

(b) The Minister may, where he considers it necessary or expedient to do so, by regulations provide for any or all of the following matters in relation to any class or classes of development to which regulations under paragraph (a) apply, namely:

    (i) the publication by a State authority of any specified notice with respect to development that it proposes to carry out or to have carried out on its behalf (hereafter in this paragraph referred to as "proposed development"),

    (ii) the giving by a State authority, to the planning authority for the area in which proposed development is to be carried out or any other specified person, of any specified notice, documents, particulars, plans or other information with respect to the proposed development,

    (iii) the making available for inspection by members of the public of any specified documents, particulars, plans or other information with respect to proposed development,

    (iv) the preparation of an environmental impact statement with respect to proposed development, the contents of such a statement and the making available for inspection or purchase by members of the public of such a statement,

    (v) the making of submissions or observations to a State authority with respect to proposed development,

    (vi) the reference to a specified person of any dispute or disagreement with respect to proposed development between a State authority and the planning authority for the area in which the proposed development is to be carried out,

    (vii) requiring a State authority, in deciding whether proposed development is to be carried out, to have regard to any specified matters or considerations.

(2) (a) Where development is proposed to be carried out by or on behalf of a Minister of the Government or the Commissioners, the Minister of the Government concerned or, in the case of development proposed to be carried out by or on behalf of the Commissioners, the Minister for Finance may, if he is satisfied that the carrying out of the development is required by reason of an accident or emergency, by order provide that the Acts or, as may be appropriate, any requirement or requirements of regulations under subsection (1)(b) specified in the order shall not apply to the development and for so long as such an order is in force the Acts or the said requirement or requirements, as the case may be, shall not apply to the development.

(b) A Minister of the Government may by order revoke an order made by him under paragraph (a).

(c) A Minister of the Government shall cause an order made by him under this subsection to be published in the *Iris Oifigiúil* and notice of the making of the order to be published in a newspaper circulating in the area of the development concerned.

(3) Regulations under subsection (1)(b) may contain such incidental, supplemental and consequential provisions as appear to the Minister to be necessary or expedient and, without prejudice to the generality of the foregoing, may include provisions modifying or adapting any enactment or instrument made under an enactment for the purpose of enabling the regulations to have full effect. **[227]**

---

2 Cross References

a   See LG(PD)R 1994 (SI 86/1994), art 156, 158.

b   See LG(PD)R 1994 (SI 86/1994), art 157.

4 Commentary

Section 2 provides that the Planning Acts apply to all developments to be undertaken by the State which is in the same position as any other person except in regard to those developments which are specifically exempted by the Minister under Regulations. These Regulations are now contained in Part XIII of the LG(PD)R 1994.

---

3.   Amendment of section 78 of Principal Act [3a]

[228]

---

3 Notes

a   Section 3 amends LG(PD)A 1963, s 78. See the amended Act.

---

4.   Application of Part IV of Principal Act to certain development

(1) Permission under Part IV of the Principal Act shall not be, and shall be deemed never to have been, required for development carried out or commenced by or on behalf of a State authority before the commencement of this section (hereinafter in this subsection referred to as "State development"):

Provided that if in any proceedings –

(i) a court has, before the commencement of this section, made a finding that permission as aforesaid was required for particular State development, or

(ii) a court, after the commencement of this section, makes such a finding and the proceedings concerned were initiated before the 26th day of May, 1993,

this subsection shall not have effect in relation to the particular State development.

(2) Permission under Part IV of the Principal Act shall not be required for –

(a) any development commenced by or on behalf of a State authority during a period of one year beginning on the commencement of this section, or[2a]

(b) any development commenced by or on behalf of a State authority after the commencement of section 5 in respect of which consultation pursuant to section 84 of the Principal Act has been completed before the commencement of section 5.   **[229]**

---

2 Cross References

a   Section 4 was brought into force on 15 June 1993 by SI 152/1993.

4 Commentary

Section 4 is a saver for those developments which were commenced before the enactment of the legislation except for the *Howard* and *Byrne* cases.

---

5.   Repeal[2a]

Section 84 of the Principal Act is hereby repealed.   **[230]**

---

2 Cross References

a   Section 5 came into force on 15 June 1994. See SI 152/1993.

---

6.   Short title, collective citation, commencement and construction

(1) This Act may be cited as the Local Government (Planning and Development) Act, 1993.

(2) The Local Government (Planning and Development) Acts, 1963 to 1992, and this Act may be cited together as the Local Government (Planning and Development) Acts, 1963 to 1993.

(3) This Act shall came into operation on such day or days as may be fixed therefor by order or orders of the Minister, either generally or with reference to any particular purpose or provision, and different days may be so fixed for different provisions of this Act.

(4) This Act and the Local Government (Planning and Development) Acts, 1963 to 1992, shall be construed together as one Act.   **[231]**

LOCAL GOVERNMENT (PLANNING AND DEVELOPMENT) ACT, 1998

(No. 9 of 1998)

ARRANGEMENT OF SECTIONS

Section

1. Amendment of Local Government (Planning and Development) Act, 1983.
2. Indemnification.
3. Continuance in office of members of Board.
4. Short title, collective citation and construction.

ACTS REFERRED TO

Civil Service Regulation Act, 1956	1956, No. 46
Local Government (Planning and Development) Act, 1976	1976, No. 20
Local Government (Planning and Development) Act, 1983	1983, No. 28
Local Government (Planning and Development) Act, 1992	1992, No. 14
Local Government (Planning and Development) Acts, 1963 to 1993	

An Act to amend and extend the Local Government (Planning and Development) Acts, 1963 to 1993, to provide for certain matters relating to An Bord Pleanála [16th April, 1998]

1. Amendment of Local Government (Planning and Development) Act, 1983[3a]

[232]

---

3 Notes

a   Section 1 substitutes LG(PD)A 1983, s 3. See the amended Act.

---

2. Indemnification

Where the Board is satisfied that a member of the Board, an employee of the Board or a person whose services are provided to the Board under sections 10(2), 13(1) and 21(3) of the Local Government (Planning and Development) Act, 1976, has discharged his or her duties in relation to the functions of the Board in a *bona fide* manner, it shall indemnify such member, employee or person against all actions or claims howsoever arising in respect of the discharge by him or her of his or her duties. **[233]**

3. Continuance in office of members of Board

Any member of the Board in office immediately prior to the passing of this Act shall continue in office as if this Act had not been enacted. **[234]**

4. Short title, collective citation and construction

(1) This Act may be cited as the Local Government (Planning and Development) Act, 1998.

(2) The Local Government (Planning and Development) Acts, 1963 to 1993, and this Act may be cited together as the Local Government (Planning and Development) Acts, 1963 to 1998.

(3) This Act and the Local Government (Planning and Development) Acts, 1963 to 1993, shall be construed together as one Act. **[235]**

LOCAL GOVERNMENT (PLANNING AND DEVELOPMENT) ACT, 1999

Number 17 of 1999

ARRANGEMENT OF SECTIONS

ACTS REFERRED TO

An Act to amend and extend the Local Government (Planning And Development) Acts, 1963 to 1998, to make better provision for the protection of the architectural heritage in the interests of the common good and to provide for related matters. [30th June, 1999]

Be it enacted by the Oireachtas as follows:

1. Interpretation

(1) In this Act, unless the context otherwise requires -

"**the Act of 1976**" means the Local Government (Planning and Development) Act, 1976;

"**architectural conservation area**" means a place, area, group of structures or townscape, taking account of building lines and heights, which -

    (a) is of special architectural, historical, archaeological, artistic, cultural, scientific, social or technical interest, or

    (b) contributes to the appreciation of protected structures;

"**attendant grounds**", in relation to a structure, includes land lying outside the curtilage of the structure;

"**endangered**" means exposed to harm, decay or damage, whether immediately or over a period of time, through neglect or through direct or indirect means;

"**occupier**", in relation to a protected structure or a proposed protected structure, means -

    (a) any person in or entitled to immediate use or enjoyment of the structure,

    (a) any person entitled to occupy the structure, and

    (c) any other person having, for the time being, control of the structure;

"**the Principal Act**" means the Local Government (Planning and Development) Act, 1963;

"**proposed protected structure**" means a structure in respect of which a notice is issued under section 6 of this Act or under Part III of the Principal Act proposing to add the structure, or a specified part of it, to a record of protected structures, and, where that notice so indicates, includes any specified feature which is within the attendant grounds of the structure and which would not otherwise be included in this definition;

"**protected structure**" means -

    (a) a structure, or

    (b) a specified part of a structure,

which is included in a record of protected structures, and, where that record so indicates, includes any specified feature which is within the attendant grounds of the structure and which would not otherwise be included in this definition;

"**protection**", in relation to a structure or part of a structure, includes conservation, preservation and improvement compatible with maintaining the character and interest of the structure or part;

"**record of protected structures**" means the record included under section 2 in a development plan;

"**registering authority**" means a registering authority within the meaning of the Registration of Title Act, 1964;

"**structure**" has the same meaning as in the Principal Act but includes -

    (a) the interior of the structure,

    (b) the land lying within the curtilage of the structure,

    (c) any other structures lying within that curtilage and their interiors, and

    (d) all fixtures and features which form part of the interior or exterior of any structure or structures referred to in paragraph (a) or (c);

"**vesting order**" means an order made under section 25.

(2) For the purposes of this Act, the definition of "works" in section 2 of the Principal Act includes any act or operation involving the application or removal of plaster, paint, wallpaper, tiles, or other material to or from the surfaces of the interior or exterior of a structure.

(3) In this Act -

    (a) a reference to a section is to a section of this Act unless it is indicated that a reference to some other enactment is intended,

    (b) a reference to a subsection or paragraph is to a subsection or paragraph of the provision in which the reference occurs unless it is indicated that a reference to some other provision is intended,

    (c) a reference to an enactment is to that enactment as amended at any time by any enactment, including this Act.   **[236]**

2. Record of protected structures

(1) For the purpose of protecting structures, or parts of structures, which are of special architectural, historical, archaeological, artistic, cultural, scientific, social or technical interest, every development plan shall include a record of protected structures and shall include in that record every structure which is in the opinion of the planning authority of such interest within its functional area.

(2) After consulting with the Minister for Arts, Heritage, Gaeltacht and the Islands, the Minister shall prescribe the form of record of protected structures.

(3) Subject to any additions or deletions made to the record either under this Act or in the course of a review of the development plan under Part III of the Principal Act, a record of protected structures shall continue to be part of that plan or any variation or replacement of the plan.

(4) Subject to this Act, Part III of the Principal Act shall apply to a record of protected structures. **[237]**

3. Guidelines for planning authorities

(1) The Minister for Arts, Heritage, Gaeltacht and the Islands shall, after consulting with the Minister, issue guidelines to planning authorities concerning development objectives -

  (a) for protecting structures, or parts of structures, which are of special architectural, historical, archaeological, artistic, cultural, scientific, social or technical interest, and

  (b) for preserving the character of architectural conservation areas,

and any such guidelines shall include the criteria to be applied when selecting proposed protected structures for inclusion in the record of protected structures.

(2) The Minister for Arts, Heritage, Gaeltacht and the Islands may, after consulting with the authorities of any religious denominations which he or she considers necessary, issue guidelines to planning authorities concerning -

  (a) the issue of declarations under section 8 in respect of protected structures which are regularly used as places of public worship, and

  (b) the consideration by planning authorities of applications for development affecting the interior of such protected structures.

(3) In considering development objectives, a planning authority shall have regard to any guidelines issued under this section.

(4) In this section "development objective" means an objective which, under section 19 of the Principal Act, a planning authority proposes to include in its development plan. **[238]**

4. Recommendations to planning authorities concerning specific structures

(1) The Minister for Arts, Heritage, Gaeltacht and the Islands may, in writing, make recommendations to a planning authority concerning the inclusion in its record of protected structures of any or all of the following:

  (a) particular structures;

  (b) specific parts of particular structures;

  (c) specific features within the attendant grounds of particular structures.

(2) A planning authority shall have regard to any recommendations made to it under this section.

(3) A planning authority which, after considering a recommendation made to it under this section, decides not to comply with the recommendation shall inform the Minister for Arts, Heritage, Gaeltacht and the Islands in writing of the reason for its decision. **[239]**

5. Additions to and deletions from record of protected structures

(1) A planning authority may add to or delete from its record of protected structures a structure, a specified part of a structure or a specified feature of the attendant grounds of a structure, where -

    (a) the authority considers that -

        (i) in the case of an addition, the addition is necessary or desirable in order to protect a structure, or part of a structure, of special architectural, historical, archaeological, artistic, cultural, scientific, social or technical interest, whether or not a recommendation has been made under section 4, or

        (ii) in the case of a deletion, the protection of the structure or part is no longer warranted,

    and

    (b) the addition or deletion is made in accordance with a review of a development plan under Part III of the Principal Act or in accordance with section 6 or 38 of this Act.

(2) The making of an addition to, or a deletion from, a record of protected structures shall be a reserved function.   **[240]**

6. Procedure for making additions or deletions

(1) A planning authority which proposes, at any time other than in the course of reviewing its development plan under Part III of the Principal Act, to make an addition to or a deletion from its record of protected structures shall -

    (a) serve on each person who is the owner or occupier of the proposed protected structure or the protected structure, as the case may be, a notice of the proposed addition or deletion, including the particulars,

    (b) send particulars of the proposed addition or deletion to the Minister for Arts, Heritage, Gaeltacht and the Islands and to any other prescribed bodies, and

    (c) cause notice of the proposed addition or deletion to be published in the Iris Oifigiuil and in at least one newspaper circulating in the area.

(2) A notice under subsection 1(a) or (c) shall state the following:

    (a) that particulars of the proposed addition or deletion may be inspected at a specified place during a specified period of not less than one month;

    (b) that, within 14 days from the end of the period for inspection, any person may make written objections or representations with respect to the proposed addition or deletion to the planning authority;

    (c) that any person making an objection or representation under paragraph (b) may include in the objection or representation a request to be afforded an opportunity to state his or her case before a person or persons appointed by the planning authority;

    (d) whether or not the proposed addition or deletion was recommended by the Minister for Arts, Heritage, Gaeltacht and the Islands;

    (e) that, if the proposed addition or deletion was recommended by the Minister for Arts, Heritage, Gaeltacht and the Islands, the planning authority shall forward to that Minister for his or her observations a copy of any objection or representation made under paragraph (b).

(3) Before making the proposed addition or deletion, the planning authority shall -

(a) consider any written objections or representations received under subsection (2)(b),

(b) comply with any request made under subsection (2)(c). and

(c) have regard to any observations received from the Minister for Arts, Heritage, Gaeltacht and the Islands concerning those objections or representations within one month after the receipt by that Minister of a copy of the objections or representations.

(4) Within 3 months after the end of the period allowed under subsection (2)(a) for inspection, the planning authority shall decide whether or not the proposed addition or deletion should be made.

(5) Within 14 days after making an addition to or a deletion from the record of protected structures, a planning authority shall serve on the owner and on the occupier of the structure concerned a notice of the addition or deletion, including the particulars. **[241]**

7. Registration under the Registration of Title Act, 1964

Where a structure, a specified part of a structure or a specified feature within the attendant grounds of a structure is included in the record of protected structures, its inclusion may be registered under the Registration of Title Act, 1964, in the appropriate register maintained under that Act as a burden affecting registered land (within the meaning of that Act).   **[242]**

8. Works affecting the character of protected structures or proposed protected structures

(1) Notwithstanding section 4(1)(g) of the Principal Act, the carrying out of works to a protected structure, or a proposed protected structure, shall be exempted development for the purposes of the Principal Act only if those works would not materially affect the character of -

(a) the structure, or

(b) any element of the structure which contributes to its special architectural, historical, archaeological, artistic, cultural, scientific, social or technical interest.

(2) An owner or occupier of a protected structure may make a written request to the planning authority within whose functional area that structure is situated to issue a declaration as to the type of works which it considers would or would not materially affect the character of the structure or of any element referred to in subsection (1)(b) of that structure.

(3) Within 3 months after receiving a request under subsection (1) or within such other period as may be prescribed, a planning authority shall issue a declaration under this section to the person who made the request.

(4) Before issuing a declaration under this section, a planning authority shall have regard to -

(a) any guidelines issued under section 3, and

(b) any recommendations made to the authority under section 4.

(5) If the declaration relates to a protected structure which is regularly used as a place of public worship, the planning authority -

(a) in addition to having regard to the guidelines and recommendations referred to in subsection (4) shall respect liturgical requirements, and

(b) for the purpose of ascertaining those requirements shall -

    (i) comply with any guidelines concerning consultation which may be issued by the Minister for Arts, Heritage, Gaeltacht and the Islands, or

    (ii) if no such guidelines are issued, consult with such person or body as the planning authority considers appropriate.

(6) When considering an application for permission or approval for the development of land under Part IV of the Principal Act which -

(a) relates to the interior of a protected structure, and

(b) is regularly used as a place of public worship,

the planning authority, and the Board on appeal, shall, in addition to any other requirements of the Local Government (Planning and Development) Acts, 1963 to 1998, respect liturgical requirements.

(7) A planning authority may at any time review a declaration issued under this section but the review shall not affect any works carried out in reliance on the declaration prior to the review.

(8) A planning authority shall cause -

(a) the details of any declaration issued by that authority under this section to be entered on the register kept by the authority under section 8 of the Principal Act, and

(b) a copy of the declaration to be made available for inspection by members of the public during office hours at the office of the authority following the issue of the declaration.

(9) A declaration under this section shall not prejudice the application of section 5 of the Principal Act to any question that arises as to what in a particular case is or is not exempted development.

(10)(a) For the avoidance of doubt, it is hereby declared that, in considering any application for permission or approval in relation to a protected structure, a planning authority. or the Board on appeal, shall have regard to the protected status of that structure.

(b) A planning authority. or the Board on appeal. shall not grant permission for the demolition of a protected structure save in exceptional circumstances.   **[243]**

9. Duty of owners and occupiers to protect structures from endangerment

(1) Each owner and each occupier shall, to the extent consistent with the rights and obligations arising out of their respective interests in a protected structure or a proposed protected structure, ensure that the structure, or any element of it which contributes to its special architectural, historical, archaeological, artistic, cultural. scientific, social or technical interest, is not endangered.

(2) The duty imposed by subsection (1) in relation to a proposed protected structure arises at the time the owner or occupier is notified under section 6 of this Act or under Part III of the Principal Act of the proposal to add the structure to the record of protected structures.

(3) Neither of the following shall be considered to be a breach of the duty imposed on each owner and each occupier under this section:

(a) development in respect of which permission under section 26 of the Principal Act has been granted;

(b) development consisting only of works of a type which, in a declaration issued under section 8(3) of this Act to that owner or occupier, a planning authority has declared would not materially affect the character of the protected structure or any element referred to in subsection (1) of this section of that structure.

(4) Any person who, without lawful authority, causes damage to a protected structure or a proposed protected structure shall be guilty of an offence.

(5) Without prejudice to any other defence that may be available, it shall be a good defence in any proceedings for an offence under subsection (4) to prove that the damage to the structure resulted from works which were -

(a) urgently required in order to secure the preservation of the structure or any part of it,

(b) undertaken in good faith solely for the purpose of temporarily safeguarding the structure, and

(c) unlikely to permanently alter the structure or any element of it referred to in subsection (1).   **[244]**

10. Power to require works to be carried out in relation to endangerment of protected structures

(1) Where, in the opinion of the planning authority, it is necessary to do so in order to prevent a protected structure situated within its functional area from becoming or continuing to be endangered, the authority shall serve on each person who is the owner or occupier of the protected structure a notice -

(a) specifying the works which the planning authority considers necessary in order to prevent the protected structure from becoming or continuing to be endangered, and

(b) requiring the person on whom the notice is being served to carry out those works within a specified period of not less than 2 months from the date the notice comes into effect under section 13.

(2) After serving notice under subsection (1) on a person, a planning authority may -

(a) at its discretion, assist the person in carrying out the works required under the notice, and

(b) provide such assistance in any form it considers appropriate. including advice, financial aid, materials, equipment and the services of the authority's staff.

(3) Any person on whom a notice under subsection (1) has been served may, within one month from the date of service of the notice, make written representations to the planning authority concerning -

(a) the terms of the notice,

(b) the provision of assistance under subsection (1), and

(c) any other material considerations.

(4) After considering any representations made under subsection (3), the planning authority may confirm, amend or revoke the notice and shall notify the person who made the representations of its decision.

(5) Particulars of a notice served under this section shall be entered in the register kept by the planning authority under section 8 of the Principal Act.   **[245]**

11. Power to require restoration of character of protected structures and other places

(1) In this section "works", in relation to a structure or any element of a structure, includes the removal, alteration or replacement of any specified part of the structure or element and the removal or alteration of any advertisement structure.

(2) A planning authority may serve a notice that complies with subsection (3) on each person who is the owner or occupier of a structure situated within its functional area, if -

    (a) the structure is a protected structure and, in the opinion of the planning authority, the character of the structure or of any of its elements ought to be restored, or

    (b) the structure forms part of a place, an area, a group of structures or a townscape which is of special architectural, historical, archaeological, artistic, cultural, scientific, social or technical interest and, in the opinion of the planning authority, it is desirable to restore the character of that place, area, group of structures or townscape, as the case may be.

(3) A notice under subsection (2) shall -

    (a) specify the works required to be carried out for the purposes of restoring the structure or element referred to in the notice,

    (b) state that the person on whom the notice is served may, within a specified period of not less than 2 months from the date of the service of the notice, make written representations to the planning authority concerning the notice,

    (c) invite that person to enter into discussions with the planning authority, within a specified period of not less than 2 months from the date of the service of the notice, concerning the notice and in particular concerning -

        (i) the provision by the planning authority of advice, materials, equipment, the services of the authority s staff or other assistance in carrying out the works specified in the notice, and

        (ii) the period within which the works are to be carried out,

        (iii) specify the period within which, unless otherwise agreed in the discussions under paragraph (c), the works shall be carried out, being a period of not less than 2 months from the end of the period allowed for entering into discussions, and

    (e) state that, to the extent that the works relate to an authorised structure or a structure which has been constructed, erected or made five years or more prior to the service of the notice, the planning authority shall pay any expenses that are reasonably incurred by that person in carrying out the works in accordance with the notice.

(4) In deciding whether to serve a notice under this section, a planning authority shall have regard to any guidelines issued under section 3 and any recommendations made under section 4.

(5) If the invitation under subsection (3)(c) to enter into discussions is accepted, the planning authority shall facilitate the holding of those discussions.

(6) After considering any representations made under subsection (3)(b) and any discussions held under subsection (5), the planning authority may confirm, amend or revoke the notice and shall notify the person who made the representations of its decision.

(7) Particulars of a notice served under this section shall be entered in the register kept by the planning authority under section 8 of the Principal Act.   **[246]**

12. Appeals against notices concerning endangerment or restoration of structures

(1) Within 14 days after being notified under section 10(4) or 11(6) of the confirmation or amendment of a notice, any person who made representations in relation to the notice may appeal against the notice to the District Court on any one or more of the following grounds:

    (a) that the person is not the owner or occupier of the structure in respect of which the notice has been served:

    (b) that, in the case of a notice under section 10(1), compliance with the requirements of the notice would involve unreasonable expense and that the person had stated in representations made to the planning authority under section 10(3) that he or she did not have the means to pay;

    (c) that the person has already taken all reasonable steps to -

        (i) in the case of a notice under section 10(1), prevent the structure from becoming or continuing to be endangered,

        (ii) in the case of a notice under section 11(2) in relation to a protected structure, restore the character of the structure or the element, or

        (iii) in the case of a notice under section 11(2) in relation to a structure that forms part of a place, area, group of structures or townscape referred to in paragraph (c) of that section assist in restoring the character of that place, area, group of structures or townscape, as the case may be;

    (d) that the time for complying with the notice is unreasonably short.

(2) Notice of an appeal under subsection (1) shall be given to the planning authority and it shall be entitled to appear, be heard and adduce evidence on the hearing of the appeal

(3) On the hearing of the appeal, the District Court may, as it thinks proper -

    (a) confirm the notice unconditionally,

    (b) confirm the notice subject to such modifications or additions as the Court thinks reasonable, or

    (c) annul the notice

(4) Where the notice is confirmed under subsection (3)(b) subject to modifications or additions, the notice shall have effect subject to those modifications or additions. **[247]**

13. Effective date of notices concerning endangerment or restoration of structures

A notice under section 10(1) or 11(2) shall not have effect until the expiry of one month from the date of service of the notice, subject to the following exceptions:

(a) if any representations have been made under section 10 or 11 in relation to the notice and no appeal is taken within the period allowed under section 12(1), the notice has effect on the expiry of the appeal period;

(b) if an appeal is taken under section 12(1) and the notice is confirmed, the notice has effect on the date on which the decision of the District Court is pronounced or the date on which that order is expressed to take effect, whichever is later;

(c) if an application is made to the District Court under section 16(1) and an order is made under section 16(2)(a), the notice has effect on the date on which the decision of the Court is pronounced or the date on which that order is expressed to take effect, whichever is later.   **[248]**

14. Offence relating to endangerment of structures

A person who fails to comply with a notice served on him or her under section 10(1) shall be guilty of an offence.   **[249]**

15. Owners' powers in relation to notices concerning endangerment or restoration of structures

Any person who is the owner of the land or structure in respect of which a notice under section 10(1) or 11(2) has been served, and his or her servants or agents, may enter that land or structure and carry out the works required under the notice.   **[250]**

16. Application to District Court for necessary consent

(1) A person served with a notice under section 10(1) or 11(2) may apply to the District Court for an order under subsection (2) of this section if -

(a) that person is unable, without the consent of another person, to carry out the works required under the notice, and

(b) the other person withholds consent to the carrying out of those works.

(2) If, on hearing an application under subsection (1), the District Court determines that the other person's consent has been unreasonably withheld -

(a) the Court may, at its discretion, deem that consent to have been given, and

(b) in that case, the person making the application shall be entitled to carry out the works required under the notice.   **[251]**

17. Jurisdiction of District Court

The jurisdiction conferred on the District Court -

(a) by section 12 in relation to an appeal against a notice, or

(b) by section 16 in relation to an application for an order deeming consent to have been given,

shall be exercised by a judge of that Court having jurisdiction in the district in which the structure that is the subject of the appeal or application is situated.   **[252]**

18. Application to court for contribution to cost of carrying out works on endangered structures

(1) A person who has been served with a notice under section (10)1 and who has carried out the works required under the notice may apply to a court of competent jurisdiction

for an order directing that all, or such part as may be specified in the order, of the cost of those works be borne by some other person who has an interest in the structure concerned.

(2) On the hearing of an application under subsection (1), the court shall make such order as it considers just having regard to all the circumstances of the case.   **[253]**

19. Carrying out of certain works to be exempted development

The carrying out of any works specified in a notice under section 10(1) or 11(2) shall be exempted development.   **[254]**

20. Planning authority's power to carry out works

Where a person on whom a planning authority has served a notice under section 10(1) or 11(2) fails to comply with the notice, the planning authority may take such steps as it considers reasonable and necessary to give effect to the terms of the notice including -

    (a) entry on land by authorised persons in accordance with section 83 of the Principal Act as applied by section 31(3) of this Act, and

    (b) the carrying out, or arranging the carrying out, of the works specified in the notice.   **[255]**

21. Recovery by planning authority of expenses for carrying out works on endangered structures

A planning authority which serves a notice under section 10(1) in respect of a protected structure may -

    (a) recover (whether as a simple contract debt in a court of competent jurisdiction or otherwise) from the owner any expenses reasonably incurred by the authority under section 20, including any assistance provided under section 10(2), and

    (b) secure those expenses by -

        (i) charging the protected structure under the Registration of Title Act, 1964, or

        (ii) an instrument vesting the ownership of the protected structure in the authority subject to a right of redemption by the owner.

[256]

22. Power to acquire protected structure

(1) A planning authority may acquire by agreement or compulsorily any protected structure situated within its functional area if -

    (a) it appears to the planning authority that it is necessary or desirable to do so for the protection of the structure, and

    (b) in the case of a compulsory acquisition, the structure is not lawfully occupied as a dwelling house by any person other than a person employed as a caretaker.

(2) In this section and sections 23 to 28, a reference to a protected structure shall be construed to include a reference to any land which -

    (a) forms part of the attendant ground of that structure, and

    (b) is, in the planning authority's opinion, necessary to secure the protection of that structure, whether or not the land lies within the curtilage of the structure or is specified as a feature in the record of protected structures.   **[257]**

23. Notice of intention to acquire protected structure compulsorily

(1) A planning authority intending to acquire any protected structure compulsorily under this Act shall -

    (a) publish in one or more newspapers circulating in its functional area a notice -

        (i) stating its intention to acquire the protected structure compulsorily under this Act,

        (ii) describing the structure to which the notice relates,

        (iii) naming the place where a map showing the location of the protected structure is deposited and the times during which it may be inspected, and

        (iv) specifying the time within which (not being less than one month) and the manner in which objections to the acquisition of the structure may be made to the planning authority,

    and

    (b) serve on every owner, lessee and occupier (except tenants for one month or a period less than one month) of the structure a notice which complies with paragraph (a).

(2) In this section, "**owner**", in relation to a protected structure, means -

    (a) a person, other than a mortgagee not in possession, who is for the time being entitled to dispose (whether in possession or reversion) of the fee simple of the protected structure, and

    (b) a person who, under a lease or agreement the unexpired term of which exceeds 5 years, holds or is entitled to the rents or profits of the protected structure.**[258]**

24. Objection to compulsory acquisition of protected structure

(1) Any person on whom a notice of the proposed compulsory acquisition of a protected structure has been served under section 23(1)(b) may, within the time and in the manner specified in the notice, submit to the planning authority concerned an objection to the proposed compulsory acquisition referred to in the notice.

(2) A person who has submitted an objection under subsection (1) may withdraw the objection by notice in writing sent to the planning authority concerned.

(3) Where an objection submitted to a planning authority under subsection (1) is not withdrawn, the planning authority shall not acquire the protected structure compulsorily without the Minister's consent.

(4) An application for the Minister's consent to the compulsory acquisition of a protected structure shall be made within one month after the expiry of the time allowed under subsection (1) for submitting an objection to that acquisition and shall be accompanied by the following:

    (a) the relevant map;

    (b) a copy of the objection made under subsection (1) to the planning authority;

    (c) the planning authority's comments (if any) on the objection;

    (d) such other documents and particulars as may be prescribed.

(5) On receipt of the planning authority's comments (if any) on the objection, the Minister shall, by notice served on the person who made the objection, send a copy of

the comments to that person who may, within 21 days from the date of the service of the notice, make observations to the Minister in relation to the comments.

(6) On application under subsection (4), the Minister may, as he or she thinks fit, grant or refuse to grant consent to the compulsory acquisition of all or part of a protected structure referred to in a notice published under section 23.   **[259]**

25. Vesting order

(1) After complying with section 24, a planning authority may, by vesting order, acquire a protected structure if -

(a) no objection is submitted to the planning authority under section 24,

(b) any objection submitted under section 24 is subsequently withdrawn, or

(c) the Minister consents to the compulsory acquisition of the structure by the planning authority.

(2) Where a planning authority becomes aware before making a vesting order in respect of a protected structure that the structure is subject (whether alone or in conjunction with other land) to -

(a) any annuity or other payment to the Minister for Agriculture and Food or to the Commissioners of Public Works in Ireland, or

(b) any charge payable to the Revenue Commissioners on the death of any person,

the planning authority shall forthwith inform the Minister for Agriculture and Food, the Commissioners of Public Works in Ireland or the Revenue Commissioners, as the case may be, of its intention to make the vesting order.

(3) Within 14 days after making a vesting order, a planning authority shall -

(a) publish in one or more newspapers circulating within its functional area a notice -

(i)   stating that the order has been made,

(ii) describing the protected structure to which it relates, and

(iii) naming a place where a copy of the order and the attached map may be seen at all reasonable times, and

(b) serve on every person appearing to the authority to have an interest in the protected structure to which the order relates a notice stating that the order has been made and the effect of the order.   **[260]**

26. Form and effect of vesting order

(1) A vesting order by which a planning authority acquires a protected structure under this Act shall be in the prescribed form and shall have attached to it a map showing the location of the protected structure.

(2) A vesting order shall be expressed and shall operate to vest the protected structure to which it relates in the planning authority in fee simple free from encumbrances and all estates, rights, titles and interests of whatsoever kind on a specified date (in this Act referred to as the vesting date) not earlier than 21 days after the making of the order.

(3) Notwithstanding subsection (2), where a planning authority has acquired by a vesting order a protected structure which is subject, either alone or in conjunction with other land, to an annual sum payable to the Minister for Agriculture and Food or the Commissioners of Public Works in Ireland, the planning authority shall become and be

liable, as from the vesting date, for the payment to that Minister or those Commissioners, as the case may be, of -

(a) that annual sum, or

(b) such portion of it as shall be apportioned by the Minister or Commissioners, as the case may be,

as if the protected structure had been transferred to the authority by the owner on that date.

(4) For the purposes of subsection (3), an **"annual sum"** means a purchase annuity, a payment in lieu of rent, or any other annual sum which is not merely a rent under a contract of tenancy. **[261]**

27. Registration of acquired title and amendment of vesting order

(1) On making a vesting order in relation to a protected structure, a planning authority shall send the order to the registering authority which on receipt of the order shall immediately cause the planning authority to be registered as owner of the land in accordance with the order.

(2) On the application of any person, a planning authority may amend a vesting order made by the authority if -

(a) the authority is satisfied that the vesting order contains an error or mistake, whether occasioned by it or otherwise, and

(b) the error or mistake may be rectified without injustice to any person.

(3) Where a copy of an order under subsection (2) amending a vesting order is lodged with the registering authority, that authority shall rectify its register in such manner as may be necessary to make the register conformable with the amending order. **[262]**

28. Compensation

(1) Any person who, immediately before a vesting order is made, has any estate or interest in, or any right in respect of, the protected structure acquired by the order may apply to the planning authority within 12 months after the making of the order for compensation in respect of the estate, interest or right.

(2) On application under subsection (1), the planning authority shall, subject to subsection (4), pay to the applicant by way of compensation an amount equal to the value (if any) of the estate, interest or right.

(3) The compensation to be paid by the planning authority under this section in respect of any estate, interest or right in respect of the protected structure shall, in default of agreement, be determined by arbitration under and in accordance with the Acquisition of Land (Assessment of Compensation) Act, 1919.

(4) Where, after a planning authority makes a vesting order in relation to a protected structure, any sum (including a sum for costs) remains due to the authority by any person under an order of a court for payment of an amount due (whether under this Act or any other Act, or whether remaining due after deducting expenses reasonably incurred by the authority under this Act in relation to the structure), the amount of any compensation payable to that person under this section shall be reduced by the amount of that sum.

(5) Sections 69 to 79 of the Lands Clauses Consolidation Act, 1845, as amended or adapted by or under the Second Schedule to the Housing of the Working Classes Act,

1890, or any other Act, shall apply in relation to compensation to be paid by a planning authority under this section as if such compensation were a price or compensation under that Act as so amended.

(6) Where money is paid into court by the planning authority under section 69 of the Lands Clauses Consolidation Act, 1845, as applied by this section, no costs shall be payable by that authority to any person in respect of any proceedings for the investment. payment of income, or payment of capital of such money.   **[263]**

29. Use of protected structure acquired by planning authority

A planning authority may -

- (a) use a protected structure acquired by it under this Act or any other enactment for any purpose connected with its functions, or
- (b) sell, let, transfer or exchange all or any part of that protected structure.   **[264]**

30. Obligations of sanitary authorities in respect of protected structures

(1) Before issuing a notice under section 3(1) of the Local Government (Sanitary Services) Act, 1964, in respect of a protected structure or a proposed protected structure, a sanitary authority shall consider -

- (a) the protected status of the structure, and
- (b) whether, instead of a notice under section 3(1) of that Act, a notice should be issued under section 10(1) of this Act or section 11 of the Derelict Sites Act, 1990.

(2) As soon as practicable after serving or proposing to serve a notice in accordance with section 3(1) of the Local Government (Sanitary Services) Act, 1964, in respect of a protected structure or a proposed protected structure, a sanitary authority shall inform the Minister for Arts, Heritage, Gaeltacht and the Islands of the particulars of the notice if he or she recommended that the structure be protected.

(3) A sanitary authority which carries out works on a protected structure, or a proposed protected structure, under section 3(2) of the Local Government (Sanitary Services) Act, 1964, shall as far as possible preserve that structure (or elements of that structure which may be of special architectural, historical, archaeological, artistic, cultural, scientific, social or technical interest) in as much as the preservation of that structure is not likely to cause a danger to any person or property.

(4) When carrying out works in accordance with section 3(2) of the Local Government (Sanitary Services) Act, 1964, on a protected structure or a proposed protected structure, a sanitary authority shall, as soon as practicable, inform the Minister for Arts, Heritage, Gaeltacht and the Islands of the works if he or she recommended that the structure be protected.   **[265]**

31. Service of notices, obligation to give information and powers of entry

(1) Section 7 of the Principal Act shall apply in respect of the issue of notices under this Act as if they were notices under that Act.

(2) Section 9 of the Principal Act shall apply in respect of any purpose arising in relation to a planning authority's functions under this Act as if it were arising in relation to the planning authority's functions under that Act.

(3) Section 83 of the Principal Act shall apply for any purpose connected with this Act as if entry for the purposes of this Act were entry for the purposes of Part IV of that Act.

(4) References in section 83 of the Principal Act to "authorised person" shall be construed to include a person who is appointed to be an authorised person for the purpose of that section as applied by subsection (3) of this section.   **[266]**

32. Repeal of section 4(1A) of Principal Act[1a]

[267]

Amendments

a   See the amended Act.

---

33. Amendment of section 19 of Principal Act[1a]

[268]

Amendments

a   See the amended Act.

---

34. Amendment of sections 21 and 21A of Principal Act[1a]

[269]

---

1 Amendments

a   See the amended Act.

---

35. Amendment of section 26(2) of Principal Act[1a]

[270]

---

1 Amendments

a   See the amended Act.

---

36. Amendment of Third Schedule to Principal Act[1a]

[271]

---

1 Amendments

a   See the amended Act.

---

37. Amendment of Local Government (Planning and Development) Act, 1990[1a]

[272]

---

1 Amendments

a   See the amended Act.

---

38. Transitional provisions

(1) Where immediately before the commencement of this section a planning authority's development plan includes any provision to preserve or to protect, or to consider the preservation or protection of, a specific structure, or a part of a specific structure, because of its artistic, architectural or historic interest, that structure (including the items referred to in paragraphs (a) to (d) of the definition of "structure" in section 1 of this Act) or that part, as the case may be, shall, on the commencement of this section, be deemed to be included in the record of protected structures and shall be a protected structure within the meaning of this Act.

(2) As soon as practicable after the commencement of this section, and in any case not later than 4 months after the date of its commencement, the planning authority concerned shall serve on each person who is the owner or occupier of a structure, or part of a structure, which is deemed under subsection (1) to be included in the record of protected structures a notice -

(a) stating that the structure or part is a protected structure and that the provisions of this Act apply,

(b) supplying general information on the provisions of this Act which relate to protected structures and on any guidelines which have been issued under section 3 and

(c) specifying the time within which (not being less than one month) written objections may be made to the planning authority concerning the inclusion of the structure or part in the record of protected structures.

(3) After considering any objections received by the planning authority under subsection (2) in relation to the protected structure and after having had regard to the guidelines, if any, issued under section 3 and the recommendations, if any, made under section 4, the planning authority shall -

(a) if, in its opinion, the structure or part is not of special architectural, historical, archaeological, artistic, cultural, scientific, social or technical interest, decide that it is no longer deemed to be included in the record of protected structures and that it ceases to be a protected structure, and

(b) if, in its opinion, the structure or part is of special architectural, historical, archaeological, artistic, cultural, scientific, social or technical interest, decide that it continues to be deemed to be included in the record of protected structures and continues to be a protected structure.

(4) Within 14 days of making a decision under subsection (3) in relation to a structure, the planning authority shall serve notice of its decision, including the reasons, on each owner and each occupier of the structure.

(5) The making of a decision under subsection (3) shall be a reserved function.

(6) Where before the commencement of this section a notice was served under section 21(1)(c) or 21A(4)(a) of the Principal Act, section 21 or 21A, as the case may be, of that Act shall continue to apply notwithstanding its amendment by this Act, save that, if the development plan, when made, includes provision to include a specific structure, or part of a specific structure, because of its artistic, architectural or historic interest -

(a) that structure (including the items referred to in paragraphs (a) to (d) of the definition of "structure" in section 1 of this Act) or that part, as the case may be, shall be deemed to be included in the record of protected structures and shall be a protected structure within the meaning of this Act,

(b) as soon as practicable after the development plan is made, the planning authority shall notify in accordance with subsection (2) of this section each person who is the owner or occupier of the protected structure, and

(c) subsections (3) to (5) of this section shall apply.

(7) Where it appears to a planning authority that, because of the number of requests made under section 8(1), it would not be possible or appropriate for it to issue a declaration under that section within the period referred to in section 8(3) in respect of a structure which has become a protected structure by virtue of this section, the planning authority shall -

(a) serve on a person who makes a request under section 8(1) in relation to that structure a notice informing that person of the reason why it would not be possible or appropriate to issue the declaration within that period,

(b) specify in the notice the date before which the planning authority intends that the declaration shall be issued, and

(c) take all such steps as are open to it to ensure that the declaration is issued before the date specified in the notice. **[273]**

39. Grants to planning authorities

With the consent of the Minister for Finance, the Minister may, out of monies provided by the Oireachtas, make grants to planning authorities in respect of any or all of their functions under this Act, including grants for the purpose of depraying all or part of the expenditure incurred by them in -

(a) assisting persons on whom notice is served under section 10(1) or 11(2) in carrying out works in accordance with the notice, and

(b) assisting any other person in carrying out works to protected structures in accordance with such conditions as may be specified by a planning authority for the receipt of such assistance. **[274]**

40. Penalties and prosecution of offences

(1) A person who is guilty of an offence under section 9(4) or 14 shall be liable -

(a) on summary conviction, to a fine not exceeding £1,500 (together with, in the case of a continuing offence, a fine not exceeding £150 for every day on which the offence is continued) or to imprisonment for a term not exceeding 12 months or, at the discretion of the court, to both such fine and such imprisonment, or

(b) on conviction on indictment, to a fine not exceeding £1,000,000 (together with, in the case of a continuing offence, a fine not exceeding £10,000 for every day on which the offence is continued) or to imprisonment for a term not exceeding 5 years or, at the discretion of the court, to both such fine and such imprisonment.

(2) Where an offence under section 9(4) or 14 is committed by a body corporate and is proved to have been so committed with the consent or connivance of or to be attributable to any neglect on the part of any person, being a director, manager, secretary or other officer of the body corporate, or a person who was purporting to act in any such capacity, that person, as well as the body corporate, shall be guilty of an offence and be

liable to be proceeded against and punished as if he or she were guilty of the first-mentioned offence.

(3) An offence under section 9(4) or 14 may be prosecuted summarily by the planning authority in whose functional area the offence is committed.[3a]   **[275]**

---

3 Notes

a   This overcomes the problem which arose in *TDI Metro Ltd v DJ Delap* High Court, unrep, 9 June 1999.

---

41. Regulations

Subject to section 2(2), the Minister may make regulations providing for any matter which is to be prescribed under this Act.   **[276]**

42. Short title, construction, citation and commencement

(1) This Act may be cited as the Local Government (Planning and Development) Act 1999.

(2) The Local Government (Planning and Development) Acts, 1963 to 1998, and this Act may be cited together as the Local Government (Planning and Development) Acts, 1963 to 1999, and shall be construed together as one.

(3) This Act shall come into operation on the first day of January, 2000.   **[277]**

Part II
The Regulations

Local Government (Planning and Development) Regulations, 1994

(SI No. 86/1994)

Arrangements of Articles

Part I

Preliminary and General

Part II

Development plans

Part III

Exempted Development

Part IV

Permission Regulations

Part V

APPEALS AND OTHER MATTERS WITH WHICH AN BORD PLEANÁLA IS CONCERNED

Chapter 1

Application of certain provisions of Act of 1992

Chapter II

Appeals against decisions of planning authorities on planning applications

Chapter III

Determinations

Chapter IV

Appeals generally and other matters

Chapter V

Oral hearings

Chapter VI

General

Part VI

EXTENSION OF DURATION OF PLANNING PERMISSION

Part VII

FEES

Chapter I

General

Chapter II

Fees payable to a planning authority in respect of planning applications

Chapter III

Fees payable to the Board

Chapter IV

Fee payable to planning authority in respect of application to extend or further extend appropriate period

Part VIII

COMPENSATION

Part XII

LICENSING UNDER SECTION 89 OF ACT OF 1963

Part XIII

PROVISIONS WITH RESPECT TO CERTAIN DEVELOPMENT BY OR ON BEHALF OF STATE AUTHORITIES

Part XIV

MISCELLANEOUS

First Schedule

REGULATIONS REVOKED

Second Schedule

EXEMPTED DEVELOPMENT

Third Schedule

PRESCRIBED FORMS

Fourth Schedule

Fifth Schedule

Sixth Schedule

Seventh Schedule

Part I

PRELIMINARY AND GENERAL

1. Citation

These Regulations may be cited as the Local Government (Planning and Development) Regulations, 1994. **[278]**

2. Commencement

(1) Subject to sub-article (2), these Regulations shall come into operation on the 16th day of May, 1994. **[279]**

(2) Parts X and XIII, and article 9(1)(a) with respect to development of classes 32, 34, 35, 46 and 47 specified in column 1 of Part I of the Second Schedule, shall come into operation on the 15th day of June, 1994.

3. Interpretation

(1) In these Regulations, any reference to a Schedule, Part or article which is not otherwise identified is a reference to a Schedule, Part or article of these Regulations.

(2) In these Regulations, any reference to a sub-article, paragraph or sub-paragraph which is not otherwise identified is a reference to the sub-article, paragraph or sub-paragraph of the provision in which the reference occurs.

(3) In these Regulations, except where the context otherwise requires –

"**the Act of 1963**" means the Local Government (Planning and Development) Act, 1963;

"**the Act of 1976**" means the Local Government (Planning and Development) Act, 1976;

"**the Act of 1982**" means the Local Government (Planning and Development) Act, 1982;

"**the Act of 1983**" means the Local Government (Planning and Development) Act, 1983;

"**the Act of 1990**" means the Local Government (Planning and Development) Act, 1990;

"**the Act of 1992**" means the Local Government (Planning and Development) Act, 1992;

"**the Act of 1993**" means the Local Government (Planning and Development) Act, 1993;

"**the Acts**" means the Local Government (Planning and Development) Acts, 1963 to 1993;

"**appeal**" means an appeal to the Board under the Acts or any order made under the Acts;

"**approval**" means an approval consequent on an outline permission or an approval which is required to be obtained under a condition subject to which a permission or an approval is granted under the Acts;

"**the Board**" means An Bord Pleanála;

["**DTI Strategy**" has the meaning assigned to it by the Dublin Transportation Office (Establishment) Order, 1995 (S.I. No. 289 of 1995);][1a]

"**the Environmental Impact Assessment Regulations**" means the European Communities (Environmental Impact Assessment) Regulations, 1989;

"**environmental impact statement**" means a statement of the effects, if any, which proposed development, if carried out, would have on the environment;

"**minerals**" means all minerals and substances in or under land of a kind ordinarily worked by underground or by surface working for removal but does not include turf;

"**the Minister**" means the Minister for the Environment;

"**oral hearing**" means an oral hearing by the Board of an appeal or reference;

"**outline application**" means an application for an outline permission;

"**outline permission**" means a permission for development subject to the subsequent approval of the planning authority;

"**permission**" includes outline permission;

"**planning application**" means an application to a planning authority for permission to develop land and includes –

(a) an outline application,
(b) an application for an approval,
(c) an application for permission for the retention of a structure, and
(d) an application for permission for the continuance of any use of any structure or other land;

"**reference**" means a reference under section 5 of the Act of 1963;

"**register**" means the register kept by a planning authority pursuant to section 8 of the Act of 1963;

"**State authority**" means any authority being a Minister of the Government or the Commissioners of Public Works in Ireland;

["**waste licence**" means a waste licence under Part V of the Waste Management Act, 1996 (No. 10 of 1996).][1b]

(4) In these Regulations, a reference to any enactment shall be construed as a reference to that enactment as amended or adapted by any subsequent enactment or instrument.   **[280]**

1 Amendments

a   The words in square brackets were inserted by the LG(PD) (No 2)R 1997 (SI 121/1997), art 4.

b   The words in square brackets were inserted by LG(PD) (No 3)R 1997 (SI 261/1997), art 4.

4.   Revocation

The Regulations mentioned in the First Schedule are hereby revoked.   **[281]**

Part II

DEVELOPMENT PLANS

5.   [Authorities prescribed under section 21(1)(a) of Act of 1963 [1a]

The prescribed authorities for the purposes of section 21(1)(a)[2a] of the Act of 1963 shall be –

- (a) Bord Fáilte Éireann,
- (b) the Central Fisheries Board,
- (c) An Chomhairle Ealaíon,
- (d) the Commissioners of Public Works in Ireland,
- (e) in the case of a planning authority any part of whose functional area is situate within an area which is affected by the DTI Strategy, the Dublin Transportation Office,
- (f) the Electricity Supply Board,
- (g) Forfás,
- (h) the appropriate health board,
- (i) the Minister for Agriculture, Food and Forestry,
- (j) the Minister for Arts, Culture and the Gaeltacht,
- (k) the Minister for Defence,
- (l) the Minister for Education,
- (m) the Minister for the Marine,
- (n) the Minister for Transport, Energy and Communications,
- (o) the National Authority for Occupational Safety and Health,
- (p) the Heritage Council,
- (q) the appropriate Regional Fisheries Board,
- (r) in the case of a planning authority any part of whose functional area is situate within the functional area of the Shannon Free Airport Development Company Ltd, that Company,
- (s) An Taisce – the National Trust for Ireland,
- (t) the Minister,
- (u) the Board,
- (v) the National Roads Authority,
- (w) every planning authority whose area is contiguous to the area of the planning authority which prepared the draft,
- (x) every local authority in the area to which the draft relates, and

(y) the regional authority established by order under section 43 of the Local Government Act, 1991 within whose region the functional area of the planning authority is situate, and any regional authority whose region is contiguous to the region of the first-mentioned authority.] **[282]**

---

1 Amendments

a   Article 5 was substituted by LG(PD) (No 2)R 1997 (SI 121/1997), art 5.

2 Cross References

a   LG(PD)A 1963, s 21(1)(a) prescribes authorities to which draft development plans or proposed variations of a development plan must be sent.

---

6. Documents prescribed under section 21(1)(a) of Act of 1963

The prescribed documents for the purposes of section $21(1)(a)^{2a}$ of the Act of 1963 shall be –

   (a) in relation to the authorities prescribed at (a) to [(s)] of article 5 $-^{1a}$

      (i) a copy of the notice of the preparation of the draft published in accordance with section 21(1)(b) of the Act of 1963,

      (ii) a copy of the written statement comprised in any draft of a proposed development plan, or of proposed variations of a development plan, and

      (iii) a copy of any plan, diagram or other illustrative material comprised in the draft.

   (b) in relation to the authorities prescribed at (t) to (y) of article 5^{1b} –

      (i) a copy of the notice of the preparation of the draft published in accordance with section 21(1)(b) of the Act of 1963,

      (ii) three copies of the written statement comprised in any draft of a proposed development plan, or of proposed variations of a development plan, and

      (iii) three copies of any plan, diagram or other illustrative material comprised in the draft. **[282]**

---

1 Amendments

a   Paragraph (a) was amended by LG(PD)(No 3)R 1997 (SI 261/1997), art 5.

b   Paragraph (b) was amended by LG(PD)(No 3)R 1997 (SI 261/1997), art 5.

2 Cross References

a   LG(PD)A 1963, s 21(1)(a) prescribes authorities to which draft development plans or proposed variations of a development plan must be sent.

---

7. Copies of development plans and extracts [3a]

(1) A planning authority shall make available for purchase by the public copies of a development plan and extracts therefrom.

(2) Where application is made to a planning authority by a member of the public for a copy of a development plan or of an extract therefrom, the copy shall be issued to the applicant on payment to the planning authority of such fee as they may fix not exceeding the reasonable cost of making the copy. **[283]**

Part III

EXEMPTED DEVELOPMENT

8. Interpretation for Part III

In this Part –

"**amusement arcade**" means premises used for the playing of gaming machines, video games or other amusement games;

"**betting office**" means premises for the time being registered in the register of bookmaking offices kept by the Revenue Commissioners under the Betting Act, 1931 (No. 27 of 1931);

"**business premises**" means –

(a) any structure or other land (not being an excluded premises) which is normally used for the carrying on of any professional, commercial or industrial undertaking or any structure (not being an excluded premises) which is normally used for the provision therein of services to persons,

(b) a hotel or public house,

(c) any structure or other land used for the purpose of, or in connection with, the functions of a State authority;

"**care**" means personal care, including help with physical or social needs;

"**day centre**" means non-residential premises used for social or recreational purposes or for the provision of care (including occupational training);

"**dwellinghouse**" does not, as regards development of classes 1, 2, 4, 6(b)(ii) or 7 specified in column 1 of Part I of the Second Schedule, include a building designed for use and used as two or more separate flats or apartments, or a flat or apartment contained within such a building;

"**excluded premises**" means –

(a) any premises used for purposes of a religious, educational, cultural, recreational or medical character,

(b) any guest house or other premises (not being a hotel) providing overnight guest accommodation, block of flats or apartments, club, boarding house or hostel,

(c) any structure which was designed for use as one or more separate dwellings, except such a structure which was used as business premises immediately before the 1st day of October, 1964 or is so used with permission under the Acts;

"**habitable house**" means a building or part of a building which –

(a) is used as a dwelling, or

(b) is not in use but when last used was used, disregarding any unauthorised use, as a dwelling, or

(c) was provided for use as a dwelling but has not been occupied;

"**illuminated**" in relation to any advertisement, sign or other advertisement structure means illuminated internally or externally by artificial lighting, directly or by reflection, for the purpose of advertisement, announcement or direction;

"**industrial building**" means a structure (not being a shop, or a structure in or adjacent to and belonging to a quarry or mine) and used for the carrying on of any industrial process;

"**light industrial building**"[3a] means an industrial building in which the processes carried on or the plant or machinery installed are such as could be carried on or installed in any residential area without detriment to the amenity of that area by reason of noise, vibration, smell, fumes, smoke, soot, ash, dust or grit;

"**industrial process**" means any process which is carried on in the course of trade or business other than agriculture and which is for or incidental to the making of any article or part of an article (including a vehicle, aircraft, ship or vessel, or a film, video or sound recording), or the altering, repairing, ornamenting, finishing, cleaning, washing, packing, canning, adapting for sale, breaking up or demolition of any article, including the getting, dressing or treatment of minerals;

"**industrial undertaker**" means a person by whom an industrial process is carried on and "**industrial undertaking**" shall be construed accordingly;

["**mobile telephony**" means public mobile telephony;][1a]

"**motor vehicle**" means a mechanically propelled vehicle for the purposes of the Road Traffic Act, 1961 (No. 24 of 1961);

"**painting**" includes any application of colour;

"**repository**" means a structure (excluding any land occupied therewith) where storage is the principal use and where no business is transacted other than business incidental to such storage;

"**shop**" means a structure used for any or all of the following purposes, where the sale, display or service is principally to visiting members of the public –

    (a) for the retail sale of goods,

    (b) as a post office,

    (c) for the sale of tickets or as a travel agency,

    (d) for the sale of sandwiches or other cold food for consumption off the premises,

    (e) for hairdressing,

    (f) for the display of goods for sale,

    (g) for the hiring out of domestic or personal goods or articles,

    (h) as a launderette or dry cleaners,

    (i) for the reception of goods to be washed, cleaned or repaired,

but does not include use for the direction of funerals or as a funeral home, or as a hotel, a restaurant or a public house, or for the sale of hot food for consumption off the premises, or any use to which class 2 or 3 of Part IV of the Second Schedule applies;

"**wholesale warehouse**" means a structure where business, principally of a wholesale nature, is transacted and goods are stored or displayed but only incidentally to the transaction of that business.

(2) In the Second Schedule, unless the context otherwise requires, any reference to the height of a structure, plant or machinery shall be construed as a reference to its height when measured, from ground level, and for that purpose "**ground level**" means the level of the ground immediately adjacent to the structure, plant or machinery or, where the

level of the ground where it is situate or is to be situate is not uniform, the level of the lowest part of the ground adjacent to it. **[284]**

---

1 Amendments

a   The words in square brackets were inserted by LG(PD)R 1997 (SI 78/1997), art 3.

3 Notes

a   See *Cork County Council v Ardfert Quarry Products Ltd* (HC) unrep, 7 December 1982. Note that this case was decided under the LG(PD)R 1977 and references to industrial use have been modified in the current regulations.

---

9.   Exempted development [3a]

(1) (a) Subject to paragraph (b) and article 10, development of a class specified in column 1 of Part I of the Second Schedule shall be exempted development for the purposes of the Acts, provided that such development complies with the conditions and limitations specified in column 2 of the said Part I opposite the mention of that class in the said column 1.

(b) Development of class 29(f) specified in column 1 of Part I of the Second Schedule which complies with the conditions and limitations specified in column 2 of the said Part I opposite the mention of that part of that class in the said column 1 shall, if commenced during the period of six months beginning on the coming into operation of this paragraph, be exempted development for the purposes of the Acts.

(2) (a) Subject to article 10, development consisting of the use of a structure or other land for the exhibition of advertisements of a class specified in column 1 of Part II of the Second Schedule shall be exempted development for the purposes of the Acts, provided that –

(i)   such development complies with the conditions and limitations specified in column 2 of the said Part II opposite the mention of that class in the said column 1, and

(ii) the structure or other land shall not be used for the exhibition of any advertisement other than an advertisement of a class which is specified in column 1 of the said Part II and which complies with the conditions and limitations specified in column 2 of the said Part II opposite the mention of that class in the said column 1.

(b) Subject to article 10, development consisting of the erection of any advertisement structure for the exhibition of an advertisement of any one of the classes specified in column 1 of Part II of the Second Schedule shall be exempted development for the purposes of the Acts, provided that –

(i)   the area of such advertisement structure which is used for the exhibition of an advertisement does not exceed the area, if any, specified in column 2 of the said Part II opposite the mention of that class in the said column 1, and

(ii) the advertisement structure is not used for the exhibition of advertisements other than advertisements of the class to which the exemption relates.

(3) Subject to article 10, in areas other than county boroughs, boroughs, urban districts, towns specified in the First Schedule to the Act of 1963 and the excluded areas as defined in section 9 of the Local Government (Reorganisation) Act, 1985 (No. 7 of 1985), development of a class specified in column 1 of Part III of the Second Schedule shall be exempted development for the purposes of the Acts, provided that such development complies with the conditions and limitations specified in column 2 of the said Part III opposite the mention of that class in the said column 1.

(4) (a) Subject to paragraph (b), the carrying out of such works as are necessary to secure compliance with the Building Regulations, 1991 (S.I. No. 306 of 1991) shall, in the case of development consisting of the construction of a dwelling or dwellings in respect of which permission under Part IV of the Act of 1963 was granted before the 1st day of June, 1992, be exempted development. [2a]

(b) Paragraph (a) shall not apply in the case of development consisting of the construction of a building designed for use as two or more separate dwellings.

(5) Development that a county council established by section 11 of the Local Government (Dublin) Act, 1993 (No. 31 of 1993) commences within the functional area of another county council established by that section before the 31st day of December, 1995 shall be exempted development for the purposes of the Acts. **[285]**

---

2 Cross References

a   See also class 38(e), Part I, Second Schedule for exemptions relating to works in compliance with a condition attached to a fire safety certificate.

3 Notes

a   This article together with Parts 1–3 of the Second Schedule establish the classes of development which will be exempted development. These exemptions are subject to the restrictions contained in art 10. Sub-article 1(a), 2 and 3, 4, 5 generally restate the previous existing provision. Sub-article 1(b) applied for 6 months from 16 May 1994.

9A. [Works consisting of or incidental to the carrying out of development referred to in section 84(4)(*a*) of the Environmental Protection Agency Act, 1992 (No. 7 of 1992) for the purpose of giving effect to a condition attached to a licence or revised licence granted by the Environmental Protection Agency under Part IV of the said Act shall be exempted development.].[1a] **[286]**

---

1 Amendments

a   Article 9A was inserted by LG(PD)R 1995 (SI 69/1995), art 3.

---

10. Restrictions on exemption

(1) Development to which article 9 relates shall not be exempted development for the purposes of the Acts –

(a) if the carrying out of such development would –

(i) contravene a condition attached to a permission under the Acts or be inconsistent with any use specified in a permission under the Acts,

(ii)   consist of or comprise the formation, laying out or material widening of a means of access to a public road the surfaced carriageway of which exceeds 4 metres in width,

(iii)   endanger public safety by reason of traffic hazard or obstruction of road users,

(iv)   except in the case of a porch to which class 7 specified in column 1 of Part I of the Second Schedule applies and which complies with the conditions and limitations specified in column 2 of the said Part I opposite the mention of that class in the said column 1, comprise the construction, erection, extension or renewal of a building on any street so as to bring forward the building, or any part of the building, beyond the front wall of the building on either side thereof or beyond a line determined as the building line in a development plan for the area or, pending the variation of a development plan or the making of a new development plan, in the draft variation of the development plan or the draft new development plan,

(v)   consist of or comprise the carrying out under a public road of works other than a connection to a wired broadcast relay service, sewer, water main, gas main or electricity supply line or cable, or any works to which class 23, 24 or 29(a) specified in column 1 of Part I of the Second Schedule applies,

(vi)   interfere with a view or prospect of special amenity value or special interest the preservation of which is an objective of a development plan for the area in which the development is proposed or, pending the variation of a development plan or the making of a new development plan, in the draft variation of the development plan or the draft new development plan,

(vii)   consist of or comprise the excavation, alteration or demolition of caves, sites, features or objects of archaeological, geological or historical interest the preservation of which is an objective of a development plan for the area in which the development is proposed or, pending the variation of a development plan or the making of a new development plan, in the draft variation of the development plan or the draft new development plan,

(viii)   consist of or comprise the extension, alteration, repair or renewal of an unauthorised structure or a structure the use of which is an unauthorised use,

(ix)   consist of or comprise the alteration, extension or demolition of a building or other structure, other than an alteration consisting of the painting of any previously painted part of such building or structure, where such building or structure is specified in a development plan for the area or, pending the variation of a development plan or the making of a new development plan, in the draft variation of the development plan or the draft new development plan, as a building or other structure, or one of a group of buildings or other structures, of artistic, architectural or historic interest:

(I) the preservation of which it is an objective of the planning authority to secure, or

(II) the preservation of which it is the intention of the planning authority to consider in the event of an application being made for permission to alter, extend or demolish the building or structure,

(x) consist of –

(I) the use for the exhibition of advertisements, other than advertisements of class 5, 9 or 15 specified in column 1 of Part II of the Second Schedule, of a building or other structure, where such building or structure is specified in a development plan for the area, or pending the variation of a development plan or the making of a new development plan, in the draft variation of the development plan or the draft new development plan, as a building or other structure, or one of a group of buildings or other structures, of artistic, architectural or historical interest the preservation of which it is an objective of the planning authority to secure,

(II) the erection of an advertisement structure, other than a structure for the exhibition of an advertisement of class 5, 9 or 15 as aforesaid, on, or within the curtilage of, a building or other structure as aforesaid,

(III) the erection on a building or other structure as aforesaid of a satellite television signal receiving antenna,

(xi) consist of the demolition or such alteration of a building or other structure as would preclude or restrict the continuance of an existing use of a building or other structure where it is an objective of the planning authority to ensure that the building or other structure would remain available for such use and such objective has been specified in a development plan for the area or, pending the variation of a development plan or the making of a new development plan, in the draft variation of the development plan or the draft new development plan,

(xii) consist of the fencing or enclosure of any land habitually open to or used by the public during the ten years preceding such fencing or enclosure for recreational purposes or as means of access to any seashore, mountain, lakeshore, riverbank or other place of natural beauty or recreational utility,

(xiii) obstruct any public right of way, or

(b) in an area to which a special amenity area order relates, if development would be development –

(i) of class, 1, 3, 15, 19, 20, 25, 26, 27 or 29 (other than paragraph (a) thereof) specified in column 1 of Part I of the Second Schedule,

(ii) consisting of the use of a structure or other land for the exhibition of advertisements of class 1, 4, 6, 11, 16 or 17 specified in column 1 of Part II of the said Schedule or the erection of an advertisement structure for the exhibition of any advertisement of any of the said classes, or

(iii) of class 3, 5, 6, 7, 8, 9, 10, 11 or 12 specified in column 1 of Part III of the said Schedule, or

   (c) if it is development –

       (i) which is of a class for the time being specified under Article 24 of the Environmental Impact Assessment Regulations, or under any provision amending or replacing the said Article 24, or

      (ii) which would be of a class referred to in sub-paragraph (i) but for not exceeding a quantity, area or other limit for the time being specified in relation to that class and which comprises or is for the purposes of an activity in relation to which a licence under Part IV of the Environmental Protection Agency Act, 1992 (No. 7 of 1992) is required,

     unless that development is required by the Environmental Impact Assessment Regulations or any other statutory provision to comply with procedures (not being procedures relating to applications for permission under Part IV of the Act of 1963 or to applications for licences under Part IV of the Environmental Protection Agency Act, 1992) for the purpose of giving effect to the Council Directive of 27 June, 1985 (No. 85/337/EEC, O.J. No. L175/40, 5 July, 1985), or

   (d) if it consists of or comprises an industrial activity or isolated storage to which Regulations 12 to 18 of the European Communities (Major Accident Hazards of Certain Industrial Activities) Regulations, 1986 (S.I. No. 292 of 1986), as amended by the European Communities (Major Accident Hazards of Certain Industrial Activities) (Amendment) Regulations, 1989 (S.I. No. 194 of 1989) and the European Communities (Major Accident Hazards of Certain Industrial Activities) (Amendment) Regulations, 1992 (S.I. No. 21 of 1992), apply.

(2) Sub-article (1)(a)(vi) shall not apply where the development consists of the construction by any electricity undertaking of an overhead line or cable not exceeding one hundred metres in length for the purpose of conducting electricity from a distribution or transmission line to any premises. **[287]**

11. Changes of use

(1) Development which consists of a change of use within any one of the classes of use specified in Part IV of the Second Schedule and which does not involve the carrying out of any works, other than works which are exempted development, shall be exempted development for the purposes of the Acts, provided that the development, if carried out, would not contravene a condition attached to a permission under the Acts or be inconsistent with any use specified or included in such a permission.

(2) Development consisting of the use of not more than four bedrooms in a dwellinghouse as overnight guest accommodation shall be exempted development for the purposes of the Acts, provided that such development would not contravene a condition attached to a permission under the Acts or be inconsistent with any use specified or included in such a permission.

(3) Development consisting of the provision within a building occupied by, or under the control of, a State authority of a shop or restaurant for visiting members of the public shall be exempted development for the purposes of the Acts.

(4) (a) A use which is ordinarily incidental to any use specified in Part IV of the Second Schedule is not excluded from that use as an incident thereto merely by

reason of its being specified in the said Part of the said Schedule as a separate use.

(b) Nothing in any class in Part IV of the Second Schedule shall include any use —²ᵃ

    (i)   as an amusement arcade,

   (ii)   as a motor service station,

  (iii)   for the sale or leasing, or display for sale or leasing, of motor vehicles,

  (iv)   for a taxi business or for the hire of motor vehicles,

   (v)   as a scrapyard, or a yard for the breaking of motor vehicles,

  (vi)   for the storage or distribution of minerals.

[(vii)   as a supermarket, the retail floor space of which exceeds 3,000 square metres.]¹ᵃ

[288]

---

1 Amendments

a   Sub-article (4)(b)(vii) was inserted by LG(PD)(No. 2)R 98 (SI 194/1998), art 3.

2 Cross References

a   See Part IV, Second Schedule. See also class 13, Part I, Second Schedule, which gives exempted development status to certain changes of use between certain classes of development specified in Part IV of the Second Schedule.

---

12. Saver for certain development

Development commenced prior to the coming into operation of this Part and which was exempted development for the purposes of the Acts by reason of a provision of regulations revoked by these Regulations shall, notwithstanding such revocation, continue to be exempted, development for the purposes of the Acts.   **[289]**

13. Prescribed development for purposes of section 4(4) of Act of 1963

The prescribed development for the purposes of subsection (4) (inserted by the Environmental Impact Assessment Regulations) of section 4 of the Act of 1963 shall be –

  (a)   the use of uncultivated land or semi-natural areas for intensive agricultural purposes, where the area involved would be greater than 100 hectares,

  [(b)   initial afforestation where the area involved, either on its own or taken together with any adjacent area planted by or on behalf of the applicant within the previous three years, would result in a total area planted exceeding 70 hectares and for the purposes of this subparagraph an area, other than an area planted before the 1st day of October, 1996, shall be deemed to be adjacent if its nearest point lies within 500 metres of any part of the area involved,

(bb) replacement of broadleaf high forest by conifer species, where the area involved would exceed 10 hectares,]¹ᵃ

  (c)   peat extraction which would involve a new or extended area of 50 hectares or more.   **[290]**

1 Amendments

a   Paragraphs (b) and (bb) were substituted by LG(PD)R 1996 (SI 100/1996), art 3.

Part IV

PERMISSION REGULATIONS

14. Notice of planning application [3a]

(1) An applicant shall –

    (a) within the period of two weeks before the making of a planning application, give notice of the intention to make the application in a newspaper in accordance with article 15, and

    (b) not later than the making of the planning application, give notice of the application by the erection or fixing of a site notice in accordance with article 16.

(2) The requirement of sub-article (1)(b) shall not apply in relation to a planning application for development consisting of the construction or erection by an electricity undertaking of overhead transmission or distribution lines for conducting electricity, or development consisting of the construction or erection by Bord Telecom Éireann – The Irish Telecommunications Board, or by any person to whom a licence under section 111 of the Postal and Telecommunications Services Act, 1983 (No. 24 of 1983) has been granted, of overhead telecommunications lines. **[291]**

3 Notes

a   This article requires an applicant to give notice of an intention to apply for planning permission both by publishing a notice in a newspaper and by the erection of a notice on the site. The only exception to this requirement is for certain development consisting of electricity and telecommunications transmission lines.

15. Notice in newspaper

(1) A notice published pursuant to article 14(1)(a) shall be published in a newspaper circulating in the district in which the land or structure to which the proposed planning application relates is situate, shall contain as a heading the name of the planning authority to which the planning application will be made and shall state –

    (a) the name of the applicant,[3a]

    (b) the nature of the application (that is, whether it is for a permission, an outline permission or an approval),

    (c) the location of the land[3b] or the address of the structure to which the application relates (as may be appropriate),

        (i) the nature and extent[3c] of the development (including, where the application relates to development consisting of or comprising the provision of dwellings, the number of dwellings to be provided), or

     (ii)   where the application relates to the retention of a structure, the nature of the proposed use of the structure and, where appropriate, the period for which it is proposed to retain the structure, or

    (iii)   where the application relates to the continuance of any use, the nature of such use and of the previous use, [3d]

  (e) where the application will be accompanied by an environmental impact statement in accordance with article 24(1):

     (i)   that such a statement will be submitted to the planning authority with the application, and

    (ii)   that the environmental impact statement, and any further information in relation to the proposed development which may be furnished to the planning authority in the course of the consideration of the application by the planning authority, will be available at the offices of the planning authority.

(2) Where a planning application relates to development which comprises or is for the purposes of an activity in relation to which a licence under Part IV of the Environmental Protection Agency Act, 1992, [or a waste licence,][1a] is required, a notice published pursuant to article 14(1)(a) shall, in addition to the requirements of sub-article (1), indicate this fact.   **[292]**

---

1 Amendments

a   The words in square brackets were inserted by LG(PD)R 1997 (SI 261/1997), art 6.

3 Notes

a   Compare McWilliam J's decision in *State (Alf-a-Bet Promotions Ltd) v Bundoran UDC* 112 ILTR 9 with the dictum of Henchy J in *State (Finglas Developments) Ltd v Dublin County Council* (SC) unrep, 17 February 1983. See also *State (Toft) v Galway Corporation* [1981] ILRM 439 and *Thomas McDonagh and Sons Ltd v Galway County Council* (SC) unrep, 17 May 1993 and *Blessington & District Community Council v Wicklow County Council* (HC) unrep, 19 July 1996 where a much more flexible approach to the issue of public notices was adopted and the approach in *Toft* followed.

b   See *Crodaun Homes Ltd v Kildare County Council* [1983] ILRM 1 where the issue in the Supreme Court was whether a notice which read "Co. Kildare – 14 Bungalows at Leixlip Gate for Crodaun Homes Limited" was sufficient for the purposes of the Regulations. In the High Court Barrington J had held the notice sufficient and in the Supreme Court O'Higgins CJ agreed with this. However, the majority (Griffin and Hederman JJ) held it insufficient. In his judgment (with which Hederman J concurred) Griffin J emphasised that notice must reach all potential objectors and "potential objectors will not therefore be confined to persons who live in the vicinity of the lands". On the other hand O'Higgins CJ thought "... that the object of these Regulations is to ensure that the location of the site to be developed is to be known in particular to people in the locality". See also *Gormley v ESB* [1985] IR 129.

c   See McMahon J in *Keleghan v Corby* 111 ILTR 144 and *Calor Teo v Sligo County Council* [1991] 2 IR 267.

d   See generally *Brady v Donegal County Council* [1989] ILRM 282; *Calor Teo v Sligo County Council* [1991] 2 IR 267; *Crodaun Homes Ltd v Kildare County Council* [1983] ILRM 1; *Cunningham v An Bord Pleanála* (HC) unrep, 3 May 1990; *Dooley v Galway County Council* (HC) unrep, 4 February 1992; *Frank Dunne Ltd v Galway County Council* [1974] IR 45; *ESB v Gormley* [1985] IR 129; [1985] ILRM 494; *Keleghan v Corby & Dublin Corporation* 111

ILTR 144; *Monaghan UDC v Alf-a-Bet Promotions Ltd* [1980] ILRM 64; *O'Donoghue v An Bord Pleanála* [1991] ILRM 750; *State (Toft) v Galway Corporation* [1981] ILRM 439 and *Malloy & Walsh v Dublin County Council* [1990] IR 90; [1990] ILRM 633.

16. Site notice [3a]

(1) A site notice erected or fixed on any land or structure pursuant to article 14(1)(b) –

    (a) shall be painted or inscribed, or printed and affixed, on a durable material, and

    (b) subject to sub-article (2), shall be securely erected or fixed in a conspicuous position on or near the main entrance to the land or structure concerned from a public road, or on any part of the land or structure adjoining a public road, so as to be easily visible and legible by persons using the public road.

(2) Where the land or structure to which a planning application relates does not adjoin a public road, a site notice shall be erected or fixed in a conspicuous position on the land or structure so as to be easily visible and legible by persons outside the land or structure.

(3) The position of a site notice on the land or structure concerned shall be shown on a plan accompanying the planning application.

(4) A site notice shall be headed "APPLICATION TO PLANNING AUTHORITY" and shall state –

    (a) the name of the applicant,

    (b) the nature of the application (that is, whether it is for a permission, an outline permission or an approval),

    (c) (i) the nature and extent of the development (including, where the application relates to development consisting of or comprising the provision of dwellings, the number of dwellings to be provided), or

        (ii) where the application relates to the retention of a structure, the nature of the proposed use of the structure and, where appropriate, the period for which it is proposed to retain the structure, or

        (iii) where the application relates to the continuance of any use, the nature of such use and of the previous use,

    (d) that the planning application may be inspected at the offices of the planning authority.

(5) A site notice shall be maintained in position on the land or structure concerned for a period of at least one month after the making of the planning application and shall be renewed or replaced if it is removed or becomes defaced or illegible within that period.[3b] **[293]**

---

3 Notes

a   A site notice must contain similar information to that contained in a newspaper notice except that there is no explicit reference in the article that where a development is subject to an EIA that this be referred to in the site notice. Such notices will be required to state that the application may be inspected at the office of the planning authority and the notice must be kept in place for at least 1 month.

b   As the public notice effectively determines the nature and extent of a proposed development it is not clear which would take priority in the event of a conflict between a site and newspaper notice but in the event that such an ambiguity led to confusion and that parties were misled, it is possible that any permission granted would be quashed.

17. Further notice [3a]

(1) (a) An applicant who proposes to submit an environmental impact statement to a planning authority pursuant to a requirement under article 25(1) or 26(1) shall, before submitting the statement, publish in a newspaper circulating in the district in which the relevant land or other structure is situate notice of the intention to submit the statement.

   (b) A notice published in a newspaper in accordance with paragraph (a) shall contain as a heading the name of the planning authority to which the planning application was made and shall state –

   (i)   the name of the applicant,

   (ii) the date on which the planning application was made and its reference number in the register,

   (iii) the location of the land or the address of the structure to which the application relates (as may be appropriate),

   (iv) (I)   that an environmental impact statement will be submitted to the planning authority in connection with the planning application, and

   (II) that the environmental impact statement, and any further information in relation to the proposed development which may be furnished to the planning authority in the course of the consideration of the application by the planning authority, will be available at the offices of the planning authority.

   (c) Where a planning application relates to development which comprises or is for the purposes of an activity in relation to which a licence under Part IV of the Environmental Protection Agency Act, 1992, [or a waste licence,][1a] is required, a notice published in a newspaper in accordance with paragraph (a) shall, in addition to the requirements of paragraph (b), indicate this fact.[3b]

   (d) An environmental impact statement submitted by an applicant pursuant to a requirement under article 25(1) or 26(1) shall be accompanied by two copies of the relevant page of the newspaper in which a notice in accordance with the foregoing paragraphs has been published.

(2) Where –[3c]

   (a) it appears to a planning authority that any notice –

   (i)   if published in a newspaper:

   (I)   has been published in a newspaper which does not have a sufficiently large circulation in the district in which the land or structure to which the planning application relates is situate, or

   (II) does not comply with the requirements of article 15 or paragraphs (b) and (c) of sub-article (1) (as may be appropriate),

   (ii) if erected or fixed on any land or structure, does not comply with the requirements of article 16,

   (iii) in either case, because of its content or for any other reason, is misleading or inadequate for the information of the public, or

    (b) a period of more than two weeks has elapsed between the publication of a notice in a newspaper pursuant to article 14(1)(a) and the making of the planning application, or

    [(c) it appears to a planning authority that a site notice has not been erected or fixed on land or a structure in accordance with article 16, or that any notice erected or fixed has not been maintained in position in accordance with sub-article (5) of the said article or has been defaced or become illegible and has not been renewed or replaced,][1b]

the planning authority shall require the applicant to give such further notice in such manner and in such terms as they may specify and to submit to them such evidence as they may specify in relation to compliance with any such requirement.

(3) Where —[3d]

    (a) plans, drawings or other particulars are submitted to a planning authority by an applicant in response to an invitation under article 35, or

    (b) further information is received from an applicant pursuant to a requirement under article 33 more than three months after the said requirement,

the planning authority may, where they consider it necessary so to do, require the applicant to give such further notice in such manner and in such terms as they may specify and to submit to them such evidence as they may specify in relation to compliance with any such requirement.[3e]   **[294]**

---

1 Amendments

a   The words in square brackets were inserted by LG(PD)R 1997 (SI 261/1997), art 6.

b   Subsection 2(c) was substituted by LG(PD)R 1995, (SI 69/1995), art 4.

3 Notes

a   Sub-article 1 applies to developments where an application for planning permission has been submitted to the planning authority which is required to be accompanied by an EIS and where the applicant has failed to submit such a statement.

b   All developments in this category will require to be accompanied by an EIS.

c   A planning authority is obliged to require the publication of a new notice where any of the inadequacies identified in sub-art 2 are identified and have no discretion in this regard.

d   Planning authorities have a discretion to require the publication of a new notice in the circumstances of that sub-article and they have a further discretion in the form of such notice.

e   See *Ardoyne House Management Co Ltd v Dublin Corporation* (HC) unrep, 6 February 1998 where it was held that a decision to grant permission in circumstances where such a notice had not been complied with was void and was quashed by Morris P. The fact that the decision was subsequently appealed did not bar the applicant's right to bring the proceedings and succeed at the trial of the action.

---

18. Content of planning applications generally

(1) A planning application shall –

    (a) (i) state the name and address, and telephone number if any, of the applicant[3a] and of the person, if any, acting on behalf of the applicant,

(ii) indicate the address to which any correspondence relating to the application should be sent,

(b) state whether the application is for a permission, an outline permission or an approval,

(c) give particulars (including the location or address, as may be appropriate) of the land or structure concerned,

(d) give particulars of the interest[3b] in the land or structure held by the applicant and, if the applicant is not the owner, state the name and address of the owner,[3c]

(e) be accompanied by two copies of the relevant page of the newspaper in which notice of the application has been published pursuant to article 14(1)(a), and of the text of the site notice erected or fixed on the land or structure pursuant to article 14(1)(b),

(f) be accompanied by four copies of a location map, to a scale of not less than 1:10,560 (which shall be indicated thereon) and marked or coloured so as to identify clearly the land or structure to which the application relates and the boundaries thereof,

(g) state:

   (i) the area of the land to which the application relates, and

   (ii) where the application relates to a building or buildings –

      (I) the number of dwellings (if any) to be provided, and

      (II) except in the case of an application for a single dwellinghouse or a number of such houses, the gross floor space of the building or buildings,

(h) if the development consists of or comprises an industrial activity or isolated storage to which Regulations 12 to 18 of the European Communities (Major Accident Hazards of Certain Industrial Activities) Regulations, 1986 (S.I. No. 292 of 1986), as amended by the European Communities (Major Accident Hazards of Certain Industrial Activities) (Amendment) Regulations, 1989 (S.I. No. 194 of 1989) and the European Communities (Major Accident Hazards of Certain Industrial Activities) (Amendment) Regulations, 1992 (S.I. No. 21 of 1992), apply, indicate this fact,

(i) if the development comprises or is for the purposes of an activity in relation to which a licence under Part IV of the Environmental Protection Agency Act, 1992, [or a waste licence,][1a] is required, indicate this fact.

(2) In sub-article (1)(g), **"gross floor space"** means the area ascertained by the internal measurement of the floor space on each floor of a building or buildings (including internal walls and partitions) disregarding any floor space provided for the parking of vehicles by persons occupying or using the building or buildings where such floor space is incidental to development to which the application primarily relates.[3d]   **[295]**

---

1 Amendments

a   The words in square brackets were inserted by LG(PD)R 1997 (SI 261/1997), art 6.

3 Notes

a   Compare *State (Alf-a-Bet Promotions Ltd) v Bundoran UDC* 112 ILTR 9 with the judgment of Henchy J in *State (Finglas Developments Ltd) v Dublin County Council* (HC) unrep 18 July 1981; (SC) unrep, 17 February 1983.

b   In *McCabe v Harding Investments Ltd* [1984] ILRM 105 O'Higgins CJ drew a distinction between regulations which prescribe what must accompany an application and those which prescribe what must be done prior to lodging an application, the context suggesting that non-compliance with the former category may not be fatal to the validity of the application. In *Keane v An Bord Pleanála* [1998] 2 ILRM 241 the Supreme Court distinguished the earlier case of *Frescati Estates Ltd v Walker* [1975] IR 177 and confined its ambit to applications not made with the consent of the owner of the lands. The fact that an applicant may not have sufficient interest to carry out a development is not a bar to the making of a valid planning application.

c   In *Hynes v An Bord Pleanála* (HC) unrep, 30 July 1998 it was held that the provisions of art 18(1)(d) are directory and not mandatory and failure to comply with this requirement did not make the application invalid.

d   See generally *Frescati Estates Ltd v Walker* [1975] IR 177 and *Scott v An Bord Pleanála* [1995] 1 ILRM 424; *Burke v Drogheda Corporation* (HC) unrep, 11 June 1982, *Molloy & Walsh v Dublin County Council* [1990] IR 90.

19. Applications for permission

Subject to article 20 –

(a) a planning application in respect of any development consisting of or mainly consisting of the carrying out of works on, in or under land or for the retention of a structure shall, in addition to the requirements of article 18, be accompanied by four copies of such plans (including a site or layout plan and drawings of floor plans, elevations and sections which comply with the requirements of article 23), and such other particulars, as are necessary to describe the works or structure to which the application relates,

(b) a planning application for any development consisting of or mainly consisting of the making of any material change in the use of any structure[3a] or other land or the continuance of any use of any structure or other land (whether instituted without a permission granted under the Acts or in accordance with a permission so granted for a limited period only) shall, in addition to the requirements of article 18, be accompanied by:

(i) a statement of the existing and of the use proposed or, where appropriate, of the former use and the use proposed to be continued, together with particulars of the nature and extent of any such proposed use,

(ii) where the development to which the application relates comprises the carrying out of works on, in or under the structure or other land – four copies of such plans (including a site or layout plan and drawings of floor plans, elevations and sections which comply with the requirements of article 23), and such other particulars, as are necessary to describe the works proposed.   **[296]**

3 Notes

a   See the observations of Finlay P in *Re Viscount Securities Ltd v Dublin County Council* 112 ILTR 17.

19A.

[(1) Article 19(a) shall not apply to a planning application for development consisting of the construction or erection by an electricity undertaking of overhead transmission or distribution lines for conducting electricity.

(2) A planning application referred to in sub-article (1) shall, in addition to the requirements of article 18, be accompanied by four copies of such plans and drawings drawn to a scale of not less than 1:100, as are necessary to describe any form of structure or apparatus which will support, or form part of, the lines referred to in the said sub-article.

(3) (a)   A reference to article 19 in any other provision of these Regulations shall, in the case of a planning application referred to in sub-article (1), be construed as a reference to this article.

(b)   Article 23(1), other than paragraphs (f), (g) and (h) thereof, shall not apply to a planning application referred to in sub-article (1).][1a]   **[297]**

---

1 Amendments

a   Article 19A was inserted by LG(PD)R 1995 (SI 69/1995), art 5.

---

20. Outline applications [3a, 3b]

(1) Notwithstanding article 19, an outline application[3c] may, in addition to the requirements of article 18, be accompanied only by such plans and particulars as are necessary to enable the planning authority to make a decision in relation to the siting, layout or other proposals for development in respect of which a decision is sought.

(2) Notwithstanding any other provision of this Part, an outline application may not be made in respect of –

(a)   the retention on land of any structure or the continuance of any use of any structure or other land,

(b)   (i)   development which is of a class for the time being specified under Article 24 of the Environmental Impact Assessment Regulations, or under any provision amending or replacing the said Article 24, or

(ii)   development which would be of a class referrred to in sub-paragraph (i) but for not exceeding a quantity, area or other limit for the time being specified in relation to that class and which comprises or is for the purposes of an activity in relation to which a licence under Part IV of the Environmental Protection Agency Act, 1992 is required,

(c)   development in relation to which notice is served by a planning authority in accordance with sub-article (3).

(3) Where an outline application is received in respect of development which would be of a class referred to in sub-article (2)(b)(i) but for not exceeding a quantity, area or other limit for the time being specified in relation to that class and which is not development referred to in sub-article (2)(b)(ii), the planning authority shall, where they consider that the development would be likely to have significant effects on the environment, by notice in writing inform the applicant that an outline application may not be made in respect of that development.   **[298]**

3 Notes

a   See the decision of Costello P in *Irish Asphalt Ltd v An Bord Pleanála* (HC) unrep, 28 July 1995 which decided that conditions on an outline provision may be modified in the subsequent grant of approval. Where there is a change in the circumstances of an area compare with *State (Pine Valley Developments Ltd) v Dublin County Council* [1984] IR 407 and *State (Kenny & Hussey) v An Bord Pleanála* (HC) unrep, 23 February 1984; (SC) unrep, 20 December 1984. See also *State (Tern Houses (Brennanstown) Ltd v An Bord Pleanála* [1985] IR 725.

b   This article confers on planning authorities an explicit discretion as to the extent of plans and particulars that must accompany an application for outline permission and this will depend on the nature of the development being proposed. See however *State (Tern Houses Ltd) v An Bord Pleanála* [1985] IR 725.

c   The grant of approval does not extend the life of the outline permission.

21. Effect of outline permission[3a]

An outline permission shall not operate so as to authorise the carrying out of any development until –

(a)   an approval has been granted consequent on an application in accordance with article 22(1), or

(b)   as respects a specified part of the development for which an outline permission was granted, an approval has been granted for such specified part consequent on an application in accordance with article 22(1), or

(c)   a further approval has been granted in any case where the terms of an approval granted consequent on an application in accordance with article 22(1), or the terms of the outline permission, require such further approval to be obtained.[3b]   **[299]**

3 Notes

a   For cases dealing with the relationship between outline planning permission and approval, see O'Sullivan and Shepherd, *Irish Planning Law and Practice,* para [3.640] *et seq.*

b   See *State (Silverhill Development Co Ltd) v An Bord Pleanála* (HC) unrep, 16 March 1984 which allows for piecemeal developments within an area granted outline permission so long as the approval is consistent with the planning unit submitted at the outline stage.

22. Applications for approval

(1)   (a)   Subject to paragraph (b), an application for an approval[3a] consequent on an outline permission shall be accompanied by such further plans and particulars as would be required under article 19 if an application for permission, other than an outline permission, were made.

(b)   An application for an approval consequent on an outline permission may be related to a specified part[3b] of the development for which an outline permission was granted and separate applications for approval may, subject to section 2 of the Act of 1982, be made in respect of other parts of the said development from time to time. [3c]

(2) An application for an approval which is required to be obtained under a condition subject to which a permission or approval was granted shall be accompanied by such plans and particulars as are necessary to enable the planning authority to make a decision in relation to the matter in respect of which the approval is sought.[3d]   **[300]**

---

3 Notes

a   An application for approval must be accompanied by the same plans and particulars as if the application were being made for full permission but approval must normally be granted if it conforms to the outline permission.

b   See however *Silverhill Development Co Ltd v An Bord Pleanála* (HC) unrep, 16 March 1984 where it is specified that the application must show the entire area covered by the outline permission.

c   See Barrington J's decision in the High Court in *State (Pine Valley Development Ltd) v Dublin County Council* [1984] IR 407.

d   Compare the observations of McMahon J in *Keleghan v Dublin Corporation* (1979) 111 ILTR 144 to the effect that a full permission granted on condition that details of access be agreed with the planning authority might constitute no more than an outline permission. Such a condition passed without comment, however, in *State (Foxrock Construction Ltd) v Dublin County Council* (HC) unrep, 18 July 1981.

---

23. Plans, drawings and maps accompanying planning applications

(1) Plans, drawings and maps accompanying a planning application shall comply with the following requirements –

   (a) site or layout plans shall be drawn to a scale of not less than 1:500 (which shall be indicated thereon), the site boundary shall be clearly delineated in colour, and buildings, roads, boundaries, septic tanks and percolation areas, bored wells and other features in the vicinity of the land or structure to which the application relates shall be shown,

   (b) other plans, elevations and sections shall be drawn to a scale of not less than 1:100, which shall be indicated thereon,[3a]

   (c) drawings of elevations of any proposed structure shall show the main features of any buildings which would be contiguous to the proposed structure if it were erected,

   (d) plans relating to works comprising reconstruction, alteration or extension of a structure shall be so marked or coloured as to distinguish between the existing structure and the works proposed,

   (e) plans and drawings of floor plans, elevations and sections shall indicate in figures the principal dimensions (including overall height) of any proposed structure and the distances of any such structure from the boundaries of the site,

   (f) any map or plan which is based on an Ordnance Survey map shall indicate the relevant Ordnance Survey sheet number,

   (g) the north point shall be indicated on all maps and plans other than drawings of floor plans, elevations and sections,

(h) plans and drawings shall indicate the name and address of the person by whom they were prepared.

(2) A planning authority may, by notice in writing, require an applicant to provide not more than two additional copies of any plan, drawing or map which accompanied the planning application.   **[301]**

---

3 Notes

a   See *Readymix (Eire) Ltd v Dublin County Council* (HC) unrep, 12 August 1970.

---

24. Certain planning applications to be accompanied by environmental impact statement [3a]

(1) Subject to sub-article (2), a planning application in respect of –

(a) development which is of a class for the time being specified under Article 24 of the Environmental Impact Assessment Regulations, or under any provision amending or replacing the said Article 24, or

(b) ...[1a]

(2) Sub-article (1) shall not apply to a planning application in respect of development as regards which an exemption is granted by the Minister in accordance with subsection (3) (inserted by the Environmental Impact Assessment Regulations and amended by the European Communities (Environmental Impact Assessment) (Amendment) Regulations, 1994) of section 25 of the Act of 1963,

(3) (a) Where the Minister has, in granting an exemption in accordance with the aforesaid subsection (3) of section 25 of the Act of 1963, applied other requirements in relation to a proposed planning application, the application when made shall –

(i)   where it relates to development which comprises or is for the purposes of an activity in relation to which a licence under Part IV of the Environmental Protection Agency Act, 1992, [or a waste licence,][1b] is required, comply with the said other requirements in so far as those requirements relate to matters other than the risk of environmental pollution from the activity, or

(ii) where it relates to development other than development referred to in sub-paragraph (i), comply with the said other requirements.

(b) Where a planning application in relation to which the Minister has applied other requirements does not, when made, comply with paragraph (a), the planning authority shall serve a notice stating that the relevant requirements have not been complied with and requiring compliance with the said requirements.[3b]   **[302]**

---

1 Amendments

a   Subsection (1)(b) was repealed by LG(PD)R 1999 (SI 92/1999), art 10.

b   The words in square brackets were inserted by LG(PD)(No 3)R 1997 (SI 261/1997), art 6.

3 Notes

a This provision largely restates the position as set out in art 7 LG(PD)R 1990. However it is now the case that all development which is subject to a requirement to obtain an integrated licence from the EPA must in addition be accompanied by an EIS even where the thresholds provided for in the EC(EIA)R 1989 have not been exceeded. The Minister's power to grant exemptions to these developments in such circumstances has been continued.

b See *Honeyclover Ltd v An Bord Pleanála* (HC) unrep, 29 January 1990.

---

25. Procedure where planning application not accompanied by environmental impact statement [3a]

(1) Subject to sub-article (2), where a planning authority receive a planning application to which article 24(1) applies and the application is not accompanied by an environmental impact statement, they shall, as soon as may be, by notice in writing –

    (a) inform the applicant that the application does not comply with the said requirement, and

    (b) require the applicant to comply with the said requirement.

(2) Where, before the service of a notice in accordance with sub-article (1), a planning authority receive notice of the grant of an exemption in accordance with subsection (3) (inserted by the Environmental Impact Assessment Regulations and amended by the European Communities (Environmental Impact Assessment) (Amendment) Regulations, 1994) of section 25 of the Act of 1963 as regards the development in respect of which the planning application has been made;

    (a) a notice in accordance with sub-article (1) shall not be served,

    (b) the planning authority shall, where other requirements have been applied in relation to the application in accordance with the said subsection (3), as soon as may be after receipt of notice of the grant of the exemption and of the other requirements applied, by notice in writing require the applicant to comply –

        (i) where the application relates to development which comprises or is for the purposes of an activity in relation to which a licence under Part IV of the Environmental Protection Agency Act, 1992 [or a waste licence,][1a] is required, with the said other requirements in so far as those requirements relate to matters other than the risk of environmental pollution from the activity, or

        (ii) where the application relates to development other than development referred to in sub-paragraph (i), with the said other requirements.

(3) (a) A notice served in accordance with sub-article (1) shall cease to have effect where an exemption is granted in accordance with subsection (3) (inserted by the Environmental Impact Assessment Regulations and amended by the European Communities (Environmental Impact Assessment) (Amendment) Regulations, 1994) of section 25 of the Act of 1963 as regards the development to which the planning application relates, on the date of the receipt by the planning authority of notice of the grant of the exemption.

    (b) Where a notice served in accordance with sub-article (1) ceases to have effect in accordance with paragraph (a), the planning authority shall, as soon as may be, by notice in writing, inform the applicant of the cesser of the notice and of the date on which it ceased to have effect, and –

(i)   where no other requirements have been applied in relation to the application in accordance with the aforesaid subsection (3) of section 25 of the Act of 1963, that the application falls to be dealt with as if the notice in accordance with sub-article (1) had been complied with on the said date, or

(ii) where other requirements have been applied in relation to the application in accordance with the aforesaid subsection (3) –

(I)   if the application relates to development which comprises or is for the purposes of an activity in relation to which a licence under Part IV of the Environmental Protection Agency Act, 1992 [or a waste licence],[1a] is required, require the applicant to comply with the said other requirements in so far as those requirements relate to matters other than the risk of environmental pollution from the activity, or

(II) if the application relates to development other than development referred to in sub-paragraph (ii)(I), require the applicant to comply with the said other requirements.

[303]

---

1 Amendments

a   The words in square brackets were inserted by LG(PD)(No 3)R 1997 (SI 261/1997), art 6.

3 Notes

a   This provision alters the previous position in that now planning authorities may consider other aspects of a development pending the submission of an EIS. Until the EIS required has been submitted the application remains invalid and given the broad nature of the information required in an EIS it is difficult to see how effective further consideration of an application which requires but is not accompanied by an EIS will be. See *Shannon Regional Fisheries Board v An Bord Pleanála* (HC) unrep, 17 November 1994.

---

26. Requirement to submit environmental impact statement in case of certain other planning applications [3a]

(1) Where a planning authority receive a planning application in respect of any development which would be of a class referred to in article 24(1)(a) but for not exceeding a quantity, area or other limit for the time being specified in relation to that class, and where they consider that the development would be likely to have significant effects on the environment, they shall, by notice in writing, require the applicant to submit an environmental impact statement.[1a]

(1A) A planning authority shall, where it receives a planning application in respect of development which would: -

(a) be of a class referred to in article 24(1)(a) but for not exceeding a quantity, area or other limit for the time being specified in relation to that class, and

(b) be located on: -

(i)   a special area of conservation,

(ii) a site notified in accordance with Regulation 4 of the European Communities (Natural Habitats) Regulations, 1997 (S.I. No. 94 of 1997),

    (iii) an area classified pursuant to paragraph (1) or (2) of article 4 of the Birds Directive,

    (iv) a site where consultation has been initiated in accordance with article 5 of the Habitats Directive,

    (v) land established or recognised as a nature reserve within the meaning of section 15 or 16 of the Wildlife Act, 1976 (No. 39 of 1976),

    (vi) land designated as a refuge for fauna under section 17 of the Wildlife Act, 1976 (No. 39 of 1976),

decide whether the development would or would not be likely to have significant effects on the environment.

(1B) A planning authority shall, where it is deciding pursuant to this article whether a proposed development would or would not be likely to have significant effects on the environment, have regard to the criteria specified for the purposes of article 27 of the European Communities (Environmental Impact Assessment) Regulations, 1989.][1b]

(2) (a) A notice served in accordance with sub-article (1) shall cease to have effect where an exemption is granted in accordance with subsection (3) (inserted by the Environmental Impact Assessment Regulations and amended by the European Communities (Environmental Impact Assessment) (Amendment) Regulations, 1994) of section 25 of the Act of 1963 as regards the development to which the planning application relates, on the date of the receipt by the planning authority of notice of the grant of the exemption.

    (b) Where a notice served in accordance with sub-article (1) ceases to have effect in accordance with paragraph (a), the planning authority shall, as soon as may be, by notice in writing, inform the applicant of the cesser of the notice and of the date on which it ceased to have effect, and –

      (i) where no other requirements have been applied in relation to the application in accordance with the aforesaid subsection (3) of section 25 of the Act of 1963, that the application falls to be dealt with as if the notice in accordance with sub-article (1) had been complied with on the said date, or

      (ii) where other requirements have been applied in relation to the application in accordance with the aforesaid subsection (3) –

        (I) if the application relates to development which comprises or is for the purposes of an activity in relation to which a licence under Part IV of the Environmental Protection Agency Act, 1992, [or a waste licence,][1c] is required, require the applicant to comply with the said other requirements in so far as those requirements relate to matters other than the risk of environmental pollution from the activity, or

        (II) if the application relates to development other than development referred to in sub-paragraph (ii)(I), require the applicant to comply with the said other requirements.

[304]

---

1 Amendments

a   Subarticle (1) was amended by LG(PD)R 1999, (SI 92/1999), art 11(a).

b   Subarticles (1A) and (1B) were inserted by LG(PD)R 1999, (SI 92/1999), art 11(b).

c   The words in square brackets were inserted by LG(PD)(No 3)R 1997 (SI 261/1997), art 6.

3 Notes

a   This article confers on planning authorities a discretion to require the submission of an EIS where they consider the development is likely to have significant effects on the environment if it is a class of activity specified in art 24(1). The Minister has the power to grant exemptions for developments in this category.

---

27. Environmental impact statement submitted where notice in accordance with article 26(1) not served [3a]

(1) Where a planning application in respect of any development which would be of a class referred to in article 24(1)(a) but for not exceeding a quantity, area or other limit for the time being specified in relation to that class is accompanied by an environmental impact statement, the planning authority shall deal with the application as if the statement had been submitted in accordance with article 24(1).[1a]

(2) A reference in these Regulations to an environmental impact statement submitted or received in accordance with article 24(1) shall include an environmental impact statement to which sub-article (1) applies.   **[305]**

---

1 Amendments

a   Subarticle (1) was amended by LG(PD) 1999, (SI 92/1992), art 12.

3 Notes

a   This provides that where an EIS has been submitted voluntarily by an applicant the application will be processed as if such an EIS was required under art 24.

---

28. Content of environmental impact statement [3a]

(1) An environmental impact statement submitted to a planning authority in accordance with a requirement of or under this Part shall comply with Article 25 of the Environmental Impact Assessment Regulations, or any provision amending or replacing the said Article 25.[3b]

(2) (a) A planning authority shall, on receipt of an environmental impact statement —[3c]

   (i)   in case the planning application relates to development which comprises or is for the purposes of an activity in relation to which a licence under Part IV of the Environmental Protection Agency Act, 1992, [or a waste licence,][1a] is required, consider whether the statement complies with sub-article (1) with regard to matters other than the risk of environmental pollution from the activity, or

   (ii) in any other case, consider whether the statement complies with sub-article (1).

   (b) (i) Where a planning authority, in the case of development referred to in paragraph (a)(i), consider that an environmental impact statement does not comply with sub-article (1) with regard to matters other than the risk of environmental pollution from the activity, they shall, by notice in writing, so inform the applicant and require the applicant to submit such further information or particulars as may be necessary to secure compliance with sub-article (1) in relation to the said matters.

(ii) Where a planning authority, in the case of development referred to in paragraph (a)(ii), consider that an environmental impact statement does not comply with sub-article (1), they shall, by notice in writing, so inform the applicant and require the applicant to submit such further information or particulars as may be necessary to secure compliance with the said sub-article.

[306]

---

1 Amendments

a   The words in square brackets were inserted by LG(PD)(No 3)R 1997 (SI 261/1997), art 6.

3 Notes

a   This provides for the examination of an EIS so as to ensure compliance with the requirements contained in art 25 EC(EIA)R 1989. Planning authorities have a duty to consider whether the statement submitted so complies but such an examination will be difficult in the case of certain developments which are subject to licencing by the EPA as planning authorities are prohibited from considering any matter which relates to the risk of environmental pollution.

b   See *Browne v An Bord Pleanála* [1989] ILRM 865 where it is clear that the courts in a judicial review will not inquire into the adequacy of an EIS but it is submitted that if it fails to comply with the legal requirements as set out in the regulations then this is a matter that should be considered.

c   Where an EIS is considered inadequate in failing to comply with the requirements of art 25 EC(EIA)R 1989 a notice under sub-art 2 is appropriate. Where the EIS meets the requirements of art 25 but is deficient in some other way a notice under art 33 is appropriate.

---

29. Procedure on receipt of planning application[3a]

(1) On receipt of a planning application, a planning authority shall –

(a) stamp the documents with the date of their receipt, and

(b) consider whether the application complies with the requirements of articles 18 and 23 and, as may be appropriate, of article 19, 20 or 22.

(2) (a) Where a planning authority consider that a planning application complies with the requirements of articles 18 and 23 and, as may be appropriate, of article 19, 20 or 22, they shall send to the applicant an acknowledgement stating the date of receipt of the application.

(b) Where a planning authority consider that a planning application does not comply with the requirements referred to in paragraph (a) which relate to the application, they may, as they consider appropriate having regard to the extent of the failure to comply with the said requirements, by notice in writing –

(i)   inform the applicant that the application is invalid and cannot be considered by the planning authority, or

(ii) require the applicant to furnish such further particulars, plans, drawings or maps as may be necessary to comply with the said requirements.

(3) Where a planning authority serve a notice in accordance with sub-article (2)(b)(i), they shall return to the applicant all particulars, plans, drawings and maps which accompanied the application. **[307]**

3 Notes

a This provision requires planning authorities to examine planning applications so as to determine whether they comply with the requirements of the Regulations. The article provides that where there is a serious failure to comply with the requirements of the Regulations the planning authority may return all the plans and other documents submitted including the fee (art 95). Alternatively they may indicate the documentation required in order to validate the application.

30. Planning authority notice ³ᵃ

(1) A planning authority shall, not later than the third working day following a particular week, make available in accordance with sub-article (2) a list of the planning applications received by the authority during that week.

(2) (a) A list referred to in sub-article (1) shall indicate in respect of each planning application received during the week to which the list relates –

    (i) the name and address of the applicant,

    (ii) the nature of the application (that is, whether it is for a permission, an outline permission or an approval),

    (iii) the location of the land or the address of the structure to which the application relates (as may be appropriate),

    (iv) (I) the nature and extent of the development (including, where the application relates to development consisting of or comprising the provision of dwellings, the number of dwellings to be provided), or

        (II) where the application relates to the retention of a structure, the nature of the proposed use of the structure and, where appropriate, the period for which it is proposed to be retained, or

        (III) where the application relates to the continuance of any use, the nature of such use and of the previous use,

    (v) the date of receipt of the application.

(b) A list referred to in sub-article (1) shall indicate those planning applications, if any –

    (i) in respect of which an environmental impact statement has been submitted to the planning authority in accordance with article 24(1), or

    (ii) which relate to development which comprises or is for the purposes of an activity in relation to which a licence under Part IV of the Environmental Protection Agency Act, 1992, [or a waste licence,]¹ᵃ is required.

(3) A list referred to in sub-article (1) shall, in addition to the requirements of sub-article (2), indicate any planning application in respect of which –

(a) an environmental impact statement has been received by the planning authority pursuant to a requirement under article 25(1) or 26(1),

(b) the planning authority have served a notice under article 29(2)(b)(i) or (ii),

    (c) further particulars, plans, drawings, maps or other information have been furnished to the planning authority pursuant to a requirement under article 28(2)(b), 29(2)(b)(ii) or 33,

    (d) revised plans, drawings or other particulars have been submitted to the planning authority pursuant to an invitation under article 35,

during the week to which the list relates.

(4) (a) A list referred to in sub-article (1) shall, for a period of not less than two months beginning on the day on which it is made available –

      (i) be displayed in or at the offices of the planning authority in a position convenient for public inspection during office hours,

      (ii) be displayed for public inspection in each public library situate in, and in each mobile public library operating in, the functional area of the planning authority.

    (b) A list referred to in sub-article (1) may, in addition to the requirements of paragraph (a), be displayed in or at any other place which the planning authority consider appropriate, or be made available for publication, or published, in a newspaper circulating in the functional area of the planning authority, or be made available by such other means as the planning authority consider appropriate.

    (c) A list referred to in sub-article (1) shall be made available to the members of the planning authority in such manner as they may by resolution direct.

(5) (a) Copies of a list referred to in sub-article (1) shall, during the period of two months referred to in sub-article (4)(a), be made available at the offices of the planning authority during office hours, free of charge or for such fee as the planning authority may fix not exceeding the reasonable cost of making the copy.

    (b) A copy of a list referred to in sub-article (1) shall, during the period of two months as aforesaid, be sent, on request, to any person or body, free of charge or for such fee, not exceeding the reasonable cost of making the copy and the cost of postage, as the planning authority may fix. **[308]**

---

1 Amendments

a   The words in square brackets were inserted by LG(PD)(No 3)R 1997 (SI 261/1997), art 6.

3 Notes

a   The requirements of planning authorities relating to the publication of weekly lists of planning applications received has been considerably expanded in terms of the information that such lists shall contain and the period for and duration of publication. See also art 42 for similar requirements relating to applications for planning permission that have been determined.

---

31. Notice to Minister of certain planning applications [3a]

(1) (a) A planning authority shall, as soon as may be after its receipt, notify the Minister of any planning application –

      (i) in respect of which an environmental impact statement has been submitted in accordance with article 24(1), or

    (ii) in respect of which they intend to require, in accordance with article 25(1) or 26(1), the submission of an environmental impact statement,

and which relates to development likely to have significant effects on the environment in another Member State of the European Communities.

  (b) A notification to the Minister pursuant to paragraph (a) shall –

    (i) state the name and address of the applicant,

    (ii) indicate the location of the land or the address of the structure to which the application relates (as may be appropriate),

    (iii) indicate the nature and extent of the development,

    (iv) state the date of receipt of the application, and

    (v) if the application relates to development which comprises or is for the purposes of an activity in relation to which a licence under Part IV of the Environmental Protection Agency Act, 1992, [or a waste licence,]¹ᵃ is required, include an indication of this fact.

(2) A planning authority shall furnish to the Minister a copy of any environmental impact statement received in respect of a planning application in relation to which notice is given to the Minister pursuant to sub-article (1).

[(3) The Minister may, in the case of a planning application in respect of which an environmental impact statement is required by or under this Part to be submitted to the planning authority, and: -

  (a) which, in his opinion, relates to development which would be likely to have significant effects on the environment in another Member State of the European Communities, or

  (b) where another Member State of the European Communities considers that the said development would be likely to have such effects and has requested that it be provided with information on the application,

require the planning authority to furnish to him such particulars, information or documents concerning the application as he may specify.]¹ᵇ

[(4) Where the Minister is notified in accordance with sub-article (1), or particulars, information or documents are furnished to him in accordance with sub-article (3), the planning authority shall notify the applicant that another Member State of the European Communities is being provided with information in relation to the planning application.]¹ᶜ   **[309]**

---

1 Amendments

a   The words in square brackets were inserted by LG(PD)(No 3)R 1997 (SI 261/1997), art 6.

b   Subarticle (3) was substituted by LG(PD)R 1999 (SI 92/1999), art 13(a).

c   Subarticle (4) was inserted by LG(PD)R 1999 (SI 92/1999), art 13(b).

3 Notes

a   This article requires planning authorities to notify the Minister of all applications for which an EIS has been submitted or is required which is likely to have significant effects on the environment of a Member State of the European Union.

32. Notice to certain bodies[3a]

(1) Where a planning authority receive a planning application, they shall, except in the case of an application in respect of which a notice in accordance with article 29(2)(b)(i) has been or will be served, send notice in accordance with sub-article (2) –

(a)   where it appears to the planning authority that the land or structure is situate in an area of special amenity, whether or not an order in respect of that area has been made under section 42 of the Act of 1963, or that the development or retention of the structure would obstruct any view or prospect of special amenity value or special interest – to An Chomhairle Ealaíon, Bord Fáilte Éireann and An Taisce – the National Trust for Ireland,

(b)   where it appears to the planning authority that the development would obstruct or detract from the value of any tourist amenity or tourist amenity works – to Bord Fáilte Éireann,

(c)   where it appears to the planning authority that the development would be unduly close to any cave, site, feature or other object of archaeological, geological, scientific or historical interest, or would detract from the appearance of any building of artistic, architectural or historical interest, or, in either case, would obstruct any scheme for improvement of the surroundings of or any means of access to any such place, object or structure – to An Chomhairle Ealaíon, Bord Fáilte Éireann, the Minister for Arts, Culture and the Gaeltacht,[1a] the National Monuments Advisory Council and An Taisce – the National Trust for Ireland,

(d)   where it appears to the planning authority that the development would obstruct or detract from the value of any existing or proposed development by a local authority – to such local authority,

(e)   where it appears to the planning authority that if permission were granted, a condition should be attached under section 26(2)(f) of the Act of 1963 – to any local authority (other than the planning authority) which would be affected under section 26(7) of that Act,

(f)   where it appears to the planning authority that the development might give rise to appreciable discharges of polluting matters to waters or be likely to cause serious water pollution or the danger of such pollution, or might otherwise affect fisheries – to the appropriate Regional Fisheries Board,

(g)   where the development consists of or comprises an industrial activity or isolated storage to which Regulations 12 to 18 of the European Communities (Major Accident Hazards of Certain Industrial Activities) Regulations, 1986 (S.I. No. 292 of 1986), as amended by the European Communities (Major Accident Hazards of Certain Industrial Activities) (Amendment) Regulations, 1989 (S.I. No. 194 of 1989) and the European Communities (Major Accident Hazards of Certain Industrial Activities) (Amendment) Regulations, 1992 (S.I. No. 21 of 1992), apply – to the National Authority for Occupational Safety and Health,

(h)   where it appears to the planning authority that the development might endanger or interfere with the safety of aircraft or the safe and efficient navigation thereof – to the Irish Aviation Authority,

(i) where the development consists of or comprises the formation, laying out or material widening of an access to a national road within the meaning of section 2 of the Roads Act, 1993 (No. 14 of 1993), not being a national road within a built-up area within the meaning of section 45 of the Road Traffic Act, 1961, or where it appears to the planning authority that the development might give rise to a significant increase in the volume of traffic using a national road – to the National Roads Authority,

[(ii) where it appears to the planning authority that the development might significantly impact on the implementation of the DTI Strategy – to the Dublin Transportation Office.]

(j) where the development comprises or is for the purposes of an activity in relation to which a licence under Part IV of the Environmental Protection Agency Act, 1992, [or a waste licence]¹ᵇ is required – to the Environmental Protection Agency.

(2) Notice given by a planning authority pursuant to sub-article (1) shall –

(a) state the name and address of the applicant,

(b) indicate the location of the land or the address of the structure to which the application relates (as may be appropriate),

(c) indicate the nature and extent of the development,

(d) state the date of receipt by the planning authority of the application, and

(e) if the application relates to development which comprises or is for the purposes of an activity in relation to which a licence under Part IV of the Environmental Protection Agency Act, 1992, [or a waste licence,]¹ᵇ is required, indicate this fact.

(3) Where an environmental impact statement is received by a planning authority in respect of a planning application in accordance with any provision of this Part, the authority shall send a copy of the statement to any body to which they are required by sub-article (1) to give notice of the application.

(4) A copy of an environmental impact statement received by a planning authority in accordance with any provision of this Part and details of the planning application concerned as specified in sub-article (2) shall, in addition to the requirements of sub-article (1), be sent –

(a) where the application relates to development for the purposes of breeding of salmonid fish – to the Minister for the Marine,

(b) where the application relates to development for the purposes of initial afforestation or the replacement of broadleaf high forest by conifer species – to the Minister for Agriculture, Food and Forestry,

(c) where it appears to the planning authority that the development might have significant effects on public health – to the appropriate Health Board,

(d) where it appears to the planning authority that the development might have significant effects in relation to nature conservation – to the Commissioners of Public Works in Ireland,

(e) where the application relates to extraction of minerals within the meaning of the Minerals Development Acts, 1940 to 1979 – to the Minister for Transport, Energy and Communications.

(5) A reference in sub-article (1) to Bord Fáilte Éireann shall, in the case of a planning application relating to land or a structure situate in the functional area of the Shannon Free Airport Development Company Ltd., be construed as a reference to that Company.

[310]

---

1 Amendments

a   The words in square brackets were inserted by LG(PD)(No 2)R 1997 (SI 121/1997), art 6.

b   The words in square brackets were inserted by LG(PD)(No 3)R 1997 (SI 261/1997), art 6.

3 Notes

a   Failure to send notice may invalidate a permission. See *P & F Sharpe Ltd v Dublin City and County Manager* [1989] IR 701 and *Nolan v Dublin Corporation* [1989] IR 701.

---

33. Further information

(1) Where a planning authority receive a planning application they may, by notice in writing, require the applicant –

(a) to submit any further information (including any plans, maps or drawings, or any information as to any estate or interest in or right over land) which they consider necessary to enable them to deal with the application,

(b) to produce any evidence which they may reasonably require to verify any particulars or information given in or in relation to the application.

[(2) A planning authority shall not require an applicant who has complied with a requirement under sub-article (1) to submit any further information, particulars or evidence save: -

(a) in case an environmental impact statement is required by or under this Part to be submitted to the authority and the proposed development would be likely to have significant effects on the environment in another Member State of the European Communities, where the authority, having regard to the views of such State, considers this to be reasonably necessary,

(b) as may be reasonably necessary to clarify the matters dealt with in the applicant's response to a requirement to submit further information, particulars or evidence, or to enable them to be considered or assessed.[3a]

[(2A) A planning authority shall, where it considers that further information, particulars or evidence submitted in accordance with a requirement under this article contains significant additional data in relation to the effects on the environment of the proposed development: -

(a) send notice of the furnishing of the further information to the authority and a copy of the further information, to any body to which notice was given in accordance with article 32 and to indicate to those bodies that submissions or observations in relation to the further information may be made in writing to the authority before a specified date,

(b) in case an environmental impact statement is required by or under this Part to be submitted to the authority: -

(i) require the applicant to publish in a newspaper circulating in the district in which the land or structure to which the relevant planning application relates is situate a notice stating that significant further information in relation to the said effects has been furnished to the authority, that the further information will be available, for inspection or for purchase at the offices of the authority, and that submissions or observations in relation to the further information may be made in writing to the authority before a specified date,

(ii) where the proposed development would be likely to have significant effects on the environment in another Member State of the European Communities, send notice of the furnishing of the further information and a copy of the further information to the Minister.][1a]

(3) Where there is a failure or refusal to comply with a requirement under [sub-article (1) or (2)][1b] within one month of such requirement, the planning authority may, if they think fit, determine the application in the absence of the information or evidence specified in the requirement.   **[311]**

---

1 Amendments

a   Sub-articles (2) and (2A) were substituted by LG(PD)R 1999 (SI 92/1999), art 14.

b   Words in square brackets substituted by by LG(PD)R 1995 (SI 69/1995), art 6.

3 Notes

a   See *O'Connor Downtown Properties Ltd v Nenagh Urban District Council* [1993] 1 IR 1 for a discussion on the limits on what a valid request for further information must contain. The request must be genuine: see Butler J in *State (Conlon Construction Ltd) v Cork County Council* (HC) unrep, 31 July 1975 and McMahon J in *State (NCE Ltd v Dublin County Council* [1979] ILRM 249.

---

34. Submissions or observations in relation to planning applications[3a]

(1) Subject to sub-article (2), any person or body may make submissions or observations in writing to a planning authority in relation to a planning application.

(2) A person or body shall not, in the case of a planning application which relates to development comprising or for the purposes of an activity in relation to which a licence under Part IV of the Environmental Protection Agency Act, 1992, [or a waste licence,][1a] is required, be entitled to make submissions or observations to a planning authority in relation to the risk of environmental pollution from the activity.   **[312]**

---

1 Amendments

a   The words in square brackets were inserted by LG(PD)(No 3)R 1997 (SI 261/1997), art 6.

3 Notes

a   This article establishes an explicit right to make observations or submissions relating to a planning application. Where the activity proposed is subject to licencing by the EPA there is no entitlement to make submissions on those aspects of the development which are properly matters to be considered in the integrated licence.

35. Revised plans, etc.[3a]

Where a planning authority, having considered a planning application, are disposed to grant a permission or an approval subject to any modification of the development to which the application relates, they may invite the applicant to submit to them revised plans or other drawings modifying, or other particulars providing for the modification of, the said development and, in case such plans, drawings or particulars are submitted, may decide to grant a permission or an approval for the relevant development as modified by all or any such plans, drawings or particulars.   **[313]**

---

3 Notes

a   This provision whereby a planning authority may invite revised plans is similar to the previous corresponding provision (art 27 LG(PD)R 1977). This should be used where a proposal is acceptable subject to certain modifications and it is not advisable to use the power contained in art 33 in these circumstances – see *O'Connor Downtown Properties Ltd v Nenagh Urban District Council* [1993] 1 IR 1. A request under art 35 will not have the effect of extending the appropriate period and if a request is made under art 35 an extension of time under s 26(4)(A) should be sought. This power is discretionary only: a planning authority is not obliged to exercise it if they consider a modified development acceptable. See D'Arcy J in *State (Abenglen Properties Ltd) v Dublin Corporation* [1984] IR 381.

---

36. Availability of documents relating to planning applications[3a]

(1) (a) Any document mentioned in section 6(a) of the Act of 1992 received or obtained by a planning authority in relation to a planning application shall be made available for inspection by members of the public during office hours at the offices of the authority from as soon as may be after receipt of the document until the application is withdrawn or the decision of the authority in respect of the application is given.

    (b) (i) Any submissions or observations in writing in relation to a planning application which are received by a planning authority shall be made available for inspection by members of the public during office hours at the offices of the authority from as soon as may be after receipt of the submissions or observations until the application is withdrawn or the expiration of a period of one month beginning on the day of the giving of the decision of the authority in respect of the application or, if an appeal or appeals is or are taken against the decision, until as regards the appeal or, as may be appropriate, each of the appeals –

        (I) it is withdrawn, or

        (II) it is determined by the Board or dismissed by it pursuant to section 11 or 14 of the Act of 1992, or

        (III) in relation to it a direction is given to the authority by the Board pursuant to section 15 of the said Act.

    (ii) This paragraph shall apply in relation to any planning application received by a planning authority after the coming into operation of this article.

(2) (a) Where a permission or an approval is granted (whether by the relevant planning authority or the Board), the documents concerned mentioned in

section 6 of the Act of 1992 relating to the planning application shall be made available for inspection by members of the public during office hours at the offices of the planning authority from the expiration of the period mentioned in section 5(1) of that Act until –

(i)   in the case of a permission for the retention on land of any structure or a permission granted either for a limited period only or subject to a condition which is of a kind described in section 26(2)(j) or 27(f) of the Act of 1963, the expiration of a period of five years beginning on the day of the grant of the permission, or

(ii)   in the case of a permission other than a permission referred to in sub-paragraph (i) or an approval, the expiration of the appropriate period within the meaning of section 2 of the Act of 1982 or, as the case may be, of that period as extended under section 4 of the said Act, for the relevant permission.

(b)   Any submissions or observations in writing which are received by a planning authority in relation to a planning application received after the coming into operation of this article shall, where a permission or an approval (as the case may be) is granted, be made available for public inspection in accordance with paragraph (a).

(3) Article 29 of the Local Government (Planning and Development) Regulations, 1977 (S.I. No. 65 of 1977), as substituted by article 9 of the Local Government (Planning and Development) (Amendment) Regulations, 1982 (S.I. No. 342 of 1982) and as amended by the Local Government (Planning and Development) Regulations, 1990 (S.I. No. 25 of 1990), and article 19 of the Local Government (Planning and Development) Regulations, 1990 shall, notwithstanding their revocation by the Local Government (Planning and Development) (No. 2) Regulations, 1992 (S.I. No. 222 of 1992), continue to apply and have effect in relation to –

(a)   any planning application received by a planning authority before the 14th day of September, 1992, until the giving of the decision of the planning authority in respect of the application,

(b)   any planning application in respect of which a permission or approval was granted (whether by the relevant planning authority or the Board) before the 14th day of September, 1992.   **[314]**

---

3 Notes

a   A member of the public is entitled to inspect all the documents submitted by the applicant and all the reports prepared by or for the planning authority. See LG(PD)A 1992, ss 5 and 6. In addition sub-articles 1(b) and 2(b) establish an additional right to inspect submissions or observations made in the course of the application. An applicant therefore will have a right to see the objections lodged against the development proposed. This provision applies to all applications including those received before 16 May 1994.

---

37. Availability for purchase of copies of environmental impact statements and extracts [3a]

Copies of an environmental impact statement submitted to a planning authority in accordance with any provision of this Part, and of extracts from such a statement, shall be made available for purchase during office hours at the offices of the planning authority, for such fee as the authority may fix not exceeding the reasonable cost of making the copy, from as soon as may be after receipt of the statement by the authority until the expiration of a period of one month beginning on the day of the giving of the decision of the authority in respect of the planning application to which the statement relates or, if an appeal or appeals is or are taken against the decision, until as regards the appeal or, as may be appropriate, each of the appeals –

(a) it is withdrawn, or

(b) it is determined by the Board or dismissed by it pursuant to section 11 or 14 of the Act of 1992, or

(c) in relation to it a direction is given to the authority by the Board pursuant to section 15 of the said Act.   **[315]**

---

3 Notes

a   This article provides for extracts as well as complete copies of an EIS to be made available for purchase at a fee not exceeding the reasonable cost of making the copy. The article further specifies precisely the periods during which an EIS is to be made available for inspection.

---

38. Notice in certain cases

Form No. 1 set out in the Third Schedule shall be the prescribed form of the notice of the intention of a planning authority to consider deciding to grant a permission in a case where the development concerned would contravene materially the development plan or any special amenity area order.   **[316]**

39. Minimum period for determination of planning application[3a]

A planning authority shall not decide to grant or to refuse a permission or an approval until after –

(a)   in case the applicant has submitted an environmental impact statement to the authority in accordance with article 24(1):

(i) where the applicant has been required pursuant to article 17 to give further notice of the application, the expiration of twenty-eight days beginning on the day on which that requirement has been complied with,

(ii) where the applicant has not been required to give further notice, the expiration of twenty eight days beginning on the day of receipt by the planning authority of the application;

(b)   in case the applicant has been required in accordance with article 25(1) or 26(1) to submit an environmental impact statement:

(i) where, on receipt by the authority of the statement, the applicant has been required pursuant to article 17 to give further notice of the application, the expiration of twenty-eight days beginning on the day on which that requirement has been complied with,

(ii) where the applicant has not been required to give further notice, the expiration of twenty-eight days beginning on the day of receipt by the planning authority of the statement;

[(bb)   in case the applicant has submitted an environmental impact statement to the authority in accordance with any provision of this Part and the proposed development would be likely to have significant effects on the environment in another Member State of the European Communities: -

(i)   the views, if any, of such State have been received, or

(ii)   a time specified in paragraph (a) or (b) (as the case may be), whichever ends the later;][1a]

(c)   in any other case:

(i)   where the applicant has been required pursuant to article 17 to give further notice of the application, the expiration of fourteen days beginning on the day on which that requirement has been complied with,[3b]

(ii)   where the applicant has not been required to give further notice, the expiration of fourteen days beginning on the day of receipt by the planning authority of the application.

[317]

---

1 Amendments

a   Subparagraph (bb) was inserted by LG(PD)R 1999, (SI 92/1999), art 15.

3 Notes

a   This article clears up the difficulty which occurred in *State (Stanford) v Dun Laoghaire Corporation* (SC) unrep, 20 February 1981.

b   See *Ardoyne House Management Co Ltd v Dublin Corporation* (HC) unrep, 6 February 1998 where a decision made by the respondent to grant permission in circumstances where a notice under art 17 had not been complied with was quashed.

---

40. Withdrawal of planning application

A planning application may be withdrawn, by notice in writing, at any time before the giving of the decision of the planning authority in respect of the application.   **[318]**

41. Notification of decision on planning application

Every notification given to an applicant by a planning authority of a decision in respect of a planning application shall specify –

(a)   the reference number of the application in the register,

(b)   the development or retention or continuance of use to which the decision relates,

(c)   the nature of the decision,

(d)   the date of the giving of the decision,

(e)   in the case of a decision to grant a permission or approval – any conditions attached thereto,

(f)   in the case of a decision to grant a permission or approval for the construction, erection or making of a structure and to specify the purposes for which the structure may or may not be used – such purposes,[3a]

(g)   in the case of a decision to grant a permission or approval for the development of land consisting of or comprising the carrying out of works – any approval or further approval required,

(h) in the case of a decision to grant a permission – any period specified by the planning authority pursuant to section 3 of the Act of 1982 as the period during which the permission is to have effect,

(i) in the case of a decision to refuse permission or approval or to grant permission or approval subject to conditions – the reasons for such refusal or for the imposition of the conditions, as may be appropriate,

(j) in the case of a decision to grant a permission or approval – that the permission or approval (as may be appropriate) shall be issued as soon as may be after the expiration of the period for the making of an appeal if there is no appeal before the Board on the expiration of the said period, and

(k) that an appeal against the decision may be made to the Board by any person within the period of one month beginning on the date of the giving of the decision of the planning authority,

[(l) in the case of a decision to grant permission, where the applicant concerned submitted an environmental impact statement to the authority in accordance with any provision of this Part, the reasons for such decisions.]¹ᵃ   **[319]**

---

1 Amendments

a   Subparagraph (l) was inserted by LG(PD)R 1999 (SI 92/1999), art 16.

3 Notes

a   See *Readymix (Eire) Ltd v Dublin County Council* Supreme Court, unrep, 30 July 1974 for a discussion of what is meant by the purpose for which a structure is designed.

---

42. Notice of decisions ³ᵃ

(1) A planning authority shall, by not later than the third working day following a particular week, make available in accordance with sub-article (2) a list of the planning applications in respect of which decisions were given by the authority during that week.

(2) A list referred to in sub-article (1) shall indicate, in addition to the matters specified in article 30(2), the nature of the decision of the planning authority in respect of the application.

(3) (a) A list referred to in sub-article (1) shall, for a period of not less than two months beginning on the day on which it is made available –

   (i) be displayed in or at the offices of the planning authority in a position convenient for public inspection during office hours,

   (ii) be displayed for public inspection in each public library situate in, and in each public mobile library operating in, the functional area of the planning authority.

  (b) A list referred to in sub-article (1) may, in addition to the requirements of paragraph (a), be displayed in or at any other place which the planning authority consider appropriate, or be made available for publication, or published, in a newspaper circulating in the functional area of the planning authority, or be made available by such other means as the planning authority consider appropriate.

  (c) A list referred to in sub-article (1) shall be made available to the members of the planning authority in such manner as they may by resolution direct.

(4) (a) Copies of a list referred to in sub-article (1) shall, during the period of two months referred to in sub-article (3)(a), be made available at the offices of the planning authority during office hours, free of charge or for such fee as the planning authority may fix not exceeding the reasonable cost of making the copy.

(b) A copy of a list referred to in sub-article (1) shall, during the period of two months as aforesaid, be sent, on request, to any person or body, free of charge or for such fee, not exceeding the reasonable cost of making the copy and the cost of postage, as the planning authority may fix. **[320]**

3 Notes

a   This requirement provides for the publication of a weekly list of decisions made on planning applications and specifies where and for how long such lists must be displayed and what information such lists must contain. See also art 30 which provides for the publication of similar lists relating to applications for planning permission received.

43. Additional notice in certain cases[3a]

(1) Where a planning authority have given notice of a planning application to a body in accordance with article 32, the authority shall send notice of the decision of the authority in respect of the application to the body within three working days of the giving of the decision.

(2) Where any person or body (not being a body to which sub-article (1) relates) has made submissions or observations in writing to a planning authority in relation to a planning application, the planning authority shall, if notice of the decision in respect of the application is not published in a newspaper by the authority in a list referred to in article 42(1) or pursuant to sub-article (3), send notice of the decision to the person or body within three working days of the giving of the decision.

(3) (a) Where a planning authority do not publish a list referred to in article 42(1) in a newspaper –

 (i) the authority shall, within seven days of giving their decision in respect of a planning application in relation to which an environmental impact statement was submitted to them in accordance with any provisions of this Part, publish notice of the decision in a newspaper circulating in the district in which the land or structure to which the planning application relates is situate,

 (ii) the authority may, in the case of any planning application other than an application referred to in paragraph (i), publish notice of their decision in respect of the application in a newspaper as aforesaid.

(b) Where a planning authority publish notice of their decision in respect of a planning application in a newspaper in accordance with paragraph (a)(ii), the notice shall be published within seven days of the giving of the decision.

[(4) (a) A planning authority shall, within three working days of giving its decision in respect of a planning application in relation to which notice was given to the Minister in accordance with article 31(1), or in relation to which particulars, information or documents were furnished to the Minister in accordance with article 31(3), send notice of the decision to: -

287

     (i) the Minister, and -

    (ii) where views in relation to the proposed development were furnished by another Member State of the European Communities, such State.

  (b) A notice sent pursuant to paragraph (a) of this sub-article shall contain the information referred to in article 41.][1a]   **[321]**

---

1 Amendments

a   Subarticle (4) was substituted by LG(PD)R 1999 (SI 92/1999), art 20.

3 Notes

a   This article prescribes the form of notice to be given to a body to which notification of a planning application was forwarded under art 32 and from whom a submission was received. For persons or bodies other than those specified in art 32, notice of the decision may be given by publishing a notice in a newspaper circulating in the area or more usually sending notice of its decision individually to each person or body. Publication in a newspaper may only be used where the list is published in accordance with the provisions of art 42(3). In *Dolan v Dublin Corporation* (HC) unrep, 19 June 1989, Barron J held invalid a decision to grant permission because of the planning authority's failure to implement this article.

---

44. Provision of forms and instructions

(1) A planning authority may provide forms and instructions for the convenience or information of any persons intending to make a planning application.

(2) The Minister may prepare and publish model forms and instructions for the use and guidance of planning authorities in dealing with planning applications.   **[322]**

45. Notice of extension of appropriate period [3a]

Where, in accordance with subsection (4AA) (inserted by the Environmental Impact Assessment Regulations) of section 26 of the Act of 1963, the Minister extends the appropriate period within the meaning of subsection (4) of that section, the planning authority shall, as soon as may be after receipt of notification of the extension, publish notice of the extension in a newspaper circulating in the district in which the relevant land or structure is situate.   **[323]**

---

3 Notes

a   Section 26(4AA) of LG(PD) 1963 was repealed by the EC(EIA)(A)R 1998, (SI 351/1998), art 4(6).

---

46. Procedure on receipt of notice of Minister's decision on request for exemption from requirement to submit environmental impact statement[3a]

A planning authority shall, on receipt of notice of the decision of the Minister on a request for an exemption under subsection (3) (inserted by the Environmental Impact Assessment Regulations and amended by the European Communities (Environmental Impact Assessment) (Amendment) Regulations, 1994) of section 25 of the Act of 1963, stamp the notice with the date of its receipt.   **[324]**

3 Notes

a   This provision is necessary because under s 25(4)(b) of the LG(PD)A 1963 the period for the determination of a planning application does not include the period beginning on the day a request for an exemption is made and ending on the day notice is given of the Minister's decision.

47. Transitional [3a]

(1) Subject to sub-articles (2) and (3) –

  (a) this Part shall not apply or have effect in relation to a planning application that is received before the coming into operation of this Part,

  (b) the provisions of the Local Government (Planning and Development) Regulations, 1977 to 1993 replaced by this Part shall, notwithstanding article 4, continue in force and have effect in relation to any planning application that is received before the coming into operation of this Part.

(2) Article 36 shall, subject to sub-articles (1)(b)(ii), (2)(b) and (3) thereof, apply and have effect in relation to planning applications whether received before or after the coming into operation of this Part.

(3) A list referred to in this article 30(1) or 42(1) shall be made available in accordance with the provisions of the article concerned in respect of the week commencing on the coming into operation of this Part and of each subsequent week.   **[325]**

3 Notes

a   This contains the transitional provisions. All articles with the exception of art 36 will only apply to applications received on or after 16 May 1994. Article 36 applies to applications received before 16 May 1994.

Part V

APPEALS AND OTHER MATTERS WITH WHICH AN BORD PLEANÁLA IS CONCERNED

Chapter 1: Application of certain provisions of Act of 1992

48. Application of certain provisions of Act of 1992 to appeals under section 27(4) of Act of 1963 [3a]

(1) (a) Sections 4, 7, 8, 9, 10 and 11 of the Act of 1992 shall apply to appeals under section 27(4) of the Act of 1963.

  (b) Where a planning authority decide under section 27 of the Act of 1963 to grant a permission and an appeal taken under subsection (4) of that section against that decision is dismissed by the Board pursuant to section 11 of the Act of 1992, the planning authority shall make the grant as soon as may be after the dismissal.

(2) Sections 6 and 16 of the Act of 1992 shall apply to appeals under section 27(4) of the Act of 1963 in the following manner –

  (a) in the said sections, a reference to a planning application shall be construed as a reference to an application for permission under section 27 of the Act of 1993,

  (b) in subsection (3)(b) of section 16, "27" shall be substituted for "26".

289

(3) Section 12 of the Act of 1992 shall apply to appeals under section 27(4) of the Act of 1963 subject to the substitution of "27(4)" for "26(5)" in subsection (2)(c) of the said section 12.

(4) Section 13 of the Act of 1992 shall apply to appeals under section 27(4) of the Act of 1963 subject to the substitution for subsection (1) of the said section 13 of the following subsection:

> "(1) The Board in determining an appeal may take into account matters other than those raised by the parties or by any person who has made submissions or observations to the Board in relation to the appeal if the matters either relate to the proper planning and development of the area of the relevant planning authority or are matters to which by virtue of section 24(2) of the Act of 1976 the Board may have regard.."

(5) Section 17 of the Act of 1992 shall apply to appeals under section 27(4) of the Act of 1963 subject to the substitution of "27(4)" for "26(5)" in subsections (1)(a) and (1)(b) of the said section 17.

(6) In the application of the Act of 1992 to appeals under section 27(4) of the Act of 1963, "**party to an appeal**" means any of the following persons, namely –

(a) the appellant,

(b) the planning authority against whose decision an appeal is made,

(c) the applicant for any permission in relation to which an appeal is made by another person (other than a person acting on behalf of the appellant),

and "**party**" shall be construed accordingly.   **[326]**

---

3 Notes

a   LG(PD)A 1963, s 27(4) provides for the making of appeals on or against decisions made by a planning authority and applications made for retention of structures which were unauthorised on or before 1 October 1964.

---

49. Application of certain provisions of Act of 1992 to certain other appeals

(1) This article shall apply to any appeal to the Board under the Act of 1963 or the Act of 1976, other than an appeal under section 26(5), 27(4) or 85(4)(b) of the Act of 1963.[2a]

(2) Sections 4, 7, 9, 10, 11 and 16 of the Act of 1992 shall apply to appeals to which this article applies.

(3) Section 8 of the Act of 1992 shall, subject to the following modifications, apply to appeals to which this article applies –

(a) the deletion from subsection (1)(b) of the words "Without prejudice to subsection (3),", and the deletion of subsection (3);

(b) the substitution for subsection (2) of the following subsection:

> "(2) The period referred to in subsection (1)(b) is the period of one month beginning on the day of receipt of the appeal by the Board or, where there is more than one appeal to the Board, on the day on which the Board last receives an appeal."

(4) Section 12 of the Act of 1992 shall, subject to the following modifications, apply to appeals to which this article applies –

(a) in the case of an appeal under section 89(4) of the Act of 1963,[2b] the substitution for subsection (2)(c) of the said section 12 of the following paragraph:

> "(c) A request by an appellant for an oral hearing of an appeal shall accompany the appeal and any request for an oral hearing received by the Board other than a request which accompanies the appeal shall not be considered by the Board.";

(b) in the case of any appeal to which this article applies other than an appeal referred to in paragraph (a), the substitution for subsection (2)(c) of the said section 12 of the following paragraph:

> "(c) Where a provision of the Principal Act or of the Act of 1976 authorising an appeal to the Board enable the appeal only to be made within, or before the expiration of, a specified period or before a specified day, a request by an appellant for an oral hearing of an appeal may only be made within, or before the expiration of, the specified period or before the specified day and any request for an oral hearing not so received by the Board shall not be considered by the Board."

(5) Section 13 of the Act of 1992 shall apply to appeals to which this article applies subject to the substitution for subsection (1) of the following subsection:

> "(1) The Board in determining an appeal may take into account matters other than those raised by the parties or by any person who has made submissions or observations to the Board in relation to the appeal if the matters either relate to the proper planning and development of the area of the relevant planning authority or are matters to which by virtue of section 24(2) of the Act of 1976 the Board may have regard."

(6) (a) (i) Where a provision of the Act of 1963 or of the Act of 1976 authorising an appeal to the Board to which this article applies enables the appeal only to be made within, or before the expiration of, a specified period or before a specified day, that provision shall be construed as including a provision that an appeal received by the Board outside, or after the expiration of, the specified period or on or after the specified day shall be invalid as not having been made in time.

(ii) Where the last day of the specified period within or before the expiration of which, or the day immediately preceding the specified day before which, an appeal may be made to the Board is a Saturday, a Sunday, a public holiday (within the meaning of the Holidays (Employees) Act, 1973 (No. 25 of 1973)) or any other day on which the offices of the Board are closed, an appeal shall, notwithstanding sub-paragraph (i), be valid as having been made in time if received by the Board on the next following day on which the offices of the Board are open.

(b) Where a requirement of or under the Act of 1992 as applied by this article requires submissions, observations or a request to be made, or documents, particulars or other information to be submitted, to the Board within, or before the expiration of, a specified period or before a specified day and the last day of the specified period or the day immediately preceding the specified day is a Saturday, a Sunday, a public holiday (within the meaning of the Holidays (Employees) Act, 1973) or any other day on which the offices of the Board are closed, the submissions, observations or request, or documents, particulars or other information (as the case may be) shall be regarded as having been received in time if received by the Board on the next following day on which the offices of the Board are open.

(7) In the application of the Act of 1992 to appeals to which this article applies, "**party to an appeal**" means any of the following persons, namely –

   (a) the appellant,

   (b) the planning authority against whose decision an appeal is made,

   (c) the applicant for any licence in relation to which an appeal is made by another person (other than a person acting on behalf of the appellant),

   (d) any person served or issued by a planning authority with a notice or order, or copy thereof, under section 30, 33, 36, 37, 44, 45 or 48 of the Act of 1963 or section 25 of the Act of 1976, in relation to which an appeal is made by another person,

and "**party**" shall be construed accordingly. **[327]**

---

2 Cross References

a   LG(PD)A 1963, s 26(5) relates to appeals against decisions made on applications for planning permissions or approval. LG(PD)A 1963, s 27(4) relates to appeals in relation to decisions on applications made for the retention of structures which existed on or before the appointed day. LG(PD)A 1963, s 85(4)(b) relates to appeals against consent being unreasonably withheld in relation to the laying of cables, pipelines or wires on lands not forming part of a public road.

b   LG(PD)A 1963, s 89(4) relates to appeals against a decision for an application for a licence to erect a structure on or along a public road.

---

50. Submission of documents, etc. to Board by planning authorities

Where an appeal to which article 49 applies is made to the Board, the planning authority concerned shall, within a period of fourteen days beginning on the day on which a copy of the appeal is sent to them by the Board pursuant to section 7 of the Act of 1992 as applied by article 49, submit to the Board any information or documents in their possession which is or are relevant to the appeal. **[328]**

51. Availability for inspection of copies of appeals

Where a copy of an appeal to which article 49 applies is given to a planning authority by the Board pursuant to section 7 of the Act of 1992 as applied by the said article, the planning authority shall, as soon as may be after receipt of the copy of the appeal, make a copy of the appeal available for inspection by members of the public during office hours at the offices of the authority until the appeal is withdrawn or is dismissed or determined by the Board. **[329]**

52. Application of certain provisions of Act of 1992 to appeals provided for by orders under section 45 of Act of 1963[2a]

Where provision is made by an order under section 45 of the Act of 1963 for the application of section 26(5) of that Act, with or without adaptations or modifications, in relation to any consent under the order and any applications therefor, the provisions of sections 1 and 4 to 17 of the Act of 1992 shall apply, as may be appropriate, in relation to any appeal to the Board against a decision of the relevant planning authority on an application for consent as if the appeal were an appeal under section 26(5) of the Act of 1963 and a reference in any of the said sections of the Act of 1992 to a planning application shall be construed as a reference to an application for consent under the order.   **[330]**

2 Cross References

a   LG(PD)A 1963, s 45 relates to appeals made relating to tree preservation orders.

53. Application of certain provisions of Act of 1992 to references [3a]

(1) Sections 4, 7 to 13 and 16 of the Act of 1992 shall, subject to the modifications and adaptations specified in this article, apply to a reference.

(2) In the application of the sections mentioned in sub-article (1) to a reference –

  (a) **"appeal"** and **"appellant"** shall be construed, respectively, as **"reference"** and **"person by whom the reference was made"**;

  (b) the reference in section 4(1)(d) to **"grounds of appeal"** shall be construed as a reference to **"grounds of the reference"**.

(3) Section 8 of the Act of 1992 shall apply to a reference subject to –

  (a) the deletion from subsection (1)(b) of the words "Without prejudice to subsection (3),", and the deletion of subsection (3);

  (b) the substitution for subsection (2) of the following subsection:

  "(2) The period referred to in subsection (1)(b) is the period of one month beginning on the day of receipt by the Board of the reference."

(4) Section 12 of the Act of 1992 shall apply to a reference subject to the substitution for subsection (2)(c) of the following paragraph:

  "(c) A request by a person making a reference for an oral hearing of the reference shall accompany the reference and any request for an oral hearing received by the Board other than a request which accompanies the reference shall not be considered by the Board.".

(5) Section 13 of the Act of 1992 shall apply to a reference subject to the substitution for subsection (1) of the following subsection:

  "(1) The Board in determining a reference may take into account matters other than those raised by the parties or by any person who has made submissions or observations to the Board in relation to the reference."

(6) Where a reference is made to he Board the planning authority concerned shall, within a period of fourteen days beginning on the day on which a copy of the reference is sent to them by the Board, submit to the Board any information or documents in their possession which is or are relevant to the reference.

(7) In the application of the Act of 1992 to references, **"party to a reference"** means any of the following persons, namely –

  (a) the person making the reference,

  (b) the planning authority for the area in which the land or structure to which the reference relates is situate,

  (c) any other person with whom the question to which the reference relates has arisen,

and **"party"** shall be construed accordingly.   **[331]**

3 Notes

a   A reference to An Bord Pleanála is provided for under LG(PD)A 1963, s 5.

Chapter II: Appeals against decisions of planning authorities on planning applications

54. Definition for Chapter II

In this Chapter, "**appeal**" means an appeal against a decision of a planning authority on a planning application.   **[332]**

55. Additional requirement as to submission of documents, etc. in case of certain planning applications

Where notice of, or particulars, information or documents in relation to, a planning application has or have been given to the Minister by a planning authority in accordance with article 31 and notice of the decision of the authority on the application has been given to the Minister in accordance with article 43(4), the planning authority shall notify the Board of this in course of their compliance with the requirements of section 6 of the Act of 1992.   **[333]**

56. Power of Board to require submission of environmental impact statement in connection with certain appeals

(1) Where an appeal is against a decision of a planning authority on a planning application which relates to development which, in the opinion of the Board, is development –

(a) of a class for the time being specified under Article 24 of the Environmental Impact Assessment Regulations (or under any provision amending or replacing the said Article 24), or

(b) ... [1a]

and an environmental impact statement was not submitted to the planning authority in respect of the planning application, the Board shall require the applicant to submit to the Board an environmental impact statement.[3a]

(2) Where an appeal is against a decision of a planning authority on a planning application which relates to development which would be of a class for the time being specified under Article 24 of the Environmental Impact Assessment Regulations (or under any provision amending or replacing the said Article 24) but for not exceeding a quantity, area or other limit specified in relation to that class and where the planning authority did not require the applicant, in accordance with article 26, to submit an environmental impact statement, the Board shall, where it considers that the development would be likely to have significant effects on the environment, require the applicant to submit to the Board an environmental impact statement.[1b]

(3) Sub-article (1) or (2) shall not apply in the case of an appeal against the decision of a planning authority on a planning application which relates to development as regards which an exemption was granted by the Minister in accordance with subsection (3) (inserted by the Environmental Impact Assessment Regulations and amended by the European Communities (Environmental Impact Assessment) (Amendment) Regulations, 1994) of section 25 of the Act of 1963.   **[334]**

1 Amendments

a   Subarticle (1)(b) was deleted by LG(PD)R 1999 (SI 92/1999), art 18(a).

b   Subarticle (2) was amended by LG(PD)R 1999 (SI 92/1999), art 18(a).

3 Notes

a   This provision resolves the previous anomalous position whereby the Board did not appear to have the power to require the submission of an EIS where the development proposed exceeded the minimum thresholds specified where this was not required by the planning authority. An explicit power has now been conferred on the Board to require the submission of an EIS in those circumstances.

57. Content of environmental impact statement

An environment impact statement submitted pursuant to a requirement under article 56 shall comply with Article 25 of the Environmental Impact Assessment Regulations, or any provision amending or replacing the said Article 25.   **[335]**

58. Consideration of adequacy of information contained in environmental impact statement [3a]

Where the Board receives an environmental impact statement in connection with an appeal in accordance with section 6 of the Act of 1992 or pursuant to a requirement under article 56, the Board shall –

> (a) in case the decision against which the appeal is brought relates to development which comprises or is for the purposes of an activity in relation to which a licence under Part IV of the Environmental Protection Agency Act, 1992, [or a waste licence,][1a] is required, consider whether the environmental impact statement complies with article 57 with regard to matters other than the risk of environmental pollution from the activity, or
>
> (b) in case the decision against which the appeal is brought relates to development other than development referred to in paragraph (a), consider whether the environmental impact statement complies with article 57.   **[336]**

1 Amendments

a   The words in square brackets were inserted by LG(PD)(No 3)R 1997 (SI 261/1997), art 6.

3 Notes

a   The position which existed under the LG(PD)R 1992 has been modified so as to prohibit the Board in assessing the adequacy of an EIS from considering matters which relate to the risk of environmental pollution in applications which are subject to licencing by the EPA.

59. Availability for inspection and purchase of environmental impact statement [3a]

(1) (a) An environmental impact statement received by the Board in accordance with section 6 of the Act of 1992 shall, in addition to the requirements of articles 36 and 37, be made available for inspection free of charge, and copies of any such statement and extracts therefrom shall be made available for purchase, at the offices of the Board or at such other convenient place as the Board may specify until, as regards the appeal or, as may be appropriate, each of the appeals

against the decision of the planning authority on the planning application in relation to which the environmental impact statement was submitted to the planning authority –

    (i)   it is withdrawn, or

    (ii) it is determined by the Board or dismissed by it pursuant to section 11 or 14 of the Act of 1992, or

    (iii) in relation to it a direction is given to the planning authority by the Board pursuant to section 15 of the said Act.

(b) Copies of an environmental impact statement referred to in paragraph (a) shall be made available for purchase in accordance with that paragraph for the fee fixed by the planning authority in accordance with article 37, and copies of extracts from any such statement shall be made available for purchase in accordance with that paragraph for such fee as the Board may fix not exceeding the reasonable cost of making the copy.

(2) (a)[3b] An environmental impact statement received by the Board pursuant to a requirement under article 56 shall be made available for inspection free of charge, and copies of any such statement and extracts therefrom shall be made available for purchase, at the offices of the planning authority and at the offices of the Board or such other convenient place as the Board may specify until, as regards the appeal in respect of which the environmental impact statement is received –

    (i)   it is withdrawn, or

    (ii) it is determined by the Board or dismissed by it pursuant to section 11 or 14 of the Act of 1992, or

    (iii) in relation to it a direction is given to the planning authority by the Board pursuant to section 15 of the said Act.

(b) Copies of an environmental impact statement referred to in paragraph (a) shall be made available for purchase in accordance with that paragraph for such fee, not exceeding the reasonable cost of making the copy, as may be fixed by the Board, and copies of extracts from any such statement shall be made available for purchase for such fee as the planning authority or the Board, as may be appropriate, may fix not exceeding the reasonable cost of making the copy.   **[337]**

---

3 Notes

a   This article modifies the position which existed under the LG(PD)R 1992 by providing that extracts of an EIS as well as the complete document are to be made available for purchase at a cost not exceeding the reasonable cost of making a copy.

b   Subarticle (2) provides for cases where the Board requires an EIS to be submitted pursuant to art 56, whereas sub-art 1 provides for cases where the EIS is transmitted from the planning authority.

---

60. Notice to Minister of certain appeals [3a]

[(1) The Board shall, as soon as may be, notify the Minister of any appeal: -

    (a) in respect of which notice in accordance with article 55 is given to the Board by the planning authority concerned, or

(b) in respect of which the Board intends to require, in accordance with article 56, an environmental impact statement, and: -

    (i) which in the opinion of the Board, relates to development likely to have significant effects on the environment in another Member State of the European Communities, or

    (ii) another Member State of the European Communities considers that the said development would be likely to have the said effects and has requested that it be provided with information in relation to the planning application.

(2) The Board shall furnish to the Minister a copy of any environmental impact statement received in relation to an appeal in respect of which notice is given to the Minister pursuant to sub-article (1)(b).]¹ᵃ **[338]**

---

1 Amendments

a   Article 60 was substituted by LG(PD)R 1999 (SI 92/1999), art 19.

---

61. Notice of certain appeals ³ᵃ

(1) The Board shall publish in at least one daily newspaper published in the State notice of any appeal in respect of which an environmental impact statement has been received by the Board in accordance with section 6 of the Act of 1992 or pursuant to a requirement under article 56.

(2) A notice published in accordance with sub-article (1) shall state –

    (a) the locations at which, and the period during which, the environmental impact statement will be available for inspection and purchase, and

    (b) that, subject 8 of the Act of 1992 –

        (i) in the case of an appeal against a decision of a planning authority on a planning application which relates to development other than development referred to in sub-paragraph (ii), submissions or observations may be made to the Board in relation to the appeal within a period of one month beginning on the day of publication of the notice,

        (ii) in the case of an appeal against a decision of a planning authority on a planning application which relates to development comprising or for the purposes of an activity in relation to which a licence under Part IV of the Environmental Protection Agency Act, 1992, [or a waste licence,]¹ᵃ is required, submissions or observations may be made to the Board in relation to matters other than the risk of environmental pollution from the activity within a period of one month beginning on the day of publication of the notice.

[339]

---

1 Amendments

a   The words in square brackets were inserted by LG(PD)(No 3)R 1997 (SI 261/1997), art 7.

3 Notes

a   The Board is required to publish a notice in a daily newspaper of any appeal which is accompanied by an EIS. Such notice must now state that in those appeals where the development is subject to licencing by the EPA that submissions which relate to the risk of environmental pollution may not be made.

62. Weekly list [2a, 3a]

(1) The Board shall, not later than the third working day following a particular week, make available in accordance with sub-article (2) a list of –

(a) the appeals received by the Board, and

(b) the appeals determined, dismissed or withdrawn or in relation to which a direction is given by the Board pursuant to section 15 of the Act of 1992,

during that week.

(2) (a) A list referred to in sub-article (1) shall indicate in respect of each of the appeals received by the Board during the week to which the list relates –

   (i) the name of the appellant,

   (ii) the date on which the appeal was received by the Board,

   (iii) the reference number of the Board in respect of the appeal,

   (iv) the nature and location of the development or retention or continuance of use to which the appeal relates,

   (v) the reference number of the planning application concerned in the register of the planning authority, and

   (vi) the name of the person by or on behalf of whom the planning application was made.

(b) A list referred to in sub-article (1) shall indicate, in respect of each appeal determined, dismissed or withdrawn or in relation to which a direction is given by the Board pursuant to section 15 of the Act of 1992 during the week to which the list relates, the matters specified in paragraph (a)(iii) to (vi) and the following additional matters –

   (i) in the case of an appeal determined by the Board, the nature of the decision of the Board and the date of the order of the Board in relation to the appeal,

   (ii) in the case of an appeal dismissed by the Board, the date of the order of the Board in relation to the appeal,

   (iii) in the case of an appeal which has been withdrawn, the date on which it was withdrawn,

   (iv) in the case of an appeal in relation to which a direction has been given by the Board pursuant to section 15 of the Act of 1992, the date of the order of the Board in relation to the appeal,

   and shall identify any appeal in respect of which an environmental impact statement was received by the Board.

(3) A list referred to in sub-article (1) shall, for a period of not less than one month beginning on the day on which it is made available, be displayed in or at the offices of the Board in a position convenient for public inspection during office hours.

(4) (a) Copies of a list referred to in sub-article (1) shall, during the period of one month referred to in sub-article (3), be made available at the offices of the Board during office hours, free of charge or for such fee as the Board may fix not exceeding the reasonable cost of making the copy.

(b) A copy of a list referred to in sub-article (1) shall, during the period of one month as aforesaid, be sent, on request, to any person or body, free of charge or for such fee, not exceeding the reasonable cost of making the copy and the cost of postage, as the Board may fix.   **[340]**

2 Cross References

a   See also art 78.

3 Notes

a   The Board is required to publish and make available a weekly list of appeals received and appeals which have been determined (or otherwise) and the article provides that certain information must be provided in this list. This list is required to be published not later than the third working day following the week to which the list relates and it must remain available for inspection for at least a month.

63. Revised plans, etc.

The Board may, when considering an appeal, invite the applicant for the permission or approval concerned to submit to the Board, in duplicate, revised plans or other drawings modifying, or other particulars providing for the modification of, the development to which the appeal relates and an applicant so invited may submit such plans, drawings or particulars to the Board.   **[341]**

64. Availability for inspection of copies of appeals

Where a copy of an appeal is given to a planning authority by the Board in accordance with section 7 of the Act of 1992, or in accordance with that section as applied by these Regulations, the planning authority shall, as soon as may be after receipt of the copy of the appeal, make a copy of the appeal available for inspection by members of the public during office hours at the offices of the authority until the appeal is withdrawn or is dismissed or determined by the Board or a direction is given to the authority in relation to it by the Board pursuant to section 15 of the Act of 1992.   **[342]**

65. Notification by Board of decision on appeal

A notification given by the Board of a decision on an appeal shall specify –

(a) the reference number of the Board in respect of the appeal,

(b) the reference number of the planning application concerned in the register of the planning authority,

(c) the development or retention or continuance of use to which the decision relates,

(d) the nature of the decision,

(e) the date of the order of the Board in relation to the appeal,

(f) in the case of a decision to grant a permission or approval – any conditions attached thereto,

(g) in the case of a decision to grant a permission or approval for the construction, erection or making of a structure and to specify the purposes for which the structure may or may not be used – such purposes,

(h) in the case of a decision to grant a permission or approval for the development of land consisting of or comprising the carrying out of works – any approval or further approval required,

(i) in the case of a decision to grant a permission – any period specified by the Board pursuant to section 3 of the Act of 1982 as the period during which the permission is to have effect, and

shall state the reasons for the decision (including, in the case of a decision to grant permission or approval subject to conditions, the reasons for the imposition of the conditions).   **[343]**

66. Notification by Board of decision on appeal – additional requirement in certain cases

[(1) The Board shall notify: -

(a) the Minister,

(b) the other Member State of the European Communities concerned,

of its decision on any appeal in respect of which notice was given to the Minister pursuant to article 60.

(2) A notification under sub-article (1) of this article shall contain the information referred to in article 65.]¹ᵃ   **[344]**

---

1 Amendments

a   Article 66 was substituted by LG(PD)R 1999 (SI 92/1999), art 20.

Chapter III: Determinations

67. Definitions for Chapter III

In this Chapter –

(a) **"determination"** means a determination by the Board of –

(i) a disagreement, question or dispute to which section 26(7) of the Act of 1963 or section 15(2) of the Act of 1990 relates, or

(ii) a contribution or other matter which, pursuant to a condition attached to a permission or approval granted under section 26 of the Act of 1963, is to be agreed between the planning authority and the person to whom the permission or approval is granted and in default of agreement is to be determined by the Board;

(b) **"party to a determination"** means –

(i) in the case of a disagreement to which section 26(7) of the Act of 1963 relates:

(I) the local authority who will be responsible for maintenance of the roads, open spaces, car parks, sewers, watermains or drains concerned,

(II) the person carrying out the works concerned;

     (ii)   in the case of a dispute or question to which section 15(2) of the Act of 1990 relates:

         (I)   the planning authority concerned,

         (II)   the person by whom the application for permission for erection of the new structure was made;

    (iii) in the case of a determination referred to in paragraph (a)(ii):

         (I)   the planning authority concerned,

         (II)   the person to whom the permission or approval was granted;

    and "**party**" shall be construed accordingly.   **[344]**

68. Power of Board to require submission of documents, etc. in case of determinations

(1) Where the Board is of opinion that any document, particulars or other information is or are necessary for the purpose of enabling it to make a determination, the Board may serve on any party a notice under this article –

    (a) requiring that party, within a period specified in the notice (being a period of not less than fourteen days beginning on the date of service of the notice) to submit to the Board such document, particulars or other information (which document, particulars or other information shall be specified in the notice), and

    (b) stating that, in default of compliance with the requirements of the notice, the Board will, after the expiration of the period so specified and without further notice to the party, make the determination pursuant to this article.

(2) Where the notice has been served under sub-article (1), the Board, at any time after the expiration of the period specified in the notice, may, having considered any document, particulars or other information submitted by the party on whom the notice has been served, without further notice to that party make the determination.   **[345]**

69. Convening of meetings

Where is appears to the Board expedient or convenient for the purposes of making a determination the Board may, in its absolute discretion, convene a meeting of the parties.   **[346]**

Chapter IV: Appeals generally and other matters

70. Notice of appeal or reference

The Board may require any party to an appeal or a reference to give such public notice in relation thereto as the Board may specify and, in particular, may require such notice to be given by publication in a newspaper circulating in the district in which the land or structure to which the appeal or reference relates is situate.   **[347]**

71. Inspections in relation to appeals, references and determinations

The Board may arrange for the carrying out of inspections in relation to appeals, references or determinations within the meaning of article 67(a), by persons appointed for that purpose by the Board either generally or for a particular appeal, reference or determination or for appeals, references or determinations of a particular class (including appeals, references or determinations relating to land in the area of a particular planning authority).   **[348]**

72. Additional requirements as to giving of notice by Board

(1) Where the Board serves notice under section 2(3)(a) of the Act of 1992 on the parties to an appeal or other matter with which the Board is concerned, the Board shall also serve such notice on each person who has made submissions or observations to the Board in relation to the appeal or other matter.

(2) Where the Board serves notice under section 12(3) of the Act of 1992, or that provision as applied by these Regulations, on a person who has requested an oral hearing of an appeal or reference and on each other party to the appeal or reference, the Board shall also serve such notice on each person who has made submissions or observations to the Board in relation to the appeal or reference.   **[349]**

72A.

[(1) (a)   Subject to paragraph (b) and sub-articles (2) and (3) –

   (i)   the documents relating to an appeal or other matter with which the Board is concerned shall be made available at the offices of the Board for inspection by members of the public, and

   (ii) copies of the documents referred to in sub-paragraph (i), and of extracts from such documents, shall be made available at the offices of the Board, free of charge or for such fee as the Board may fix not exceeding the reasonable cost of making the copy.

   (b) Paragraph (a)(ii) shall not apply in relation to plans or other drawings, or photographs.

(2) The documents to which sub-article (1)(a) applies shall be made available in accordance with the said provision for a period of five years commencing on the third working day following the day on which –

   (a) the appeal or other matter with which the Board is concerned is determined or dismissed by the Board, or

   (b) in the case of an appeal against a decision of a planning authority on a planning application, a direction in relation to it is given by the Board pursuant to section 15 of the Act of 1992.

(3) This article shall apply and have effect in relation to any appeal or other matter with which the Board is concerned that is received by the Board on or after the 10th day of April, 1995, other than any such appeal or other matter that is withdrawn or is regarded, pursuant to section 16 of the Act of 1992 or that section as applied by these Regulations, as having been withdrawn.]¹ᵃ   **[350]**

---

1 Amendments

a   Article 72A was inserted by LG(PD)R 95 (SI 75/1995), art 2.

Chapter V: Oral hearings

73. Interpretations for Chapter V

(1) In this Chapter, a reference to an oral hearing means an oral hearing, within the meaning of section 12 of the Act of 1992 or that provision as applied by these Regulations, of an appeal or a reference.

(2) In this Chapter, "**relevant persons**" means the parties to an appeal or a reference and any persons who have made submissions or observations to the Board in relation to an appeal or reference in accordance with section 8 of the Act of 1992 or that provision as applied by these Regulations. **[351]**

74. Oral hearings – general [3a]

(1) A request for an oral hearing may be withdrawn at any time.

(2) Where the Board decides to hold an oral hearing, the Board shall –

(a) inform relevant persons and give such persons not less than seven days' notice of the time and place of the opening of the oral hearing or such shorter notice as may be accepted by all such persons,

(b) give each relevant person a copy of all correspondence, documents, particulars or other information received from other relevant persons in accordance with the provisions of the Act of 1992 or those provisions as applied by these Regulations and not previously given to that relevant person.

(3) The Board may, at any time before the opening of an oral hearing, alter the time or place of the opening of the hearing and, in the event of such alteration, the Board shall give relevant persons not less than seven days' notice of the new time and place or such shorter notice as may be accepted by all such persons.

(4) Where relevant persons have been informed that an oral hearing is to be held and where, following the withdrawal of a request for an oral hearing, the appeal or reference falls to be determined without an oral hearing, the Board shall give notice accordingly to such persons.

(5) An oral hearing shall be conducted by the Board or by a person appointed for that purpose by the Board either generally or for a particular appeal or reference or for appeals or references of a particular class (including appeals or references relating to land in the area of a particular planning authority). **[352]**

---

3 Notes

a   See *Max Developments v An Bord Pleanála* [1994] 2 IR 121 and *Simunovich v An Bord Pleanála* (HC) unrep, 23 April 1993.

---

75. Procedure at oral hearing [3a]

(1) The Board or other person conducting an oral hearing shall have discretion as to the conduct of the hearing and in particular shall –

(a) conduct the hearing without undue formality,

(b) decide the order of appearance of relevant persons,

(c) permit any relevant person to appear in person or to be represented by another person.

(2) Where the Board has given notice in accordance with section 13(2)(a) of the Act of 1992, or that provision as applied by these Regulations, of its intention to take into account matters other than those raised by the parties to an appeal or reference or by any person who has made submissions or observations to the Board in relation to an appeal or reference, the parties and any such person shall be permitted, if present, to make

submissions in relation to the said matters to the Board or other person conducting the oral hearing.

(3) The Board or other person conducting an oral hearing shall have discretion to hear a person other than a relevant person, where it is considered appropriate in the interests of justice to allow the person to be heard.   **[353]**

---

3 Notes

a   Discretion is now given to a person conducting an oral hearing to hear a person other than a person who is a party or who has made a submission to the appeal where the interests of justice so require.

---

76. Adjournment or re-opening of oral hearing [3a]

(1) Subject to sub-articles (2) and (3), the Board or other person conducting an oral hearing may adjourn or re-open any hearing or, notwithstanding that any relevant person has failed to attend a hearing, proceed with the hearing.

(2) Notice of the time and place of the re-opening of an oral hearing or resumption of an oral hearing that has been adjourned indefinitely shall be given by the Board to each relevant person and to any person who has been heard at the hearing in accordance with article 75(3) not less than seven days before the said time unless all such persons accept shorter notice.

(3) Unless the Board considers it expedient to do so and so directs, an oral hearing shall not be re-opened after the report thereon has been submitted to the Board.   **[354]**

---

3 Notes

a   See *Max Developments v An Bord Pleanála* [1994] 2 IR 121.

---

77. Replacement of person appointed to conduct oral hearing

If, for any reason, the person appointed is unable or fails to conduct, or to complete the conduct of, an oral hearing or, for any reason, is unable or fails to furnish a report on an oral hearing to the Board, the Board may appoint another person to conduct the oral hearing or to conduct a new oral hearing.   **[355]**

Chapter VI: General

78. Transitional [3a]

(1) Subject to sub-article (2) –

   (a) this Part shall not apply or have effect in relation to any appeal or other matter that is received by the Board before the coming into operation of this Part,

   (b) the provisions of the Local Government (Planning and Development) (No. 2) Regulations, 1992 shall, notwithstanding article 4, continue in force and have effect in relation to any appeal or other matter that is received by the Board before the coming into operation of this Part.

(2) A list referred to in article 62 shall be made available in accordance with that article in respect of the week commencing on the coming into operation of this Part and of each subsequent week.   **[356]**

3 Notes

a   This is a transitional provision and is of little relevance now.

Part VI

EXTENSION OF DURATION OF PLANNING PERMISSION

79. Interpretation for Part VI[3a]

(1) In this Part, **"the appropriate period"** has the meaning assigned to it by section 2(5) of the Act of 1982.

(2) In this Part, any reference to a decision to extend or further extend the appropriate period as regards a particular permission shall include a reference to such a decision which is regarded as having been given by virtue of section 4(2) of the Act of 1982 and cognate expressions shall be construed accordingly.   **[357]**

3 Notes

a   Two important decisions clarify the position relating to such applications: *Frenchurch Properties v Wexford County Council* [1991] ILRM 769 and *Garden Village Construction Company Ltd v Wicklow County Council* (SC) unrep, 28 July 1994.

80. Time at which application to extend or further extend appropriate period may be made

An application under section 4 of the Act of 1982 to extend or further extend the appropriate period as regards a particular permission shall be made not earlier than one year before the expiration of the appropriate period sought to be extended or further extended.   **[358]**

81. Content of application to extend appropriate period

An application under section 4 of the Act of 1982 to extend the appropriate period as regards a particular permission shall be made in writing and shall contain the following particulars –

(a) (i)   the name and address, and telephone number if any, of the applicant and of the person, if any, acting on behalf of the applicant,

    (ii) the address to which any correspondence relating to the application should be sent,

(b) the location of the land or the address of the structure to which the permission relates (as may be appropriate),

(c) the development to which the permission relates,

(d) particulars of the interest held in the relevant structure or other land by the applicant,

(e) the date of the permission and its reference number in the register,

(f) in the case of an outline permission, the date and reference number in the register of the subsequent approval or approvals,

(g) the date on which the permission will cease, or ceased,[2a] to have effect,

(h) the date of commencement of the development to which the permission relates,

(i) particulars of the substantial works[3a] carried out or which will be carried out pursuant to the permission before the expiration of the appropriate period,

(j) the additional period by which the permission is sought to be extended, and

(k) the date on which the development is expected to be completed.[2b]   **[359]**

---

2 Cross References

a   See LG(PD)A 1982, s 4(6).

b   See LG(PD)A 1982, s 4(1).

3 Notes

a   Works carried out in breach of permission will not satisfy the requirements of s 4, and the applicant will not be entitled to an extension. See *McCoy v Dun Laoghaire Corporation* (HC) unrep, 1 June 1984.

---

82. Content of application to further extend appropriate period

An application under section 4 of the Act of 1982 to further extend the appropriate period as regards a particular permission shall be made in writing and shall contain the particulars referred to at paragraphs (a) to (h) inclusive of article 81 and the following additional particulars –

(a) particulars of the works (if any) carried out pursuant to the permission since the permission was extended or further extended,

(b) the period by which the permission is sought to be further extended,

(c) the date on which the development is expected to be completed, and

(d) the circumstances beyond the control of the person carrying out the development due to which the development has not been completed.[2a]   **[360]**

---

2 Cross References

a   See LG(PD)A 1982, s 4(3)(a)(iii).

---

83. Procedure on receipt of application to extend or further extend appropriate period [3a]

(1) On receipt of an application to extend or further extend the appropriate period as regards a particular permission, a planning authority shall –

(a) stamp the document with the date of their receipt, and

(b) consider whether the application complies with the requirements of article 81 or 82, as the case may require.

(2) (a) Where a planning authority consider that an application to extend or further extend the appropriate period as regards a particular permission complies with the requirements of article 81 or 82, as may be appropriate, they shall send to the applicant an acknowledgement stating the date of receipt of the application.

(b) Where a planning authority consider that an application to extend or further extend the appropriate period as regards a particular permission does not comply with the requirements of article 81 or 82, as may be appropriate, they shall, by notice in writing, require the applicant to furnish such further particulars as may be necessary to comply with the said requirements.   **[361]**

3 Notes

a   This provision sets out the procedure to be adopted on receipt of an application to extend or further extend the duration of a planning permission. The procedure is similar to that employed where a planning application is received and planning authorities have a similar duty to consider whether the application complies with the requirements contained in the Regulations relating to such applications.

84. Further information

(1) Where a planning authority receive an application to extend or further extend the appropriate period as regards a particular permission, they may, by notice in writing, require the applicant –

(a) to submit such further information as they may require to consider the application (including any information regarding any estate or interest in or right over land), or

(b) to produce any evidence which they may reasonably require to verify any particulars or information given in or in relation to the application.

(2) A planning authority shall not require an applicant who has complied with a requirement under sub-article (1) to submit any further information, particulars or evidence save as may be reasonably necessary to clarify the matters dealt with in the applicant's response to the said requirement or to enable those matters to be considered or assessed.

(3) Where an applicant fails or refuses to comply with any requirement under this article within one month of such requirement, the planning authority may, if they think fit, refuse the application.   **[362]**

85. Notification of decision on application to extend or further extend appropriate period[3a]

Every notification given by a planning authority of a decision on an application to extend or further extend the appropriate period as regards a particular permission shall specify –

(a) the date of the permission and its reference number in the register,

(b) the location of the land or the address of the structure to which the permission relates (as may be appropriate),

(c) the development to which the decision relates,

(d) the date of the decision,

(e) the nature of the decision,

(f)   in the case of a decision to extend or further extend the appropriate period, the additional period by which that period has been extended, and

(g) in the case of a decision to refuse to extend or further extend the appropriate period, the reasons for such refusal.   **[363]**

3 Notes

a   There is no provision for an appeal against the decision of the planning authority on such applications.

Part VII

FEES

Chapter I: General

86. Definition for Part VI

In this Part –

"**commercial development**" means development for the purposes of any professional, commercial or industrial undertaking, development in connection with the provision for reward of services to persons or undertakings, or development consisting of the provision of two or more dwellings, but does not include development for the purposes of agriculture;

"**the 1984 Regulations**" means the Local Government (Planning and Development) (Fees) Regulations, 1984 (S.I. No. 358 of 1984);

"**the 1991 Regulations**" means the Local Government (Planning and Development) (Fees) (Amendment) Regulations, 1991 (S.I. No. 187 of 1991);

"**the 1993 Regulations**" means the Local Government (Planning and Development) (Fees) (Amendment) Regulations, 1993 (S.I. No. 349 of 1993).   **[364]**

87. Transitional

(1) Where a planning application is received by a planning authority before the coming into operation of this Part, the fee to be paid to the planning authority shall, notwithstanding this Part, be the fee payable under the 1984 Regulations as amended by the 1991 Regulations and the 1993 Regulations.

(2) Where an application under section 4 of the Act of 1982 for an extension or further extension as regards a particular permission of the appropriate period within the meaning of section 2(5) of that Act is received by a planning authority before the coming into operation of this Part, the fee to be paid to the planning authority shall, notwithstanding this Part, be the fee payable under the 1984 Regulations as amended by the 1993 Regulations.   **[365]**

Chapter II: Fees payable to a planning authority in respect of planning applications

88. Fee for planning application

Subject to the following provisions of this Part, a fee shall be paid to a planning authority by an applicant in respect of a planning application.[3a]   **[366]**

3 Notes

a   In *Calor Teo v Sligo County Council* [1991] 2 IR 267 it was made clear that an application will remain invalid until the full fee is paid.

89. Exemption

(1) Where a planning application relates in whole or in part to development which in the opinion of the planning authority is development proposed to be carried out by or on behalf of a voluntary organisation, and which in the opinion of the planning authority –

(a) is designed or intended to be used for social, recreational, educational or religious purposes by inhabitants of a locality generally or by people of a particular group or religious denomination and is not to be used mainly for profit or gain,

(b) is designed or intended to be used as a hostel, workshop or other accommodation for persons with a disability and is not to be used mainly for profit or gain, or

(c) is ancillary to development referred to in paragraph (a) or (b),

a fee shall not be payable in respect of any such development.

(2) Where a planning application relates in whole or in part to development which is proposed to be carried out by or on behalf of a body standing approved of for the purposes of section 6 of the Housing (Miscellaneous Provisions) Act, 1992 (No. 18 of 1992) and which in the opinion of the planning authority –

(a) is designed or intended to be used for the accommodation of poor or homeless persons or persons who would otherwise be likely to require housing accommodation provided by a housing authority, and is not to be used mainly for profit or gain, or

(b) is ancillary to development referred to in paragraph (a),

a fee shall not be payable in respect of any such development.   **[367]**

90. Standard fee

The amount of the fee payable in respect of a planning application shall, subject to articles 91, 92 and 93 and Section III of the Fourth Schedule, be the amount indicated in column 2 of Section II of the Fourth Schedule opposite the mention of the relevant class of development in column 1 of Section II of the said Schedule.[2a]   **[368]**

---

2 Cross References

a   See Fourth Schedule (substituted by LG(PD)(F)(A)R 1998 (SI 119/1998).

---

91. Fee for certain planning applications relating to retention of structures or continuance of use [2a]

Subject to Section III of the Fourth Schedule, the amount of the fee payable in respect of an application for permission for the retention on land of any structure or for the continuance of any use of any structure or other land, other than an application to which article 93(2)(b) or (c) applies, shall be the amount indicated in column 2 of Section II of the Fourth Schedule opposite the mention of the relevant class of development in column 1 of Section II of the said Schedule, increased by one half.   **[369]**

---

2 Cross References

a   The fees payable in this regard were modified by LG(PD)(F)(A)R 1998 (SI 119/1998) which came into effect on 1 May 1998. However, these Regulations were subsequently revoked by

LG(PD)(F)(A)(No 2)R 1998 (SI 128/1998) but the scale of fees and date of effect remains the same except in so far as they relate to appeals to An Bord Pleanála.

92. Outline application fee [3a]

Subject to Section III of the Fourth Schedule, the amount of the fee payable in respect of an outline application shall be three quarters of the amount indicated in column 2 of Section II of the Fourth Schedule opposite the mention of the relevant class of development in column 1 of Section II of the said Schedule.   **[370]**

3 Notes

a   At the stage of an outline application the floor area being applied for must be established which means that often full design drawings must be prepared at this stage. This is often expensive and unnecessary when in reality what is sought is the decision in principle that the development is acceptable.

93. Reduced fee [3a]

(1) Subject to sub-article (3) and Section III of the Fourth Schedule, the amount of the fee payable in respect of an application mentioned in sub-article (2) shall be one quarter of the amount indicated in column 2 of Section II of the Fourth Schedule opposite the mention of the relevant class of development in column 1 of Section II of the said Schedule.

(2) The applications referred to in sub-article (1) are –

(a)   an application for an approval,

(b)   an application for permission for the retention of any structure or for the continuance of any use of land without complying with a condition subject to which a previous permission was granted for the development,

(c)   an application for permission for the retention of any structure or for the continuance of any use of land in respect of which a previous permission has been granted for a limited period only or subject to a condition which is of a kind described in section 26(2)(j) or 27(2)(f) of the Act of 1963 and which is made not less than two months before the expiration of the previous permission,

(d)   an application which relates to development which differs from development authorised by a previous permission by reason only of –

(i)   a change in the type of dwelling proposed to be constructed, erected or made, or

(ii)   the modification of the design or of the external appearance of a building or other structure proposed to be constructed, erected or made.

(3) This article shall have effect only where a fee under this Part or under the 1984 Regulations as amended by the 1991 Regulations and the 1993 Regulations has been paid in relation to the relevant previous permission or approval.   **[371]**

3 Notes

a   The scale of fees payable was modified by LG(PD)(F)(A)R 1998 (SI 119/1998) which was in turn revoked by LG(PD)(F)(A)(No 2)R 1998 (SI 128/1998) but the scale of fees introduced is the same in both sets of regulations. See the revised Schedules.

94. Refund of fee in case of certain repeat applications

(1) Where a planning application (not being an application for an approval) is either –

(a) withdrawn before a decision to grant or to refuse the relevant permission is made by the planning authority, or

(b) determined by the planning authority or by the Board,

and a subsequent such application is made by or on behalf of the same applicant, the planning authority shall, subject to sub-article (3) and article 96 and to paragraph 5 of Section III of the Fourth Schedule, refund three quarters of the fee paid to them in respect of the subsequent application if, and only if, each of the conditions mentioned in sub-article (2) is complied with.

(2) The conditions referred to in sub-article (1) are –

(a) the authority are satisfied that the subsequent application relates to development of the same character or description as the development to which the earlier application related, and

(b) a fee under this Part (or under the 1984 Regulations as amended by the 1991 Regulations and the 1993 Regulations) in respect of the class or classes of development to which the subsequent application relates has been paid in respect of the earlier application, and

(c) the period between the withdrawal or determination of the first application and the making of the subsequent application does not exceed twelve months, and

(d) the authority are satisfied that the subsequent application relates to land substantially consisting of the site or part of the site to which the earlier application related, and

(e) no previous refund under sub-article (1) or under article 10 of the 1984 Regulations has at any time been made to the same applicant in respect of an application which related substantially to the same land and to development of the same character or description as that to which the subsequent application relates, and

(f) the case is not a case where a reduced fee has been paid under article 93 or under article 9 of the 1984 Regulations.

(3) A refund under this article shall be made on a claim in that behalf made in writing to the planning authority and received by them within (but not after) the period of two months beginning on the day of the giving of the decision of the planning authority in respect of the subsequent application.   **[372]**

95. Refund of fee in certain other cases [3a]

Where a planning authority serve a notice in accordance with article 20(3) or 29(2)(b)(i), they shall refund the fee paid to them in respect of the planning application.   **[373]**

3 Notes

a   This provision requires a planning authority to refund the fee paid where an application is submitted for outline planning permission which may or may not be considered by a planning authority (in the circumstances outlined in art 20) or if the application is returned for a gross failure to comply with application requirements (art 29 2(b)(i)).

96. Discretionary power to refund fee in certain limited circumstances

(1) Notwithstanding any other provision of this Part, but subject to paragraph 5 of Section III of the Fourth Schedule, a planning authority shall have an absolute discretion to refund a part of the fee payable in respect of a particular planning application where they are satisfied that the payment in full of the fee would not be just and reasonable having regard to any of the following –

   (a) the limited extent of the development,

   (b) the limited cost of the development,

   (c) the fee payable in respect of an application for any other development of a similar character, extent or description.

(2) A decision under sub-article (1) shall contain a statement specifying the reasons for the decision.   **[374]**

97. Applications involving mixed development

(1) Subject to sub-article (2), where a planning application relates to development which is within more than one of the classes mentioned in column 1 of Section II of the Fourth Schedule –

   (a) an amount shall be calculated in accordance with this Part in respect of the development which is within each such class, and

   (b) the aggregate of the amounts so calculated shall, subject to Section III of the Fourth Schedule, be taken as the amount of the fee payable in respect of the development to which the application relates.

(2) Sub-article (1) shall not have effect in relation to development comprising the provision of roads, car parks, services, open spaces or any structures or other works which are included in the planning application and are incidental to development of the class or classes to which the application primarily relates.

(3) Where a planning application referred to in sub-article (1) relates to a building which is to contain floor space which it is proposed to use (or which is designed for use or is capable of use) for the purposes of providing common access or common services or facilities for persons occupying or using the building, the amount of such common floor space appropriate to each class of development mentioned in column 1 of Section II of the Fourth Schedule shall be taken, for the purposes of the calculation referred to in sub-article (1)(a), to be such proportion of the common floor space as the amount of floor space coming directly within the class bears to the total amount of gross floor space in the building.   **[375]**

98. Applications involving multi-purpose development

Where a planning application relates to development which is designed for, or capable of, or intended for, use for one of several purposes, the amount of the fee payable in respect of each of the relevant classes of development mentioned in column 1 of Section II of the Fourth Schedule shall be calculated and the fee payable shall, subject to Section III of the Fourth Schedule, be the highest of those amounts. **[376]**

99. Applications involving alternative plans

Where a planning application includes proposals for materially different layouts or designs relating to the proposed development, the fee payable in respect of the application shall be calculated as if each proposal constituted a separate planning application. **[377]**

100. Calculation of site area and gross floor space

(1) Where, in respect of any class of development mentioned in column 1 of Section II of the Fourth Schedule, the amount of the fee is to be calculated by reference to the site area, that area shall be taken as consisting of the area of land to which the application relates.

(2) Where, in respect of any class of development mentioned in column 1 of Section II of the Fourth Schedule, the amount of the fee is to be calculated by reference to the area of gross floor space to be provided, that area shall be ascertained by the internal measurement of the floor space on each floor of a building or buildings (including internal walls and partitions), disregarding any floor space provided for the parking of vehicles by persons occupying or using the building or buildings where such floor space is incidental to development to which the application primarily relates.

(3) Where the area referred to in sub-article (1) or (2) is less than the unit of measurement specified in respect of the relevant class of development or is not an exact multiple of that unit, the fraction of a unit remaining after division of the total area by the unit of measurement shall be treated, for the purposes of calculating the fee payable in respect of the application, as the complete unit. **[378]**

Chapter III: Fees payable to the Board

101. Fee for appeals[3a]

(1) A person making an appeal shall pay a fee to the Board.

(2) Subject to article 104, the amount of the fee payable to the Board shall be the amount indicated in column 2 of the Fifth Schedule opposite the appropriate mention of an appeal in column 1 of the said Schedule. **[379]**

---

3 Notes

a Appeals in this context are broader than mere appeals against planning decisions and includes appeals against revocation of permission, hedge removal notices, tree preservation orders, conservation orders, creation of public rights of way and erection of wires/cables: LG(PD)A 1976, s 25 and LG(PD)A 1963, ss 30, 36, 37, 44, 45, 46, 48, 85 and 89.

---

102. Fee for references [2a]

(1) A person making a reference to the Board shall pay a fee to the Board.

(2) Subject to article 104, the amount of the fee payable to the Board shall be the amount indicated in column 2 of the Fifth Schedule opposite the mention of a reference in column 1 of the said Schedule. **[380]**

2 Cross References

a   A "reference" in this regard will be brought under LG(PD)A 1963, s 5. See art 3. See the Fifth
     Schedule, as amended by LG(PD)(F)(A)(No 2)R 1998 (SI 128/1998). See also art 104.

103. Fee for requests for determinations[2a]

(1) A person making a request to the Board for a determination referred to in article
67(a) shall pay a fee to the Board.

(2) Subject to article 104, the amount of the fee payable to the Board shall be the amount
indicated in column 2 of the Fifth Schedule opposite the mention of a request for a
determination in column 1 of the said Schedule.   **[381]**

2 Cross References

a   For precisely what constitutes a determination see art 67(a) and see Fifth Schedule.

104. Reduced fee payable in certain circumstances

Where an appeal, a reference or a request for a determination to which article 103
applies is made to the Board by –

  (a)   a planning authority,

  (b)   An Chomhairle Ealaíon,

  (c)   Bord Fáilte Éireann,

  (d)   An Taisce – the National Trust for Ireland,

  (e)   the National Monuments Advisory Council,

  (f)   the Royal Irish Academy,

  (g)   the Central Fisheries Board,

  (h)   a Regional Fisheries Board,

the fee to be paid to the Board in respect of the appeal, reference or request shall be the
amount indicated in column 2 of the Fifth Schedule opposite the mention of a reduced
fee in column 1 of the said Schedule.   **[382]**

105. Fee for submissions or observations to the Board

(1) (a)   Subject to sub-articles (2) and (3), a fee shall be paid to the Board by a person
          or body of persons making submissions or observations to the Board as regards
          an appeal, a reference or a determination to which article 103 applies, and by a
          person who is heard at an oral hearing in accordance with article 75(3).

  (b)   The amount of the fee payable to the Board shall be the amount indicated in
         column 2 of the Fifth Schedule opposite the mention of submissions or
         observations in column 1 of the said Schedule.

(2) Sub-article (1) shall not apply where the person by or on whose behalf submissions
or observations are made is –

  (a)   the appellant or person making the reference to, or request for a determination
         by, the Board,

  (b)   the applicant for the permission, approval or licence in relation to which the
         appeal is made,

(c) any person served or issued by a planning authority with a notice or order, or copy thereof, under section 30, 33, 36, 37, 44, 45 or 48 of the Act of 1963 or section 25 of the Act of 1976, in relation to which an appeal is made by another person,[2a]

(d) a body referred to in article 104 or a State authority, or

(e) a Member State of the European Communities.

(3) Where a fee has been paid under this article or under article 23 of the 1984 Regulations by or on behalf of a person or body of persons making submissions or observations as regards a particular appeal, reference or determination, a fee shall not be payable in respect of any further submissions or observations made by or on behalf of the same person or body of persons in accordance with the Act of 1992, or that Act as applied by Part V, as regards that appeal, reference or determination. **[383]**

---

2 Cross References

a   Section 30 relates to the revocation or modification of planning permission.

Section 33 relates to a notice served in respect of an unauthorised development existing immediately before 1 October 1964.

Section 36 relates to notices requiring the removal or alteration of a structure.

Section 37 relates to notices requiring the discontinuance of any use of land.

Section 44 relates to notices requiring the removal or alteration of hedges.

Section 45 relates to tree preservation orders.

Section 48 relates to the compulsory creation of a public right of way.

LG(PD)A 1976 s 25 relates to the enforcement of planning controls in relation to open space.

---

106. Fee for requests for oral hearings [3a]

(1) A person making a request to the Board for an oral hearing of an appeal or reference shall, in addition to the fee prescribed by article 101 or 102, as may be appropriate, pay a fee to the Board in respect of the request.

(2) The amount of the fee payable to the Board shall be the amount indicated in column 2 of the Fifth Schedule opposite the mention of a request for an oral hearing in column 1 of the said Schedule. **[384]**

---

3 Notes

a   The requirement for the payment of a fee where an oral hearing is requested was provided for under the LG(PD)R 1992 and where such a fee does not accompany such a request the Board may not consider the request – see LG(PD)A 1992, s 12(2)(b)(i).

Chapter IV: Fee payable to planning authority in respect of application to extend or further extend appropriate period

107. Fee for application to extend or further extend appropriate period

(1) A fee shall be paid to a planning authority by an applicant in respect of an application under section 4 of the Act of 1982 for an extension or further extension, as regards a particular permission, of the appropriate period within the meaning of section 2(5) of that Act.

(2) The amount of the fee payable in respect of an application mentioned in sub-article (1) shall be the amount indicated in column 2 of the Sixth Schedule opposite the mention of such an application in column 1 of the said Schedule.   **[385]**

Part VIII

COMPENSATION

108. Definition for Part VIII

In this Part, "**compensation claim**" means a claim for compensation under the Act of 1990.   **[386]**

109. Compensation claim[3a]

(1) A compensation claim shall be made to the planning authority in writing and shall include –

    (a) the name and address of the claimant and a statement of his interest in the land to which the claim relates,

    (b) a statement of the matter in respect of which the claim is made, the provision of the Act of 1990 under which it is made, the amount of compensation claimed and the basis on which that amount has been calculated, and

    (c) the names and addresses of all other persons (so far as they are known to the claimant) having an interest in the land to which the claim relates, or, where the claimant does not know of any such persons, a statement to that effect.

(2) Where a planning authority receive a compensation claim which fails to comply with a requirement of sub-article (1), the authority shall, by notice in writing, require the claimant to comply with such requirement and may defer consideration of the claim until the claimant has complied with such requirement.   **[387]**

---

3 Notes

a   This lays down the requirements for compensation claims under the LG(PD)A 1990 and provides that where a claim for compensation does not comply with art 109(1) or 109(2), a planning authority is required to serve a notice on the claimant to comply with the requirement. In such circumstances the planning authority is permitted to defer consideration of the claim until the claimant has complied with the requirements.

---

110. Notice of claim

(1) Within one month of the receipt by a planning authority of a compensation claim, or within one month of compliance with a requirement under article 109(2), the planning authority shall, unless the claim is withdrawn, give notice in writing to every person, other than the claimant, appearing to them to have an interest in the land to which the claim relates.

(2) A notice under sub-article (1) shall state the name and address of the claimant, the land to which the claim relates, the matter in respect of which the claim is made and, where the relevant period under section 4 of the Act of 1990 for the making of a compensation claim has not expired, the date having regard to the said section 4 after which a further claim for compensation in respect of that matter cannot be made.

(3) Where more than one compensation claim in respect of the same matter has been received by a planning authority, the provisions of sub-article (1) shall not apply in

respect of such persons as are claimants or have already been given notice of a claim in respect of that matter under that sub-article.   **[388]**

111. Provision of certain evidence and information

Where a compensation claim is made, the planning authority may, by notice in writing, require the claimant to provide evidence in support of the claim and evidence as to the claimant's interest in the land to which the claim relates and may defer consideration of the claim under the claimant has complied with such requirement.   **[389]**

112. Application under section 14 of Act of 1990

(1) Where an application is made to the Minister under section 14 of the Act of 1990 for an order declaring that he is satisfied that it would not be just and reasonable in the particular circumstances that payment of compensation should be prevented by the provisions of section 12 or 13 of that Act, the applicant shall submit to the Minister –

   (a) his name and address and a statement of his interest in the land to which the application relates,

   (b) a statement of the date of notification of the decision refusing, or granting subject to conditions relating to any of the matters set out in paragraphs 8 and 9 of the Fourth Schedule of the Act of 1990, permission to develop the land to which the application relates, and

   (c) a statement of the reasons why, in the opinion of the applicant, such an order should be made.

(2) (a) An applicant for an order under section 14 of the Act of 1990 shall send to the Minister such documents and information relevant to the application and in the applicant's possession or procurement as the Minister may require.

   (b) The planning authority concerned shall send to the Minister such documents and information relevant to an application for an order under section 14 of the Act of 1990 and in their possession or procurement as the Minister may require.   **[390]**

113. Notice under section 13 of Act of 1990

A notice under section 13 of the Act of 1990 served on a person by whom or on behalf of whom a compensation claim under section 11 of that Act has been made shall contain –

   (a) a statement of the land to which the notice relates,

   (b) a statement that, notwithstanding the refusal of permission to develop the land or the grant of such permission subject to conditions (as the case may be), the land in question is, in the opinion of the planning authority, capable of other development for which permission under Part IV of the Act of 1963 ought to be granted.

   (c) a statement in outline of the nature and extent of the other development (being other development within the meaning of section 13 of the Act of 1990) of which, in the opinion of the planning authority, the land is capable,

   (d) a statement that the notice shall continue in force for a period of five years commencing on the day of service of the notice unless before the expiration of that period:

      (i) the notice is withdrawn by the planning authority, or

   (ii)   a permission is granted under Part IV of the Act of 1963 to develop the land to which the notice relates in a manner consistent with the other development specified in the notice, subject to no conditions or to conditions of a class or description set out in the Fourth Schedule of the Act of 1990, or

   (iii)   the notice is annulled by virtue of section 13 (5) of the Act of 1990, and

  (e) a statement that compensation shall not be payable on the claim in respect of the land in question where:

   (i)   the notice is in force; or

   (ii)   an application for permission under Part IV of the Act of 1963 to develop the land to which the notice relates in a manner consistent with the other development specified in the notice has not been made before the expiration of the notice, or

   (iii)   permission is granted under Part IV of the Act of 1963 to develop the land to which the notice relates in a manner consistent with the other development specified in the notice, subject to no conditions or to conditions of a class or description set out in the Fourth Schedule of the Act of 1990. **[390]**

Part IX

Environmental Impact Assessment of Certain Development by or on behalf of Local Authorities

114. Definition for Part IX

In this Part, **"local authority"** means a local authority for the purposes of section 78 of the Act of 1963. **[391]**

115. Restriction of application of Part IX

[(1) This Part shall not apply to development proposed to be carried out by or on behalf of a local authority outside the functional area of the local authority or development of a facility in relation to which a waste licence is required.][1a]

(2) In this article, **"functional area"** means, in the case of a county council, the county exclusive of any borough or urban district therein. **[392]**

---

1 Amendments

a   Article 115(1) was substituted by LG(PD)(No 3)R 1997 (SI 261/1997), art 8.

---

116. Environmental impact statement to be prepared in respect of certain proposed development [3a]

Where development proposed to be carried out by or on behalf of a local authority is of a class for the time being specified under Article 24 of the Environmental Impact Assessment Regulations, or under any provision amending or replacing the said Article 24, the local authority shall cause an environmental impact statement to be prepared in respect of that development. **[393]**

3 Notes

a   See *Shannon Regional Fisheries Board v An Bord Pleanála* (HC) unrep, 17 November 1994; see also *Honeyclover Ltd v An Bord Pleanála* (HC) unrep, 29 January 1990.

117. Requirement to prepare environmental impact statement in respect of certain other proposed development

Where development proposed to be carried out by or on behalf of a local authority would be of a class referred to in article 116 but for not exceeding a quantity, area or other limit for the time being specified in relation to that class, the Minister shall, where he considers that the said development would be likely to have significant effects on the environment, require the local authority to cause an environmental impact statement to be prepared in respect of that development.   **[394]**

118. Content of environmental impact statement [3a]

An environmental impact statement prepared in accordance with article 116 or pursuant to a requirement under article 117 shall comply with Article 25 of the Environmental Impact Assessment Regulations, or any provision amending or replacing the said Article 25.   **[395]**

3 Notes

a   See *Browne v An Bord Pleanála* [1991] 2 IR 209.

119. Certain development not to be carried out without certification of Minister

Proposed development in respect of which an environmental impact statement has been prepared in accordance with article 116 or pursuant to a requirement under article 117 shall not be carried out unless the Minister has certified, following an application to him in accordance with article 123, that the proposed development (or the proposed development as varied or modified by him in accordance with article 127), in his opinion, will not have significant adverse effects on the environment, or will embody the best practicable means to prevent or limit such effects.   **[396]**

120. Notice of application for certification

Before making an application in accordance with article 123 for the certification of the Minister, a local authority shall publish in a newspaper circulating in the area in which the proposed development would be situate a notice –

(a)   indicating the nature and location of the proposed development,

(b)   stating that:

   (i)   they propose to make the application for certification,

   (ii)   an environmental impact statement has been prepared in respect of the proposed development,

   (iii)   the environmental impact statement will be available, for inspection free of charge and for purchase, at the offices of the local authority at specified times during a specified period (which shall be not less than one month beginning on the day of publication of the notice),

(iv) submissions or observations in relation to the effects on the environment of the proposed development may be made in writing to the Minister before a specified date (which shall be not less than two weeks after the end of the period for inspection and purchase specified pursuant to sub-paragraph (iii)).

[397]

121. Availability for purchase of copies of environmental impact statements and extracts

Copies of an environmental impact statement prepared in respect of proposed development in accordance with article 116 or pursuant to a requirement under article 117, and of extracts from any such statement, shall be made available for purchase during the period specified pursuant to article 120(b)(iii) for such fee as the local authority may fix not exceeding the reasonable cost of making the copy.   **[398]**

122. Notice of application for certification to certain bodies

(1) Before making an application in accordance with article 123 for the certification of the Minister, a local authority shall send notice of the proposed application and a copy of the environmental impact statement prepared in respect of the proposed development to the relevant body or bodies specified in sub-article (3).

(2) A notice in accordance with sub-article (1) shall state that submissions or observations in relation to the effects on the environment of the proposed development may be made in writing to the Minister before a specified date (which shall be not less than two weeks after the end of the period for inspection and purchase specified pursuant to article 120(b)(iii)).

(3) A notice in accordance with sub-article (1) shall be sent –

(a) where it appears to the local authority that the proposed development would be situate in an area of special amenity, whether or not an order in respect of that area has been made under section 42 of the Act of 1963 – to An Chomhairle Ealaíon, Bord Fáilte Éireann and An Taisce – the National Trust for Ireland,

(b) where it appears to the local authority that the proposed development would affect the value of any tourist amenity or tourist amenity works – to Bord Fáilte Éireann,

(c) where it appears to the local authority that the proposed development would affect any cave, site, feature or other object of archaeological, geological, scientific or historical interest or any building of artistic, architectural or historical interest – to An Chomhairle Ealaíon, Bord Fáilte Éireann, [the Minister for Arts, Culture and the Gaeltacht,][1a] the National Monuments Advisory Council and An Taisce – the National Trust for Ireland,

(d) where it appears to the local authority that the area of another local authority would be affected by the proposed development – to the local authority concerned,

(e) where it appears to the local authority that the development might endanger or interfere with the safety of aircraft or the safe and efficient navigation thereof – to the Irish Aviation Authority,

(f) where it appears to the local authority that the proposed development might give rise to appreciable discharges of polluting matters to waters – to the appropriate Regional Fisheries Board,

(g) where it appears to the local authority that the proposed development might have significant effects on public health – to the appropriate Health Board,

[(gg)where it appears to the local authority that the proposed development might significantly impact on the implementation of the DTI Strategy – to the Dublin Transportation Office.]¹ᵇ

(h) where it appears to the local authority that the proposed development might have significant effects in relation to nature conservation – to [the Minister for Arts, Culture and the Gaeltacht.]¹ᵃ

(4) A reference in sub-article (3) to Bord Fáilte Éireann shall, in the case of proposed development which would be situate in the functional area of the Shannon Free Airport Development Company Ltd., be construed as a reference to that Company. **[399]**

---

1 Amendments

a   The words in square brackets were substituted by LG(PD)R 1997 (SI 121/1997).

b   Sub-article (gg) was inserted by LG(PD)(No 2)R 1997 (SI 121/1997), art 6.

---

123. Application for certification of Minister

Where an environmental impact statement has been prepared in respect of proposed development in accordance with article 116 or pursuant to a requirement under article 117, the local authority shall, as soon as may be after compliance with the requirements of articles 120 and 122, apply to the Minister for the certification mentioned in article 119, and send to the Minister –

(a) three copies of the environmental impact statement prepared in respect of the proposed development,

(b) a copy of the notice published pursuant to article 120, and

(c) details of any body to which notice was given pursuant to article 122, the date on which such notice was given and the period specified in the notice for the making of submissions or observations to the Minister. **[400]**

124. Further information

(1) The Minister may, where he considers it necessary so to do, require a local authority who have applied in accordance with article 123 for certification for proposed development to furnish to him such further information in relation to the effects on the environment of the proposed development as the Minister may specify.

(2) (a) The Minister shall, where he considers that further information received pursuant to a requirement under sub-article (1) contains significant additional data in relation to the effects on the environment of the proposed development, require the local authority –

(i) to publish in a newspaper circulating in the area in which the proposed development would be situate a notice stating that further information in relation to the effects of the proposed development has been furnished to the Minister, that the further information will be available, for inspection free of charge and for purchase, at the offices of the local authority at specified times during a period of three weeks beginning on the day of publication of the notice and that submissions or observations in relation to the further information may be made to the Minister before the expiration of the said period,

(ii) to send notice of the furnishing of the further information to the Minister, and a copy of the further information, to any body to which notice was given pursuant to article 122, and to indicate to the body concerned that submissions or observations in relation to the further information may be made to the Minister before the expiration of a period of three weeks beginning on the day on which the notice is sent to the body concerned by the local authority.

(b) Copies of further information in respect of which notice is published pursuant to a requirement under sub-article (2)(a)(i) shall be made available for purchase during the period referred to in sub-article (2)(a)(i) for such fee as the local authority may fix not exceeding the reasonable cost of making the copy. **[401]**

125. Consultation with other Member States of European Communities

Where the Minister considers that proposed development in respect of which an application for certification has been made in accordance with article 123 would have significant effects on the environment in another Member State of the European Communities, or where another Member State likely to be significantly affected so requests, the Minister shall consult that Member State in relation to the effects on the environment of the proposed development. **[402]**

126. Minister to have regard to certain matters in considering application for certification

The Minister shall, when considering an application for certification made in accordance with article 123, have regard to the environmental impact statement prepared in respect of the proposed development in accordance with article 116 or pursuant to a requirement under article 117 (including any additional information furnished by the local authority pursuant to a requirement under article 124(1)), to any submissions or observations made to him in accordance with this Part, and to the views of other Member States of the European Communities arising from consultation, if any, in accordance with article 125. **[403]**

127. Power of Minister to vary or modify proposed development

(1) The Minister may, in certifying proposed development in accordance with article 119, direct that the proposed development shall be varied or modified in such manner as he considers necessary or appropriate to ensure that the proposed development, in his opinion, will not have significant adverse effects on the environment, or will embody the best practicable means to prevent or limit such effects.

(2) Where the Minister in certifying proposed development directs that the proposed development shall be varied or modified, the development shall not be carried out save in conformity with that direction.

[(3) Sub-article (2) shall not operate to prejudice, restrict or affect in any way any condition attached to a waste licence granted in respect of a development certified in accordance with Article 119.]¹ᵃ **[404]**

---

1 Amendments

a   Sub-article (3) was inserted by LG(PD)(No 3)R 1997 (SI 261/1997), art 8.

---

128. Notice of Minister's decision in relation to application for certification

[(1) The Minister shall cause notice of his decision in relation to an application for certification in accordance with article 123 to be published in a newspaper circulating in the area in which the proposed development would be situate.

(2) When the Minister makes a decision referred to in sub-article (1), the relevant local authority shall make the environmental impact statement concerned and the decision available for inspection at specified times during a specified period (which shall be not less than one month beginning on the day of publication of the notice).

(3) Where there has been consultation with another Member State of the European Communities in accordance with article 125 in relation to the effects on the environment of a proposed development, notice of the Minister's decision in relation to the application for certification shall be given to that Member State.]   **[405]**

---

1 Amendments

a   Article 128 was substituted by LG(PD)R 1999 (SI 92/1999), art 21.

---

129. Transitional

Part IV of the Local Government (Planning and Development) Regulations, 1990, as amended by article 2(b) of the Local Government (Planning and Development) Regulations, 1992 (SI No. 209 of 1992), shall, notwithstanding article 4, continue in force and have effect in relation to any application for the certification of the Minister made in accordance with the said Part before the coming into operation of this Part.**[406]**

Part X

REQUIREMENTS IN RESPECT OF SPECIFIED DEVELOPMENT BY OR ON BEHALF OF LOCAL AUTHORITIES

130. Development to which Part X applies

(1) This Part shall, subject to sub-articles (2) and (3) and article 136, apply to the following classes of cases of development, being development specified pursuant to section 78(1) of the Act of 1963 and hereafter in this Part referred to as "proposed development"–

  (a) the construction or erection of a house or other dwelling,
  (b) the construction of a new road or the widening or realignment of an existing road, where the length of the new road or of the widened or realigned portion of the existing road, as the case may be, would be –
    (i)   in the case of a road in an urban area, 100 metres or more, or
    (ii) in the case of a road in any other area, 1 kilometre or more,
  (c) the construction of a bridge or tunnel,
  (d) the construction or erection of pumping stations, treatment works, holding tanks or outfall facilities for waste water or storm water,

(e) the construction or erection of water intake or treatment works, overground aqueducts, or dams or other installations designed to hold water or to store it on a long-term basis,

(f) drilling for water supplies,

(g) the construction of a swimming pool,

(h) the use of land, or the construction or erection of any installation or facility, for the disposal of waste [not being development which comprises or is for the purposes of an activity in relation to which a waste licence is required,][1a]

(i) the use of land as a burial ground,

(j) the construction or erection of a fire station, a library or a public toilet, and

[(k) any other development, the estimated cost of which exceeds £50,000, not being —[1b]

    (i) development of a class specified in any of the foregoing paragraphs, or

    (ii) ...[1c]

    (iii) development consisting of the laying underground of sewers, mains, pipes or other apparatus.]

[(2) (a)   (i) Subject to sub-paragraph (ii) and paragraph (b), this Part shall not apply to proposed development that a local authority propose to carry out outside the functional area of the local authority.

    (ii) Notwithstanding sub-paragraph (i), this Part shall apply to development of a class specified in paragraph (b) or (c) of sub-article (1) that a local authority propose to carry out outside the functional area of the local authority.][1d]

(b) This Part shall, subject to sub-article (3) and article 136, apply to proposed development that a county council established by section 11 of the Local Government (Dublin) Act, 1993 proposed to carry out within the functional area of another county council established by that section during the period commencing on the coming into operation of this Part and terminating on the 31st day of December, 1995.

(c) In this sub-article, "**functional area**" means, in the case of a county council, the county exclusive of any borough or urban district therein.

(3) This Part shall not apply to proposed development if –

(a) the development consists of works of maintenance or repair, or

(b) the development is necessary for dealing forthwith with any situation which the manager considers is an emergency situation calling for immediate action without regard to the provisions of this Part, or

(c) the development is required by Part IX or any other statutory provision to comply with procedures for the purpose of giving effect to the Council Directive of 27 June, 1985 (No. 85/337/EEC, O.J. No. L175/40, 5 July, 1985), or

(d) the development consists of works which the local authority are required by or under statute or by order of a Court to undertake, or

(e) ...[1e]

(4) In this article, "**manager**" means –

(a) as respects the corporation of a county borough, the manager for the purposes of the Acts relating to the management of the county borough, and

(b) as respects the council of a county or an elective body for the purposes of the County Management Acts, 1940 to 1993, the manager for the purposes of the said Acts.   **[407]**

---

1 Amendments

a   Sub-article 1(h) was amended by LG(PD)(No 3)R 1997 (SI 261/1997), art 9.

b   Sub-article 1(k) of sub-art (1) was inserted by LG(PD)R 1995 (SI 69/1995), art 7.

c   Sub-paragraph (ii) of sub-art (1)(k) was deleted by LG(PD)R 1998 (SI 124/1998), art 2.

d   Sub-article 2(a) was substituted by LG(PD)R 1995, (SI 69/1995), art 7.

e   Sub-article 3(e) was deleted by LG(PD)R 1995 (SI 69/1995), art 7.

---

131. Notice of proposed development

(1) A local authority shall publish notice of proposed development in a newspaper circulating in the area in which the proposed development would be situate.

(2) A notice published in accordance with sub-article (1) shall –

(a) indicate the location, nature and extent of the proposed development, and

(b) state that:

    (i) plans and particulars of the proposed development will be available for inspection at the offices of the local authority at specified times during a specified period (which shall be not less than one month beginning on the day of publication of the notice),

    (ii) submissions or observations with respect to the proposed development, dealing with the proper planning and development of the area in which the development would be situate, may be made in writing to the local authority before a specified date (which shall be not less than two weeks after the end of the period for inspection of plans and particulars specified pursuant to sub-paragraph (i)).

                                                                       [408]

132. Notice of proposed development to certain bodies

(1) A local authority shall send notice of proposed development to any relevant body or bodies specified in sub-article (3).

(2) A notice in accordance with sub-article (1) shall -

(a) indicate the location, nature and extent of the proposed development,

(b) be accompanied by a copy of the plans and particulars of the proposed development made available for inspection by members of the public in accordance with article 133,

(c) state that submissions or observations with respect to the proposed development, dealing with the proper planning and development of the area in which the development would be situate, may be made in writing to the local authority before a specified date (which shall be not less than two weeks after the end of the period for inspection of plans and particulars specified pursuant to article 131(2)(b)(i)).

(3) A notice in accordance with sub-article (1) shall be sent –

(a) where it appears to the local authority that the proposed development would be situate in an area of special amenity, whether or not an order in respect of that area has been made under section 42 of the Act of 1963 – to An Chomhairle Ealaíon, Bord Fáilte Éireann and An Taisce – the National Trust for Ireland,

(b) where it appears to the local authority that the proposed development would affect the value of any tourist amenity or tourist amenity works – to Bord Fáilte Éireann,

(c) where it appears to the local authority that the proposed development would affect any cave, site, feature or other object of archaeological, geological, scientific or historical interest or any building of artistic, architectural or historical interest – to An Chomhairle Ealaíon, Bord Fáilte Éireann, [the Minister for Arts, Culture and the Gaeltacht,]¹ᵃ the National Monuments Advisory Council and An Taisce – the National Trust for Ireland,

(d) where it appears to the local authority that the area of another local authority would be affected by the proposed development – to the local authority concerned,

(e) where it appears to the local authority that the proposed development might endanger or interfere with the safety of aircraft or the safe and efficient navigation thereof – to the Irish Aviation Authority,

(f) where it appears to the local authority that the proposed development might give rise to appreciable discharges of polluting matters to waters – to the appropriate Regional Fisheries Board,

[(ff) where it appears to the local authority that the proposed development might significantly impact on the implementation of the DTI Strategy – to the Dublin Transportation Office,]¹ᵇ

(g) where it appears to the local authority that the proposed development might have significant effects on public health – to the appropriate [the minister for Arts, Culture and the Gaeltacht,]¹ᵃ

(h) where it appears to the local authority that the proposed development might have significant effects in relation to nature conservation – to the [Minister for Arts, Culture and the Gaeltacht.]¹ᵃ

(4) A reference in sub-article (3) to Bord Fáilte Éireann shall, in the case of proposed development which would be situate in the functional area of the Shannon Free Airport Development Company Ltd., be construed as a reference to that Company.   **[409]**

---

1 Amendments

a   The words in square brackets were substituted by LG(PD)(No 2)R 1997 (SI 121/1997), art 8.

b   Sub-article 3(ff) was inserted by LG(PD)(No 2)R 1997 (SI 121/1997), art 8.

---

133. Availability for inspection of plans and particulars

A local authority shall make available for inspection by members of the public, at the times and during the period specified pursuant to article 131(2)(b)(i) –

(a) a document describing the nature and extent of the proposed development and the principal features thereof,

(b) a location map, drawn to a scale of not less than 1:10,560 and marked or coloured so as to identify clearly the land on which it is proposed to carry out the proposed development,

[(c) except in the case of development of a class specified in article 130 (1)(b) or (c) –

    (i) a site layout plan, drawn to a scale of not less than 1:500, showing the boundary of the site on which it is proposed to carry out the proposed development and the buildings or other structures, and roads or other features, in the vicinity of the site, and

    (ii) such other plans and drawings, drawn to a scale of not less than 1:100, as are necessary to describe the proposed development,

(d)   (i) in the case of development of a class specified in article 130(1)(b), such plans and drawings, drawn to a scale of not less than 1:2500, as are necessary to describe the proposed development, and

    (ii) in the case of development of a class specified in article 130(1)(c), such plans and drawings, drawn to a scale of not less than 1:200, as are necessary to describe the proposed development.][1a]

[410]

---

1 Amendments

a   Paragraphs (c) and (d) were substituted by LG(PD)R 1995 (SI 69/1995), art 8.

---

134. Report with respect to proposed development

(1) A local authority shall, after the expiration of the period or periods (as the case may be) during which submissions or observations with respect to proposed development may be made to the local authority in accordance with this Part, prepare a report in relation to proposed development.

(2) A report prepared in accordance with sub-article (1) shall –

(a) describe the nature and extent of the proposed development and the principal features thereof,

(b) evaluate the likely implications, if any, of the proposed development with respect to the proper planning and development of the area in which the development would be situate,

(c) list the persons or bodies who made submissions or observations with respect to the proposed development in accordance with this Part,

(d) summarise the issues with respect to the proper planning and development of the area in which the proposed development would be situate raised by persons or bodies who made submissions or observations in accordance with this Part, and give the response of the local authority thereto, and

(e) indicate whether it is proposed to proceed with the proposed development, to proceed with the proposed development as varied or modified in a manner indicated in the report, or not to proceed with the proposed development.

(3) A report prepared by a local authority in accordance with sub-article (1) shall be submitted to the members of the local authority and may, subject to any resolution adopted by the members of the local authority pursuant to section 2 (8) of the City and County Management (Amendment) Act, 1955 (No. 12 of 1955), be so submitted in the course of compliance with section 2(7) of the said Act.   **[411]**

135. Notice following compliance with requirements of Part X

(1) Where the preceding requirements of this Part have been complied with respect to proposed development, a local authority shall –

- (a) send notice in accordance with sub-article (2) to any body to which notice of the proposed development was sent pursuant to article 132, and

- (b) send notice in accordance with the said sub-article to any other persons or bodies who made submissions or observations with respect to the proposed development in accordance with this Part, or publish a notice in accordance with the said sub-article in a newspaper circulating in the area in which the proposed development would be situate.

(2) A notice referred to in sub-article (1) shall indicate that the local authority will proceed with the proposed development, or proceed with the proposed development subject to variations or modifications, or not proceed with the proposed development, as the case may be.   **[412]**

136. Transitional

This Part shall not apply to proposed development where –

- (a) the members of the local authority have been informed of the works comprising the proposed development pursuant to section 2(7) of the City and County Management (Amendment) Act, 1955 before the coming into operation of this Part, and

- (b) (i) in the case of proposed development which will be carried out by the local authority, the development has commenced before the 31st day of December, 1994, or

    (ii) in the case of proposed development which will be carried out on behalf of the local authority, a contract for the carrying out of the development has been signed before the 31st day of December, 1994.   **[412]**

Part XI

APPOINTMENT OF CHAIRMAN AND ORDINARY MEMBERS OF AN BORD PLEANÁLA

137. Definitions for Part XI

In this Part –

"**chairman**" means the chairman of the Board;

"**the committee**" means the committee referred to in section 5 of the Act of 1983. **[413]**

138. Procedure where request under section 5(7) of Act of 1983 made to committee

(1) Whenever a request under section 5(7) of the Act of 1983 is made to the committee for the selection of candidates for appointment to be the chairman –

- (a) the committee shall meet on a day and at a time and place determined by the President of the High Court, who shall cause to be communicated to the other members of the committee the day, time and place of the meeting, and

(b) the committee shall, before selecting candidates for appointment to be the chairman pursuant to the request, cause an advertisement to be published inviting application for appointment to such office.

(2) An advertisement published pursuant to sub-article (1)(b) shall specify a period of not less than twenty-one days for the making of applications and any application which is not received by the committee within the period so specified shall be invalid. **[414]**

139. Content of application

An application for selection by the committee shall include a curriculum vitae and particulars of the special knowledge and experience and other qualifications and personal qualities which the applicant considers relevant to the application. **[415]**

140. Requirement to submit further particulars

Where the committee receive an application for selection by the committee they may require the applicant to submit, within a period of not more than twenty-one days, such further particulars as they may require (including any evidence which the committee may reasonably require to verify any particulars given by the applicant in or in relation to the application). **[416]**

141. Interviewing of applicants

(1) Where the committee consider it necessary for the purposes of selecting candidates they may, subject to sub-article (2), invite applicants to attend for interview on a day and at a time and place specified by the committee.

(2) Where the committee decide to invite applicants to attend for interview pursuant to sub-article (1), the committee may, in their absolute discretion, having examined the information contained in the applications in the context of the matters referred to in section 5(7)(b) of the Act of 1983, invite to attend for interview only those applicants who appear to them to be likely to be suitable to be considered for selection as candidates for appointment to be the chairman. **[417]**

142. Cesser of entitlement to further consideration by committee

An applicant who does not attend for interview on the day and at the time and place specified by the committee or who does not furnish such particulars or evidence as may be required by the committee pursuant to article 140 within the period specified pursuant to that article shall not be entitled to further consideration by the committee for selection as a candidate for appointment to be the chairman. **[418]**

143. Procedure of committee

(1) The committee shall hold such meetings as may be necessary for the performance of their functions.

(2) The quorum for a meeting of the committee shall be four.

(3) The President of the High Court shall preside at meetings of the committee at which he is present.

(4) If the President of the High Court is not present at a meeting of the committee, a member of the committee selected by the committee shall preside at the meeting.

(5) Every question at a meeting of the Committee shall be determined by a majority of votes of member present.

Subject to the foregoing provisions of this article, the committee shall regulate their own procedure.   **[419]**

144. Secretary of committee

An officer of the Minister designated by the Secretary of the Department of the Environment shall act as secretary of the committee.   **[420]**

145. Prescribed organisations for purposes of section 7(2)(a) of Act of 1983

The prescribed organisations for the purposes of section 7(2)(a) of the Act of 1983 shall be –

(a) the Irish Planning Institute,

(b) the Royal Town Planning Institute, Irish Branch – Southern Section,

(c) the Institution of Engineers of Ireland,

(d) the Society of Chartered Surveyors in the Republic of Ireland, and

(e) the Royal Institute of the Architects of Ireland.   **[421]**

146. Prescribed organisations for purposes of section 7(2)(b) of Act of 1983 [3a]

The prescribed organisations for the purposes of section 7(2)(b) of the Act of 1983 shall be –

(a) An Taisce – the National Trust for Ireland,

(b) Bord Fáilte Éireann,

(c) the Irish Architectural Archive,

(d) the Irish Resource Development Trust,

(e) the Royal Irish Academy, and

(f) the County and City Managers' Association.   **[422]**

147. Prescribed organisations for purposes of section 7(2)(c) of Act of 1983 [3a]

The prescribed organisations for the purposes of section 7(2)(c) of the Act of 1983 shall be –

(a) the Construction Industry Federation,

(b) the Irish Congress of Trade Unions,

(c) Forfás,

(d) the Irish Business and Employers' Confederation, and

(e) the Chambers of Commerce of Ireland.   **[423]**

148. Prescribed organisations for purposes of section 7(2)(d) of Act of 1983

The prescribed organisations for the purposes of section 7(2)(d) of the Act of 1983 shall be –

(a) Aontacht Cumann Riartha Aitreabhthóirí (The Association of Combined Residents' Associations),

(b) the National Association of Tenants' Organisations,

(c) the National Youth Council of Ireland,

(d) the Irish Farmers' Association,

(e) the Irish Creamery Milk Suppliers' Association,

(f) the Irish Countrywomen's Association, and

(g) the Council for the Status of Women.   **[424]**

149. Duty of prescribed organisation on receipt of request pursuant to section 7(3) of Act of 1983

Where a request is made to a prescribed organisation pursuant to section 7(3) of the Act of 1983 the organisation shall, before the expiration of two months commencing on the day on which the request is made –

(a) select two candidates for appointment as ordinary members of the Board;

(b) inform the Minister:

  (i)   of the names of the candidates selected, and

  (ii) of the reasons why, in the opinion of the organisation, each candidate is suitable for appointment as an ordinary member of the Board;

(c) send to the Minister:

  (i)   a curriculum vitae in relation to each candidate, and

  (ii) the written consent of each candidate to his selection in accordance with the request.

[425]

Part XII

LICENSING UNDER SECTION 89 OF ACT OF 1963

150. Definition for Part XII

In this Part, "**specified appliance or structure**" means an appliance or structure referred to in section 89(1) of the Act of 1963[2a] or any additional appliance or structure specified in article 151.   **[426]**

---

2 Cross References

a   LG(PD)A 1963, s 89 provides for the granting of a licence to construct or maintain structures or appliances on or along a public road.

---

151. Appliances and structures suitable for being licensed

The following appliances and structures are hereby specified as suitable for being licensed under section 89 of the Act of 1963 –

(a) a petrol, oil or other storage tank (together with any associated manhole, inlet, outlet, or pipe for connection with a pump),

(b) a delivery pipe or hose attached to a petrol pump or oil pump, which is erected in a permanent position and which is not on a public road,

(c) a moveable pump or other appliance for dispensing any oil or oil derivative or mixture thereof,

(d) a case, rack, shelf or other appliance or structure for displaying articles for the purposes of advertisement or of sale in or in connection with any adjacent business premises,

(e) tables and chairs outside a hotel, restaurant or public house,[3a]

(f) a cabinet used as part of a wired broadcast relay service by a person licensed under the Wireless Telegraphy (Wired Broadcast Relay Licence) Regulations, 1974 (S.I. No. 67 of 1974),

(g) a lamp-post,

(h) a bridge, arch, tunnel, passage or other similar structure which is used or intended for use other than by the public and was constructed on or after the 1st day of October, 1964,

(i) a cellar or other underground structure constructed on or after the 1st day of October, 1964,

(j) a coin-operated machine other than a vending machine, and

(k) an advertisement consisting of any symbol, emblem, model, device or logo. **[427]**

---

3 Notes

a   See further, Second Schedule, Part I class 44. To place any items listed under art 151 on or near a public road without the required licence is an offence. See LG(PD)A 1963, s 89(8).

---

152. Fees for licences under section 89 of Act of 1963[2a]

(1) Where a licence under section 89 of the Act of 1963 is granted by a planning authority –

(a) to erect, construct, place and maintain, or

(b) to maintain

a specified appliance or structure referred to in Part I or II of the Seventh Schedule, the amount of the fee to be paid to the planning authority shall, subject to the provisions of article 153, be –

(i) where the licence is for a period of one year, the appropriate amount indicated in the second column of that Schedule opposite the reference in the first column of that Schedule to the specified appliance or structure,

(ii) where the licence is for a period of more than one year, an amount equal to the fee for one year for each year or part of a year for which the licence is granted, and

(iii) where the licence is for a period of less than a year, an amount equal to one tenth of the fee for one year for each month or part of a month for which the licence is granted, or £5, whichever is the greater.

(2) Where a licence under section 89 of the Act of 1963 is granted by a planning authority to erect, construct, place and maintain a specified appliance or structure referred to in Part III of the Seventh Schedule, the amount of the fee to be paid to the planning authority shall be the amount indicated in the second column of that Schedule opposite the reference in the first column of that Schedule to the specified appliance or structure and no fee shall be payable in respect of any renewal of a licence for such an appliance or structure. **[428]**

---

2 Cross References

a   See the Seventh Schedule.

---

153. Additional fee for advertising use

In the case of –

(a) any pump, machine or similar appliance or structure, more than one quarter of the surface area of which is used for advertising purposes,

(b) any town or landscape map more than one third of the surface area of which is used for advertising purposes, and

(c) any other appliance or structure any part of the area of which is used for advertising purposes,

the amount of the fee under article 152 shall be increased by the amount of the fee payable under that article in respect of an advertisement structure which is on a public road.   **[429]**

154. Disposal of licence fees

Licence fees received by planning authorities in respect of specified appliances and structures referred to in the Seventh Schedule shall be paid into the county fund in the case of a council of a county and into the municipal fund in the case of a corporation of a county or other borough or the council of an urban district.   **[430]**

155. Transitional

Where an application for a licence is received by a planning authority before the coming into operation of this Part, the fee to be paid to the planning authority shall, notwithstanding article 4, be the fee payable under Part VII of the Local Government (Planning and Development) Regulations, 1977 and the Fourth Schedule to those Regulations.   **[431]**

Part XIII

PROVISIONS WITH RESPECT TO CERTAIN DEVELOPMENT BY OR ON BEHALF OF STATE AUTHORITIES

156. Specified development for purposes of section 2(1)(a)(i) of Act of 1993

(1) The specified classes of development for the purposes of section 2(1)(a)(i) of the Act of 1993 shall be –

(a) development consisting of the provision of:

(i) Garda stations or other buildings, or other premises or installations, or other structures or facilities, used for the purposes of or in connection with the operations of An Garda Síochána,

(ii) prisons or other places of detention,

(iii) courthouses,

(iv) barracks or other buildings, or other premises or installations (including airfields and naval yards), or other structures or facilities, used for the purposes of or in connection with the operations of the Defence Forces,

(v) office buildings or other premises used for the purposes of or in connection with the business of Uachtarán na h-Éireann, Dáil Éireann, Seanad Éireann, the Department of the Taoiseach, the Office of the Tánaiste, the Department of Defence, the Department of Foreign Affairs, the Department of Justice, the Office of the Attorney General, the Chief State Solicitor's Office and the Office of the Director of Public Prosecutions;

(b) (i) development consisting of the provision of an extension of any building referred to in paragraph (a), where such extension will be situate, in whole or in part, outside the curtilage of the existing building or, where the building is situate within a premises or other installation referred to in the said paragraph, outside the curtilage of the premises or other installation,

(ii) development consisting of the provision of an extension of a premises or other installation, other than a building, referred to in paragraph (a) which will extend the premises or other installation beyond the curtilage of the existing premises or other installation;

(c) (i) development consisting of the carrying out of any works, for reasons of national security, within, or bounding, the curtilage of any building, premises or other installation occupied by, or under the control of, a State authority, other than a building, premises or other installation referred to in paragraph (a),

(ii) development consisting of the carrying out, by or on behalf of a State authority, for reasons of national security, of any works within, or bounding, the curtilage of the residence of a holder, or former holder, of a public office or any other public servant or former public servant.

(2) For the purposes of this article, a building, premises, installation, structure or facility may be provided by the carrying out of works or by the making of a material change in the use of a building, premises, installation, structure or facility.   **[432]**

157. Specified development for purposes of section 2(1)(a)(ii) of Act of 1993

The specified class of development for the purposes of section 2(1)(a)(ii) of the Act of 1993 shall be the carrying out by the Commissioners of Public Works in Ireland, with such additions, omissions, variations and deviations as may be found necessary in the course of the works, of works specified in a drainage scheme confirmed by the Minister for Finance under Part II of the Arterial Drainage Act, 1945 (No. 3 of 1945).   **[433]**

158. Notice of proposed development

(1) This article shall apply to the classes of development specified in article 156(1)(a) or (b), other than development consisting of the construction or erection of such temporary structures for the purposes of or in connection with the operations of the Defence Forces as are urgently required for reasons of national security, and the development to which this article applies is hereafter in this Part referred to as "proposed development".

(2) A State authority shall –

(a) publish notice of proposed development in a newspaper circulating in the area in which the development would be situate, and

(b) erect or fix a site notice of proposed development on the land or structure where the development would be situate.

(3) A notice published pursuant to sub-article (2)(a) shall contain as a heading the name of the State authority by which the development is proposed to be carried out and shall state –

(a) the location, nature and extent of the proposed development,

(b) that plans and particulars of the proposed development will be available for inspection, at the offices of the State authority in Dublin and at a specified location in the area in which the development would be situate, at specified times during a period of one month beginning on the day of publication of the notice,

(c) that submissions or observations with respect to the proposed development, dealing with the proper planning and development of the area in which the development would be situate, may be made in writing to the State authority within a period of six weeks beginning on the day of publication of the notice.

(4) (a) A site notice erected or fixed pursuant to sub-article (2)(b) shall contain as a heading the name of the State authority by which the development is proposed to be carried out and shall state –

    (i) the nature and extent of the proposed development,

    (ii) the locations and the times at which, and the period during which, plans and particulars of the proposed development will be available for inspection, and

    (iii) the period during which submissions or observations with respect to the proposed development, dealing with the proper planning and development of the area in which the development would be situate, may be made in writing to the State authority.

(b) A site notice erected or fixed pursuant to sub-article (2)(b) –

    (i) shall be painted or inscribed, or printed and affixed, on a durable material, and

    (ii) subject to paragraph (c), shall be securely erected or fixed in a conspicuous position on or near the main entrance to the land or structure concerned from a public road, or on any other part of the land or structure adjoining a public road, so as to be easily visible and legible by persons using the public road.

(c) Where the land or structure concerned does not adjoin a public road, a site notice shall be erected or fixed in a conspicuous position on the land or structure so as to be easily visible and legible by persons outside the land or structure.

(d) A site notice shall be erected or fixed on the land or structure concerned not later than the day of publication of notice of the proposed development in a newspaper pursuant to sub-article (2)(a), shall be maintained in position for a period of at least one month after publication of the said notice and shall be renewed or replaced if it is removed or becomes defaced or illegible within that period.   **[434]**

159. Notice of proposed development to planning authority

(1) A State authority shall send notice of proposed development to the planning authority for the area in which the proposed development would be situate.

(2) A notice in accordance with sub-article (1) shall –

(a) indicate the location, nature and extent of the proposed development,

(b) be accompanied by a copy of the plans and particulars of the proposed development made available for inspection by members of the public in accordance with article 160, and

(c) state that submissions or observations with respect to the proposed development, dealing with the proper planning and development of the area in which the development would be situate, may be made in writing to the State authority within a period of six weeks beginning on the day on which the notice is sent to the planning authority.   **[435]**

160. Availability for inspection of plans and particulars

A State authority shall make available for inspection by members of the public, at the locations and times and during the period of one month beginning on the day of publication of notice of proposed development pursuant to article 158(2)(a) –

   (a) a document describing, in general terms, the nature and extent of the proposed development,

   (b) a location map, drawn to a scale of not less than 1:10,560 and marked or coloured so as to identify clearly the land on which it is proposed to carry out the development, and

   (c) plans or drawings describing, in outline, the external appearance of the building, or other premises or installation, or other structure or facility, to be provided or extended (as the case may be).   **[436]**

161. State authority to have regard to certain matters

(1) A State authority shall, in deciding whether proposed development is to be carried out, have regard to any submissions or observations made by a planning authority or by any other person or body in accordance with this Part.

(2) A State authority may, following compliance with sub-article (1), decide, as it considers appropriate, that the proposed development will be carried out, with or without variations or modifications, or will not be carried out.   **[437]**

162. Notice of decision with respect to proposed development

(1) A State authority shall, within three working days of making its decision with respect to proposed development, send notice of the decision to the planning authority for the area in which the proposed development would be situate.

(2) Where any person or body, other than the planning authority for the area in which proposed development would be situate, has made submissions or observations to a State authority with respect to the proposed development in accordance with this Part, the State authority shall, where notice of its decision with respect to the proposed development is not published in a newspaper pursuant to sub-article (3), send notice of the decision to the person or body within three working days of the making of its decision.

(3) (a) A State authority may publish notice of its decision with respect to proposed development in a newspaper circulating in the area in which the proposed development would be situate.

   (b) A notice published pursuant to paragraph (a) shall be published within seven days of the making of the decision of the State authority with respect to the proposed development.   **[438]**

Part XIV

MISCELLANEOUS

163. Prescribed authorities for purposes of section 46 of Act of 1963 [2a]

The prescribed authorities for the purposes of section 46 of the Act of 1963 (being the authorities which must be consulted by a planning authority before they make an order under that section) shall be –

    (a) [the Minister for Arts, Culture and the Gaeltacht,][3a]

    (b) the Royal Irish Academy,

    (c) Bord Fáilte Éireann, and

    (d) An Taisce – the National Trust for Ireland.   **[439]**

---

1 Amendments

a   The words in square brackets were substituted by LG(PD)(No 2)R 1997 (SI 121/1997), art 9.

2 Cross References

a   LG(PD)A 1963, s 46 provides for the making of conservation orders relating to flora or fauna in an area to which a special amenity order relates.

---

164. Public authorities for purposes of sections 5 of Act of 1976[2a]

Each of the following bodies is hereby declared to be a public authority for the purposes of section 5 of the Act of 1976 –

    (a) Bord Fáilte Éireann,

    (b) Bord Telecom Éireann – The Irish Telecommunications Board,

    (c) An Chomhairle Ealaíon,

    (d) Córas Iompair Éireann,

    (e) the Electricity Supply Board,

    (f) Forfás,

    (g) the National Monuments Advisory Council,

    (h) the National Roads Authority,

    (i) An Post – the Post Office,

    (j) the Shannon Free Airport Development Company Limited, and

    (k) Udarás na Gaeltachta.   **[440]**

---

2 Cross References

a   LG(PD)A 1976, s 5 provides that An Bord Pleanála shall keep itself informed of the policies and objectives of certain bodies as set out in this Article.

---

165. Vesting order

Form No. 2 set out in the Third Schedule, or a form substantially to the like effect, shall be the prescribed form of vesting order to be made by a planning authority in exercise of the powers conferred on them by section 25(5) of the Act of 1976.   **[441]**

166. Persons to whom section 32 of Act of 1976 applies[2a]

(1) The following classes, descriptions and grades of employees of the Board and other persons are hereby prescribed for the purposes of section 32 of the Act of 1976 –

    (a) every employee of the Board, other than an employee the qualifications for whose employment are not wholly or in part professional or technical and the maximum remuneration for whose employment is less than the maximum remuneration for the office of Executive Officer in the Civil Service;

    (b) (i) every officer of the Minister who, pursuant to arrangements made under section 21(3) of the Act of 1976, and

       (ii) every other person employed in a part-time capacity by the Board in accordance with section 10(2) of the Act of 1976 who,

    is engaged in duties relating to appeals, contributions, questions or disputes which fall to be determined by the Board or in duties relating to the functions of the Board under section 29 of the Act of 1963.

(2) The following classes, descriptions and grades of offices under a planning authority are hereby prescribed for the purposes of section 32 of the Act of 1976 –

    (a) the offices of County Manager, City Manager and Town Clerk, Assistant County Manager, Assistant City Manager, County Secretary, Town Clerk and Assistant Town Clerk;

    (b) any other office under a planning authority the holder of which is assigned duties which relate to the performance of any functions of a planning authority under the Acts.   **[442]**

---

2 Cross References

a   LG(PD)A 1976 s 32 provides for the making of declarations of interests by members and employees of An Bord Pleanála and members and officers of planning authorities.

---

167. Form of declaration under section 32 of Act of 1976

(1) Form No. 3 set out in the Third Schedule shall be the prescribed form of a declaration to be given to the Board under section 32 of the Act of 1976.

(2) Form No. 4 set out in the Third Schedule shall be the prescribed form of a declaration to be given to a planning authority under section 32 of the Act of 1976.**[443]**

168. Register fee

The prescribed fee for a copy of an entry in the register shall be the amount indicated in column 2 of the Sixth Schedule opposite the mention of such a copy in column 1 of the said Schedule.   **[444]**

First Schedule

REGULATIONS REVOKED

Number and Year	Title
65 of 1977	Local Government (Planning and Development) Regulations, 1977.
231 of 1980	Local Government (Planning and Development) (Amendment) Regulations, 1980.
154 of 1981	Local Government (Planning and Development) (Amendment) Regulations, 1981.
342 of 1982	Local Government (Planning and Development) (Amendment) Regulations, 1982.
285 of 1983	Local Government (Planning and Development) (An Bord Pleanála) Regulations, 1983.
403 of 1983	Local Government (Planning and Development) (Postal and Telecommunications) (Exempted Development) Regulations, 1983.
348 of 1984	Local Government (Planning and Development) (Exempted Development and Amendment) Regulations, 1984.
358 of 1984	Local Government (Planning and Development) (Fees) Regulations, 1984.
130 of 1985	Local Government (Planning and Development) (Exempted Development) Regulations, 1985.
287 of 1987	Local Government (Planning and Development) (Exempted Development) Regulations, 1987.
338 of 1989	Local Government (Planning and Development) (Fees) (Amendment) Regulations, 1989.
25 of 1990	Local Government (Planning and Development) Regulations, 1990.
144 of 1990	Local Government (Planning and Development) (Compensation) Regulations, 1990.
187 of 1991	Local Government (Planning and Development) (Fees) (Amendment) Regulations, 1991.
3 of 1992	Local Government (Planning and Development) (Fees) (Amendment) Regulations, 1992.
209 of 1992	Local Government (Planning and Development) Regulations, 1992.
222 of 1992	Local Government (Planning and Development) (No. 2) Regulations, 1992.
349 of 1993	Local Government (Planning and Development) (Fees) (Amendment) Regulations, 1993.
402 of 1993	Local Government (Planning and Development) Regulations, 1993.

[445]

Second Schedule: Part I

EXEMPTED DEVELOPMENT – GENERAL[3A]

Column 1 Description of Development	Column 2 Conditions and Limitations
Development within the curtilage of a dwellinghouse CLASS 1 The extension of a dwellinghouse, by the construction or erection of an extension (including a conservatory) to the rear of the dwellinghouse or by the conversion for use as part of the dwellinghouse of any garage, store, shed or other similar structure attached to the rear or to the side of the dwellinghouse.	1. (a) Where the dwellinghouse has not been extended previously, the floor area of any such extension shall not exceed 23 square metres. (b) Where the dwellinghouse has been extended previously, the floor area of any such extension, taken together with the floor area of any previous extension or extensions, shall not exceed 23 square metres. [2.(a) Subject to sub-paragraph (b), the height of the walls of any such extension, exclusive of any gable, shall not exceed the height of the rear wall of the dwellinghouse. (b) Where the rear wall of the dwellinghouse includes a gable, the height of the walls of any such extension, exclusive of any gable, shall not exceed the height of the side walls of the dwellinghouse. (c) The height of the highest part of the roof of any such extension shall not exceed the height of the highest part of the roof of the dwellinghouse.][1a] 3. The construction or erection of any such extension to the rear of the dwellinghouse shall not reduce the area of private open space of the dwellinghouse to the rear of the dwellinghouse to less than 25 square metres.
CLASS 2 The provision, as part of a central heating system of a dwellinghouse, of a chimney, boiler house or oil storage tank.	The capacity of any such oil storage tank shall not exceed 3,500 litres.
CLASS 3 The construction, erection or placing within the curtilage of a dwellinghouse of any tent, awning, shade or other object, greenhouse, garage, store, shed or other similar structure.	1. No such structure shall be constructed, erected or placed forward of the front wall of the dwellinghouse.

Column 1 Description of Development	Column 2 Conditions and Limitations
	2. The total area of such structures constructed, erected or placed within the curtilage of a dwellinghouse shall not, taken together with any other such structures previously constructed, erected or placed within the said curtilage, exceed 25 square metres.
	3. The construction, erection or placing within the curtilage of a dwellinghouse of any such structure shall not reduce the amount of private open space of the dwellinghouse to the rear or to the side of the dwellinghouse to less than 25 square metres.
	4. The external finishes of any garage or other structure constructed, erected or placed to the side of a dwellinghouse, and the roof covering where any such structure has a tiled or slated roof, shall conform with those of the dwellinghouse.
	5. The height[2a] of any such structure shall not exceed, in the case of a building with a tiled or slated pitched roof, 4 metres or, in any other case, 3 metres.
	6. The structure shall not be used for human habitation or for the keeping of pigs, poultry, horses, ponies or pigeons or for any other purpose other than a purpose incidental to the enjoyment of the dwellinghouse as such.
CLASS 4 (a) The erection of a wireless or television antenna, other than a satellite television signal receiving antenna, on the roof of a dwellinghouse.	The height of the antenna above the roof of the dwellinghouse shall not exceed 6 metres.
(b) The erection on, or within the curtilage of, a dwellinghouse of a satellite television signal receiving antenna	1. Not more than one such antenna shall be erected on, or within the curtilage of, a dwellinghouse.
	2. The diameter of any such antenna shall not exceed 1 metre.
	3. No such antenna shall be erected on, or forward of, the front wall of the dwellinghouse.

Column 1 Description of Development	Column 2 Conditions and Limitations
	4. No such antenna shall be erected on the front roof slope of the dwellinghouse or higher than the highest part of the roof of the dwellinghouse.
CLASS 5 The construction, erection or alteration, within or bounding the curtilage of a dwellinghouse, of a gate, gateway, railing or wooden fence or a wall constructed of brick, stone, blocks with decorative finish, other concrete blocks or mass concrete.	1. The height of any such structure shall not exceed 2 metres or, in the case of a wall or fence within or bounding any garden or other space in front of a dwellinghouse, 1.2 metres.
	2. Every wall other than a dry stone wall shall be capped and the external surface of every wall of mass concrete or of concrete blocks, other than blocks with decorative finish, bounding any garden or other space between a dwellinghouse and a road shall be plastered.
CLASS 6 (a) The construction of any path, drain or pond or the carrying out of any landscaping works within the curtilage of a dwellinghouse.	The level of the ground shall not be altered by more than 1 metre above or below the level of the adjoining ground.

(b) Any works within the curtilage of a dwellinghouse for –
 	
  (i) the provision to the rear of the dwellinghouse of a hard surface for use for any purpose incidental to the enjoyment of the dwellinghouse as such.
 	
  (ii) the provision to the front or side of the dwellinghouse of a hard surface for the parking or not more than two motor vehicles used for a purpose incidental to the enjoyment of the dwellinghouse as such.	

CLASS 7 The construction or erection of a porch outside any external door of a dwellinghouse.	1. Any such structure shall be situate not less than 2 metres from any road.
	2. The floor area of any such structure shall not exceed 2 square metres.
	3. The height of any such structure shall not exceed, in the case of a structure with a tiled or slated pitched roof, 4 metres or, in any other case, 3 metres.

Column 1 Description of Development	Column 2 Conditions and Limitations
Sundry minor works **CLASS 8** The construction, erection, renewal or replacement, other than within or bounding the curtilage of a dwellinghouse, of any gate or gateway.	The height of any such structure shall not exceed 2 metres.
CLASS 9 The plastering or capping of any wall of concrete blocks or mass concrete.	
CLASS 10 The construction, erection, lowering, repair or replacement, other than within or bounding the curtilage of a dwellinghouse, of – (i) any fence (not being a hoarding or sheet metal fence), or (ii) any wall of brick, stone, blocks with decorative finish, other concrete blocks or mass concrete.	1. The height of any new structure shall not exceed 1.2 metres or the height of the structure being replaced, whichever is the greater, and in any event shall not exceed 2 metres. 2. Every wall, other than a dry stone wall, constructed or erected bounding a road shall be capped and the external surface of every wall of mass concrete or of concrete blocks, other than blocks with decorative finish, bounding a road shall be plastered.
CLASS 11 Any alteration consisting of the painting of any external part of any building or other structure.	Such painting may not, except in the case of a hoarding or other temporary structure bounding land on which development consisting of works is being or will be carried out in pursuance of a permission granted under Part IV of the Act of 1963 or as exempted development, be for the purposes of creating a mural.
CLASS 12 The repair or improvement of any private street, road or way, being works carried out on land within the boundary of the street, road or way, and the construction of any private footpath or paving.	The width of any such private footpath or paving shall not exceed 3 metres.
Change of use **CLASS 13** Development consisting of a change of use – (a) from use for the sale of hot food for consumption off the premises, or for the sale or leasing or display for sale or leasing of motor vehicles, to use as a shop, (b) from use as a public house to use as a shop, (c) from use for the direction of funerals, as a funeral home, as an amusement arcade or a restaurant, to use as a shop,	

Column 1 Description of Development	Column 2 Conditions and Limitations
(d) from use to which class 2 of Part IV of this Schedule applies to use as a shop,	
(e) from use as two or more dwellings to use as a single dwelling of any structure previously used as a single dwelling,	
[(f) from use as a dwellinghouse to use as a residence for persons with an intellectual or physical disability or a mental illness and persons providing care for such persons.][1b]	The number of persons with an intellectual or physical disability [or a mental illness][1c] living in any such residence shall not exceed 6 and the number of resident carers shall not exceed 2.

Temporary structures and uses

CLASS 14

Occasional use for social or recreational purposes of any school, hall, club, art gallery, museum, library, reading room, gymnasium or any structure normally used for public worship or religious instruction.

CLASS 15

The erection, construction or placing on land on, in, or under which or on land adjoining which development consisting of works (other than mining) is being or is about to be carried out in pursuance of a permission granted under Part IV of the Act of 1963 or as exempted development, of structures, works, plant or machinery needed temporarily in connection with that development during the period in which it is being carried out.	Such structures, works, plant or machinery shall be removed at the expiration of the period and the land shall be forthwith reinstated save to such extent as may be authorised or required by a permission under Part IV of the Act of 1963.

[CLASS 15A

The erection, construction or placing on land, on, in, or under which or on land adjoining which development consisting of mining is to be carried out in pursuance of a permission granted under Part IV of the Act of 1963, of structures, works, plant or machinery needed temporarily in connection with preparation for the aforesaid mining.][1d]	Such structures, works, plant or machinery shall be removed prior to commencement of the mining.

CLASS 16

The placing or maintenance on a public road of any moveable appliance licensed under section 89 of the Act of 1963.

Column 1 Description of Development	Column 2 Conditions and Limitations
CLASS 17 The use of premises in connection with an election to the office of President of Ireland, an election of members of Dáil Éireann, the Parliament of the European Communities, a local authority of Údarás na Gaeltachta, or a referendum within the meaning of the Referendum Act, 1942.	The use shall be discontinued after a period not exceeding 30 days.
CLASS 18 The keeping or storing of a caravan or boat within the curtilage of a dwellinghouse.	1. Not more than one caravan or boat shall be so kept or stored. 2. The caravan or boat shall not be used for the storage, display, advertisement or sale of goods or for the purposes of any business. 3. No caravan or boat shall be so kept or stored for more than nine months in any year or occupied as a dwelling while so kept or stored.

Development for industrial purposes
CLASS 19
(a) Development of the following descriptions, carried out by an industrial undertaker on land occupied and used by such undertaker for the carrying on and for the purposes of any industrial process, or on land used as a dock, harbour or quay for the purposes of any industrial undertaking —
 	
  (i) the provision, rearrangement, replacement or maintenance of private ways or private railways, sidings or conveyors,
 	
  (ii) the provision, rearrangement, replacement or maintenance of sewers, mains, pipes, cables or other apparatus,
 	
  (iii) the installation or erection by way of addition or replacement of plant or machinery, or structures of the nature of plant or machinery.
 	
(b) Any works for the provision within the curtilage of an industrial building of a hard surface to be used for the purposes of or in connection with the industrial process carried on in the building.
	1. Any such development shall not materially alter the external appearance of the premises of the undertaking.
	
	2. The height of any plant or machinery, or any structure in the nature of plant or machinery, shall not exceed 15 metres or the height of the plant, machinery or structure replaced, whichever is the greater.

Column 1 Description of Development	Column 2 Conditions and Limitations
CLASS 20 Storage within the curtilage of an industrial building, in connection with the industrial process carried on in the building, of raw materials, products, packing materials or fuel, or the deposit of waste arising from the industrial process.	The raw materials, products, packing materials, fuel or waste stored shall not be visible from any public road contiguous or adjacent to the curtilage of the industrial building.

Development by statutory undertakers

CLASS 21

The carrying out by any railway undertaking of development required in connection with the movement of traffic by rail in, on, over or under the operational land of the undertaking except –

(i) the construction or erection of any railway station or bridge, or of any residential structure, office, or structure to be used for manufacturing or repairing work, which is not situate wholly within the interior of a railway station, or

(ii) the reconstruction or alteration of any of the aforementioned structures so as materially to affect the design or external appearance thereof.

CLASS 22

The carrying out by any harbour authority of development being –

(i) works authorised by a harbour works order in pursuance of section 134 of the Harbours Act, 1946 (No. 9 of 1946), which consist of the construction, reconstruction, extension or removal of docks, graving docks, quays, wharves, jetties, piers, embankments, breakwaters, roads, viaducts, tramways, railways or aerodromes, (but not the construction or erection of sheds, transit sheds, transhipment sheds, silos, stores and other structures or the reconstruction or alteration of such excepted structures so as materially to affect the design or external appearance thereof), or

Column 1 Description of Development	Column 2 Conditions and Limitations
(ii) the cleaning, scouring, deepening, improving or dredging of their harbour or the approaches thereto or the removal of any obstruction within the limits of their harbour, and the use of land for the disposal of dredged material in accordance with an objective in a development plan for the area in which the land is situate.	

CLASS 23

The carrying out –

(a) pursuant to and in accordance with a consent given by the Minister for Transport, Energy and Communications under section 8 of the Gas Act, 1976 (No. 30 of 1976), by the Irish Gas Board of development consisting of the construction of underground pipelines for the transmission of gas (but not the construction or erection of any apparatus, equipment or other thing ancillary to such a pipeline save cathodic protection equipment and marker posts), or

(b) pursuant to and in accordance with an order made by the Minster for Transport, Energy and Communications under section 2 of the Gas (Amendment) Act, 1987 (No. 9 of 1987), by the Irish Gas Board of development consisting of the laying underground of mains, pipes, cables or other apparatus, or

(c) in accordance with requirements of the Minister for Transport, Energy and Communications under section 40 of the Gas Act 1976, of development consisting of the construction of an underground pipeline for the transmission of gas (but not the construction or erection of any apparatus, equipment or other thing ancillary to such a pipeline save cathodic protection equipment and marker posts), or

(d) by any gas undertaking (other than the Irish Gas Board) of development consisting of the laying underground of mains, pipes, cables or other apparatus for the purposes of the undertaking.

Column 1 Description of Development	Column 2 Conditions and Limitations
CLASS 24 The carrying out by any electricity undertaking of development consisting of the laying underground of mains, pipes, cables or other apparatus for the purposes of the undertaking.	
CLASS 25 The carrying out by any electricity undertaking of development consisting of the construction of overhead transmission or distribution lines for conducting electricity at a voltage not exceeding a nominal value of 20kV.	
CLASS 26 The carrying out by any electricity undertaking of development for the purposes of the undertaking consisting of the construction or erection of an overhead transmission line not more than 40 metres from a position in respect of which permission for such line was granted and which otherwise complies with such permission, but not a line in respect of which a condition attached to the relevant permission imposed a contrary requirement.	
CLASS 27 The carrying out by any electricity undertaking of development consisting of the construction or erection of a unit substation for the distribution of electricity at a voltage not exceeding a nominal value of 20kV.	The volume above ground level of any such unit substation shall not exceed 11 cubic metres, measured externally.
CLASS 28 The carrying out by An Post – The Post Office of development consisting of the provision of – (a) pillarboxes or other forms of letter box, (b) roadside boxes for the delivery of mail, (c) deposit boxes for the temporary storage of mail for local delivery, (d) machines for the supply of stamps or printed postage labels.	
CLASS 29 The carrying out, by Bord Telecom Éireann - The Irish Telecommunications Board, or by any person to whom a licence under section 111 of the Postal and Telecommunications Services Act, 1983 has been granted, of development consisting of the provision of –	

Column 1 Description of Development	Column 2 Conditions and Limitations
(a) underground telcommunications structures or other underground telecommunications works (including the laying of mains and cables and the installation underground of any apparatus or equipment),	
(b) overhead telecommunications lines,	Where such lines are attached to poles the height of the poles shall not exceed 10 metres.
(c) telephone kiosks or other public telephone facilities in a public place,	No such kiosk or facility shall be situated within 10 metres of the curtilage of any dwellinghouse, save with the consent in writing of the owner and occupier thereof.
(d) equipment for transmitting or receiving telecommunications messages from satellites in space,	1. No such equipment shall exceed 10 metres in height. 2. The width of any antenna shall not exceed 5 metres. 3. No such equipment shall be situated within 10 metres of the curtilage of any dwellinghouse save with the consent in writing of the owner and occupier thereof, or within 10 metres of the window of a workroom of any other structure.
(e) permanent telecommunications exchange and radio station containers,	1. No such container shall exceed 10 metres in length, 3 metres in width or 3 metres in height. 2. No such container shall be situated within 10 metres of the curtilage of any dwellinghouse save with the consent in writing of the owner and occupier thereof, or within 10 metres of the window of a workroom of any other structure.
(f) antenna support structures,[2b]	The height of any such structure shall not – (a) if constructed or erected on the ground, exceed 15 metres, (b) if constructed or erected on the roof of a building, exceed 7 metres above the roof.
(g) cabinets forming part of a telecommunication system,	The volume above ground level of any such cabinet shall not exceed 1.5 cubic metres, measured externally.
(h) transportable radio links.	1. The link shall be removed from the land on which it is provided not later than twelve months from the date on which it was provided. 2. No such link shall exceed 30 metres in height above ground level or, where it is erected on a roof, 7 metres above the roof.

Column 1 Description of Development	Column 2 Conditions and Limitations
	3. No such link shall be situated within 10 metres of the curtilage of any dwellinghouse or of the window of a workroom of any other structure.
[(i) antennae for mobile telephony by way of attachment to an existing antenna support structure used in connection with radio transmission or reception.]	1. The number of such antennae shall not exceed twelve, of which not more than four shall be of the dish type (whether shielded or not).
	2. (i) The dimensions of any such antenna provided shall not exceed the greatest length, width or depth of any antenna for mobile telephony of corresponding type already attached to the structure.
	(ii) Otherwise, the dimensions of any such antenna provided shall not exceed:
	(a) in the case of any panel type antenna, 1,500 x 400 x 150 (Length x Width Depth in mm),
	(b) in the case of any co-linear type antenna, 5,000 x 100 x (Length Diameter in mm), and
	(c) in the case of any dish type antenna (whether shielded or not), 1,800mm in diameter.
	3. The attachment of such antennae shall not result in the field strength of the non-ionising radiation emissions from the radio installations on the site exceeding the limits for non-ionising radiation emissions included as a condition of the granting of a licence under section 111 of the Postal and Telecommunications Services Act, 1983.
	4. The attachment of such antennae may be carried out by way of a platform only where the antenna support structure already incorporates a platform.
	5. The height of the existing structure (including any antenna thereon) shall not be exceeded.
(j) an antenna support structure in place of an existing antenna support structure.	1. The replacement shall take place within a period of not longer than one month following the removal of the existing structure.
	2. (i) The height of the replacement structure shall not exceed the height of the replaced structure.

Column 1 Description of Development	Column 2 Conditions and Limitations
	(ii) The width of the replacement structure shall not exceed the width of the replaced structure except where the replaced structure was two metres or less in width, in which case the width of the replacement may be up to 100 per cent greater than the width of the replaced structure, all measurements to be taken at the widest point. (iii) Where the replaced structure did not incorporate an antenna platform, the replacement shall not incorporate such a platform. 3. (i) The antenna to be attached to the replacement structure shall not exceed the number of antennae on the replaced structure and, an additional 12 antennae for mobile telephony, of which not more than four of the additional 12 shall be of the dish type (whether shielded or not). (ii) The dimensions of any replacement antenna shall not exceed the greatest length, width or depth of any replaced antenna of corresponding type. 4. (i) The dimensions of any additional antenna for mobile telephony provided shall not exceed the greatest length, width or depth of any antenna for mobile telephony of corresponding type on the replaced structure. (ii) Otherwise, the dimensions of any antenna provided shall not exceed: (a) in the case of any panel type antenna, 1,500 x 400 x 150 (Length x Width x Depth in mm), (b) in the case of any co-linear type antenna, 5,000 x 100 (Length x Diameter in mm), and (c) in the case of any dish type antenna (whether shielded or not), 1,800mm in diameter.

Column 1 Description of Development	Column 2 Conditions and Limitations
	5. The replacement of an antenna support structure together with any replacement or additional antenna shall not result in the field strength of the non-ionising radiation emissions from the radio installations on the site exceeding the limits for non-ionising radiation emissions included as a condition of the granting of a licence under section 111 of the Postal and Telecommunications Services Act, 1983.][1e]
Development for amenity or recreational purposes CLASS 30 Development consisting of the laying out and use of land – (a) as a park, private open space or ornamental garden,	
(b) as a roadside shrine,	The area of any such shrine shall not exceed two square metres, the height shall not exceed two metres above the centre of the road opposite the structure and it shall not be illuminated.
(c) for athletics or sports (other than golf or pitch and putt or sports involving the use of motor vehicles, aircraft or firearms), where no charge is made for admission of the public to the land. CLASS 31 Development consisting of – (a) the carrying out by or on behalf of a statutory undertaker of any works for the maintenance, improvement, reconstruction or restoration of any watercourse, canal, river, lake or other inland waterway, or any lock, quay, mooring, harbour, pier, dry-dock or other structure forming part of the inland waterway or associated therewith, and any development incidental thereto,	
(b) the erection or construction by or on behalf of a statutory undertaker of facilities required in connection with the operation, use or management of a watercourse, canal, river, lake or other inland waterway.	1. The floor area of any building constructed or erected shall not exceed 40 square metres. 2. The height of any building constructed or erected shall not exceed, in the case of a building with a pitched roof, 6 metres or, in any other case, 3 metres.

Column 1 Description of Development	Column 2 Conditions and Limitations
	3. Any car park provided or constructed shall incorporate parking space for not more than 24 cars.
CLASS 32³ᵈ (a) Development consisting of the carrying out by or on behalf of a State authority or other public body, or land used by the authority or body as a public park, of works incidental to that use, including the provision, construction or erection of any structure which is in connection with or for the purposes of the enjoyment of the park as such or which is required in connection with or for the purposes of the management or operation of the park.	1. The floor area of any building constructed or erected shall not exceed 40 square metres.
(b) Development consisting of the carrying out by or on behalf of [a State Authority or other public body,]¹ᶠ on a nature reserve established in accordance with section 15 of the Wildlife Act, 1976 (No. 39 of 1976), of works (including the provision, construction or erection of structures) which are in connection with or for the purposes of the enjoyment of the reserve as such or which are required in connection with the management or operation of the reserve.	2. The height of any building or other structure constructed or erected shall not exceed 10 metres. 3. Any car park provided or constructed shall incorporate parking space for not more than 40 cars.
Miscellaneous CLASS 33 Development consisting of the use of land for any fair, funfair, bazaar or circus or any local event of a religious, cultural, educational, political, social, recreational or sporting character and the placing or maintenance of tents, vans or other temporary or moveable structures or objects on the land in connection therewith.	1. The land shall not be used for any such purposes either continuously for a period exceeding 15 days or occasionally for periods exceeding in aggregate 30 days in any year. 2. On the discontinuance of such use the land shall be forthwith reinstated save to such extent as may be authorised or required by a permission granted under Part IV of the Act of 1963.
CLASS 34 Development consisting of the placing or erection on, or within the curtlage of, a building, or on any other land, occupied by, or under the control of, a State authority, of flags, banners or national emblems and any structures for the display of flags, banners or national emblems.	

Column 1 Description of Development	Column 2 Conditions and Limitations
CLASS 35[3e] Development consisting of the provision, construction or erection by or on behalf of a State authority of temporary structures or other temporary facilities required in connection with a visit of a foreign dignitary or delegation.	The temporary structures and facilities shall be removed after the conclusion of the visit and the land concerned shall be forthwith reinstated.
CLASS 36 The erection, placing or keeping on land of any lighthouse, beacon, buoy or other aid to navigation on water or in the air.	Any such lighthouse, beacon, buoy or other navigational aid shall not exceed 40 metres in height.
CLASS 37 Works incidental to the use or maintenance of any burial ground, churchyard, monument, fairgreen, market, schoolyard or showground except – (a) the erection or construction of any wall, fence or gate bounding or abutting on a public road, (b) the erection or construction of any building other than a stall or store which is wholly enclosed within a market building, or (c) the reconstruction or alteration of any building other than a stall or store which is wholly enclosed within a market building.	
CLASS 38[3f] Works consisting of or incidental to – (a) the carrying out of any works on land which are in accordance with and necessary for compliance with the terms of any licence granted under section 34 of the Local Government (Sanitary Services) Act, 1948, but not including the erection of any building, hut or chalet or the construction of any road or hardstanding, (b) the removal of any structure or object or the carrying out of any works required by a planning authority under the provisions of any enactment, (c) the carrying out of development in compliance with a notice under section 12 of the Local Government (Water Pollution) Act, 1977 (No. 1 of 1977), (d) the carrying out of development in compliance with a notice under section 26 of the Air Pollution Act, 1987 (No. 6 of 1987),	

Column 1 Description of Development	Column 2 Conditions and Limitations
(e) the carrying out of development in compliance with a condition or conditions attached to a fire safety certificate granted in accordance with Part III of the Building Control Regulations, 1991 (S.I. No. 305 of 1991), other than the construction or erection of an external fire escape or water tank. [(f) the carrying out of development in compliance with a notice under section 55 of the Waste Management Act, 1996 (No. 10 of 1996).][1g] CLASS 39 The excavation for the purposes of research or discovery – (a) pursuant to and in accordance with a licence under section 26 of the National Monuments Act, 1930 (No. 2 of 1930), of a site, feature or other object of archaeological or historical interest, (b) of a site, feature or other object of geological interest. CLASS 40 The sinking of a well, drilling of a borehole, erection of a pump, or construction of a pumphouse, or other works necessary for the purpose of providing a domestic water supply, or a group water supply scheme in accordance with a plan or proposal approved by the Minister or a local authority for the purpose of making a grant towards the cost of such works. CLASS 41 Any drilling or excavation for the purpose of surveying land or examining the depth and nature of the subsoil, other than drilling or excavation for the purposes of minerals prospecting.	

Column 1 Description of Development	Column 2 Conditions and Limitations
CLASS 42[3g] Development consisting of the provision, construction or erection by the Commissioners of Public Works in Ireland or the Environmental Protection Agency, or by a local authority outside the functional area of the authority, of any equipment or structure for or in connection with the collection of information on the levels, volumes and flows of water in rivers or other watercourses, lakes or groundwaters, and any development incidental thereto.	The floor area of any building or other structure provided, constructed or erected shall not exceed 8 square metres and the height of any such building or other structure shall not exceed 4 metres.
CLASS 43 The connection of any premises to a wired broadcast relay service, sewer, watermain, gas main or electricity supply line or cable, including the breaking open of any street or other land for that purpose.	
CLASS 44 The construction or erection by a person licensed under the Wireless Telegraphy (Wired Broadcast Relay Licence) Regulations, 1974 of a cabinet as part of a wired broadcast relay service.	The volume above ground level of any such cabinet shall not exceed 1 cubic metre, measured externally.

CLASS 45
(a) The demolition of a building or other structure, other than:
  (i) a habitable house, or
  (ii) a building which forms part of a terrace of buildings, or
  (iii) a building which abuts on another building in separate ownership.
(b) the demolition of part of a habitable house in connection with the provision of an extension or porch in accordance with class 1 or 7, respectively, of this Part of this Schedule or in accordance with a permission for an extension or porch granted under Part IV of the Act of 1963.	

CLASS 46[2c] The carrying out by the Commissioners of Public Works in Ireland of any works for the maintenance of works and structures for which, by virtue of the Arterial Drainage Act, 1945 or any order made thereunder, the Commissioners are responsible, and any development incidental thereto.	

Column 1 Description of Development	Column 2 Conditions and Limitations
CLASS 47 Development consisting of the carrying out of any works within, or bounding, the curtilage of a building, premises or installation specified in article 156(1)(a).	
CLASS 48[2d] Development consisting of the carrying out by or on behalf of An Garda Síochána, for security reasons, of any works within, or bounding, the curtilage of the residence of a person in receipt of protection from An Garda Síochána, other than a person referred to in article 156(1)(c)(ii).	
CLASS 49 Development consisting of the construction or erection by a Regional Fisheries Board of –	
(a) a footbridge	Any such footbridge shall not exceed 1.2 metres in width or 8 metres in length.
(b) a fish pass	
(c) a fish screen or barrier	
(d) a walkway or fishing stand	Any such walkway shall not exceed 1.2 metres in width, and any such fishing stand shall not exceed 10 square metres in area.
CLASS 50 [The carrying out of development below the high water mark pursuant to and in accordance with a licence under the Fisheries (Amendment) Act, 1997 (No. 23 of 1997) (including a licence deemed to be granted under that Act or the Fisheries and Foreshore (Amendment) Act, 1998 (No 54 of 1998))][1h]	

---

1 Amendments

a   Paragraph 2 of Column 2 of Class 1 which relates to the determination of height was substituted by LG(PD)R 1995, (SI 69/1995), art 9.

b   Paragraph (f) of class 13 was substituted by LG(PD)R 1995 (SI 69/1995), art 9.

c   The words in square brackets were inserted by LG(PD)R 1995 (SI 69/1995), art 9.

d   Class 15A was inserted by LG(PD)R 1995 (SI 69/1995), art 9(3).

e   Paragraphs (i) and (j) of Class 29 were inserted by SI 78/1997, art 4.

f   Class 32, para (b) was amended by LG(PD)(No 2)R 1997 (SI 121/1997), art 10.

g   Class 38, para (f) was inserted by of SI 261/1997, art 10.

h   Class 50 was inserted by LG(PD)R 1999 (SI 92/1999), art 22.

2 Cross References

a   For a construction of the term "height" see art 8(2).

b   See article 9(1)(b) which provides that this exemption will only apply until 16 December 1994 and structures erected after this period will be subject to planning control. It is not immediately clear why such a time limit was given.

c   Arterial drainage works are generally exempted development; see art 157, Part XIII. The exemption relates primarily to the maintenance of such works.

d   Article 156(1)(c)(ii) provides for exemptions for works which are required by An Garda Síochána at the residence of a person in receipt of Garda protection.

3 Notes

a   For an in-depth consideration of this class of exemptions see *Smyth v Colgan* Supreme Court, unrep, 15 July 1998 where phrases such as "habitable house", "dwelling house", "floor area" and "gable" were all considered.

b   This provides for such premises to be used for any purposes in relation to such elections and not just as offices as was previously the case under the previous corresponding provision.

c   Under this provision boats are now subject to the same restrictions as caravans and a limit of 1 boat or caravan has been imposed.

d   This exemption was necessary following the decision of the Supreme Court in *Howard v Commissioners of Public Works* Supreme Court, unrep, 26 May 1993.

e   This exemption was necessary following the decision of *Howard v Commissioners of Public Works* Supreme Court, unrep, 26 May 1993.

f   This class of exemptions has been significantly changed. The exemptions for works under the derelict sites act has been omitted. The Derelict Sites Act 1990 provides that works carried out pursuant to that act will be exempted development. Part (d) and (e) relating to the Air Pollution Act 1987 and BCA 1990 are new. It is surprising that in view of parts (b)–(e) that a similar exemption was not provided for relating to conditions imposed by the Environment Protection Agency.

g   This exemption was necessary to some extent following the decision of *Howard v Commissioners of Public Works* Supreme Court, unrep, 26 May 1993.

h   The structures referred to here require a licence under s 89 LG(PD)A 1963.

i   Article 156(1)(A) relates to the categories of development which the Minister may specify as being outside the scope of general planning control under s 2(*a*)(i) LG(PD)A 93.

Part II

EXEMPTED DEVELOPMENT – ADVERTISEMENTS

Column 1 Description of Development	Column 2 Conditions and Limitations
CLASS 1 Advertisements (other than those specified in classes 2, 3 or 5 of this Part of this Schedule) exhibited on business premises, wholly with reference to all or any of the following matters: the business or other activity carried on or the goods or services provided on those premises.	1. The total area of such advertisements exhibited on or attached or affixed to the front of any building on the premises shall not exceed an area equal to 0.3 square metres for every metre length of such front, less the total area of any such advertisements exhibited on the premises but not exhibited on or attached or affixed to a building, and in any event shall not exceed 5 square metres. 2. The total area of such advertisements exhibited on or attached or affixed to any face of a building on the premises other than the front thereof shall not exceed 1.2 square metres and the total area of any such advertisements on such face which are illuminated shall not exceed 0.3 square metres. 3. The total area of such advertisements which are not exhibited on or attached or affixed to a building on the premises shall not exceed 3 square metres, of which not more than 1.5 square metres shall consist of advertisements which are illuminated. 4. (a) No part of any such advertisement which is not exhibited on or attached or affixed to a building on the premises, or of an advertisement structure on which it is exhibited, shall be more than 2.5 metres in height. (b) No part of any such advertisement which is exhibited on or attached or affixed to a building on the premises shall be more than 4 metres in height above the ground level. 5. Where any such advertisement projects more than 5 centimetres over any public road, the sign or other advertisement structure on which it is exhibited shall not be less than 2 metres above the level of such road and shall not project more than 1 metre over such road.

Column 1 Description of Development	Column 2 Conditions and Limitations
	6. Where any such advertisement consists of a circular sign and projects more than 5 centimetres over any public road, the diameter of such sign shall not exceed 1 metre and no other such advertisement shall be exhibited on a sign or other advertisement structure projecting more than 5 centimetres over such road.
	7. Where any one or more such advertisements are exhibited on a swinging or fixed sign or other advertisement structure (other than a circular sign) projecting more than 5 centimetres from any external face of a building, the total area of such advertisements shall not exceed 1.2 square metres and the area of any face of any such advertisement shall not exceed 0.4 square metres.
	8. No such advertisement shall contain or consist of any symbol, emblem, model, logo or device exceeding 0.6 metres in height or any letter exceeding 0.3 metres in height.
	9. No such advertisement shall cover any part of any window or door of any building on which the advertisement is exhibited or to which it is attached or affixed.
CLASS 2 Illuminated advertisements exhibited as part of any shop or other window display on business premises and other advertisements affixed to the inside of the glass surface of a window of a business premises or otherwise exhibited through a window of such premises.	The total area of any advertisements so exhibited shall not exceed one quarter of the area of the window through which the advertisements are exhibited.
CLASS 3 Advertisements displayed within a business premises and which are not visible from outside the premises.	
CLASS 4 An advertisement in the form of a flag which is attached to a single flagstaff fixed in an upright position on the roof of a business premises and which bears no inscription or emblem other than the name, device or logo of a person or business occupying the business premises.	Not more than one such advertisement shall be exhibited on a business premises.

Column 1 Description of Development	Column 2 Conditions and Limitations
CLASS 5 Advertisements, exhibited at the entrance to any premises, relating to any person, partnership or company carrying on a public service or a profession, business or trade at the premises.	1. No such advertisement shall exceed 0.3 square metres in area. 2. Not more than one such advertisement, or, in the case of premises with entrances on different road frontages, one such advertisement for each such frontage, shall be exhibited in respect of each such person, partnership or company on the premises.
CLASS 6 Advertisements relating to any institution of a religious, educational, cultural, recreational or medical or similar character, any guesthouse or other premises (other than a hotel) providing overnight guest accommodation or public house, block of flats, club, boarding house or hostel, situate on the land on which any such advertisement is exhibited.	1. Any such advertisement shall not exceed 0.6 square metres in area. 2. No part of any such advertisement or an advertisement structure on which it is exhibited shall be more than 2.5 metres in height above ground level. 3. Not more than one such advertisement or, in the case of premises with entrances on different road frontages, one such advertisement for each such frontage, shall be exhibited in respect of any such premises.
CLASS 7 Advertisements exhibited on land wholly or for the most part enclosed within a hedge, fence, wall or similar screen or structure (not being land which is a public park, public garden or other land held for the use and enjoyment of the public, or a part of a railway undertaking's enclosed land normally used for the carriage of passengers or goods by rail) and not readily visible from land outside the enclosure wherein it is exhibited.	
CLASS 8 Advertisements exhibited within a railway station, bus station, airport terminal or ferry terminal and which are not readily visible from outside the premises.	
CLASS 9 Advertisements relating to the sale or letting of any structure or other land (not being an advertisement structure) on which they are exhibited.	1. The area of any such advertisements shall not exceed – (a) in the case of an advertisement relating to the sale or letting of a dwelling, 0.6 square metres,

Column 1 Description of Development	Column 2 Conditions and Limitations
	(b) in the case of an advertisement relating to the sale or letting of any other structure or land, 1.2 square metres.
	2. Not more than one such advertisement shall be exhibited on the structure or other land.
	3. No such advertisement shall be exhibited, and no advertisement structure erected for the purpose of exhibiting such advertisement shall remain on the structure or land, for more than seven days after the sale or letting to which the advertisement relates.
CLASS 10 Advertisements relating to the sale on or before a date specified therein of goods or livestock, and exhibited on land where such goods or livestock are situate or where such sale is held, not being land which is normally used, whether at regular intervals or otherwise, for the purpose of holding sales of goods or livestock.	1. No such advertisement shall exceed 0.6 square metres in area. 2. Not more than one such advertisement shall be exhibited on the land concerned. 3. No such advertisement shall be exhibited, and no advertisement structure erected for the purpose of exhibiting such advertisement shall remain on the land, for more than seven days after the date specified.
CLASS 11 Advertisements relating to the carrying out of building or similar works on the land on which they are exhibited, not being land which is normally used, whether at regular intervals or otherwise, for the purpose of carrying out such works.	1. Where only one advertisement is exhibited, such advertisement shall not exceed 3.5 square metres in area and shall not be exhibited more than 6 metres above ground level. 2. Where more than one advertisement is exhibited, no such advertisement shall exceed 0.6 square metres in area, the total area of such advertisements shall not exceed 3.5 square metres and no such advertisement shall be exhibited more than 4 metres above ground level. 3. No such advertisement shall be exhibited, and no advertisement structure erected for the purpose of exhibiting such advertisement shall remain on the land, for more than seven days after the completion of the works.

Column 1 Description of Development	Column 2 Conditions and Limitations
CLASS 12 Advertisements for the purposes of announcement or direction or warning exhibited by a statutory undertaker in relation to the operation of the statutory undertaking.	
CLASS 13 Advertisements for the purposes of identification, direction or warning with respect to the land or structures on which they are exhibited.	No such advertisement shall exceed 0.3 square metres in area.
CLASS 14 Advertisements relating to an election to the office of President of Ireland, an election of members of Dáil Éireann, the Parliament of the European Communities, a local authority or Údarás na Gaeltachta, or a referendum within the meaning of the Referendum Act, 1942.	No such advertisement shall be exhibited, and no advertisement structure erected for the purpose of exhibiting such advertisement shall be left in place, for more than seven days after the date of the election or referendum to which the advertisement relates.
CLASS 15 Advertisements required to be exhibited by or under any enactment, including (but without prejudice to the generality hereof) advertisements the exhibition of which is so required as a condition of the valid exercise of any power, or proper performance of any function, given or imposed by such enactment, or for compliance with any procedure prescribed by or under any enactment.	
CLASS 16 Advertisements other than advertisements specified in class 17 of this Part of this Schedule, announcing any local event of a religious, cultural, educational, political, social, recreational or sporting character, and advertisements relating to any temporary matter in connection with any local event of such a character, not in either case being an event promoted or carried on for commercial purposes.	1. No such advertisement shall exceed 1.2 square metres in area. 2. No such advertisement shall be exhibited more than 2.5 metres above ground level or be glued, pasted or otherwise affixed to any structure other than an advertisement structure. 3. No such advertisement shall be exhibited, and no advertisement structure erected for the purpose of exhibiting such advertisement shall be left in place, for more than seven days after the conclusion of the event or matter to which it relates.
CLASS 17 Advertisements consisting of placards, posters or bills relating to the visit of any travelling circus, funfair, carnival, show, musicians, players or others travelling entertainment.	1. No such advertisement shall exceed 1.2 square metres in area.

Column 1 Description of Development	Column 2 Conditions and Limitations
	2. No such advertisement shall be exhibited more than 2.5 metres above ground level or be glued, pasted or otherwise affixed to any structure other than an advertisement structure.
	3. No such advertisement shall be exhibited, and no advertisement structure erected for the purpose of exhibiting such advertisement shall be left in place, for more than seven days after the last performance or closing of the entertainment.
CLASS 18 An advertisement relating to any demonstration of agricultural methods or processes on the land on which the advertisement is exhibited.	1. No such advertisement shall exceed 0.6 square metres in area.
	2. Not more than one such advertisement shall be exhibited on the land concerned.
	3. No such advertisement shall be exhibited, and no advertisement structure erected for the purpose of exhibiting such advertisement shall remain on the land, for more than seven days after the date of the demonstration to which it relates.

Part III

EXEMPTED DEVELOPMENT – RURAL

Column 1 Description of Development	Column 2 Conditions and Limitations
Limited use for camping CLASS 1 Temporary use of any land for the placing of any tent or caravan or for the mooring of any boat, barge or other vessel used for the purpose of camping.	1. Not more than one tent or caravan shall be placed within 100 metres of another tent or caravan at any time.
	2. No tent, caravan or vessel shall remain on the land for a period greater than 10 days.
	3. No tent, caravan or vessel shall be used for the storage, display, advertisement or sale of goods or for the purposes of any business.
	4. No tent or caravan shall be placed on land within 50 metres of any public road unless the land is enclosed by a wall, bank or hedge, or any combination thereof, having an average height of not less than 1.5 metres.

Column 1 Description of Development	Column 2 Conditions and Limitations
CLASS 2 Temporary use of land by a scouting organisation for a camp.	The land shall not be used for such purposes for any period or periods exceeding 30 days in any year.
Minor works and structures **CLASS 3** Works relating to the construction or maintenance of any gully, drain, pond, trough, pit or culvert, the widening or deepening of watercourses, the removal of obstructions from watercourses and the making or repairing of embankments in connection with any of the foregoing works.	
CLASS 4 The construction or erection or any wall or fence, other than a fence of sheet metal or a wall or fence within or bounding the curtilage of a dwellinghouse.	1. The height of the wall or fence, other than a fence referred to in paragraph 2, shall not exceed 2 metres. 2. The height of any fence for the purposes of deer farming or conservation shall not exceed 3 metres.
Minerals and petroleum prospecting **CLASS 5** (a) The carrying out of works on any land for the purpose of minerals prospecting and the erection or placing on land of any structures required for that purpose, where the prospecting is carried out pursuant to and in accordance with the terms and conditions of a licence granted by the Minster for Transport, Energy and Communications under the Minerals Development Acts, 1940 to 1979. (b) The carrying out of works on any land for the purpose of searching for petroleum and the erection or placing on land of any structures required for that purpose, where the searching is carried out pursuant to and in accordance with the terms and conditions of an exploration licence, a petroleum prospecting licence or a reserved area licence granted by the Minster for Transport, Energy and Communications under the Petroleum and Other Minerals Development Act, 1960 (No. 7 of 1960).	

Column 1 Description of Development	Column 2 Conditions and Limitations
Agricultural Structures CLASS 6 Works consisting of the provision of a roofed structure for the housing of pigs, cattle, sheep, goats, poultry, donkeys, horses, deer or rabbits, having a floor area not exceeding 300 square metres (whether or not by extension of an existing structure), and any ancillary provision for effluent storage.	1. No such structure shall be used for any purpose other than the purpose of agriculture. 2. The total area of such structure together with any other such structures situated within the same farmyard complex or within 100 metres of that complex shall not exceed 450 square metres floor area in aggregate. 3. Effluent storage facilities adequate to serve the structure having regard to its size, use, location and the need to avoid water pollution shall be provided. 4. No such structure shall be situated, and no effluent from such structure shall be stored, within 10 metres of any public road. 5. No such structure within 100 metres of any public road shall exceed 8 metres in height. 6. No such structure shall be situated, and no effluent from such structure shall be stored, within 100 metres of any dwellinghouse (other than the dwellinghouse of the person providing the structure) or other residential building or school, hospital, church or building used for public assembly, save with the consent in writing of the owner and, as may be appropriate, the occupier or person in charge thereof.
CLASS 7 Works consisting of the provision of roofless cubicles, open loose yards, self-feed silo or silage areas, feeding aprons, assembly yards, milking parlours, sheep dipping units, effluent storage facilities or structures for the making or storage of silage, or any other structures of a similar character or description, having an aggregate floor area not exceeding 300 square metres, and any ancillary provision for effluent storage.	1. No such structure shall be used for any purpose other than the purpose of agriculture. 2. The total area of such structures together with any other such structures situated within the same farmyard complex or within 100 metres of that complex shall not exceed 450 square metres floor area in aggregate. 3. Effluent storage facilities adequate to serve the structure having regard to its size, use, location and the need to avoid water pollution shall be provided.

Column 1 Description of Development	Column 2 Conditions and Limitations
	4. No such structure shall be situated, and no effluent from such structure shall be stored, within 10 metres of any public road.
	5. No such structure within 100 metres of any public road shall exceed 8 metres in height.
	6. No such structure shall be situated, and no effluent from such structure shall be stored, within 100 metres of any dwellinghouse (other than the dwellinghouse of the person providing the structure) or other residential building or school, hospital, church or building used for public assembly, save with the consent in writing of the owner and, as may be appropriate, the occupier or person in charge thereof.
CLASS 8 Works consisting of the provision of any store, barn, shed, glass-house or other structure, not being of a type specified in class 6 or 7 of this Part of this Schedule, and having a floor area not exceeding 300 square metres.	1. No such structure shall be used for any purpose other than the purpose of agriculture or forestry, but excluding the housing of animals or the storing of effluent.
	2. The total area of such structures together with any other such structures situated within the same farmyard complex or complex of such structures or within 100 metres of that complex shall not exceed 900 square metres floor area in aggregate.
	3. No such structure shall be situate within 10 metres of any public road.
	4. No such structure within 100 metres of any public road shall exceed 8 metres in height.
	5. No such structure shall be situated within 100 metres of any dwellinghouse (other than the dwellinghouse of the person providing the structure) or other residential building or school, hospital, church or building used for public assembly, save with the consent in writing of the owner and, as may be appropriate, the occupier or person in charge thereof.

Column 1 Description of Development	Column 2 Conditions and Limitations
Land Reclamation CLASS 9³ᵃ Development consisting of the carrying out, on land which is used only for the purpose of agriculture or forestry, of any of the following works – (a) field drainage, (b) land reclamation, (c) the removal of fences, (d) the improvement of existing fences, (e) the improvement of hill grazing, or (f) the reclamation of estuarine marsh land or of callows, where the preservation of such land or callows is not an objective of a development plan for the area.	
Miscellaneous CLASS 10³ᵇ Works consisting of the provision of a roofed structure for the housing of horses, other than horses kept for use in the farming of land, or ponies, having a floor area not exceeding 100 square metres (whether or not by extension of an existing structure), and any ancillary provision for effluent storage.	1. No such structure shall be used for any purpose other than the housing of horses or ponies. 2. The total area of such structure together with any other such structures situated within a premises or within 100 metres of that premises shall not exceed 150 square metres floor area in aggregate. 3. Effluent storage facilities adequate to serve the structure having regard to its size, use, location and the need to avoid water pollution shall be provided. 4. No such structure shall be situated, and no effluent from such structure shall be stored, within 10 metres of any public road. 5. No such structure within 100 metres of any public road shall exceed 8 metres in height. 6. No such structure shall be situated, and no effluent from such structures shall be stored, within 100 metres of any dwellinghouse (other than the dwellinghouse of the person providing the structure) or other residential building or school, hospital, church or building used for public assembly, save with the consent in writing of the owner and, as may be appropriate, the occupier or person in charge thereof.

Column 1 Description of Development	Column 2 Conditions and Limitations
CLASS 11 Works consisting of the provision of a roofed structure for housing greyhounds, having a floor area not exceeding 50 square metres (whether or not by extension of an existing structure), and any ancillary provision for effluent storage.	1. No such structure shall be used for any purpose other than the keeping of greyhounds. 2. The total area of such structure together with any other such structures situated within a premises or within 100 metres of that premises shall not exceed 75 square metres floor area in aggregate. 3. Effluent storage facilities adequate to serve the structure having regard to its size, use, location and the need to avoid water pollution shall be provided. 4. No such structure shall be situated, and no effluent from such structure shall be stored, within 10 metres of any public road. 5. No such structure within 100 metres of any public road shall exceed 8 metres in height. 6. No such structure shall be situated, and no effluent from such structures shall be stored, within 100 metres of any dwellinghouse (other than the dwellinghouse of the person providing the structure) or other residential building or school, hospital, church or building used for public assembly, save with the consent in writing of the owner and, as may be appropriate, the occupier or person in charge thereof.
CLASS 12 Works consisting of the provision of a roofless hard-surfaced yard, or of a roofless hard-surfaced enclosed area, having an area not exceeding 100 square metres (whether or not by extension of an existing yard or area), and any ancillary provision for effluent storage.	1. No such structure shall be used for any purpose other than in connection with the keeping of horses, ponies or greyhounds. 2. Effluent storage facilities adequate to serve the structure having regard to its size, use, location and the need to avoid water pollution shall be provided. 3. The total area of such structure or structures together with any other such structures situated within the same complex or within 100 metres of that complex shall not exceed 150 square metres floor area in aggregate.

Column 1 Description of Development	Column 2 Conditions and Limitations
	4. No such structure shall be situated, and no effluent from such structure shall be stored, within 10 metres of any public road.
	5. No structure shall be situated, and no effluent from such structure shall be stored, within 100 metres of any dwellinghouse (other than the dwellinghouse of the person providing the structure) or other residential building or school, hospital, church or building used for public assembly, save with the consent in writing of the owner and, as may be appropriate, the occupier or person in charge thereof.

2 Cross References

a   See art 9(3) for the areas to which Part III relates.

3 Notes

a   See *Tralee UDC v Stack* High Court, unrep, 13 January 1984 and *Lennon v Kingdom Plant Hire* High Court, unrep, 13 December 1991.

b   The exemptions in classes 10-12 are necessary given the limited definition of "Agriculture" in s 2(1) of LG(PD)A 1963 Act as it relates to the keeping of horses and greyhounds.

Part IV

CLASSES OF USE[3a]

CLASS 1

Use as a shop.[2a]

CLASS 2

Use for the provision of –

    (a) financial services;

    (b) professional services (other than health or medical services);

    (c) any other services (including use as a betting office);

where the services are provided principally to visiting members of the public.

CLASS 3

Use as an office, other than a use to which class 2 of this Part of this Schedule applies.

CLASS 4

Use as a light industrial building.

CLASS 5

Use as a wholesale warehouse or as a repository.

CLASS 6

Use as a residential club, guest house or a hostel (other than a hostel where care is provided).

CLASS 7

Use –

    (a) for public worship or religious instruction;

    (b) for the social or recreational activities of a religious body;

    (c) as a monastery or convent.

CLASS 8

Use –

    (a) as a health centre or clinic or for the provision of any medical or health services (but not the use of the dwellinghouse of a consultant or practitioner, or any building attached to the dwellinghouse or within the curtilage thereof, for that purpose);

    (b) as a creche;

    (c) as a day nursery;

    (d) as a day centre.

CLASS 9

    (a) for the provision of residential accommodation and care to people in need of care (but not the use of a dwellinghouse for that purpose);

    (b) as a hospital or nursing home;

    (c) as a residential school, residential college or residential training centre.

CLASS 10

Use as –

    (a) an art gallery (but not for the sale or hire of works of art);

    (b) a museum;

    (c) a public library or public reading room;

    (d) a public hall;

    (e) an exhibition hall;

    (f) a social centre, community centre or non-residential club;

but not as a dance hall or concert hall.

CLASS 11

Use as –

    (a) a theatre;

    (b) a cinema;

    (c) a concert hall;

    (d) a bingo hall;

    (e) a skating rink or gymnasium or for other indoor sports or recreation not involving the use of motorised vehicles or firearms. **[446]**

2 Cross References

a   See the definition of "shop" in art 8. Article 11(4)(b) is also relevant in this regard and should be read in conjunction with class 1.

3 Notes

a   This Part allows for a change of use within any of the classes set out in Part IV to be exempted subject to such change not requiring works which are not exempted. See also art 11 and class 13 Part I. It is not automatic that a change from one class to an other is automatically in development – it is only such if there is a *material* change of use.

Third Schedule

PRESCRIBED FORMS

Form No. 1   *Article 38*

Notice of proposed material contravention of development plan or special amenity area order.

LOCAL GOVERNMENT (PLANNING AND DEVELOPMENT) ACTS, 1963 TO 1993

MATERIAL CONTRAVENTION

[1]OF DEVELOPMENT PLAN FOR

_____ [2]

OF _____ [2] SPECIAL AMENITY AREA ORDER MADE ON

_____

Ref. No. in register _____

Notice is hereby given pursuant to section 26(3) of the Local Government (Planning and Development) Act, 1963, as amended by section 39(d) of the Local Government (Planning and Development) Act, 1976 and section 45 of the Local Government Act, 1991, that ....[3] intend to consider deciding to grant a permission for

_____ [4]

at ——————————————————————————————— [5]

Such development/retention[1] would contravene materially the development plan/special amenity area order[1] referred to above. Particulars of the development/retention[1] may be inspected at _____ [6] during office hours. Any objections or representations received not later than 21 days after the _____ day of _____ [7] will be duly considered by the planning authority.

Signed _____

County Secretary/Town Clerk[1]

Date _____

Directions for completing this form

1. Omit words which do not apply.
2. Insert title of development plan or special amenity area order (as appropriate).
3. Insert name of planning authority.
4. Indicate nature of development.
5. Indicate location of land or structure concerned.
6. Insert address of office of planning authority.
7. Insert date of first publication of notice.

Form No. 2   *Article 165*

Form of Vesting Order

LOCAL GOVERNMENT (PLANNING AND DEVELOPMENT) ACT, 1976

SECTION 25 (AS AMENDED)

_____ (insert name of planning authority).

VESTING ORDER

WHEREAS development is being/has been[1] carried out pursuant to a permission granted on _____ under section 26 (as amended) of the Local Government (Planning and Development) Act, 1963 (Reference No. in Register _____).

[2] AND WHEREAS a condition requiring the provision or maintenance of land as open space, being open space to which section 25 (as amended) of the Local Government (Planning and Development) Act, 1976 (hereinafter called "the Act") applies, was attached to the permission;

AND WHEREAS it was implicit/explicit[1] in the application for the permission that land would be provided or maintained as open space, being open space to which section 25 (as amended) of the Local Government (Planning and Development) Act, 1976 (hereinafter called "the Act") applies;

AND WHEREAS on the _____ day of _____ 19 ___, the _____[3] (hereinafter referred to as "the planning authority") served

on the owner of the land a written request that within a period of _____ commencing on that day he would provide, level, plant or otherwise adapt or maintain the said land in a manner specified in the request, being a manner which in the opinion of the planning authority would make it suitable for the purpose for which the open space was to be provided;

AND WHEREAS the owner has failed to comply or to secure compliance with such request within such period;

AND WHEREAS the planning authority have, in accordance with section 25(1) of the Act, published an acquisition notice in relation to the said land and have, in accordance with section 25(2) of the Act, served a copy of the notice on the owner of the land within ten days of the date of publication of the said notice;

[2] AND WHEREAS no appeal has been taken under 25(3) of the Act;

AND WHEREAS an appeal has been taken under section 25(3) of the Act and the appeal has been withdrawn;

AND WHEREAS an appeal has been taken under section 25(3) of the Act and the said acquisition notice has been confirmed in relation to the land described in the Schedule hereto;

NOW THEREFORE, the planning authority, in exercise of the powers conferred on them by section 25(5) of the Act, hereby order that the land described in the Schedule hereto, being the land to which the said acquisition notice (as confirmed)[1] relates, and which is shown on the map attached hereto which said map has been marked _____[4] and sealed with the seal of the planning authority, shall, on the _____ day of _____, 19 ___,[5] vest in the planning authority for all the estate, term or interest for which immediately before the date of this order the said land was held by the owner together with all rights and liabilities which, immediately before the said date, were enjoyed or incurred in connection therewith by the owner together with an obligation to comply with the request made under section 25(1)(*c*) of the Act.

SCHEDULE

Description of land[6]

The official seal of the planning authority was affixed hereto this _____ day of _____, 19____, in the presence of:

_____[7]   _____[7]

_____[7]

Directions for completing this form.

1.   Delete words which do not apply.

2.   Delete recitals which do not apply.

3.   Insert full description of planning authority.

4.   The map should be sealed and marked by a heading containing a reference to the order e.g. "Map referred to in order made under section 25 (as amended) of the Local Government (Planning and Development) Act, 1976 on the _____ day of _____, 19 ____, by _____"

5.   The vesting date can be the date of the order or any subsequent date.

6.   The quantity, description and situation of the land should be set out, with an appropriate reference to the manner in which the land is shown on the map.

7.   The description of the persons in whose presence the seal is affixed should be stated e.g. "Lord Mayor", "Mayor", "Chairman", "Nominated Member", "City Manager and Town Clerk", "Manager", etc.

Form No. 3   *Article 167*

Declaration to the Board of estate or interest

LOCAL GOVERNMENT (PLANNING AND DEVELOPMENT) ACT, 1976

SECTION 32

I, _____, hereby give to An Bord Pleanála

the following declaration of interests in compliance with the requirements of section 32 of the Local Government (Planning and Development) Act, 1976:

   (a) Particulars* of any estate or interest which I have in any land:–

   _____

   _____

   (b) Particulars of any business of dealing in or developing land in which I am engaged or employed and of any such business carried on by a company or other body of which I am, or any nominee of mine is, a member:–

   _____

   _____

   (c) Particulars of any profession, business or occupation in which I am engaged, whether on my own behalf or otherwise, and which relates to dealing in or developing land:–

   _____

   _____

I hereby declare that the foregoing is a true and complete declaration of every interest of mine which is an interest to which section 32 of the Local Government (Planning and Development) Act, 1976 applies.

Signature _____

Date _____

*Including the area of the planning authority in which the land is situate.

Form No. 4   *Article 167*

Declaration to a planning authority of estate or interest

LOCAL GOVERNMENT (PLANNING AND DEVELOPMENT) ACT, 1976 SECTION 32

I, _____ , hereby give to the planning authority,

*of which I am a member,

under which I hold the office of _____,

the following declaration of interests in compliance with the requirements of section 32 of the Local Government (Planning and Development) Act, 1976:

(a) Particulars of any estate or interest which I have in land situated in the area of the planning authority:–

_____

_____

(b) Particulars of any business of dealing in or developing land in which I am engaged or employed and of any such business carried on by a company or other body of which I am, or any nominee of mine is, a member:–

_____

_____

(c) Particulars of any profession, business or occupation in which I am engaged, whether on my own behalf or otherwise, and which relates to dealing in or developing land:–

_____

_____

[I hereby declare that the foregoing is a true and complete declaration of every interest of mine which is an interest to which section 32 of the Local Government (Planning and Development) Act, 1976 applies.][1a]

Signature _____

Date _____

*Delete words which do not apply.

---

1 Amendments

a   The words in square brackets were inserted byLG(PD)R 1995 (SI 69/1995), art 10.

[Fourth Schedule[1a]

FEES FOR PLANNING APPLICATIONS

Section I: Interpretation

1. For the purposes of this Schedule, a dwelling, building or other structure or thing may be provided by –

    (a) the carrying out of works,

    (b) the making of a material change in the use of a structure,

    (c) the retention on land of a structure already constructed, erected or made, or

    (d) the continuance of a use of any structure,

and "**provision**" shall be construed accordingly.

2.   (a) Subject to paragraph (b), at references 7, 8, 13 and 14 of column 1 of Section II of this Schedule "**use of land**" shall include the continuance of a use of land, and the carrying out of works, or the retention of structures, on, in or under the land which are incidental to the use.

    (b) At reference 13 of column 1 of Section II of this Schedule "**use of land**" shall not include the carrying out of works for the provision of a club house or related facilities for persons using the golf course or pitch and putt course, or the retention of any such structures.   **[447]**

SECTION II: SCALE OF FEES FOR PLANNING APPLICATIONS

Column 1	Column 2
Class of Development	Amount of Fee
1. The provision of dwellings.	£47 for each dwelling.
2.(a)Any works for the carrying out of maintenance, improvement or other alteration of an existing dwelling (including any works for the provision of an extension or the conversion for use as part of the dwelling of any garage, store, shed or other structure).	£24
(b) Any other works, including the erection of structures, within the curtilage of an existing dwelling, for purposes ancillary to the enjoyment of the dwelling as such.	£24
(c) The erection, construction or alteration within or bounding the curtilage of an existing dwelling of gates, railings, fences, walls, or other means of enclosure.	£24
3. The provision of buildings or other structures for the purposes of agriculture.	(i) In the case of buildings, £58, or £0.75 for each square metre of gross floor space to be provided in excess of 300 square metres, whichever is the greater, (ii) in the case of any other structures, £58, and subject to a maximum of £218.

Column 1	Column 2
Class of Development	Amount of Fee
4. The provision of buildings or other structures for the purposes of the keeping of horses (other than horses kept for use in the farming of land), ponies or greyhounds.	(i) In the case of buildings, £58, or £0.75 for each square metre of gross floor space to be provided in excess of 100 square metres, whichever is the greater, (ii) in the case of any other structures, £58, and subject to a maximum of £218.
5. The provision of buildings other than buildings coming within class 1, 2, 3 or 4.	£58, or £2.60 for each square metre of gross floor space to be provided, whichever is the greater
6 (a) The use of uncultivated land or semi-natural areas for intensive agricultural purposes.	£218
(b) Initial afforestation.	£3.65 for each hectare of site area.
(c) The replacement of broadleaf high forest by conifer species.	£58, or £3.65 for each hectare of site area, whichever is the greater.
(d) Peat extraction.	£3.65 for each hectare of site area.
7. The use of land for – (a) the winning and working of minerals, (b) the deposit of refuse or waste.	£364, or £36.40 for each 0.1 hectare of site area, whichever is the greater.
8. The use of land for – (a) the keeping or placing of any tents, caravans or other structures (whether or not moveable or collapsible) for the purpose of caravanning or camping or the sale of goods, (b) the parking of vehicles, (c) the open storage of vehicles or other objects or substances.	£58, or £36.40 for each 0.1 hectare of site area, whichever is the greater.
9. The provision on, in or under land of plant or machinery, or of tanks other structures (other than buildings) for storage purposes.	£146, or £36.40 for each 0.1 hectare of site area, whichever is the greater.
10. The provision of a petrol filling station.	£146.
11. The provision of an advertisement structure or the use of an existing structure or other land for the exhibition of advertisements.	£58, or £15 for each square metre, or part thereof, of advertising space to be provided, whichever is the greater.
12. The provision of overhead transmission or distribution lines for conducting electricity, or overhead telecomunications lines.	£58, or £36.40 per 1,000 metres length, or part thereof, whichever is the greater.
13 The use of land as a golf course or a pitch and putt course.	£36.40 for each hectare of site area.
14. The use of land as a burial ground.	£146, or £36.40 for each hectare of site area, whichever is the greater.
15. Development not coming within any of the foregoing classes.	£58, or £7.30 for each 0.1 hectare of site area, whichever is the greater.

[448]

Section III Maximum and minimum fees for planning applications

1. The maximum fee payable to a planning authority by an applicant in respect of an outline application shall be £11,250.

2. The maximum fee payable to a planning authority by an applicant in respect of an application to which article 93 applies shall be £3,750.

3. The maximum fee payable to a planning authority by an applicant in respect of an application to which article 91 applies shall be £22,500.

4. The maximum fee payable to a planning authority by an applicant in respect of any planning application other than an application mentioned in paragraph 1, 2 or 3 shall be £15,000.

5. The minimum fee payable to a planning authority by an applicant in respect of a planning application shall be £24 and in any case where the planning authority make a refund in respect of a planning application the refund shall not be such as to reduce the balance of the fee to less than £24.]

1 Amendments

a   This Fourth Schedule was substituted by the LG(PD)(F)(A)(No. 2)R 1998 (SI 128/1998), First Schedule which came into effect on 15 June 1998.

[Fifth Schedule[1a]

FEES PAYABLE TO THE BOARD

Column 1	Column 2
	Amount of Fee
(a) Appeal against a decision of a planning authority on a planning application relating to commercial development, made by the person by whom the planning application was made.	£300
(b) Appeal other than an appeal mentioned at (a).	£120
(c) Reference.	£120
(d) Request for a determination.	£120
(e) Reduced fee.	£60
(f) Submissions or observations.	£36
(g) Request for an oral hearing.	£60

1 Amendments

a   This Fifth Schedule was inserted by the LG(PD)(R)(A)(No. 2)R 98 (SI 128/1998), Second Schedule which came into effect on 15 June 1998.

[449]

[Sixth Schedule[1a]

MISCELLANEOUS FEES

Column 1	Column 2 Amount of Fee
Application under section 4 of Act of 1982.	£45
Copy of any entry in the register.	£7.30

1 Amendments

a   This Sixth Schedule was substituted by LG(PD)(F)(A)(No. 2)R 1998 (SI 128/1998) which came into effect on 15 June 1998, First Schedule.

[450]

[Seventh Schedule[1a]

LICENCE FEES UNDER SECTION 89 OF ACT OF 1963 IN RESPECT OF SPECIFIED APPLIANCES AND STRUCTURES

Column 1 Appliance or Structure	Column 2 Licence Fee
Part 1 Appliances and structures for servicing vehicles:	
(a) A petrol or oil pump (including any delivery hose, air pipe, waterpipe or other attachment).	£45
(b) A movable pump or other appliance for dispensing any oil or oil derivative or mixture thereof.	£22
(c) A delivery pipe or hose attached to a petrol or oil pump which is not on a public road.	£22
(d) A petrol, oil or other storage tank (whether sub-divided or not) together with any associated manhole, inlet, outlet or pipe for connection with a pump.	£4.50 for each 5,000 litres capacity or part thereof.
(e) A pipe or an appliance with a pipe attachment for dispensing air or water not being a pipe or appliance attached to a petrol or oil pump for which a fee is prescribed under paragraph (a) above.	£6
Part II Other appliances and structures:	
(a) A vending machine or other coin operated machine (not being a weighing machine) which is on a public road.	£45

Column 1	Column 2
Appliance or Structure	Licence Fee
(b) An appliance or any type referred to in Part I of this Schedule which is not used for servicing vehicles.	£22
(c) A case, rack, shelf or other appliance or structure for displaying articles for the purpose of advertisement or sale in or in connection with any adjacent business premises.	£22
(d) An advertisement consisting of any symbol, emblem, model, device or logo which is on a public road.	£22
(e) An advertisement structure which is on a public road.	£22
(f) A hoarding, fence or scaffold (not being a hoarding, fence or scaffold bounding a public road).	£22
(g) A town or landscape map on a public road.	£6
(h) A weighing machine on a public road.	£6
(i) A cable, wire or pipeline (not being a cable for conducting electricity for domestic or agricultural purposes or a drain or waterpipe).	£11 per 800 metres length or part thereof.
(j) Tables and chairs outside a hotel, restaurant or public house.	£45
Part III	
(a) A bridge, arch, tunnel, passage or other similar structure used or intended for use other than by the public and constructed on or after the 1st day of October, 1964.	£22
(b) A cellar or other underground structure constructed on or after the 1st day of October, 1964.	£22
(c) A lamp-post	£11
(d) A cable for conducting electricity for domestic or agricultural purposes.	£11
(e) A cabinet used as part of a wired broadcast relay system by a person licensed under the Wireless Telegraphy (Wired Broadcast Relay Licence) Regulations, 1974.	£11

[451]

Amendments

a   This Seventh Schedule was substituted by LG(PD)(F)(A)(No 2)R 1998 (SI 128/1998), First Schedule.

LOCAL GOVERNMENT (PLANNING AND DEVELOPMENT) REGULATIONS, 1999

S.I. No. 92 of 1999

The Minister for the Environment and Local Government, in exercise of the powers conferred on him by section 10 of the Local Government (Planning and Development) Act, 1963 (No. 28 of 1963), and by section 25 of that Act (as amended by section 39 of the Local Government (Planning and Development) Act, 1976 (No. 20 of 1976), article 7 of the European Communities (Environmental Impact Assessment) Regulations, 1989 (S.I. No. 349 of 1989), article 5 of the European Communities (Environmental Impact Assessment) (Amendment) Regulations, 1994 (S.I. No. 84 of 1994), article 3 of the European Communities (Environmental Impact Assessment) (Amendment) Regulations, 1998 (S.I. No. 351 of 1998) and article 4 of the European Communities (Environmental Impact Assessment)(Amendment) Regulations, 1999), section 78 of that Act (as amended by article 10 of the European Communities (Environmental Impact Assessment) Regulations, 1989 (S.I. No. .349 of 1989), section 3 of the Local Government (Planning and Development) Act, 1993 (No. 12 of 1993), article 8 of the European Communities (Environmental Impact Assessment) (Amendment) Regulations, 1994 (S.I. No. 84 of 1994), article 5 of the European Communities (Environmental Impact Assessment) (Amendment) Regulations, 1998 (S.I. No. 351 of 1998) and article 5 of the European Communities (Environmental Impact Assessment) (Amendment) Regulations, 1999), and section 7A of the Local Government (Planning and Development) Act, 1992 (No. 14 of 1992) (as inserted by article 6 of the European Communities (Environmental Impact Assessment) (Amendment) Regulations, 1999), hereby makes the following regulations:

Part I

PRELIMINARY AND GENERAL

1.(1) These Regulations may be cited as the Local Government (Planning and Development) Regulations, 1999.

(2) These Regulations and the Local Government (Planning and Development) Regulations, 1994 to 1998, may be cited together as the Local Government (Planning and Development) Regulations, 1994 to 1 999. **[452]**

2.(1) Subject to sub-articles (2) and (3) of this article, these regulations shall come into operation on the 1st day of May, 1999.

(2) Part II of these regulations shall not apply to an application for planning permission, an appeal to An Bord Pleanála or an application for certification under Part IX of the 1994 Regulations, as the case may be, made before the date referred to in sub-article (1) of this article.

(3) Where an application for planning permission, an appeal to An Bord Pleanála or an application for certification under Part IX of the 1994 Regulations is made before the date referred to in sub-article (1) of this article, the provisions of the 1994 Regulations, before they were amended by Part III of these regulations, shall continue to apply to the application or appeal concerned. **[453]**

3. In these Regulations: -

"the Act of 1963" means the Local Government (Planning and Development) Act, 1963 (No. 28 of 1963);

"the Act of 1992" means the Local Government (Planning and Development) Act, 1992 (No. 14 of 1992);

"the Birds Directive" means Council Directive No. 79/409/EEC of 2 April, 1979, on the conservation of wild birds (O.J. No. L 103, 25 April, 1979);

"Habitats Directive" means Council Directive 92/43/EEC of 21 May, 1992, on the conservation of natural habitats and of wild fauna and flora (O.J. No. L 206, 22 July, 1992);

"the Local Government (Planning and Development) Regulations, 1994 to 1998" has the meaning assigned to it in the Local Government (Planning and Development) (No. 2) Regulations, 1998 (S.I. No. 194 of 1998);

"special area of conservation" has the meaning assigned to it in Regulation 2 of the European Communities (Natural Habitats) Regulations, 1997 (S.I. No. 94 of 1997);

"the 1989 Regulations" means the European Communities (Environmental Impact Assessment) Regulations, 1989 (S.I. No. 349 of 1989);

"the 1994 Regulations" means the Local Government (Planning and Development) Regulations, 1994 (S.I. No. 86 of 1994).   **[454]**

Part II

Scoping of Environmental Impact Statements

4. A request by an applicant or a person intending to apply for permission under Part IV of the Act of 1963 to a planning authority for a written opinion on the information to be contained in an environmental impact statement (referred to in this Part as a "written opinion") shall state: -

    (a)   the name, address and telephone number of the person making the request,

    (b)   the location of the land to which the request relates,

    (c)   a brief description of the nature of the proposed development and of its possible effects on the environment,

    (d)   if the proposed development comprises or is for the purposes of an activity in relation to which a licence under Part IV of the Environmental Protection Agency Act, 1992 (No. 7 of 1992), or a licence under Part V of the Waste Management Act, 1996 (No. 10 of 1996), is required, this fact.   **[455]**

5. Where a planning authority, having received a request for a written opinion, considers that it has insufficient information to enable it to give the written opinion concerned, it shall require the person making the request to provide such further information or documentation as it considers necessary.   **[456]**

6.(1) A planning authority shall, not later than 3 weeks after having received a request for a written opinion or, where further information or documentation was required pursuant to article 5, not later than 3 weeks after such requirement was complied with: -

    (a)   give notice of having received the request concerned to the bodies referred to in article 32 of the 1994 Regulations (as amended), as appropriate, indicating that submissions or observations in relation to the information to be contained in the environmental impact statement concerned may be made to the authority within a period of one month beginning on the date of the notice, and

(b) give notice to the person who made the request concerned that a submission or observations in relation to the information to be contained in the environmental impact statement concerned may be made to the authority within a period of one month beginning on the date of the notice.

(2) A notice given by a planning authority pursuant to paragraph (a) of sub-article (1) of this article shall contain the information referred to in article 4.   **[457]**

7. A planning authority shall, not later than 3 weeks after: -

(a) the expiry of the periods referred to in sub-article (1) of article 6, or

(b) a requirement to provide further information or documentation pursuant to article 5 has been complied with,

whichever is the later, give a written opinion to the person who made the request concerned.   **[458]**

8. (1) A planning authority shall, subject to sub-article (2) of this article, in dealing with a request for a written opinion have regard to: -

(a) article 25 (as amended) of the 1989 Regulations,

(b) such information and documentation as has been provided to it pursuant to articles 4 and 5, and

(c) any submissions or observations received by it in response to a notice issued pursuant to article 6.

(2) If the proposed development comprises or is for the purposes of an activity in relation to which a licence under Part IV of the Environmental Protection Agency Act, 1992 (No. 7 of 1992), or a licence under Part V of the Waste Management Act, 1996 (No. 10 of 1996), is required, the planning authority shall have regard to the matters referred to in sub-article (1) only insofar as those matters do not relate to the risk of environmental pollution from the activity.

(3) A written opinion shall indicate which of the information described in paragraph 2 of the Second Schedule to the 1989 Regulations (as amended) should be contained in the environmental impact statement concerned.

(4) In the case of proposed development referred to in sub-article (2), a planning authority shall, in giving a written opinion, notify the person who made the request concerned of any submissions or observations relating to the risk of environmental pollution from the activity.   **[459]**

9.(1) Where a person makes a request to the Board for a written opinion on the information to be contained in an environmental impact statement to be submitted to the Board in accordance with a requirement of or under the Act of 1992, the provisions of this Part shall apply as if the Board were a planning authority.

(2) Where a local authority makes a request to the Minister for a written opinion on the information to be contained in an environmental impact statement to be prepared in accordance with a requirement of or under section 78 of the Act of 1963, the provisions of this Part shall apply as if the Minister were a planning authority and the local authority were a person making the request.   **[460]**

Part III

AMENDMENT OF THE LOCAL GOVERNMENT

(PLANNING AND DEVELOPMENT) REGULATIONS, 1994 TO 1998[3a]

[461]

3 Notes

a   See the amended LG(PD)R 1994.

Index

[Note: References in Index are to paragraph numbers]